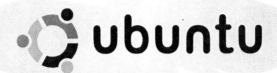

8

Server

Administration
and
Reference

To my nephew,
Christopher

Ubuntu 8 Server Administration and Reference

Richard Petersen

Surfing Turtle Press

Alameda, CA

www.surfingturtlepress.com

Please send inquires to: editor@surfingturtlepress.com

ISBN 0-9817778-3-X

ISBN-13 978-0-9817778-3-2

Library of Congress Control Number: 2008906908

included code cannot and do not warrant the performance or results that may be obtained by using the code.

Preface

This book is designed as an Ubuntu server administration and reference, covering the Ubuntu servers and their support applications. Server tools are covered as well as the underlying configuration files and system implementations. The emphasis is on what administrators will need to know to perform key server support and management tasks. Topics covered include software management, Upstart service management and runlevels, AppArmor security, and the Network Time Protocol. Key servers are examined, including Web, FTP, CUPS printing, NFS, and Samba Windows shares. Network support servers and applications covered include the Squid proxy server, the Domain Name System (BIND) server, DHCP, and IPtables firewalls.

The book is organized into five parts: getting started, services, shared resources, network support, and shells.

Part 1 focuses on basic tasks such as installing the Ubuntu Server CD, managing software from the Ubuntu repository, and basic usage for desktops and the command line interface.

Part 2 examines Internet servers as well as how all services are managed by Upstart using runlevels. Configuration and implementation of the Postfix mail server, the vsftpd FTP server, the Apache Web server, as well as news and database servers are covered in detail.

Part 3 deals with servers that provide shared resources on a local network or the Internet. Services examined include the Cups printing server, NFS Linxu network file server, and Samba Windows file and printing server, and the GFS distributed file system.

Part 4 covers servers that provide network support, like the Squid proxy server, the Bind Domain Name System (DNS) server, DHCP servers, IPtables firewalls, and IPv6 support.

Part 5 provides a review of shell commands, including those used for managing files. The Ubuntu Server CD only installs a command line interface, with no desktop. To manage your system and its files you will need to know the shell command.

It is possible to run servers from a host using the GNOME desktop interface, though this can degrade performance. Just install the Ubuntu desktop and then install the servers you want from the Ubuntu repository. The kernel installed by the Ubuntu server CD is optimized for server support. Appendix B covers basic desktop usage, and Appendix C reviews the Ubuntu desktop install.

Overview

Part 1: Getting Started

Part 2: Services

Contents

Part 1
Getting Started

4. Managing Software 77

Part 2

Services

9. News and Database Services 167

Part 3

Shared Resources

10. Print Services 175

Part 4

Network Support

Part 5

Shells

Appendices

ubuntu

Part 1: Getting Started

Introduction

Installation

Usage Basics

Software Management

1. Introduction to Ubuntu Linux

Ubuntu Linux is currently one of the most popular end-user Linux distributions (**www.ubuntu.com**). Ubuntu Linux is managed by the Ubuntu foundation, which is sponsored by Cannonical, Ltd (**www.cannonical.com**), a commercial organization that supports and promotes open source projects. Ubuntu is based on Debian Linux, one of the oldest Linux distributions dedicated to incorporating cutting edge developments and features (**www.debian.org**). The Ubuntu project was initiated by Mark Shuttleworth, a South African and Debian Linux developer. Debian Linux is primarily a development Linux project, trying out new features. Ubuntu provides a Debian based Linux distribution that is stable, reliable, and easy to use.

Ubuntu is designed as a Linux operating system that can be used easily by everyone. The name Ubuntu means "humanity to others". As the Ubuntu project describes it: "Ubuntu is an African word meaning 'Humanity to others', or 'I am what I am because of who we all are'. The Ubuntu distribution brings the spirit of Ubuntu to the software world."

The official Ubuntu philosophy lists the following principles.

1. Every computer user should have the freedom to download, run, copy, distribute study, share, change, and improve their software for any purpose, without paying licensing fees.

2. Every computer user should be able to use their software in the language of their choice.

3. Every computer user should be given every opportunity to use software, even if they work under a disability.

The emphasis on language reflects Ubuntu's international scope. It is meant to be a global distribution, not focused on any one market. Language support has been integrated into Linux in general by its internationalization projects, denoted by the term i18n. These include sites like **www.li18nux.net** and **www.openi18n.org**.

Making software available to all users involves both full accessibility support for disabled users as well as seamless integration of software access using online repositories, making massive amounts of software available to all users at the touch of a button. Ubuntu also makes full use of recent developments in automatic device detection, greatly simplifying installation as well as access to removable devices and attached storage.

Ubuntu aims to provide a fully supported and reliable, open source and free, easy to use and modify, Linux operating system. Ubuntu makes these promises about its distribution.

> ➢ Ubuntu will always be free of charge, including enterprise releases and security updates.

> ➢ Ubuntu comes with full commercial support from Canonical and hundreds of companies around the world.

> ➢ Ubuntu includes the very best translations and accessibility infrastructure that the free software community has to offer.

> ➢ Ubuntu CDs contain only free software applications; we encourage you to use free and open source software, improve it and pass it on.

Ubuntu releases

Ubuntu provides both long term and short term releases. Long term support releases (LTS) are released every two years. Ubuntu 8.04 is a long term support release. Short term releases are provided every six months between the LTS versions. These are designed to make available the latest application and support for the newest hardware. Each has its own nickname, like Hardy Heron for the 8.04 LTS release. The long term releases are supported for three years for the desktop and five years for the servers, whereas short term releases are supported for 18 months. Canonical also provides limited commercial support for companies that purchase it.

Installing Ubuntu has been significantly simplified. A core set of applications are installed, and you add to them as you wish. Following installation, added software is taken from online repositories. Install screens have been reduced to just a few screens, moving quickly through default partitioning, user setup, and time settings. The hardware like graphics cards and network connections are now configured and detected automatically.

The Ubuntu distribution of Linux is available online at numerous sites. Ubuntu maintains its own site at **www.ubuntu.com/getubuntu** where you can download the current release of Ubuntu Linux, both desktp and server versions.

Ubuntu Editions

Ubuntu is released in several editions, each designed for a distinct group of users or functions (see Table 1-1). Editions install different collections of software such as the KDE desktop, the XFce desktop, servers, educational software, and multimedia applications. Table 1-2 lists Web sites where you can download ISO images for these editions. ISO images can be downloaded directly or using a BitTorrent application.

The Ubuntu Desktop edition provides standard functionality for end users. The standard Ubuntu release provides a Live CD using the GNOME desktop. Most users would install this edition. This is the CD image that you download from the Get Ubuntu download page at:

www.ubuntu.com/getubuntu/download

Those that want to run Ubuntu just as a server, providing an Internet service like a Web site, would use the Server edition. The Server edition provided only a simple command line interface; it does not install the desktop. It is designed to primarily run servers. Keep in mind that you could install the desktop first, and later download server software from the Ubuntu repositories, running them from a system that also has a desktop. You do not have to install the Server edition to install and run servers. The Server edition can be downloaded from the Ubuntu download page, like the Desktop edition.

Ubuntu Editions	Description.
Ubuntu Desktop	Live CD using GNOME desktop, **ubuntu.com/getubuntu**.
Server Install	Install server software (no desktop) **ubuntu.com/getubuntu**.
Alternate Install	Install enhanced features **releases.ubuntu.com**.
Kubuntu	Live CD using the KDE desktop, instead of GNOME, **www.kubuntu.org**.
Xubuntu	Uses the Xfce desktop instead of GNOME, **www.xubuntu.org**. Useful for laptops.
Edubuntu	Installs Educational software: Desktop, Server, and Server add-on CDs, **edubuntu.org**
goubuntu	Uses only open source software, no access to restricted software of any kind. See the **goubuntu** link at **www.ubuntu.com**
ubuntustudio	Ubuntu desktop with multimedia and graphics production applications, **www.ubuntustudio.org**.
mythubuntu	Ubuntu desktop with MythTV multimedia and DVR applications, **mythbuntu.org**.

Table 1-1: Ubuntu Editions

Users that want more enhanced operating system features like RAID arrays or file system encryption would use the Alternate edition. The Alternate edition, along with the Desktop and Server editions, can be downloaded directly from.

```
http://releases.ubuntu.com
```

Other editions use either a different desktop or a specialized collection of software for certain groups of users. Links to the editions are listed on the www.ubuntu.com Web page. From there you can download their live/install CDs. The Kubuntu edition used the KDE desktop instead of GNOME. Xubuntu uses the XFce desktop instead of GNOME. This is a stripped down highly efficient desktop, ideal for low power use on laptops and smaller computer. The Edubuntu edition provides educational software. It can also be used with a specialized Edubuntu server to provide educational software on a school network. The Goubuntu edition is a modified version of the standard edition that includes only open source software, with no access to commercial software of any kind, including restricted vendor graphics drivers like those from Nvidia or ATI. Only Xorg open source display drivers are used. The ubuntustudio edition is a new edition that provides a collection of multimedia and image production software. The mythubuntu edition is designed just to install and run the MythTV software, letting you use Ubuntu as Multimedia DVR and Video playback system. All these editions can be downloaded from their respective Web sites, as well as from the following site. Follow the directory links to the **hardy** directory. You can also download the primary Ubuntu editions from this sites **releases** directory.

`http://cdimage.ubuntu.com`

Keep in mind that all these editions are released as Live CDs or DVD install discs, for which there are two versions, a 32 bit x 86 versions and a 64 bit x86_64 version. Older computers may only support a 32 bit version, whereas most current computers will support the 64 bit versions. Check your computer hardware specifications to be sure. The 64 bit version should run faster, and most computer software is now available in stable 64 bit packages.

URL	Internet Site
www.ubuntu.com/getubuntu/download	Primary download site for Desktop and Servers
http://releases.ubuntu.com	Download sites for Alternate, Server, and Desktop CDs and the Install DVD, as well as BitTorrent files
http://cdimage.ubuntu.com	Download site for Ubuntu editions, including Kubuntu, Xubuntu, Edubuntu, mythubuntu, goubuntu, and ubuntustudio. Check also their respective Web sites.
http://torrent.ubuntu.com	Ubuntu BitTorrent site for BitTorrent downloads of Ubuntu distribution ISO images

Table 1-2: Ubuntu CD ISO Image locations

Note: In addition, Ubuntu provides different releases for different kinds of installation on hard drives. These include a Server disc for installing just servers, and an Alternate disc for supporting specific kinds of file systems and features during an installation, like RAID and LVM file systems.

Ubuntu 8 Server Install Options

There are several ways to install the Ubuntu server software. It is recommended that you install using the Ubuntu Server CD. This release holds a version of the Linux kernel that has been optimized for use by servers. The Server CD though does not install a desktop. You are provided the command line interface only. The aim is to provide a streamlined and efficient server with as little overhead as possible. Desktops, with their X Windows System, include a lot of overhead.

One important drawback to the Server CD, is that, without the desktop, you will not be able to use any of the available desktop server configuration tools. These tools often provide a very effective and simple way to configure yoru servers. Ubuntu will perform basic automatic configuration designed for Ubuntu. With the just the command line interface, though, you will have to perform any additional configuration using just the command line editors working directly on the various server configuration files.

Server on the desktop install

As an alternative you could install the Desktop CD/DVD and then just install the server kernel and the server packages from the Ubuntu repository, instead of from the Server CD. All the servers are available on the Ubuntu repository, as well as the optimized server kernel.

The name of the server kernel package is:

```
linux-server
```

Once installed, an entery will be placed for it in the GRUB menu. Your desktop kernel will remain. You can choose to boot with either.

This configuration still starts up the X Windows System, involving much more overhead. You end to running much more software that the servers actually need to use.

If you are running servers for a small or home network, the overhead involved with the desktop is not significant. Most likely your servers will be lightly used. At the same time the additional support provided by the desktop server configuration tools would be extremely helpful.

One option is to turn off the X Server at start up, and use start up with just the command line interface. You can then use the **startx** command to start up the deskto whenever you need it. To prevent the X sever from starting up, you can use the **sysv-rc-conf** tool to deselect the gdm server (GNOME Display Manager). It is the gdm server that starts up the X server. You will then start up in the command line, and can use the startx command when you want the desktop. When you Quit from the desktop, the X server shuts down and you return to the command line.

Desktop on the Server install

You could install the Server CD and then later install the Ubuntu desktop from the repository. This would provide you with the optimized server kernel, and still give you desktop support. You install the Ubuntu desktop using the ubuntu-desktop meta-package.

```
sudo apt-get install ubuntu-desktop
```

The problem with this approach is that it also installs the GDM, the GNOME Desktop Manager. This is a login screen that will automatically start up the X Window System whenever your system starts. To prevent the X sever from starting up, you can use the **sysv-rc-conf** tool to deselect the **gdm** server.

You would then login from the command line, but then you can start up the desktop with the **startx** command. This way you only start the X Windows System when you want to use the desktop.

```
sudo startx
```

When you Quit from the desktop, the X server shuts down and you return to the command line

Server install options

To recap, your options are:

➤ Server CD only with server optimized kernel, but using the command line interface alone. No support or access to server desktop configuration tools.

➢ Server CD first, giving you the server optimized kernel, and then installing the Ubuntu Desktop from the Ubuntu repository (**ubuntu-desktop**). Will implement automatic X Window System startup for GDM

➢ Server CD first, giving you the server optimized kernel, and the installing the Ubuntu Desktop from the Ubuntu repository, but disabling the GDM to avoid automatic X Window System startup. Can use the desktop with the **startx** command, allowing use of server desktop configuration tools as well as desktop text editing.

➢ Desktop CD/DVD first, and then install server packages from the Ubuntu repository using Synaptic Package Manager. You will always have the X Window System running as additional overhead, and you will not be using the optimized server kernel. But you can use server desktop configuration tools and desktop editors. Efficiency degradation would be minor for a small or home network.

➢ Desktop CD/DVD first, and then install server kernel (**linux-server**) and server packages from the Ubuntu repository using Synaptic Package Manager. You will always have the X Window System running as additional overhead. But you can use server desktop configuration tools and desktop editors. Efficiency degradation would be minor for a small or home network.

➢ Desktop CD/DVD first, and then install server kernel (**linux-server**) and server packages from the Ubuntu repository using Synaptic Package Manager. Then disable the GDM to avoid automatic X Window System startup. You can use the desktop with the **startx** command, allowing use of server desktop configuration tools as well as desktop text editing.

Choose the option that works best for you. Keep in mind that you do not need the Server CD to run servers. All the servers on the Server CD are available on the Ubuntu repository and can be run from any desktop install. What you would loose is the optimized server kernel, which is not needed for small or home networks.

Also, unless you are performing a professional install or are comfortable with editing configuration files directly, you should not underestimate the help that server desktop configuration tools can provide. There are very good tools for local network servers like NFS, CUPS, and Samba. There are few for Internet servers like Apache and FTP, and most of these are too simple with few options. For most heavy duty Internet servers, direct editing will be required.

Ubuntu 8

Ubuntu 8includes the following features.

➢ PolicyKit authorization for users, allowing limited controlled administrative access to users for administration tools, and for storage and media devices.

➢ Brasero GNOME CD/DVD burner

➢ Kernel-based Virtualization Machine (KVM) support is included with the kernel. KVM uses hardware virtualization enabled processors like Intel VT (Virtualization Technology)

and AMD SVM (Secure Virtual Machine) processors to support hardware-level guest operating systems. Most standard Intel and AMD processors already provide this support.

➢ Use Virtual Machine Manger to manage and install both KVM and Xen virtual machines.

➢ The java-gcj-compat collection provides Java runtime environment compatibility. It consists of GNU Java runtime (libgcj), the Eclipse Java compiler (ecj), and a set of wrappers and links (java-gcj-compat).

➢ New applications like Transmission BitTorrent client, Vinagre Virtual Network Client, and the World Clock applet with weather around the world.

➢ Features automatic detection of removable devices like USB printers, digital cameras, and card readers. CD/DVD discs are treated as removable devices, automatically displayed and accessed when inserted.

➢ GNOME supports GUI access to all removable devices and shared directories on networked hosts, including Windows folders, using the GNOME Virtual File System, **gvfs**. Gvfs replaces gnomevfs.

➢ Any NTFS Windows file systems on your computer are automatically detected and mounted using **ntfs-3g**. Mounted file systems are located in the **/media** directory.

➢ Ubuntu also provides full IPv6 network protocol support, including automatic addressing and renumbering.

➢ With the Network Monitor, you can automatically select wireless connections. NetworkMonitor will automatically detect your network connections.

➢ Information about hotplugged devices is provided to applications with the Hardware Abstraction Layer (HAL) from **freedesktop.org**. This allows desktops like GNOME to easily display and manage removable devices.

➢ All devices are now treated logically as removable, and automatically configured by udev. Fixed devices are simply ones that cannot be removed. This feature is meant to let Linux accommodate the wide variety of devices now becoming available, such as digital cameras, PDAs, and cell phones. PCMCIA and Network devices are managed by udev and HAL directly.

➢ The Update Manager automatically updates your Ubuntu system and all its installed applications, from the Ubuntu online repositories.

➢ Software management (Synaptic Package Manager) accesses and installs software directly from all your configured online Ubuntu repositories.

➢ The current version of Office.org provides very effective and MS Office–competitive office applications, featuring support for document storage standards.

➢ Ubuntu has a complete range of system and network administration tools featuring easy-to-use GUI interfaces (see Chapters 4 and 5).

➢ Wine Windows Compatibility Layer lets you run most popular Windows applications directly on your Ubuntu desktop.

Ubuntu Software

For Ubuntu, you can update to the latest software from the Ubuntu repository using the update manager. The Ubuntu distribution provides an initial selection of desktop software. Additional applications can be downloaded and installed from online repositories, ranging from office and multimedia applications to Internet servers and administration services. Many popular applications are included in separate sections of the repository. During installation, your system is configured to access Ubuntu repositories.

All Linux software for Ubuntu is currently available from online repositories. You can download applications for desktops, Internet servers, office suites, and programming packages, among others. Software packages are primarily distributed in through Debian-enabled repositories, the largest of which is the official Ubuntu repository. Downloads and updates are handled automatically by your desktop software manager and updater.

A complete listing of software packages for the Ubuntu distribution, along with a search capability is located at.

`packages.ubuntu.com`

In addition, you could download from third-party sources software that is in the form of compressed archives or in DEB packages. DEB packages are those archived using the Debian Package Manager. Compressed archives have an extension such as **.tar.gz**, whereas Debian packages have a **.deb** extension. You could also download the source version and compile it directly on your system. This has become a simple process, almost as simple as installing the compiled DEB versions.

Due to licensing restrictions, multimedia support for popular operations like MP3, DVD, and DivX are included with Ubuntu in a separate section of the repository called multiverse. Ubuntu does include on its restricted repository Nvidia and ATI vendor graphics drivers. Ubuntu also provides as part of its standard installation, the generic X.org which will enable your graphics cards to work.

All software packages in different sections and Ubuntu repositories are accessible directly with the Install and Remove Software and the Synaptic Package Manager.

Ubuntu Linux Help and Documentation

A great deal of help and documentation is available online for Ubuntu, ranging from detailed install procedures to beginners questions (see Table 1-3). The two major sites for documentation are help.ubuntu.com and the Ubuntu forums at ubuntuformus.org. In additions there are blog and news sites as well as the standard Linux documentation. Also helpful is the Ubuntu Guide Wiki at **www.ubuntuguide.org**. Links to Ubuntu documentation, support, blogs, and news are listed at **www.ubuntu.com/community**. Here you will also find links for the Ubuntu community structure including the code of conduct. A Contribute section links to sites where you can make contributions in development, artwork, documentation, support. For mailing lists, check **lists.ubuntu.com**. There are lists for categories like Ubuntu announcements, community support for specific editions, and development for areas like the desktop, servers, or mobile implementation.

help.ubuntu.com	Help pages
packages.ubuntu.com	Ubuntu software package list and search
ubuntuforums.org	Ubuntu forums
ubuntuguide.org	Guide to Ubuntu
fridge.ubuntu.com	News and developments
planet.ubuntu.com	Member and developer blogs
blog.canonical.com	Latest Canonical news
www.tldp.org	Linux Documentation Project Web site
www.ubuntuguide.org	All purpose guide to Ubuntu topics
www.ubuntugeek.com	Specialized Ubuntu modifications
www.ubuntu.com/community	Links to Documentation, Support, News, and Blogs
lists.ubuntu.com	Ubuntu mailing lists

Table 1-3: Ubuntu help and documentation

help.ubuntu.com

Ubuntu-specific documentation is available at **help.ubuntu.com**. Here on tabbed pages you can find specific documentation for different releases. Always check the release help page first for documentation. The documentation though may be sparse. It covers mainly changed areas. The Ubuntu release usually includes desktop, installation, server guides. The guides are very complete and will cover most topics. The desktop guide covers these main topics: text editing, using terminals, sudo administrative access, software management, music and video applications, Internet application including mail and instant messaging, office applications, graphics and photos, printing, and games. Advanced topics are covered like programming, partitions, and font management.

The Ubuntu server guid is currently located located at:

```
http://doc.ubuntu.com/ubuntu/serverguide/C/index.html
```

The installation guide provides a very detailed discussion of install topics like system requirements, obtaining the CDs, boot parameters, partitioning, and automatic installs.

The short term support releases tend to have just a few detailed documentation topics like software management, desktop customization, security, multimedia and Internet applications, and printing. These will vary depending on what new features are included in the release.

One of the most helpful pages is the last, Community Docs page. Here you will find detailed documentation on installation of all Ubuntu releases, using the desktop, installing software, and configuring devices. Always check the page for your Ubuntu release first. The page has these main sections:

> ➢ Getting Help: links to documentation and FAQs. The official documentation link displays the tabbed page for that release on **help.ubuntu.com**.

➢ Getting Ubuntu: Link to Install page with sections on desktop, server, and alternate installation. Also information on how to move from using other operating systems like Windows or Mac.

➢ Using and Customizing your System: Sections on managing and installing software, Internet access, configuring multimedia applications, and setting up accessibility, the desktop appearance (eye candy), server configuration, and development tools (programming).

➢ Maintain your Computer: Links to system administration, security, and trouble shooting pages. System administration cover topics like adding users, configuring the GRUB boot loader, setting the time and date, and installing software. The Security page covers much lower level issues like IPtables for firewalls and how GPG security works. Of particular interest is the LUKS encrypted file system howtos.

➢ Connecting and Configuring Hardware: Links to pages on drives and partitions, input devices, wireless configuration, printers. sound, video, and laptops.

ubuntuforums.org

Ubuntu forums provide detailed online support and discussion for users. An Absolute Beginner section provides an area where new users can obtain answers to questions. Sticky threads include both quick and complete guides to installation for the current Ubuntu release. You can use the search feature to find discussions on your topic of interest.

The main support categories section covers specific support areas like networking, multimedia, laptops, security, and 64 bit support.

Other community discussions cover ongoing work such as virtualization, art and design, gaming, education and science, Wine, assistive technology, and even testimonials. Here you will also find community announcements and news. Of particular interest are third party projects that include projects like Mythubuntu (MythTV on Ubuntu), Ubuntu Podcast forum, Ubuntu Women, and Ubuntu Gamers.

The forum community discussion is where you talk about anything else. The **ubuntuforums.org** site also provides a gallery page for posted screenshots as well as RSS feeds for specific forums.

ubuntuguide.org

The Ubuntu Guide is a kind of all purpose HowTo for frequently asked questions. It is independent of the official Ubuntu site and can deal with topics like how to get DVD-video to work. Areas cover topics like popular add-on applications like Flash, Adobe Reader, and Mplayer. The Hardware section deals with specific hardware like Nvidia drivers and Logitech mice. Emulators like Wine and VMWare are also discussed.

Ubuntu news and blog sites

Several news and blog sites are accessible from the News pop-up menu on the www.ubuntu.com site.

➤ **fridge.ubuntu.com** The Fridge site lists the latest news and developments for Ubuntu. It features the Weekly newsletter, latest announcements, and upcoming events.

➤ **planet.ubuntu.com** Ubuntu blog for members and developers

➤ **blog.canonical.com** Canonical news

Linux documentation

Linux documentation has also been developed over the Internet. Much of the documentation currently available for Linux can be downloaded from Internet FTP sites. A special Linux project called the Linux Documentation Project (LDP), headed by Matt Welsh, has developed a complete set of Linux manuals. The documentation is available at the LDP home site at **www.tldp.org**. The Linux documentation for your installed software will be available at your **/usr/share/doc** directory.

2. Installing Ubuntu Server

Installing Ubuntu Linux has become a very simple procedure with just a few screens with default entries for easy installation. A pre-selected collection of software is installed. Most of your devices, like your monitory and network connection, are detected automatically. The most difficult part would be a manual partitioning of the hard drive, but you can use a Guided partitioning for installs that use an entire hard disk, as is usually the case. As an alternative, you can now install Ubuntu on a virtual hard disk on your Windows system, avoiding any partition issues.

Install CD and DVDs

In most cases, installation is performed using an Ubuntu LiveCD that will install the GNOME desktop along with a pre-selected set of software packages for multimedia players, office applications, and games. The Ubuntu LiveCD is designed to run from the CD, while providing the option to install Ubuntu on your hard drive. This is the disc you will download from the Ubuntu download site. The CD has both 32 and 64 bit versions. If you are want to use the 64 bit version, be sure you have CPU that is 64 bit compatible (all current CPUs are).

```
http://www.ubuntu.com/getubuntu/download
```

You can also download CD and DVD images directly from:

```
http://releases.ubuntu.com
```

Ubuntu Server CD

The Ubuntu server CD is designed for hardware servers, systems that will run only servers and not perform any other tasks like desktop applications. The Ubuntu desktops are not installed. You will be presented with just a command line interface and command line tools like the Vi editor to manage your server configuration. You will have to know how to manually edit server configuration files, typing in your entries.

Servers, thought, do not have to be installed from the Server CD. You can directly download and install any server from the Ubuntu repository. Should you wish, you can install the Ubuntu desktop and then use GNOME based GUI tools like Synaptic Package Manager to install the servers you want. You can also use GUI server configuration tools to manage your servers. These are not available on a direct Server CD install.

The downside of installing from the desktop is that you incur the overhead of running the desktop interface, namely GNOME. Most commercial and professional enterprise servers are time critical managing a massive number of transactions. A desktop interface can seriously degrade performance. However, for a simple home sever, which would have relatively few transactions, the desktop would incur little or not overhead. It would also make managing your sever much easier.

Server Install

The server install CD includes all the servers available for use on Linux. These include the Samba Windows network server, mail servers, and database servers. All these are also included with the Install DVD. The Server CD is designed for stripped down servers that are used to just run servers, not provide any desktop support. In fact, the GNOME and KDE desktops are not included or installed with the Server CD. This is a very specialized server installation.

The server CD uses the same text based install interface as the Alternate install, with TABs, spacebar, and arrow keys used to make selections. Before the software is installed, a Software selection screen is displayed which lets you select the servers you want to install. Use the arrow keys to move to a selection, and the spacebar to make a selection.

When you startup a server installation, you will be using the command line interface. The desktop is not installed. Desktops are considered unnecessary overhead for a server. The user enters a user name at the Ubuntu login: prompt, followed by the password at the Password prompt.

Installing Dual-Boot Systems

The boot loader, GRUB, already supports dual-booting. Should you have both Linux and Windows systems installed on your hard disks, GRUB will let you choose to boot either the Linux system or a Windows system. During installation GRUB will automatically detect any other operating systems installed on your computer and configure your boot loader menu to let you access them. You do not have to perform any configuration yourself.

If you want a Windows system on your computer, you should install it first if it is not already installed. Windows would overwrite the boot loader that a previous Linux system installed, cutting off access to the Linux system.

To install Windows after Ubuntu, you need to boot from your Ubuntu disk and select the "Boot from hard disk" option. Then run the **grub-install** command with the device name of your hard disk to reinstall the boot loader for GRUB.

Hardware, Software, and Information Requirements

Most hardware today meets the requirements for running Linux. Linux can be installed on a wide variety of systems, ranging from the very weak to the very powerful. The install procedure will detect most of your hardware automatically. You will only need to specify your keyboard, though a default is automatically detected for you.

Hardware Requirements

Listed here are the minimum hardware requirements for installing a standard installation of the Linux system on an Intel-based PC:

➢ A 32-bit or 64-bit Intel- or AMD-based personal computer. At least an Intel or compatible (AMD) microprocessor is required. A 400 MHz Pentium II or more is recommended for a graphical interface and 200 MHz for text.

➢ For 64-bit systems, be sure to use the 64-bit version of Ubuntu, which includes a supporting kernel.

➢ A CD-ROM or DVD-ROM drive. Should you need to create a bootable DVD/CD-ROM, you will need a DVD/CD-RW drive.

➢ Normally you will need at least 64MB RAM for text, and 192MB for a graphical interface, with 256MB recommended. For 64-bit systems, you will need 128MB for text and 256MB for graphical, with 512MB recommended. (Linux can run on as little as 12MB RAM.) 3GB or more is recommended for desktop installation and 700MB for a command line interface–only installation. You will also need 64MB to 2GB for swap space, depending on the amount of RAM memory you have.

Hard Drive Configuration

These days, Linux is usually run on its own hard drive, though it can also be run on a hard drive that contains a separate partition for a different operating system such as Windows.

If you have already installed Windows on your hard drive and configured it to take up the entire hard drive, you would resize its partition to free up unused space. The freed space could then be used for a Linux partition. You can use a partition management software package, such as **Parted** or **PartitionMagic**, to free up space.

Tip: You can also use the Ubuntu Live CD to start up Linux and perform the needed hard disk partitioning using GParted for QTParted.

Hardware and Device Information

If you are not installing Linux on your entire hard drive, decide how much of your hard drive (in megabytes) you want to dedicate to your Linux system. If you are sharing with Windows, decide how much you want for Windows and how much for Linux. Install Windows first.

Know where you live so that you can select the appropriate time zone.

Mice are now automatically detected. Ubuntu no longer supports serial mice. If you should need to later configure your mouse, you can use the GNOME or KDE mouse configuration tool.

Monitor and graphics cards are now detected automatically by the Xorg service. Should you need to teak or modify your configuration later, you can use either the Vendor configuration tools (ATI or Nvidia) supplied by restricted drivers, or the GNOME **displayconfig-gtk** tool (System | Administration | Screens and Graphics).

Network connections are automatically detected and configured using NetworkManager. Most network connection use DHCP or IPv6 which will automatically set up your network connection. For dial-up and wireless you may have to later configure access.

Installing Ubuntu from the Server DVD

Installing Linux involves several processes, beginning with creating Linux partitions, and then loading the Linux software, selecting a time zone, and creating new user accounts. The installation program used on Ubuntu is a screen-based program that takes you through all these processes, step-by-step, as one continuous procedure. You can use the keyboard to make selections. You can also use TAB, the arrow keys, SPACEBAR, and ENTER to make selections. The TAB key moves you to the GO Back and Continue buttons at the bottom of the screen.

When you finish with a screen, either just press ENTER or tab to the Continue button at the bottom and then press ENTER, to move to the next screen. If you need to move back to the previous screen, tab to the Go Back button and press ENTER. You have little to do other than make selections and choose options.

Tip: To boot from a CD-ROM or DVD-ROM, you may first have to change the boot sequence setting in your computer's BIOS so that the computer will try to boot first from the CD-ROM. This requires some technical ability and knowledge of how to set your motherboard's BIOS configuration.

Installation Overview

Installation is a straightforward process. A graphical installation is very easy to use, providing full mouse support and explaining each step.

➤ Most systems today already meet hardware requirements and have automatic connections to the Internet (DHCP).

➤ They also support booting a DVD-ROM or CD-ROM disc, though this support may have to be explicitly configured in the system BIOS.

➤ Also, if you know how you want Linux installed on your hard disk partitions, or if you are performing a simple update that uses the same partitions, installing Ubuntu is a fairly simple process. Ubuntu features an automatic partitioning function that will perform the partitioning for you.

➤ A preconfigured set of packages are installed, except for the servers you want installed.

For a quick installation you can simply start up the installation process, placing your DVD or CD disc in your optical drive and starting up your system. Graphical installation is a simple matter of following the instructions in each window as you progress. Installation follows seven easy steps:

1. **Language Selection**   A default is chosen for you, like English, so you can usually just press ENTER.

2. Country

3. **Keyboard Layout**   You can choose to automatically detect the layout by pressing some keys, or choose one from a list, first by country and then by type. A default is chosen for you; you can usually press ENTER.

4. **Network Detecton**. Automatic DHCP configuration or manual configuration.. You will be prompted to enter a host name.

5. **Time Zone**   You then select your time zone.

6. **Prepare partitions**   Disks are scanned and the partitioner starts up. For automatic partitioning you have the option of using a Guided partition which will set up your partitions for you. You can choose to use LVM or LVM encrypted file systems.You have the option to perform manual partitioning, setting up partitions yourself.

7. The base system is then installed.

8. **User name** Set up a user name for your computer, as well as a password for that user.

9. **Select server software**   Choose the server packages you want installed. LAMP includes the Apaceh Web server and the MySQL database server.

10. **Finish the Installation**   After the install, you will be asked to remove your DVD/CD-ROM. You then press ENTER.

Starting the Installation Program

If your computer can boot from the DVD/CD-ROM, you can start the installation directly from the CD-ROMs or the DVD-ROM. Just place the CD-ROM in the CD-ROM drive, or the DVD-ROM in the DVD drive, before you start your computer. After you turn on or restart your computer, the installation program will start up.

The Ubuntu Server CD is designed for installing the server. The installation program will present you with a menu listing the following options (see Figure 2-1):

```
Install Ubuntu Server
Check CD for defects
Rescue broken system
Test Memory
Boot from first hard disk
```

. "Install Ubuntu Server" will start up the installation Welcome screen immediately, beginning the install process (see the next section).

"Check CD for defects" will check if your CD burn was faulty.

"Rescue a broken system" will start Ubuntu and let you mount a broken system. You can then make changes to the system configuration.

"Memory Test" will check your memory.

"Boot from first hard disk" will let your LiveCD work as boot loader, starting up an operating system on the first hard disk, if one is installed. Use it to boot a system that the boot loader is not accessing for some reason.

Along the bottom of the screen are options you can set for the installation process. These are accessible with the function keys, 1 through 6.

F1 Help F2 Language F3 Keymap F4 Vga F5 Accessibility F6 Other Options

Figure 2-1: Install disk start menu for Server DVD

A description of these options is listed here:

➢ **Help** Boot parameters and install prerequisites

➢ **Languages** List of languages , pop up menu

➢ **Keymap** Languages for keyboard, pop up menu

➢ **Modes** Lists possible install modes: There is currently only the normal mode.

➢ **Accessibility**   Contrast setting, Magnifier, On screen keyboard, and Braille support

➢ **Other options**, Opens an editable text line listing the options of the current selected menu choice. You can add other options here, or modify or remove existing ones. As you move down the list of choices you will see the text listed options change, showing the boot options for that choice. Press ESC to return, or enter to start.

Use the arrow keys to move from one menu entry to another, and then press ENTER to select the entry. Should you need to add options, say to the Install or Upgrade entry, press the TAB key. A command line is displayed where you can enter the options. Current options will already be listed. Use the backspace key to delete and arrow keys to move through the line. Press the ESC key to return to the menu.

Tip: Pressing ESC from the graphics menu places you at the boot prompt, boot: , for text mode install.

The OEM install mode (Modes) is used for organizations that will be installing Ubuntu on several machines, but want to later add their own applications and configurations to the install. The OEM install will set up an OEM default user with a password provided by the installer. When the installer is ready to turn over control to a regular user, then can run the **oem-prepare** command that will set up a normal user and password, removing the OEM user.

Starting up Ubuntu

Your system then detects your hardware, providing any configuration specifications that may be needed. For example, if you have an IDE CD-RW or DVD-RW drive, it will be configured automatically.

If you cannot start the install process and you are using an LCD display, you should press F6 on the Install entry and enter **nofb** (no frame buffer) in the options command line.

nofb

As each screen appears in the installation, default entries will be already selected, usually by the auto-probing capability of the installation program. Selected entries will appear highlighted. If these entries are correct, you can simply click Forward to accept them and go on to the next screen.

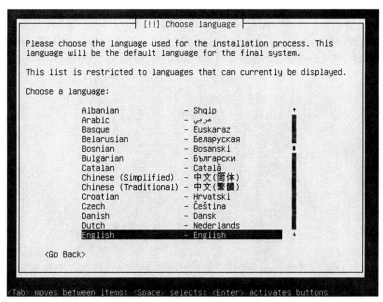

Figure 2-2: Language

Installation Steps

First you select your Language (see Figure 2-2).

Then you select your country or region (see Figure 2-3).

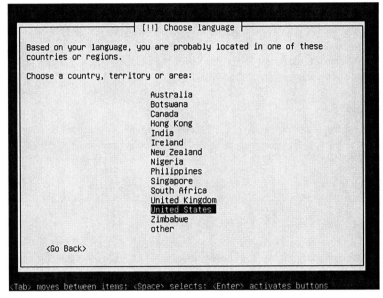

Figure 2-3: location

You will then be asked to select a keyboard—the default is already selected, such as U.S. English (see Figure 2-4). You can have it automatically detected by typing keys.

Figure 2-4: Keyboard Layout

If there is more than one keyboard layout for yoru region, you are prompted to select one. The USE keyboard will have several such as Macintosh, Dvorak, or International, as well as the standard.

Network Configuration

You then configure our network interface. If you are using a DCHP server to configure your network information, you will be prompted just to enter a host name for your server (see Figure 2-5).

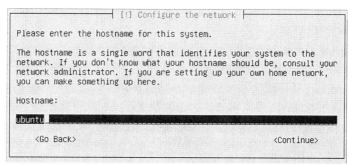

Figure 2-5: Network Configuration

If you are using a fixed IP address for your server, select Go Back and select the "Configure network manually" entry to configure your network information manually. Following screens will prompt for:

> IP address for the server

> Your network netmask

> IP address for the network gateway (address for router connected to the Internet)

> IP addresses for the name servers (DNS servers)

> Your server's host name

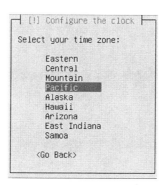

Figure 2-6: Time Zone

Time Zone

You then configure your time zone (see Figure 2-6).

Partitions

Then you will be asked to designate the Linux partitions and hard disk configurations you want to use on your hard drives.

No partitions will be changed or formatted until you select your packages later in the install process. You can opt out of the installation at any time until that point, and your original partitions will remain untouched.

The options will change according to the number of hard disks on your system. If you have several hard disks, they will be listed. You can also select the disk on which to install Ubuntu.

Ubuntu provides automatic partitioning options if you just want to use available drives and free space for your Linux system. LVM, RAID, and encrypted file systems are supported.

The Ubuntu Server provides three guided options, setting up default configurations for an entire disk. You will have to have an entire blank disk free for use for your Ubuntu server (see Figure 2-7). Each is preceded with the term Guided.   These are:

> ➢ Guided - use the entire disk

> ➢ Guided - use the entire disk and set up LVM

> ➢ Guided _use the entire disk and set up encrypted LVM.

Windows and Linux **/home** partitions will not be overwritten in a Guided partition. The Guided option, though, requires free space on your hard disk on which to install your system.

If you already have partitions set up on your hard disk, and want to overwrite existing Linux partitions, you should select the Manual option so you can edit those partitions, designating them for formatting and installation.

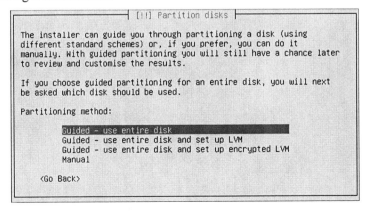

Figure 2-7: Partition options

If you selected a Guided options, you are then asked to select the disk to set up the partitions on (see Figure 2-8).

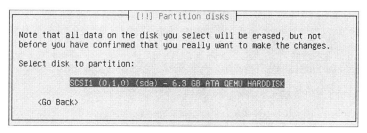

Figure 2-8: Selecting hard disk for partitioning

Before the partitions are created, the partition set up is displayed and you are prompted to accept them. This is your last chance to back out of the partitioning.

The default Guided partitioning will set up two partitions, one as the swap partition and an ext3 partition for the entire file system (/).

A default LVM partitioning will set up an ext3 file system for the boot directory, and then an LVM file system (Group) with two LVM volumes, one for the swap partition and one for the root (the Ubuntu system except for the **boot** directory), see Figure 2-9.

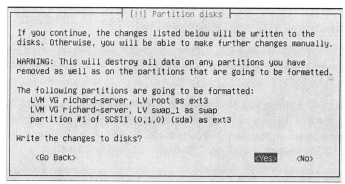

Figure 2-9: Creating partitions

Encrypted LVM will add a further prompt for the password for your encrypted file systems. Your LVM root and swap files systems will be encrypted, not your boot file systems. Whenever your systems boots up, you will be prompted to enter the passphrase for your encrypted file systems. Encryption adds a further level of security, especially for publicly access file systems like those used for servers. The effect on performance is a negligible.

Tip: If you already have a Linux system, you will most likely have several Linux partitions already. Some of these may be used for just the system software, such as the boot and root partitions. These should be formatted. Others may have extensive user files, such as a **/home** partition that normally holds user home directories and all the files they have created. You should *not* format such partitions.

To manually configure your hard drive, first plan what partitions you want to set up and what their size should be. You can set up different partitions for any directory on your system. Many systems set up separate partitions for **/home**, **/var**, **/srv**, as well as / (root) and **/boot**. You will, of course, need a swap partition.

> ➢ **/var** directory holds data that constantly changes like printer spool files.

> ➢ **/srv** directory holds server data, like Web server pages and FTP sites

> ➢ **/home** directory holds users files along with any user data.

> ➢ **/** the root directory is the system directory. All other file systems and partitions attach to it.

> ➢ **/boot** the boot directory holds the Linux kernel and the boot configuration (cannot be an LVM volume)

Except for the boot partition, all of these can be LVM volumes. LVM volumes may work better than ordinary ext3 partitions, since you can expand or replace them easily. With a standard ext3 partition you are limited to the size you specify when you first set up your partition. Also, a normal SATA hard drive is limited to just 4 partitions. If you want more on a single hard drive, you would have to set up an LVM group and implement the partitions as LVM volumes. There is no limit to the number of LVM volumes you can have in a group.

You are then prompted to create a new partition.

Specify the size of the partition in either MB or GB. The term max will use all remaining free space. The choose whether it should be primary or logical, and then at the end or beginning of the disk.

On the partition settings screen you specify the mount point, file system type (Use as), and the label. Pressing the ENTER key on the Use as entry will display a dialog listing file system types from which to choose. A standard Linux partition would use ext3, a swap partition would use swap area, and an LVM partition would use "Physical volume for LVM".

For the mount point, a dialog will list common mount points, like / for the root file system, **/home** for users, and **/boot** for a boot partition.

If you are setting up an LVM partition, select "physical volume for LVM" for the Use as option. The Partitions disk screen will then have an added entry for "Configure the Logical Volume Manager". Choose this to set up your volume group and its logical volumes. You are first prompted to create a volume group, specifying its device and a label. Then create the logical volumes (Create a logical volume). Enter a label and the size for each. You then return to the partitioner which will list all your logical volumes. Select and press enter on each to then select a file system type and mount point (a swap partition will not have a mount point).

Once all your partitions have been configured, with mount points specified, you can select the "Finish partitioning and write changes to disk" option to make the actual changes. A dialog is displayed showing the partitions that will be formatted.

Install base system and system user

The base system is then installed (see Figure 2-10).

Installing the base system
6%
Validating libstdc++6...

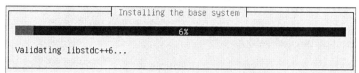

Figure 2-10: install base system

On the following screens you enter the user's full name, the user log in name, that user's password (see Figures 2-11, 12, and 13). The user you are creating will have administrative access, allowing you to change your system configuration, add new users and printers, and install new software. You are also prompted if you need an HTTP proxy.

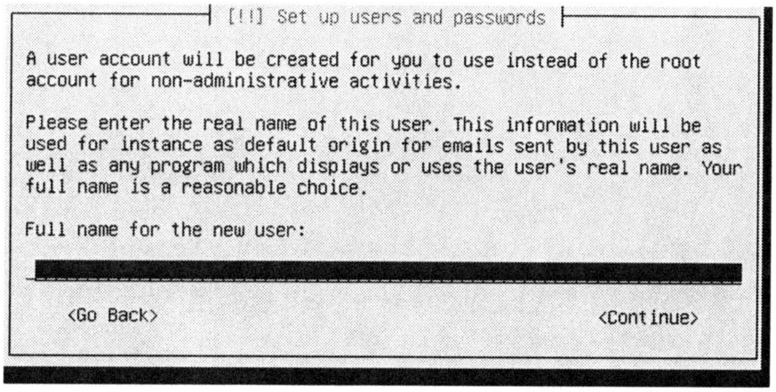

[!!] Set up users and passwords
A user account will be created for you to use instead of the root account for non-administrative activities.
Please enter the real name of this user. This information will be used for instance as default origin for emails sent by this user as well as any program which displays or uses the user's real name. Your full name is a reasonable choice.
Full name for the new user:
<Go Back>
<Continue>

Figure 2-11: create user

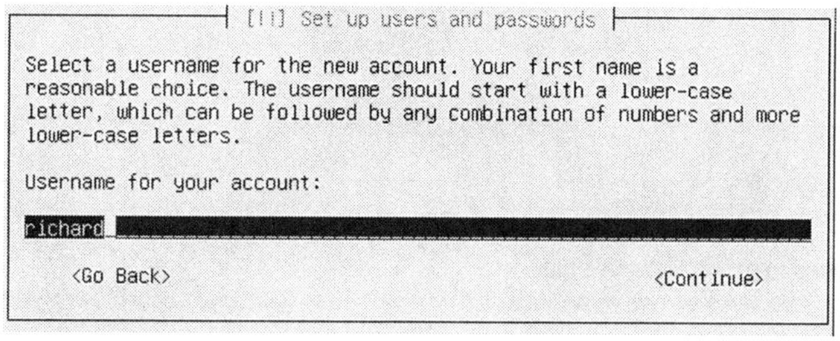

[!!] Set up users and passwords
Select a username for the new account. Your first name is a reasonable choice. The username should start with a lower-case letter, which can be followed by any combination of numbers and more lower-case letters.
Username for your account:
richard
<Go Back>
<Continue>

Figure 2-12: create user name

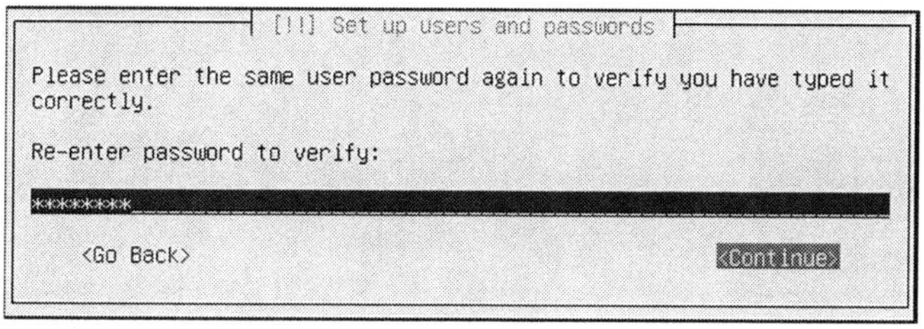

[!!] Set up users and passwords
Please enter the same user password again to verify you have typed it correctly.
Re-enter password to verify:
****
<Go Back>
<Continue>

Figure 2-13: create user password

Select server software

For access to the Ubuntu online repository, you are then prompted to enter an http proxy server, should your network connection require it.

You then select the sever packages you want to install. The LAMP server sets up a Web server with supporting software. It includes the Apache Web server, MySQL database server, and the PHP server for Web support (**L**inux, **A**pache, **M**ySQL, **P**HP). Samba provides Windows file system access. PostgreSQL is an optional database server. The Mail sever used is Postfix and the Printer server is Cups.

On a Software Selection screen, you are then prompted to select the servers you want installed (see Figure 2-14). Use the Arrow keys to move to a selection and press the spacebar to select it:

```
DNS server
Lamp Server
Mail server
OpenSSH server
PostreSQL database
Print server
Samba File server
```

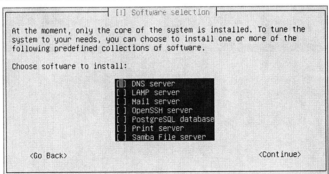

Figure 2-14: Select server packages

For MySQL (LAMP), you are prompted for a password.

```
                          [!!] Finish the installation
                            Installation complete
Installation is complete, so it is time to boot into your new system.
Make sure to remove the installation media (CD-ROM, floppies), so
that you boot into the new system rather than restarting the
installation.
      <Go Back>                                          <Continue>
```

Figure 2-15: Finishing install

For Postfix (Mail server), select the type of configuration, the options are no configuration or Internet, with a detailed explanation of both. For the Internet option, you will need to enter the domain name for your server's network (as in **surfingturtlepress.com**).

The installation then finishes (see Figure 2-15).

Remaining configuration and boot loader installation is performed for you. The server disk is ejected and you are prompted to reboot.

Server disk install start

If you installed from the server disk, no desktop is installed. When you start up, a command line interface is presented. Install messages will show the servers being installed (see Figure 2-16).

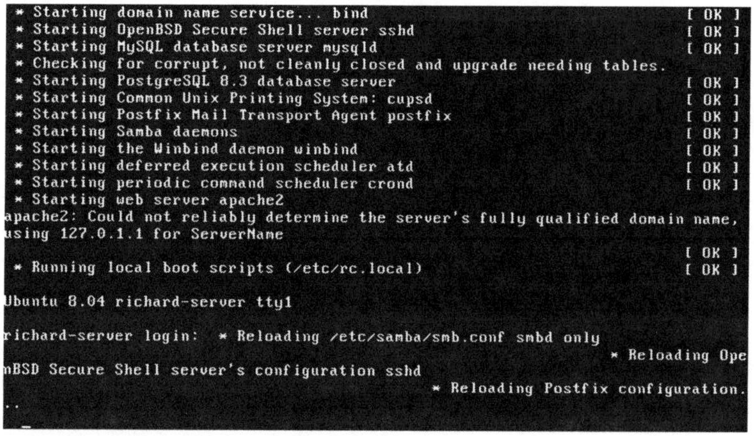

Figure 2-16: Server start up

The login prompt then prompts you to enter your user name. This is the user name you set up during installation (see Figure 2-17).

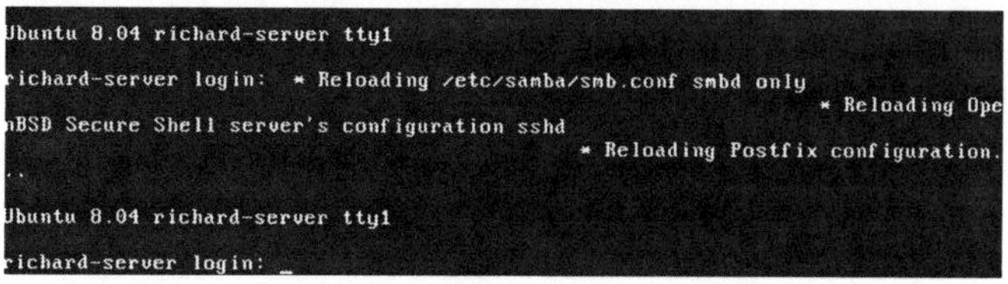

Figure 2-17: Server login prompt

For Postfix (Mail server), select the type of configuration, the options are no configuration or Internet, with a detailed explanation of both. For the Internet option, you will need to enter the domain name for your server's network (as in **surfingturtlepress.com**).

The installation then finishes (see Figure 2-15).

After you enter your user name, you will be prompted to enter the password. Once logged in, you can then run commands (see Figure 2-18).

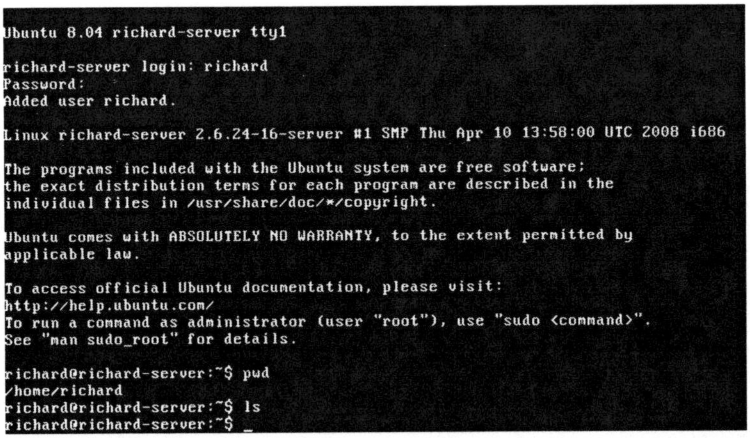

Figure 2-18: Server login

To shut down the system enter the halt command with the sudo command. You will be x

Tip: If you are using a desktop interface, you can use CTRL-ALT-F3 to shift to a command line prompt and log in to check out your system, shutting down with the **halt** command (the CTRL-A LT-F7 keys would return you to the desktop interface).

Grub selection and editing

When your system restarts, the GRUB boot loader will quickly select your default operating system and start up its login screen. If you have just installed Ubuntu, the default operating system will be Ubuntu.

Grub with the Grub menu work just as they would for the desktop. You will have an additional option for a recovery mode that loads without any servers. Press the ESC key to display the Grub menu (see Figure 2-19).

If you have more than one operating system, you can select using the GRUB menu You first need to display the GRUB menu at start up. You will have about a 3 second chance to do this. A quick message will be displayed saying that GRUB is starting up your operating system. At this point, press the ESC key. Your GRUB menu will be displayed as shown in Figure 2-19.

The GRUB menu will list Ubuntu and other operating systems you specified, such as Windows. Use the arrow keys to move to the entry you want, if it is not already highlighted, and press ENTER.

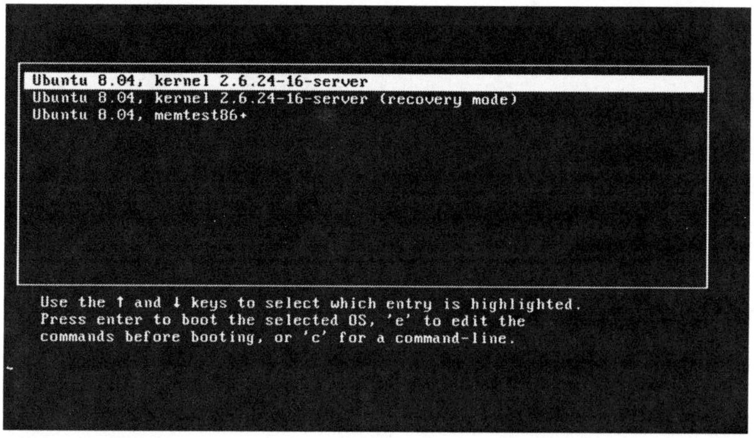

```
Ubuntu 8.04, kernel 2.6.24-16-server
Ubuntu 8.04, kernel 2.6.24-16-server (recovery mode)
Ubuntu 8.04, memtest86+




    Use the ↑ and ↓ keys to select which entry is highlighted.
    Press enter to boot the selected OS, 'e' to edit the
    commands before booting, or 'c' for a command-line.
```

Figure 2-19: Grub menu

For graphical installations, some displays may have difficulty running the graphical start up display. If you have this problem, you can edit your Linux GRUB entry and remove the **splash** term at the end of the Grub start up line. Press the **e** key to edit a Grub entry (see Figure 2-20).

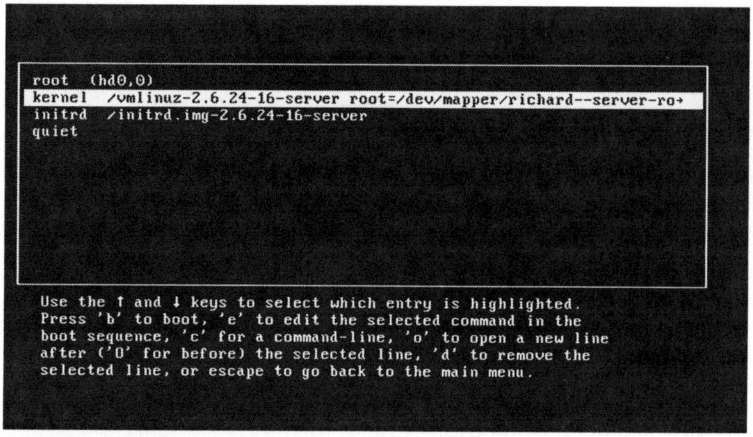

```
root    (hd0,0)
kernel  /vmlinuz-2.6.24-16-server root=/dev/mapper/richard--server-ro+
initrd  /initrd.img-2.6.24-16-server
quiet




    Use the ↑ and ↓ keys to select which entry is highlighted.
    Press 'b' to boot, 'e' to edit the selected command in the
    boot sequence, 'c' for a command-line, 'o' to open a new line
    after ('O' for before) the selected line, 'd' to remove the
    selected line, or escape to go back to the main menu.
```

Figure 2-20: Edit a Grub entry

To change a particular line, select it and then press the **e** key. The end of the line is then displayed (see Figure 2-21). You can use the arrow keys to move along the line. the Backspace key will delete characters and simply typing will insert characters. All changes are temporary. Permanent changes can only be made by directly editing the **/boot/grub/menu.lst** file.

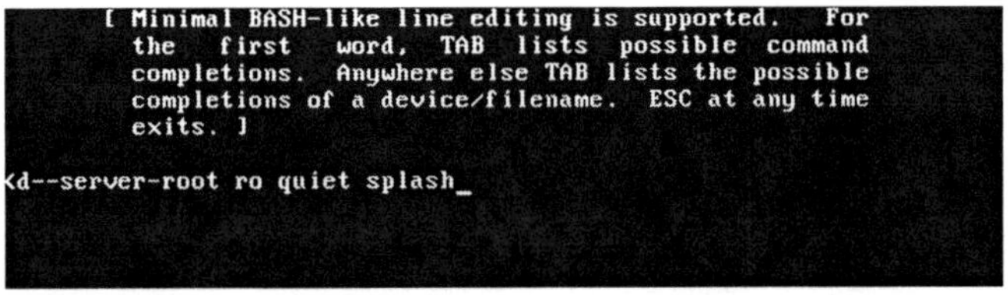

```
[ Minimal BASH-like line editing is supported.  For
the  first  word,  TAB  lists  possible  command
completions.  Anywhere else TAB lists the possible
completions of a device/filename.  ESC at any time
exits. ]

Kd--server-root ro quiet splash_
```

Figure 2-21: Edit Grub line

Once edited, press ENTER key to return to the Grub entry screen, and then press the b key to boot from the Grub entry

Initial Configuration Tasks

There are a few configuration tasks you many want to configure right away. These include:

➢ The Date And Time using the date command.

➢ Create Users using the useradd command.

➢ Firewall and Virus Projection using UFW and ClamAV for virus protection

Recovery

If for some reason you are not able to boot or access your system, it may be due to conflicting configurations, libraries, or applications. In this case, you can boot your Linux system in a recovery mode and then edit configuration files with a text editor such as Vi, remove the suspect libraries, or reinstall damaged software. To enter the recovery mode, press the ESC key on start up to display the GRUB boot menu. Then select the recovery entry.

Re-Installing the Boot Loader

If you have a dual-boot system, where you are running both Windows and Linux on the same machine, you may run into a situation where you have to re-install your GRUB boot loader. This problem occurs if your Windows system completely crashes beyond repair and you have to install a new version of Windows, or you are adding Windows to your machine after having installed Linux. Windows will automatically overwrite your boot loader (alternatively, you could install your boot loader on your Linux partition instead of the MBR). You will no longer be able to access your Linux system.

All you need to do is to reinstall your boot loader. First boot from your Linux DVD/CD-ROM installation disk, and at the menu select Rescue broken system. This boots your system in rescue mode. Then use **grub-install** and the device name of your first partition to install the boot loader. Windows normally wants to be on the first partition with the MBR, the master boot record. You would specify this partition. At the prompt enter

```
grub-install /dev/sda1
```

This will re-install your current GRUB boot loader, assuming that Windows is included in the GRUB configuration. You can then reboot, and the GRUB boot loader will start up. If you are adding Windows for the first time, you will have to add an entry for it in the **/boot/grub/menu.lst** file to have it accessible from the boot loader.

Automating Installation with Kickstart

Kickstart is a method for providing a predetermined installation configuration for installing Ubuntu. Instead of having a user enter responses on the install screens, the responses can be listed in a kickstart file the install process can read from. You will need to create a kickstart configuration file on a working Ubuntu system. (Kickstart configuration files have the extension **.cfg**.) A kickstart file is created for every Ubuntu system that holds the install responses used for that installation. It is located in the root directory at

```
/root/anaconda-ks.cfg
```

If you plan to perform the same kind of install on computers that would be configured in the same way, say on a local network with hosts that have the same hardware, you could use this kickstart file as a model for performing installations. It is a text file that you can edit, with entries for each install response, like the following for keyboard and time zone:

```
keyboard us
timezone America/LosAngeles
```

More complex responses may take options such as **network**, which uses **--device** for the device interface and **bootproto** for the boot client.

```
network --device eth0 --bootproto dhcp
```

Display configuration is more complex, specifying a video card and monitor type, which could vary. You can have the system skip this with **xskip**.

The first entry is the install source. This will be **cdrom** for a CD/DVD-ROM install. If you want to use an NFS or Web install instead, you could place that here, specifying the server name or Web site.

Tip: IF you are using a desktop interface, you can use the **system-config-kickstart** file to create your kickstart file. This provides a graphical interface for each install screen. First install it. Then to start it select Applications | System Tools | Kickstart. The help manual provides a detailed description on how to use this tool.

The name of the configuration file should be **ks.cfg**. Once you have created your kickstart file, you can copy it to CD/DVD or to a floppy disk. You could also place the file on a local hard disk partition (such as a Windows or Linux partition), if you already have one. For a network, you could place the file on an NFS server, provided your network is running a DHCP server to enable automatic network configuration on the install computer.

When you start the installation, at the boot prompt you specify the kickstart file and its location. In the following example, the kickstart file will be located on a floppy disk as **/dev/fd0**.

```
linux ks=floppy
```

You can use **sd:***device* to specify a particular device such as a hard drive or second CD-ROM drive. For an NFS site, you would use **nfs:**.

3. Usage Basics: Login, Help, and Software

Using Linux has become an almost intuitive process, with easy-to-use interfaces, including graphical logins and graphical user interfaces (GUIs) like GNOME and KDE. Even the standard Linux command line interface has become more user-friendly with editable commands, history lists, and cursor-based tools. To start using Linux, you have to know how to access your Linux system and, once you are on the system, how to execute commands and run applications. Access is supported through a graphical login. A simple window appears with menus for selecting login options and a text box for entering your username and password. Once you access your system, you can then interact with it using the windows, menus, and icons..

Linux is noted for providing easy access to extensive help documentation. It's easy to obtain information quickly about any Linux command and utility while logged in to the system. You can access an online manual that describes each command or obtain help that provides more detailed explanations of different Linux features. A complete set of manuals provided by the Linux Documentation Project is on your system and available for you to browse through or print. Both the GNOME and KDE desktops provide help systems that give you easy access to desktop, system, and application help files.

It is possible to first install the Ubuntu server, and then later install the Ubuntu desktop. This would provide you with al the configuration files for the Ubuntu server, as well as the GUI configuration tools available for those servers.

The entire Ubuntu desktop can be downloaded using the **ubuntu-desktop** metapackage. Should you want to install the Ubuntu desktop on your server, you can issue the following command.

```
sudo apt-get install ubuntu-desktop
```

Download and setup can take an hour or more.

You then logout and restart your system. The GDM will start up as shown in Figure 3-1.. The first time you start up, be sure to select GNOME from the Options Sessions menu. Click on Option and select Sessions from the pop-up menu. This displays possible interfaces to use. Select GNOME. You will be prompted to determine if you want GNOME for just this session.

Accessing Your Linux System

If you have installed the boot loader GRUB, when you turn on or reset your computer, the boot loader first decides what operating system to load and run. The boot loader then loads the default operating system, which will be Ubuntu. Ubuntu will use a graphical interface by default, presenting you with a graphical login window at which you enter your username and password.

If other operating systems, like Windows, are already installed on your computer, then you can press the spacebar at start up to display a boot loader menu showing those systems as boot options. If a Windows system is listed, you can choose to start that instead.

The Command Line Interface

The Ubuntu server CD, for efficiency reasons, will not install a desktop interface. Instead you use the traditional Unix command line interface, accessing your system from a login prompt and typing commands form your keyboard on a command line.

Accessing Linux from the Command Line Interface

For the command line interface, you are initially given a login prompt. The login prompt is preceded by the hostname you gave your system. In this example, the hostname is **turtle**. When you finish using Linux, you first log out. Linux then displays exactly the same login prompt, waiting for you or another user to log in again. This is the equivalent of the login window provided by the GDM. You can then log in to another account.

Once you log in to an account, you can enter and execute commands. Logging in to your Linux account involves two steps: entering your username and then entering your password. Type in the username for your user account. If you make a mistake, you can erase characters with the BACKSPACE key. In the next example, the user enters the username **richard** and is then prompted to enter the password:

```
Ubuntu 8 turtle server tty

turtle server login: richard
Password:
```

When you type in your password, it does not appear on the screen. This is to protect your password from being seen by others. If you enter either the username or the password incorrectly, the system will respond with the error message "Login incorrect" and will ask for your username again, starting the login process over. You can then reenter your username and password.

Once you enter your username and password correctly, you are logged in to the system. Your command line prompt is displayed, waiting for you to enter a command. Notice the command line prompt is a dollar sign (**$**), not a number sign (**#**). The **$** is the prompt for regular users, whereas the **#** is the prompt solely for the root user. In this version of Ubuntu, your prompt is preceded by the hostname and the directory you are in. Both are bounded by a set of brackets.

```
[turtle /home/richlp]$
```

To end your session, issue the **logout** or **exit** command. This returns you to the login prompt, and Linux waits for another user to log in.

```
[turtle /home/richlp]$ logout
```

To, instead, shut down your system from the command line, you enter the **halt** command. This command will log you out and shut down the system. It requires administrative access.

```
$ sudo halt
```

Using the Command Line Interface

When using the command line interface, you are given a simple prompt at which you type in your command. Even with a GUI, you sometimes need to execute commands on a command line. You can do so in a terminal window. The terminal window is accessed from the Applications | Accessories menu. You can add the terminal window icon to the desktop by right-clicking on the menu entry and selecting Add launcher to the desktop.

Linux commands make extensive use of options and arguments. Be careful to place your arguments and options in their correct order on the command line. The format for a Linux command is the command name followed by options, and then by arguments, as shown here:

```
$ command-name options arguments
```

An *option* is a one-letter code preceded by one or two hyphens, which modifies the type of action the command takes. Options and arguments may or may not be optional, depending on the command. For example, the **ls** command can take an option, **-s**. The **ls** command displays a listing of files in your directory, and the **-s** option adds the size of each file in blocks. You enter the command and its option on the command line as follows:

```
$ ls -s
```

An *argument* is data the command may need to execute its task. In many cases, this is a filename. An argument is entered as a word on the command line after any options. For example, to display the contents of a file, you can use the **more** command with the file's name as its argument. The **less** or **more** command used with the filename **mydata** would be entered on the command line as follows:

```
$ less mydata
```

The command line is actually a buffer of text you can edit. Before you press ENTER, you can perform editing commands on the existing text. The editing capabilities provide a way to correct mistakes you may make when typing in a command and its options. The BACKSPACE and DEL keys let you erase the character you just typed in. With this character-erasing capability, you can BACKSPACE over the entire line if you want, erasing what you entered. CTRL-U erases the whole line and enables you to start over again at the prompt.

You can use the UP ARROW key to redisplay your last-executed command. You can then re-execute that command, or you can edit it and execute the modified command. This is helpful when you have to repeat certain operations over and over, such as editing the same file. This is also helpful when you've already executed a command you entered incorrectly.

Accessing USB drives from the Command line Interface on a Server.

When you attach a USB drive, HAL will automatically detect it, but not mount it. A message will be displayed indicating the device name for the drive. If you have one hard drive which would be labeled device sda, then the USB device would be sdb. USB drives are normally formatted as **vfat** file systems. Your file system would be located on the first file system, which would be **sdb1** in this example.

To access the USB drive you have to create a directory on which to mount it. Then use the mount command to mount the file system. Creating the directory you do only once. Use the **mkdir** command to create the directory.

```
mkdir myusb
```

To mount a USB drive to that directory you enter a mount command with the **vfat** type, mounting the **/dev/sdb1** device to the **myusb** directory. You have to have administrative access, so you need to use the **sudo** command.

```
mount -t vfat  /dev/sdb1  myusb
```

You can then access the USB drive by accessing the mymedia directory.

```
cd myusb
ls
```

Write operations would still have to be run with administrative access.

```
sudo cp mydata  myusb
```

To write whole directories and their subdirectories, you need to add the **-R** option to **cp**.

```
sudo cp -R mydatadir  myusb
```

Once finished with the USB drive, be sure to unmount it first before removing it.

```
sudo umount /dev/sdb1.
```

The USB drive's directory cannot be your working directory.

Setting the date and time

You can set the system date and time either manually or by referencing an Internet time server. You could also use your local hardware clock. To set the system time manually, you use the **date** command. The date command has several options for adjusting both the date and time. You can set the time by month or minutes with the **--set** option. You can use a sequence of numbers to set a specific time beginning with the month, day, hour, minute, and year. The following sets the date to July 22, 8:15 AM 2008.

```
sudo date 072208152008
```

The date command also has formatting options for the day, month, or year.

To use a time server, you use the **ntpdate** command and the address of the time server.

```
sudo ntpdate  ntp.ubuntu.com
```

To access the hardware clock, you use the **hwclock** command. The command itself will display the hardware clock time.

```
hwclock
```

The **--hctosys** option will set the system clock using the hardware clock's time, and the **--systohc** option resets the hardware clock using the system time. Use the **--set** and **--date** options to set the hardware clock to a certain time.

```
sudo hwclock --systohc
```

The time zone was set when you installed your system. If you need to change it, you can copy a new time zone from the files in the /usr/share/zoneinfo subdirectories. They are arranged by location and city. Copy the new time zone to the **/etc/localtime** file.

```
sudo cp /usr/share/zoneinfo/Europe/London  /etc/localtime
```

Help Resources accessible from the command line

A great deal of support documentation is already installed on your system, as well as accessible from online sources. Both the GNOME and KDE desktops feature Help systems that use a browser-like interface to display help files. To start the GNOME or KDE Help browser, select the Help entry in the main menu or click help icon on the panel. The Help browsers now support the Ubuntu Help Center, which provides Ubuntu specific help, as well as the GNOME desktop and system man page support.

If you need to ask a question, you can select the Get online help entry in the Help menu to access the Hardy help support at **answers.launchpad.net**. Here you can submit your question, as well as check answered questions and Ubuntu

Application Documentation

On your system, the **/usr/share/doc** directory contains documentation files installed by each application. Within each directory, you can usually find HOW-TO, README, and INSTALL documents for that application.

The Man Pages

You can also access the Man pages, which are manuals for Linux commands available from the command line interface, using the `man` command. Enter `man` with the command on which you want information. The following example asks for information on the `ls` command:

```
$ man ls
```

Pressing the SPACEBAR key advances you to the next page. Pressing the B key moves you back a page. When you finish, press the Q key to quit the Man utility and return to the command line. You activate a search by pressing either the slash (/) or question mark (?). The / searches forward; the ? searches backward. When you press the /, a line opens at the bottom of your screen, and you then enter a word to search for. Press ENTER to activate the search. You can repeat the same search by pressing the N key. You needn't reenter the pattern.

Tip: You can also use either the GNOME or KDE Help system to display Man and info pages.

The Info Pages

Online documentation for GNU applications, such as the gcc compiler and the Emacs editor, also exist as *info* pages accessible from the GNOME and KDE Help Centers. You can also access this documentation by entering the command `info`. This brings up a special screen listing different GNU applications. The info interface has its own set of commands. You can learn more about it by entering `info info`. Typing `m` opens a line at the bottom of the screen where you can enter the first few letters of the application. Pressing ENTER brings up the info file on that application.

Using the Desktop Interface

If you decided to install the desktop, either from the desktop CD/DVD or from the Ubuntu repository, you can then use the GNOME desktop to manage your servers. If you installed from a desktop CD/DVD, keep in mind, that you will loose the server efficient kernel that the Server CD installs.

The Display Manager: GDM

The desktop CD/DVD will install the GDM graphical login. With the graphical login, your GUI interface (X server) starts up immediately and displays a login window with box for your username. When you enter your username, press ENTER, and then enter your password in the same box. Upon pressing ENTER, your default GUI starts up. On Ubuntu, this is GNOME by default. A constantly running X server will impose a performance hit on a server system.

For Ubuntu, graphical logins are handled by the GNOME Display Manager (GDM). The GDM manages the login interface along with authenticating a user password and username, and then starting up a selected desktop. If problems ever occur using the GUI interface, you can force an exit of the GUI with the CTRL-ALT-BACKSPACE keys, returning to the Login screen. Also, from the GDM, you can shift to the command line interface with the CTRL-ALT-F1 keys, and then shift back to the GUI with the CTRL-ALT-F7 keys.

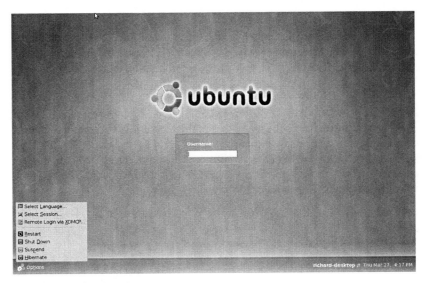

Figure 3-1: GDM Login Window

When the GDM starts up, it shows a login window with a box for login (see Figure 3-1). Various GDM themes are available, which you can select using the GDM configuration tool. The default theme currently used is the Ubuntu Human theme. An Options pop-up menu at the lower left of the screen shows entries to shutdown, restart, suspend, or hibernate your system. In addition there are Language and Session entries that display dialogs for selecting the language or user interface you want to use like GNOME or KDE.

Tip: You can also force your system to reboot at the login prompt, by holding down the CTRL and ALT keys and then pressing the DEL key (CTRL-ALT-DEL). Your system will go through the standard shutdown procedure and then reboot your computer.

To log in, enter your username in the entry box labeled Username and press ENTER. You are then prompted to enter your password. Do so, and press ENTER. By default, the GNOME desktop is then started up.

Tip: You can configure your GDM login window with different features like background images and user icons. The GDM even has its own selection of themes to choose from. Select Login Window entry on the System | Administration menu to configure your login window.

When you log out from the desktop, you return to the GDM login window. To shut down your Linux system, select Quit or the Shutdown entry in the Options menu. To restart, select Restart from the Options menu. Alternatively, you can also shut down from GNOME. From the System menu, select the Quit entry, or click the Quit button on the top panel to the right. GNOME will display a dialog screen with two rows of buttons. The buttons on the lower row show Suspend, Hibernate, Restart, or Shut Down options. Selecting Restart will shut down and restart your system.

From the Select Sessions entry in the Options menu, you can select the desktop or window manager you want to start up. A dialog box is displayed showing all installed possible user interfaces. Here you can select KDE to start up the K Desktop, for example, instead of GNOME. The KDE option will not be shown unless you have already installed it. Failsafe entries for both Gnome and the terminal provide a stripped down interface you could use for troubleshooting. The Run Xclient script lets you run just your X Windows System configuration script. This script will normally start up Gnome or KDE, but it could be specially configured for other desktops or Window managers. Normally you would have the Last session entry selected which starts up the interface you use previously. Once you have selected your interface, click the Change Session button (you can opt out of any change by clicking the Cancel button).

The List language entry opens a dialog with a pop-up menu that lists a variety of different languages that Linux supports. Choose one can click the Change Language button to change the language your interface will use.

The User Switcher

The User Switcher lets you switch to another user, without having to log out or end your current user session. The User Switcher is installed automatically as part of your basic Gnome desktop configuration. The switcher will appear on the right side of the top panel as the name of the currently logged in user. If you left-click the name, a list of all other users will be displayed (see Figure 3-2). Check boxes next to each show which users are logged in and running. To switch a user, select the user from this menu. If the user is not already logged in, the login manager (GDM) will appear and you can enter that user's password. If the user is already logged in, then the login window for the lock screen will appear (you can disable the lock screen). Just enter the user's password. The user's original session will continue with the same open windows and applications running when the user switched off. You can easily switch back and forth between logged-in users, with all users retaining their session from where they left off. When you switch off from a user, that user's running programs will continue in the background.

Figure 3-2: User Switcher

Right-clicking the switcher will list several user management items, like configuring the Login screen, managing users, or changing the user's password and personal information. The Preferences item lets you configure how the User Switcher is displayed on your panel. Instead of the user's name, you could use the term Users or a user icon. You can also choose whether to use a lock screen when the user switches. Disabling the lock screen option will let you switch seamlessly between logged-in users.

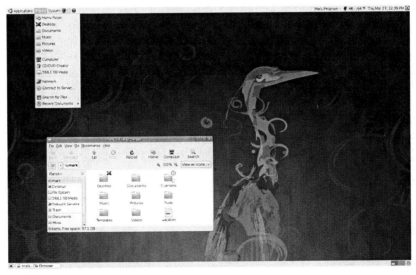

Figure 3-3: Ubuntu GNOME desktop

The GNOME Desktop

Ubuntu supports both the GNOME and KDE desktops. The default Ubuntu live CD will install GNOME, whereas the Kubuntu live CD will install KDE. The Ubuntu DVD lets you install both, and you can later install one or the other using a Synaptic meta package. GNOME uses the Ubuntu Human theme for its interface with the Ubuntu screen background and menu icon as its default (see Figure 3-3).

It is important to keep in mind that though the GNOME and KDE interfaces appear similar, they are really two very different desktop interfaces with separate tools for selecting preferences. The Preferences menus on GNOME and KDE display a very different selection of desktop configuration tools.

GNOME also includes a window manager called compiz that provides 3-D effects. To use compiz, select System | Preferences | Appearances, Desktop Effects panel, and then Advanced Effects. You can select Windows wobble and Workspace cubes. When you log in to GNOME again, compiz will be used with your desktop effects enabled.

The Ubuntu GNOME desktop display, shown in Figure 3-3, initially displays two panels at the top and bottom of the screen, as well as any file manager folder icons for your home directory and for the system. The top panel is used for menus, application icons, and notification tasks like your clock (see Figure 3-4). There are three menus:

- **Applications** With category entries like Office and Internet, these submenus will list the applications installed on your system. Use this menu to start your applications. The Install/Remove Software entry will start the Install and Remove Applications tool for basic package install operations.

- **Places** This menu lets you easily access commonly used locations like your home directory, the desktop folder for any files on your desktop, and the Computer window, through which you can access devices and removable disks, and Network for accessing shared file systems. It also has entries for searching for files (Search For Files), accessing recently used documents, and logging in to remote servers, such as NFS and FTP servers. The Places menu has a CD/DVD creator entry for using Nautilus to burn data CD/DVD-ROMs. A Recent Documents menu lists all your recently accessed files.

- **System** This includes Preferences and Administration menus. The Preferences menu is used for configuring your GNOME settings, such as the theme you want to user and the behavior of your mouse. The Administration menu holds all the Ubuntu system configuration tools used to perform administrative tasks like adding users, setting up printers, configuring network connections, and managing network services like a Web server or Samba Windows access. This menu also holds entries for locking the screen (Lock) and logging out of the system (Logout).

Next to the menus are application icons for commonly used applications. These include Firefox (the Fox and World logo), the mail utility, and the help icon. Click one to start that application. You can also start applications using the Applications menu. On the right you will see icons and text for the quit button, date/time, the user switcher, and the sound volume control.

The bottom panel is used for interactive tasks like selecting workspaces and docking applications (see Figure 3-3). The workspace switcher for virtual desktops appears as four squares in the lower-left corner. Clicking a square moves you to that area. To the right of the workspace switcher is the trash space that shows what items you have in your trash.

To move a window, left-click and drag its title bars. Each window supports Maximize, Minimize, and Close buttons. Double-clicking the title bar will maximize the window. Each window will have a corresponding button on the bottom panel. You can use this button to minimize and restore the window. The desktop supports full drag-and-drop capabilities (see Table 3-1). You can drag folders, icons, and applications to the desktop or other file manager windows open to other folders. The move operation is the default drag operation (you can also press the SHIFT key while dragging). To copy files, press the CTRL key and then click and drag before releasing the mouse button. To create a link, hold both the CTRL and SHIFT keys while dragging the icon to where you want the link, such as the desktop.

Key press	Action
SHIFT	Move a file or directory, default
CTRL	Copy a file or directory
CTRL-SHIFT	Create a link for a file or directory

Table 3-1: Desktop Click-and-drag operations

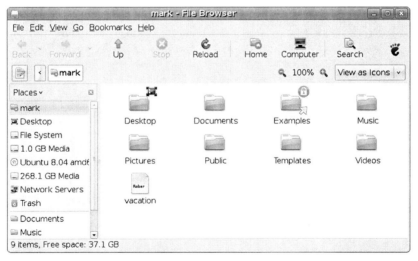

Figure 3-2: File manager for home folder

You can access your home directory from its entry in the Places menu. A file manager window opens showing your home directory. Your home directory will already have default directories created for commonly used files. These include Pictures, Documents, Music, and Videos. Your office applications will automatically save files to the Documents directory by default. A Pictures directory is where image and photo applications will place images files. The Desktop folder will hold all files and directories saved to your desktop.

Tip: If your desktop becomes too cluttered with open windows and you want to clear it by just minimizing all the windows, you can click on the Show Desktop Button at the left side of the lower panel.

The file manager window will display several components, including a browser toolbar, location box, and sidebar commonly found on most traditional file managers. When you open a new directory, the same window is used to display it, and you can use the forward and back arrows to move through previously opened directories. In the location window, you can enter the pathname for a directory to move directly to it. Figure 3-2 shows the file manager window.

Figure 3-5: GNOME Add to Panel window to add applets

Note: For both GNOME and KDE, the file manager is Internet-aware. You can use it to access remote FTP directories and to display or download their files, though in KDE the file manager is also a fully functional Web browser.

To quit the GNOME desktop, either click the Quit button on the right side of the top panel, or select the Quit entry from the System menu. This displays a dialog that includes buttons for Logout, Switch User, Restart, and Shut Down. Click the Shut Down button to shut down the system. Click Log Out to return to the login screen where you login again as a different user. Switch User will keep you logged in while you login to another user. Your active programs will continue to run in the background. The Restart button will shut down and the restart the system.

Note: Ubuntu provides several tools for configuring your GNOME desktop. These are listed in the System | Preferences menu. The Help button on each preference window will display detailed descriptions and examples. Some of the commonly used tools are discussed in the Desktop Operations section later in this chapter.

GNOME applets are small programs that operate off your panel. It is very easy to add applets. Right-click the panel and select the Add to Panel entry. This lists all available applets (see Figure 3-5). Some helpful applets are dictionary lookup, the current weather, the system monitor, which shows your CPU usage, the CPU Frequency Scaling Monitor for Cool and Quiet processors, and Search for Files, which searches your system for files. For most applets, you will have to perform basic configuration. To do this, right-click on the applet and select Preferences. This will open the Preferences window for that applet.

Note: The K Desktop Environment (KDE) displays a panel at the bottom of the screen that looks very similar to one displayed on the top of the GNOME desktop. The file manager appears slightly different but operates much the same way as the GNOME file manager.

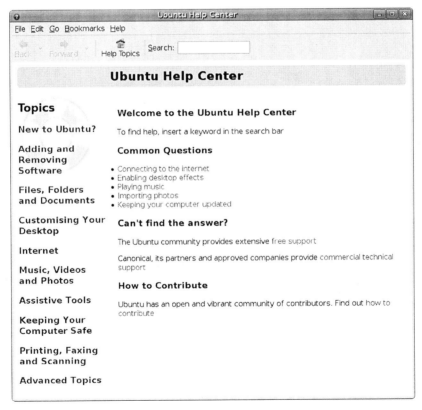

Figure 3-6: Ubuntu Help Center

Help from the desktop: the Ubuntu Help Center

To start the Ubuntu Help Center, click the Help button on the panel (the **?** icon on the top panel). This starts the GNOME help browser (Yelp) which now presents the Ubuntu Help Center (see Figure 3-6). The GNOME Help browser supports bookmarks for pages you want to access directly. The Help Topics button will return you to the start page. For detailed documentation and tutorial on the GNOME help browser, just select Contents from the Help menu or press F1.

The GNOME Help Center display topics geared to Ubuntu. Links range from adding software, managing files and folders, to printing and scanning. A help page will display detailed information on the left, and a sidebar of links for more information on the right. These will include any associated links.

As you progress through a document collection, its bookmarks appear at the top of the page. Figure 3-7 shows the import photos from dial camera, with bookmarks for "Music, video and photos" and "Photos and cameras". The sidebar links expand as you progress through the document collection

The GNOME help browser contents will also show a sidebar listing direct links to all the major help topics (Help | Contents), rather than the Ubuntu specific links on the Ubuntu Help Center page. These topics include An Introduction to the Desktop, Basic Skills, Desktop Overview, Using the panels, Tools and Utilities, and Configuring your desktop. The Introduction to the Desktop provides a comprehensive set of links to desktop pages. Many of these topics will also appear as links in pages you access through the Ubuntu Help Center (see Figure 3-8).

You can easily bring up documentation and manuals on different applications by performing a search on their names. A search on "archive" will show link to the Archive Manager Manual. A search on "system monitor" will show a link to the System Monitor manual.

The Advanced Topic link will display links for accessing the Man and Info pages.

Figure 3-7: Help Center bookmarks and sidebar

Figure 3-8: Introduction to desktop

Tip: Both GNOME and KDE, along with applications, provide context-sensitive help. Each KDE and GNOME application features detailed manuals that are displayed using their respective Help browsers. Also, system administrative tools feature detailed explanations for each task.

4. Managing Software

Installing software is an administrative function performed by a user with administrative access. Unless you chose to install all your packages during your installation, only some of the many applications and utilities available for users on Linux were installed on your system. On Ubuntu, you can easily install or remove software from your system with the Install and Remove Applications tool, the Synaptic Package Manager, or the **apt** command. Alternatively, you can install software by downloading and compiling its source code.

APT (Advanced Package Tool) is integrated as the primary install packages tool. When you install a package with Package Manger or with Synaptic, APT will be invoked and it will automatically select and download the package from the appropriate online repository. This is a major change that users may not be aware of at first glance. After having installed your system, when you then want to install additional packages, the install packages tool will now use APT to install from an online repository, though it will check your CD or DVD ROM first if you wish. This will include the entire Ubuntu online repository, including the main repository as well as Universe and Multiverse ones.

A DEB software package files all the files needed for a software application. A Linux software application often consists of several files that must be installed in different directories. The program itself is most likely placed in a directory called **/usr/bin**, online manual files go in another directory, and library files go in yet another directory.

Note: Be careful not to mix distributions. The distribution segments of all your
sources.list entries should be the same: hardy if you are using Ubuntu 8.04,
gutsy for 7.10, edgy for 7.05, dapper for 6.06, and so on.

Ubuntu Package Management Software

Though all Ubuntu software packages have the same DEB format, they can be managed and installed using different package management software tools. The primary software management tool is APT.

- ➢ APT (Advanced Package Tool): Synaptic, Package Manager, update-manager, dpkg and apt-get are front ends fro APT.

> ➢ Synaptic Package Manager: Graphical front end for managing packages, repository info at **/var/cache/apt**, same as APT

> ➢ Update Manager: Ubuntu graphical front end for updating installed software, uses APT.

> ➢ Install and Remove Applications tool, **gnome-app-install**: GNOME Graphical front end for managing packages, repository info at **/var/cache/apt**, same as APT

> ➢ **dpkg** older command line tool to install, update, remove, and query software packages. Uses own database, **/var/lib/dpkg**, , repository info at **/var/cache/apt**, same as APT

> ➢ **apt-get** primary command line tool to install, update, and remove software, uses own database, **/var/lib/apt/**, repository info at **/var/cache/apt**

> ➢ **aptitude** Front end for tools like dpkg or apt-get, cursor based, uses own database, **/var/lib/aptitude**

Ubuntu Software Repositories

There are four main components or sections to the Ubuntu repository: main, restricted, universe, and multiverse. These components are described in detail at:

ubuntu.com/ubuntu/components

To see a listing of all packages in the Ubuntu repository check **packages.ubuntu.com**. To see available repositories and their sections, open Synaptic, click Repositories from Settings menu.

Repository Sections

The repository sections for the main Ubuntu repository are as follows:

> ➢ main: Officially supported Ubuntu software (canonical), includes gstreamer good.

> ➢ restricted: Commonly used and required for many applications, but not open source or freely licensed, like proprietary graphics card drivers from Nvidia and ATI. Needed for hardware support, because not open source, they are not guaranteed to work.

> ➢ universe: All open source Linux software not directly supported by Ubuntu, would include Gstreamer bad.

> ➢ multiverse: Linus software that does not meet licensing requirements. But is not considered essential. It may not necessarily work. For example, the Gstreamer ugly package is in this repository. Check **ubuntu.com/community/ubuntustory/licensing**.

Repositories

In addition to the main repository, Ubuntu maintains several other repositories, primarily for maintenance and support for existing packages. The updates repository holds updated packages for a release. The security updates repository contains critical security package updates every system will need.

> ➢ Main repository: Collection of Ubuntu compliant software packages for releases.

➢ Updates: Corresponding updates for packages in the main repository, both main and restricted sections. Universe and Multiverse sections are not updated.

➢ Backports: Software under development for the next Ubuntu release, but packaged for use in the current one. Not guaranteed or fully tested.

➢ Security updates: security fixes for main software.

In addition, the backports repository provides un-finalized or development versions for new or current software. They are not guaranteed to work, but may provide needed features.

Note: for added repositories be sure your have installed the correct signature key as well as a valid URL for the repository.

TIP: Though it is possible to add the Debian Linux distribution repository, it is not advisable. Packages are designed for specific distributions. Combining them and lead to irresolvable conflicts.

Ubuntu Repository Configuration file: sources.list

Repository configuration is managed by APT using configuration files in the **/etc/apt** directory. The **/etc/apt/sources.list** file holds repository entries. The main and restricted sections are enabled by default. An entry consists of a single line with the following format:

```
format URI   distribution   component
```

The format is normally **deb**, for Debian package format. The URI (universal resource identifier) provides the location of the repository, such as an FTP or Web URL. The distribution is the official name of a particular Ubuntu distribution like dapper or gutsy. Ubuntu 8.04 has the name hardy. The component can be one or more terms that identify a section in that distribution repository, like main for the main repository and restricted for the restricted section. You can also list individual packages if you want.

```
deb http://archive.ubuntu.com/ubuntu/  hardy  main restricted
```

Corresponding source code repositories will have a **deb-src** format.

```
deb-src http://us.archive.ubuntu.com/ubuntu/ hardy main restricted
```

Update sections of a repository are referenced by the **-updates** suffix, as in hardy-updates.

```
deb http://archive.ubuntu.com/ubuntu/  hardy-updates  main restricted
```

Security sections for a repository have the suffix **-security**.

```
deb http://archive.ubuntu.com/ubuntu/  hardy-security  main restricted
```

Both Universe and Multiverse repositories should already be enabled. Each will have an updates repository as well as corresponding source code repositories, like those shown here for Universe.

```
deb http://us.archive.ubuntu.com/ubuntu/ hardy universe
deb-src http://us.archive.ubuntu.com/ubuntu/ hardy universe
deb http://us.archive.ubuntu.com/ubuntu/ hardy-updates universe
deb-src http://us.archive.ubuntu.com/ubuntu/ hardy-updates universe
```

Comments begin with a # mark. You can add comments of your own if you wish. Commenting an entry effectively disables that component of a repository. Placing a # mark before a repository entry will effectively disable it.

Commented entries are included for the backports and Cannonical partners repositories. Backports holds applications being developed for future Ubuntu releases and may not work. Partners include companies like Vmware and Parallels. To activate these repositories, just edit the **/etc/apt/sources.list** file using any text editor, and then remove the # at the beginning of the line.

```
# deb http://us.archive.ubuntu.com/ubuntu/ hardy-backports main \
                    restricted universe multiverse
```

You can edit the file directly with the following command.

```
gksu gedit /etc/apt/sources.list
```

Software Management with DEB, APT, and DKPG

Both the Debian distribution and Ubuntu use the Debian package format (DEB) for their software packages. Two basic package managers are available for use with Debian packages: the Advanced Package Tool (APT) and the Debian Package tool (dpkg). APT is designed to work with repositories and is used to install and maintain all your package installations on Ubuntu. Though you can install packages directly as single files with just dpkg, it is always advisable to use APT. Information and package files for Ubuntu compliant software can be obtained from **packages.ubuntu.com**.

You can also download source code versions of applications and then compile and install them on your system. Where this process once was complex, it has been significantly streamlined with the addition of *configure scripts.* Most current source code, including GNU software, is distributed with a configure script. The configure script automatically detects your system configuration and generates a *Makefile,* which is used to compile the application and create a binary file that is compatible with your system. In most cases, with a few Makefile operations you can compile and install complex source code on any system.

Managing software with APT

APT is designed to work with repositories, and will handle any dependencies for you. It uses **dpkg** to install and remove individual packages, but can also determine what dependent packages need to be installed, as well as query and download packages from repositories. There are several popular front ends for APT that let you manage your software easily, like synaptic, gnome-apt, aptitude, and deselect

For APT, you can also use the **apt-get** tool to manage your packages. **apt-get** can even download packages as well as compile source code versions for you. Using the **apt-get** command on the command line you can install, update, and remove packages. Check the **apt-get** man page for a detailed listing of **apt-get** commands (see Table 4-1).

```
apt-get  command  package
```

The **apt-get** tool takes two arguments: the command to perform and the name of the package. Other APT package tools follow the same format. The command is a term such as **install** for installing packages or **remove** to uninstall a package. Use the **install**, **remove**, or

update commands respectively. You only need to specify the software name, not the package's full file name. APT will determine that. To install the Mplayer package you would use:

```
sudo apt-get install mplayer
```

To make sure that apt-get has current repository information, use the **apt-get update** command.

```
sudo apt-get update
```

To remove packages, you use the **remove** option.

```
sudo apt-get remove mplayer
```

You can use the **-s** option to check the remove or install first, especially to check if there are any dependency problems. For remove operations you can use **-s** to find out first what dependent packages will also be removed.

```
sudo apt-get remove -s mplayer
```

A complete log of all install, remove, and update operations are kept in the **/var/log/dpkg.log** file. You can consult this file to find out exactly what files were installed or removed.

Configuration for APT is held in the **/etc/apt** directory. Here the **sources.list** file lists the distribution repositories from where packages are installed. Source lists for additional third party repositories (like that for Wine) are kept in the **/etc/sources.list.d** directory. GPG database files hold validation keys for those repositories. Specific options for apt-get are kept in either a **/etc/apt.conf** file or in various files located in the **/etc/apt.conf.d** directory.

Command	Description
update	Download and resynchronize the package listing of available and updated packages for APT supported repositories. APT repositories updated are those specified in **/etc/apt/sources.list**
upgrade	Update packages, install new versions of installed packages if available.
dist-upgrade	Update (upgrade) all your installed packages to a new release
install	Install a specific package, using its package name, not full package file name.
remove	Remove a software package from your system.
source	Download and extract a source code package
check	Check for broken dependencies
clean	Removes the downloaded packages held in the repository cache on your system. Used to free up disk space.

Table 4-1: apt-get commands

Command Line Search and Information :dpkg-query and atp-cache tools

The **dpkg-query** command lets you list detailed information about your packages. They operate on the command line (terminal window). **dpkg-query** with the -l option will list all your packages.

```
dpkg-query  -l
```

The dpkg command can operate as a front end for dpkg-query, detecting its options to perform the appropriate task. The previous command could also be run as:

```
dpkg  -l
```

To list a particular package requires and exact match on the package name, unless you use pattern matching operators. The following lists the **wine** package (Windows Compatibility Layer).

```
dpkg-query  -l wine
```

A pattern matching operator, like *, placed after a patter will display any packages beginning with that pattern. The pattern with operators needs to be quoted to prevent an attempt by the shell to use the pattern to match on filenames on your current directory. The following example finds all packages beginning with the pattern "wine". This would include packages line **wine-doc** and **wine-utils**.

```
dpkg-query  -l  'wine*'
```

You can further refine the results by using **grep** to perform an additional search. The following operation first outputs all packages beginning with **wine**, and from those results, the **grep** operations lists only those with the pattern **utils** in their name, like **wine-utils**.

```
dpkg  -l  'wine*' | grep 'utils'
```

Use the **-L** option to just list the files that a package has installed.

```
dpkg-query  -L wine
```

To see the status information about a package, including its dependencies and configuration files, use the **-s** option. Fields will include Status, Section, Architecture, Version, Depends (dependent packages), Suggests, Conflicts (conflicting packages), and Conffiles (configuration files).

```
dpkg-query -s  wine
```

The status information will also provide suggested dependencies. These are packages not installed, but like to be used. For the wine package, the **msttcorefonts** Windows font's package is suggested.

```
dpkg-query  -s  wine | grep Suggests
```

Use the **-S** option to find what package a particular file belongs to.

```
dpkg-query  -S filename
```

You can also obtain information with the **apt-cache** tool. Use the search command with **apt-cache** to perform a search.

```
apt-cache search wine
```

To find dependencies for a particular package, use the **depends** command.

```
apt-cache depends wine
```

To just display the package description use the **show** command.

```
apt-cache show wine
```

Note: If you have installed aptitude, you can use the **aptitude** command with the **search** and **show** options to find and display information about packages.

Managing Software from the Ubuntu Desktop

If you have install the Ubuntu desktop (either from the Server install or directly from a Desktop CD), you can use desktop-based software management tools for installing, updating, and removing software.

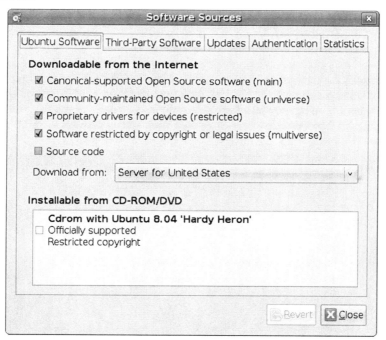

Figure 4-1: Software Sources Ubuntu Software repository sections.

Software Sources managed from Ubuntu Desktop

If you have installed a desktop interface, you can manage your repositories with the Software Sources tool. With the Software Sources you can enable or disable repository sections, as well as add new entries. This tool edits the **/etc/apt/sources.list** file directly. Choose System | Administration | Software Sources entry. This opens the Software Sources window with four panels: Ubuntu Software, Third-Party Software, Updates, Authentication, and Statistics (see Figure 4-1). The Ubuntu Software panel will list all your current repository section entries. These include the main repository, universe, restricted, and multiverse, as well as source code. Those that are enabled will be checked. You can enable or disable a repository section by simply checking or uncheck it entry. From a pop-up menu you can select the server to use. To install from a CD/DVD disc, just insert it.

On the Third-Party Software panel, you can add repositories for third party software. The repository for Ubuntu Software Partners will already be listed, but not checked. Check that entry if you want access software from the Partners. To add a third party repository click the Add button. This opens a dialog window where you enter the complete APT entry, starting with the deb format, followed by the URL, distribution, and components or packages. This is the line as it will appear in the **/etc/apt/sources.list** file. Once entered, click the Add Channel button.

The Updates panel lets you configure how updates are handled (see Figure 4-2). The panel specifies both your update sources and how automatic updates are handled. You have the option to install security (hardy-security), recommended (hardy-updates, pre-released (hardy-proposed), and unsupported (hardy-backports) updates. The security and recommended updates will already be selected. These cover updates for the entire Ubuntu repository. Pre-released and unsupported updates useful if you have installed any packages from the backports or development repositories.

Your system is already configured to check for updates automatically on a daily basis. You can opt to not check for updates at all by un-checking the Check or updates box. You also have options for how updates are to be handled. You can install any security updates automatically, without confirmation. You can download updates in the background. Or you can just be notified of available updates, and then manually choose to install them when you wish. The options are exclusive.

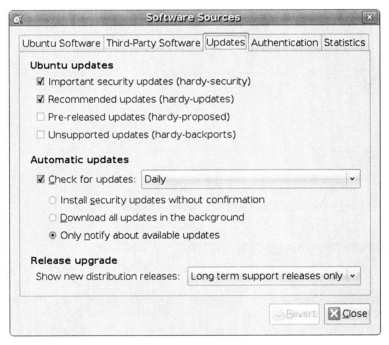

Figure 4-2: Software Sources Update configuration

The Authentication panel shows the repository software signature keys that are installed on your system (see Figure 4-3). Signature keys will already be installed for Ubuntu repositories, including your CD/DVD-ROM. If you are adding a third party repository, you will need to add its signature key. Click Import Key File button to browse for and locate a downloaded signature key file.

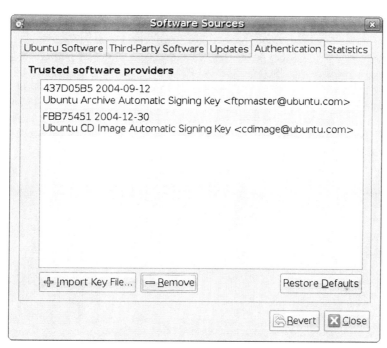

Figure 4-3: Software Sources Authentication, package signature keys

Ubuntu requires a signature key for any package that it installs. Signature keys for all the Ubuntu repositories are already installed, and will be listed on this panel. For third party repositories you will have to locate their signature key on their Web site, download it to a file, and then import that file. Most repositories will provide a signature key file for you to download and import. Click the Import Key File to open a file browser where you can select the downloaded key file. This procedure is the same as the **apt-key add** operation. Both add keys that APT then uses to verify DEB software packages downloaded from repositories before it installs them.

The Statistics package lets you provide Ubuntu with software usage information, letting them know what software is being used.

After you have made changes and click the Close button, the Software Sources tool will notify you that your software package information is out of date, displaying a Reload button. Click on the Reload button to make the new repositories or components available on your package managers like the Synaptic Package Manager. If you do not click Reload, you can run apt-get update or perform the Check operation on the Synaptic Package Manager to reload the repository configuration.

Synaptic Package Manager

The Synaptic Package Manager provides more control over all your packages. Packages are listed by name and include supporting packages like libraries as well as system critical packages. You can start up Synaptic from System | Administration | Synaptic Package Manager entry.

Buttons on the lower left of the Synaptic Package Manager window provide options for organizing and refining the list of packages shown (see Figure 4-4). Five options are available: Sections, Status, Origin, Custom Filters, and Search results. The dialog pane above the buttons will change depending on which option you choose. Clicking on the Sections button will list section categories for your software such as Base System, Communications, or Development. The Status button will list options for installed and not installed software. The Origin button shows entries for different repositories, as well as those locally installed (manual or disk based installations). Custom filters lets you choose a filter to use for listing packages. You can create your own filter and use it to display selected packages. Search results will list your current and previous searches, letting you move from one to the other.

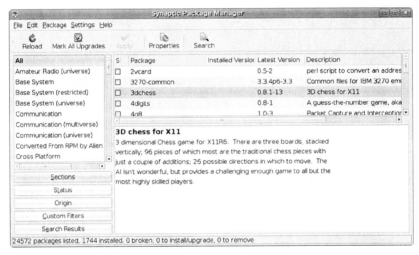

Figure 4-4: Synaptic Package Manager

The Sections option is selected by default. You can choose to list all packages, or refine your listing using categories provided in the pane. The All entry in this pane will list all available packages. Packages are organized into categories like Base System, Cross Platform, and Communications. Each category is in turn subdivided by multiverse, universe, and restricted software.

Status entries further refine installed software as auto-removable or as local or obsolete. Local software consists of packages you download and install manually.

With the Origins options, Ubuntu compliant repositories may further refine access according to multiverse, universe, and restricted software. A main entry selects Ubuntu supported software. Both the Ubuntu and Ubuntu security repositories are organized this way.

The method for locating software that you are most likely to use most often is the Search function. To perform a search, click the Search button on the toolbar. This opens a Search dialog with a text box where you can enter your search terms. A pop-up menu lets you specify what features of a package to search. The "Description and Name" feature is used most commonly. You can search other package features like just the Name, the maintainer name, the package version, packages it may depend on, or provided (associated) packages.

You can search by keyword. Both the package name and the package description will be searched. To perform a search, click on the Search button and enter the search term or terms. The results will be displayed with the repository list now replaced by a list of your searches. You can move back and forth between search results by clicking on the search entries in this listing (see

Properties

To find out information about a package, select the package and click the properties button. This opens a window with panels for Common, Dependencies, Installed files, Versions, and Description. The Common pane provides section, versions, and maintainer information. The Installed files panel show you exactly what files are installed, useful for finding the exact location and names fro configuration files as well as commands. Description information displays a detailed paragraph about the software. Dependencies will show all dependent software packages needed by this software, usually libraries.

Installing packages

To install a package, click on its entry to display a pop-up menu and select the Mark for installation entry. Should there be any dependent packages, a dialog opens listing those packages. Click the Mark button to also mark those packages for installation. The package entry will then have its checkbox marked.

Once you have selected the packages you want to install, click the Apply button on the toolbar to begin the installation process. A Summary dialog opens up showing all the packages to be installed. You have the option to just download the package files. The number of packages to be installed is listed, along with the size of the download and the amount of disk space used. Click Apply button on the dialog to download and install the packages. A download window will appear showing the progress of your package installations. You can choose to show the progress of individual packages, which opens a terminal window listing each package as it is downloaded and installed.

Once downloaded, the dialog changes to Installing Software label. You can choose to close the dialog automatically when finished.

Sometimes installation requires user input to set up a configuration for the software. You will be prompted to enter the information.

On the submenu that opens when you right-click, you also have the options to Mark Suggested for Installation or Mark Recommended for Installation. These will mark applications that can enhance your selected software, though they are not essential.

Certain software, like desktops or office suites that require a significant number of packages, can be selected all at once using metapackages. A metapackage has configuration files that select, download, and configure the range of packages needed for such complex software like a desktop.

Removing packages

To remove a package, just locate it. Then right-click and select the "Mark package for removal" entry. This will leave configuration files untouched Alternatively, you can mark a package for complete removal which will also remove any configuration files. Dependent packages will not be removed.

Once you have marked packages fro removal, click the Apply button. A summary dialog will display the packages for removal. Click Apply to remove them.

Synaptic may not remove dependent packages, especially shared libraries that might or might not be used by other applications. This means that your system could eventually have installed packages that are never being used. Their continued presence will not harm anything, but if you want to conserve space, you can clean them out using the **deborphan** tool. **deborphan** will output a listing of packages no longer needed by other packages or no longer used. You can then use this list to remove the packages.

Source code files

Though you can install source code files directly, the best way to install one is to use **apt-get**. Use the **source** command with the package name. Packages will be downloaded and extracted.

```
sudo apt-get source mplayer
```

The **--download** option lets you just download the source package without extracting it. The **--compile** option will download, extract, compile, and package the source code into a Debian binary package, ready for installation.

No dependent packages will be downloaded. If you have a software packages that requires any dependent packages to run, you will have to download and compile those also. To obtain needed dependent files, you use the **build-dep** option. All your dependent files will be located and downloaded for you automatically.

```
sudo apt-get build-dep mplayer
```

Installing from source code requires that supporting development libraries and source code header files be installed. You can to this separately for each major development platform like GNOME, KDE, or just the kernel. Alternatively you can run the APT metapackage **build-essential** for all the Ubuntu development packages. You will only have to do this once.

```
sudo apt-get install build-essential
```

Managing non-repository packages with dpkg

You can use **dpkg** to install a software package you have already downloaded directly, not with an APT enabled software tool like **apt-get** or **Synaptic**. In this case you are not installing from a repository. Instead, you have manually downloaded the package file from a Web or FTP site to a folder on your system. Such a situation would be rare, reserved for software not available on the Ubuntu or any APT enabled repository. Keep in mind that most software is already on your Ubuntu or an APT enabled repository. Check there first before performing a direct download and install with **dpkg**. The **dpkg** configuration files are located in the **/etc/dpkg** directory. Configuration is held in the **dpkg.cfg** file. See the **dpkg** man page for a detailed listing of **dpkg** options.

One situation where you would use dpkg, is for packages you have built yourself, like those created when converting a package in another format to a Debian package. This is the case when converting a RPM package (Red Hat Package Manager) to a Debian package format.

For **dpkg**, you use the **-i** option to install a package and **-r** to remove it.

```
sudo dpkg -i package.deb
```

The major failing for **dpkg** is that it provides no dependency support. It will inform you of needed dependencies, but you will have to install them separately. **dpkg** installs only the specified package. It is ideal for packages that have no dependencies.

You use the **-I** option to obtain package information directly from the DEB package file.

```
sudo dpkg -I package.deb
```

To remove a package you use the **-r** option with the package software name. You do not need version or extension information like **.386** or **.deb**. With **dpkg**, when removing a package with dependencies, you first have to remove all its dependencies manually. You will not be able to uninstall the package until you do. Configuration files are not removed.

```
sudo dpkg -r packagename
```

If you install a package that requires dependencies, and then fail to also install these dependencies, then your install database will be marked as having broken packages. In this case APT will not allow new packages to be installed until the broken packages are fixed. You can enter the **apt-get** command with the **-f** and install options. This will fix all broken packages at once.

```
sudo apt-get -f install
```

Installing Software from Compressed Archives: .tar.gz

Linux software applications in the form of source code are available at different sites on the Internet. You can download any of this software and install it on your system. Recent releases are often available in the form of compressed archive files. Applications will always be downloadable as compressed archives if they don't have an RPM version. This is particularly true for the recent versions of GNOME or KDE packages. RPM packages are only intermittently generated.

Decompressing and Extracting Software in One Step

Though you can decompress and extract software in separate operations, you will find that the more common approach is to perform both actions with a single command. The `tar` utility provides decompression options you can use to have `tar` first decompress a file for you, invoking the specified decompression utility. The `z` option automatically invokes `gunzip` to unpack a `.gz` file, and the `j` option unpacks a `.bz2` file. Use the `Z` option for `.z` files. For example, to combine the decompressing and unpacking operation for a `tar.gz` file into one `tar` command, insert a `z` option to the option list, **xzvf** (see the later section "Extracting Software" for a discussion of these options). The next example shows how you can combine decompression and extraction in one step:

```
tar xvzf antigrav_0.0.3.orig.tar.gz
```

For a **.bz2**-compressed archive, you use the **j** option instead of the **z** option.

```
tar xvjf antigrav_0.0.3.orig.tar.bz2
```

Decompressing Software Separately

Many software packages under development or designed for cross-platform implementation may not be in an RPM format. Instead, they may be archived and compressed. The filenames for these files end with the extension **.tar.gz**, **.tar.bz2**, or **.tar.Z**. The different extensions indicate different decompression methods using different commands: **gunzip** for **.gz**, **bunzip2** for **.bz2**, and **decompress** for **.Z**. In fact, most software with an RPM format also has a corresponding **.tar.gz** format. After you download such a package, you must first decompress it and then unpack it with the **tar** command. The compressed archives can hold either source code that you then need to compile or, as is the case with Java packages, binaries that are ready to run.

A *compressed archive* is an archive file created with **tar** and then compressed with a compression tool like **gzip**. To install such a file, you must first decompress it with a decompression utility like **gunzip** utility and then use **tar** to extract the files and directories making up the software package. Instead of the **gunzip** utility, you could also use **gzip -d**. The next example decompresses the **antigrav_0.0.3.orig.tar.gz** file, replacing it with a decompressed version called **antigrav_0.0.3.orig.tar**:

```
ls
 antigrav_0.0.3.orig.gz
gunzip antigrav_0.0.3.orig.tar.gz
ls
antigrav_0.0.3.orig.tar
```

You can download compressed archives from many different sites, including those mentioned previously. Downloads can be accomplished with FTP clients such as NcFTP and gFTP or with any web browser. Once downloaded, any file that ends with **.Z**, **.bz2**, **.zip**, or **.gz** is a compressed file that must be decompressed.

For files ending with **.bz2**, you use the **bunzip2** command. The following example decompresses a **bz2** version:

```
ls
 antigrav_0.0.3.orig.tar.bz2
bunzip2 antigrav_0.0.3.orig.tar.bz2
ls
antigrav_0.0.3.orig.tar
```

Files ending with **.bin** are self-extracting archives. Run the bin file as if it were a command. You may have to use **chmod** to make it executable.

Selecting an Install Directory

Before you unpack the archive, move it to the directory where you want it. Source code packages are often placed in a directory like **/usr/local/src**, and binary packages go in designated directories. When source code files are unpacked, they generate their own subdirectories from which you can compile and install the software. Once the package is installed, you can delete this directory, keeping the original source code package file (**.tar.gz**).

Packages that hold binary programs ready to run, like Java, are meant to be extracted in certain directories. Usually this is the **/usr/local** directory. Most archives, when they unpack, create a subdirectory named with the application name and its release, placing all those files or directories making up the software package into that subdirectory. For example, the file **antigrav_0.0.3.orig.tar** unpacks to a subdirectory called **antigrav_0.0.3.orig**. In certain cases, the software package that contains precompiled binaries is designed to unpack directly into the system subdirectory where it will be used.

Extracting Software

First, use **tar** with the **t** option to check the contents of the archive. If the first entry is a directory, then when you extract the archive, that directory is created and the extracted files are placed in it. If the first entry is not a directory, you should first create one and then copy the archive file to it. Then extract the archive within that directory. If no directory exists as the first entry, files are extracted to the current directory. You must create a directory yourself to hold these files.

```
# tar tvf antigrav_0.0.3.orig.tar
```

Now you are ready to extract the files from the tar archive. You use **tar** with the **x** option to extract files, the **v** option to display the pathnames of files as they are extracted, and the **f** option, followed by the name of the archive file:

```
# tar xvf antigrav_0.0.3.orig.tar
```

You can also decompress and extract in one step using the **-z** option for **gz** files and **-j** for **bz2** files.

```
# tar xvzf antigrav_0.0.3.orig.tar.gz
```

The extraction process creates a subdirectory consisting of the name and release of the software. In the preceding example, the extraction created a subdirectory called **antigrav_0.0.3.orig**. You can change to this subdirectory and examine its files, such as the **README** and **INSTALL** files.

```
# cd antigrav_0.0.3.orig
```

Installation of your software may differ for each package. Instructions are usually provided along with an installation program. Be sure to consult the **README** and **INSTALL** files, if included. See the following section on compiling software for information on how to create and install the application on your system.

Compiling Software

Some software may be in the form of source code that you need to compile before you can install it. This is particularly true of programs designed for cross-platform implementations. Programs designed to run on various Unix systems, such as Sun, as well as on Linux, may be distributed as source code that is downloaded and compiled in those different systems. Compiling such software has been greatly simplified in recent years by the use of configuration scripts that automatically detect a given system's hardware and software configuration and then allow you to compile the program accordingly. For example, the name of the C compiler on a system could be gcc or cc. Configuration scripts detect which is present and select it for use in the program compilation.

Note: Some software will run using scripting languages like Python, instead of programming language code like C++. These may require only a setup operation (a setup command), not compiling. Once installed, they will run directly using the scripting language interpreter, like Python.

A configure script works by generating a customized Makefile, designed for that particular system. A Makefile contains detailed commands to compile a program, including any preprocessing, links to required libraries, and the compilation of program components in their proper order. Many Makefiles for complex applications may have to access several software subdirectories, each with separate components to compile. The use of configure and Makefile scripts vastly automates the compile process, reducing the procedure to a few simple steps.

First, change to the directory where the software's source code has been extracted:

```
# cd /usr/local/src/antigrav_0.0.3.orig
```

Before you compile software, read the **README** or **INSTALL** files included with it. These give you detailed instructions on how to compile and install this particular program.

Most software can be compiled and installed in three simple steps. Their fist step is the ./configure command, which generates your customized Makefile. The second step is the make command, which uses a Makefile in your working directory (in this case, the Makefile you just generated with the ./configure command) to compile your software. The final step also uses the make command, but this time with the install option. The Makefile generated by the ./configure command also contains instructions for installing the software on your system. Using the install option runs just those installation commands. To perform the installation, you have to be logged in as the root user, giving you the ability to add software files to system directories as needed. If the software uses configuration scripts, compiling and installing usually involves only the following three simple commands:

```
# ./configure
# make
# make install
```

In the preceding example, the ./configure command performs configuration detection. The make command performs the actual compiling, using a Makefile script generated by the ./configure operation. The make install command installs the program on your system, placing the executable program in a directory, such as **/usr/local/bin**, and any configuration files in **/etc**. Any shared libraries it created may go into **/usr/local/lib**.

Once you have compiled and installed your application, and you have checked that it is working properly, you can remove the source code directory that was created when you extracted the software. You can keep the archive file (tar) in case you need to extract the software again. Use rm with the -rf options so that all subdirectories will be deleted and you do not have to confirm each deletion.

Tip: Be sure to remember to place the period and slash before the `configure` command. The `./` references a command in the current working directory, rather than another Linux command with the same name.

Configure Command Options

Certain software may have specific options set up for the `./configure` operation. To find out what these are, you use the `./configure` command with the `--help` option:

```
$  ./configure --help
```

A useful common option is the `-prefix` option, which lets you specify the install directory:

```
$  ./configure -prefix=/usr/bin
```

Tip: Some older X applications use `xmkmf` directly instead of a configure script to generate the needed Makefile. Although `xmkmf` has been officially replaced, in this case, enter the command `xmkmf` in place of `./configure`. Be sure to consult the **INSTALL** and **README** files for the software.

Development Libraries

If you are compiling an X, GNOME, or KDE-based program, be sure their development libraries have been installed. For X applications, be sure the `xmkmf` program is also installed. If you chose a standard install when you installed your distribution system, these most likely were not installed. For distributions using RPM packages, these come in the form of a set of development RPM packages, usually with the word "development" or "develop" in their names. You need to install those using `rpm`. GNOME, in particular, has an extensive set of RPM packages for development libraries. Many X applications need special shared libraries. For example, some applications may need the `xforms` library or the `qt` library. Some of these you may need to obtain from online sites.

Shared and Static Libraries

Libraries can be static, shared, or dynamic. A *static* library is one whose code is incorporated into the program when it is compiled. A *shared* library, however, has its code loaded for access whenever the program is run. When compiled, such a program simply notes the libraries it needs. Then when the program is run, that library is loaded and the program can access its functions. A *dynamic* library is a variation on a shared library. Like a shared library, it can be loaded when the program is run. However, it does not actually load until instructions in the program tell it to. It can also be unloaded as the program runs, and another library can be loaded in its place. Shared and dynamic libraries make for much smaller code. Instead of a program including the library as part of its executable file, it only needs a reference to it.

Libraries made available on your system reside in the **/usr/lib** and **/lib** directories. The names of these libraries always begin with the prefix **lib** followed by the library name and a suffix. The suffix differs, depending on whether it is a static or shared library. A shared library has the extension **.so** followed by major and minor version numbers. A static library simply has the **.a** extension. A further distinction is made for shared libraries in the old **a.out** format. These have the extension **.sa**. The syntax for the library name is the following:

```
libname.so.major.minor
libname.a
```

The *name* can be any string, and it uniquely identifies a library. It can be a word, a few characters, or even a single letter. The name of the shared math library is **libm.so.5**, where the math library is uniquely identified by the letter **m** and the major version is **5**, and **libm.a** is the static math library. The name of the X Window library is **libX11.so.6**, where the X Window library is uniquely identified with the letters **X11** and its major version is 6.

Most shared libraries are found in the **/usr/lib** and **/lib** directories. These directories are always searched first. Some shared libraries are located in special directories of their own. A listing of these is placed in the **/etc/ld.conf** configuration file. These directories will also be searched for a given library. By default, Linux first looks for shared libraries, then static ones. Whenever a shared library is updated or a new one installed, you need to run the **ldconfig** command to update its entries in the **/etc/ld.conf** file as well as links to it (if you install from an RPM package, this is usually done for you).

Checking Software Package Digital Signatures

One very effective use for digital signatures is to verify that a software package has not been tampered with. A software package could be intercepted in transmission and some of its system-level files changed or substituted. Software packages from your distribution, as well as those by reputable GNU and Linux projects, are digitally signed. The signature provides modification digest information with which to check the integrity of the package. The digital signature may be included with the package file or posted as a separate file. To import a key that APT can use to check a software package, you use the **apt-key** command. APT will automatically check for digital signatures. To check the digital signature of a software package file that is not part of the APT repository system, you use the **gpg** command with the **--verify** option. These would include packages like those made available as compressed archives, **.tar.gz**, whereas APT can check all DEB packages itself.

Importing Software Public keys with apt-key

First, however, you will need to make sure that you have the signer's public key. The digital signature was encrypted with the software distributor's private key; that distributor is the signer. Once you have that signer's public key, you can check any data you receive from them. In the case of third party software repositories, you have to install their public key. Once the key is installed, you do not have to install it again.

Ubuntu includes and installs its public keys with its distribution. For any packages on the Ubuntu repositories, the needed public keys are already installed and checked by APT automatically. For other sites, like Wine (the Linux Windows emulator), you may need to download the public key from their site and install it (**www.winehq.org**). You may also have to add repository support to access their Ubuntu compatible software. The Wine public key is available from winhq.org, with the public key for Ubuntu located at **wine.budgetdedicated.com/apt/387EE263.gpg** You could download the public key and then install it on your system with the apt-key command.

```
wget -q http://wine.budgetdedicated.com/apt/387EE263.gpg
```

Once downloaded you can then use the **apt-key** command to install the pubic key for use by APT in software verification. Ubuntu uses the **apt-key** command to maintain public keys for software packages. Use the **apt-key** command with the **add** option to add the key.

```
sudo apt-key add 387EE263.gpg
```

You can combine both operations into one as:

```
wget -q http://wine.budgetdedicated.com/apt/387EE263.gpg -O- | sudo apt-key add -
```

To actually access the software repository you would have to also install its APT configuration file in the **/etc/apt/sources.list.d** directory.. For wine this is named **winehq.ist**. Check the Wine site for download instructions..

Checking Software Compressed Archives

Many software packages in the form of compressed archives, **.tar.gz** or **tar.bz2**, will provide signatures in separate files that end with the **.sig** extension. To check these, you use the `gpg` command with the `--verify` option. For example, the most recent Sendmail package is distributed in the form of a compressed archive, **.tar.gz**. Its digital signature is provided in a separate **.sig** file. First you download and install the public key for Sendmail software obtained from the Sendmail website (the key may have the year as part of its name). Sendmail has combined all its keys into one armored text file, **PGPKEYS**.

```
gpg --import PGPKEYS
```

You can also use the **gpg** command with the **--search-key** and **--keyserver** options to import the key. Keys matching the search term will be displayed in a numbered list. You will be prompted to enter the number of the key you want. The 2007 Sendmail key from the results from the following example would be 7. This is the key used for 2007 released software.

```
$ gpg --keyserver pgp.mit.edu --search-keys Sendmail
```

Instead of using **gpg**, you could use Encryptions and Password Keys application to find and import the key (Applications | Accessories | Encryption and Password Keys).

To check a software archive, a **tar.gz**, file, you need to also download its digital signature files. For the compressed archive (**.tar.gz**) you can use the **.sig** file ending in **.gz.sig**, and for the uncompressed archive use **.tar.sig**. Then, with the `gpg` command and the `--verify` option, use the digital signature in the **.sig** file to check the authenticity and integrity of the software compressed archive.

```
$ gpg --verify sendmail.8.14.2.tar.gz.sig sendmail.8.14.2.tar.gz
gpg: Signature made Wed 31 Oct 2007 08:23:07 PM PDT using RSA key ID 7093B841
gpg: Good signature from "Sendmail Signing Key/2007 <sendmail@Sendmail.ORG>"$
```

You can also specify just the signature file, and `gpg` will automatically search for and select a file of the same name, but without the **.sig** or **.asc** extension.

```
# gpg --verify sendmail.8.14.2.tar.gz.sig
```

In the future, when you download any software from the Sendmail site that uses this key, you just have to perform the `--verify` operation. Bear in mind, though, that different software packages from the same site may use different keys. You will have to make sure that you have imported and signed the appropriate key for the software you are checking.

Tip: You can use the `--fingerprint` option to check a key's validity if you wish. If you are confident that the key is valid, you can then sign it with the `--sign-key` command.

Part 2: Services

Managing Services

Mail Servers

FTP Servers

Web Servers

News and Database Servers

5. Managing Services

A single Linux system can provide several different kinds of services, ranging from security to administration and including more obvious Internet services like web and FTP sites, e-mail, and printing. Security tools such as SSH and Kerberos run as services, along with administrative network tools such as DHCP and LDAP. The network connection interface is itself a service that you can restart at will. Each service operates as a continually running daemon looking for requests for its particular services. In the case of a web service, the requests will come from remote users. You can turn services on or off by starting or shutting down their daemons.

The process of starting up or shutting down a service is handled by service scripts, described in detail in this chapter. It applies to all services, including those discussed in the "Security', "System Administration", and "Internet Services" sections of this book. It is covered at this point since you will most likely use them to start and stop Internet services like web and mail servers. The service scripts are now managed by a new start up and shutdown service, Upstart.

Upstart

Linux systems traditionally used the Unix System V init daemon to manage services by setting up runlevels at which they could be started or shutdown. Ubuntu has since replaced the SystemV init deamon with the Upstart init daemon, while maintaining the System V init runlevel structure for compatibility purposes. Whereas the System V init daemon would start certain services when the entire system started up or shutdown, Upstart is entirely event driven. When an event occurs invoking the need for a service, then the service is started. This even oriented approach is designed to work well with removable devices. When a device is added or removed, this change becomes an event that the Upstart daemon detects and then runs any appropriate associated scripts. System V init daemon only ran scripts when its runlevels changed. It saw only runlevels, not events.

Structurally, Upstart can detect and respond to any event. Eventually it may implement scheduled events, replacing cron, atd, an anacron schedulers, as well as support for on demand service now managed by xinetd and inetd. You can find out more about Upstart at:

upstart.ubuntu.com

Upstart will detect events, and run scripts in the **/etc/event.d** directory for those events. These scripts define jobs that Upstart can then run. Jobs that can be performed by Upstart are defined in scripts in Upstart event directory, **/etc/event.d**. Here you will finds Upstart job scripts for emulating runlevels like the rc2 script, as well as system services like TTY terminal connections. In effect, Upstart jobs replace the entries that used to be in the SysVinit's **/etc/inittab** file.

Upstart operates by running jobs. These jobs are defined in job definition files located in the **/etc/event.d** directory. Jobs are already defined for System V init runlevel emulation, TTY system services, and for certain tasks like Ctrl-Alt-Delete event to restart your system. A job script will specify an event, the action to take for that event, and any commands to run for that event. The commands can be either a single command run by an exec operation, or a set of command encased in **script** and **end script** stanza.

Note: An Upstart job definition script does not have to have a **start on** directive. I could just be started manually with the **start** command.

To have a job started automatically when a certain event occurs you place a **start on** directive in its job file, specifying the event. You can use a stop on directive to stop the event automatically. You can have several start on directives, each for different events. The **start on** directive for the control-alt-delete job is shown here.

```
start on control-alt-delete
```

In the control-alt-delete job, you have a control-alt-delete event that runs the shutdown command with the **-r** option to restart. The **exec** command is used to run a shell command directly..

```
start on control-alt-delete
    exec shutdown -r -now
```

Many jobs defined both a start on and stop on directive, for starting and stopping the job. The event can also take an argument. In the **rc2** job definition which control runlevel 2 emulation has start and stop event as shown here:

```
start on runlevel 2
stop on runlevel [!2]
```

The rc2 job will start when a runlevel event occurs with the argument 2. It will stop when any runlevel even occurs that has an number other than 2, **[!2]**.

A **stopped** or **started** event indicates when some other job has been started or stopped. The following start on directive would star its job whenever the **myjob** job started.

```
start on started myjob
```

The **startup** event indicates system startup. The **rcS** job (single user mode) will be started up initially whenever you system starts up. In its **/etc/event.d/rcS** job definition file you will find:

```
start on startup
```

The **rc-default** job is started when the **rcS** job stops.

```
start on stopped rcS
```

The TTY1 job used for terminal services will have several start and stop directives, automatically starting at runlevel 2, 3, 4, and 5 events, and stopping on runlevel 0, 1, and 6 events.

```
start on runlevel 2
start on runlevel 3
start on runlevel 4
start on runlevel 5

stop on runlevel 0
stop on runlevel 1
stop on runlevel 6

respawn
exec /sbin/getty 38400 tty1
```

To run several command you encase the command in a **script** stanza. A script stanza begins with the **script** keyword and ends with **end script**. Most complex jobs use a the script stanza. The rc2 job script shown here will start on a runlevel event with the 2 argument. Then the commands in the script structure are run, setting the runlevel to 2 with the runlevel command. Then the **/etc/init.d/rc** script is run with the 2 argument to start up any **/etc/init.d** service scripts for runlevel 2, emulating a runlevel change to 2. The **rc2** job is started when **telinit** triggers a runlevel event with a 2 argument. For any runlevel events that are not 2, the **rc2** job will be stopped. The **console** directive specifies where the job output goes, usually to the console (**output**).

```
start on runlevel 2
stop on runlevel [!2]

console output
script
    set $(runlevel --set 2 || true)
    if [ "$1" != "unknown" ]; then
        PREVLEVEL=$1
        RUNLEVEL=$2
        export PREVLEVEL RUNLEVEL
    fi

    exec /etc/init.d/rc 2
end script
```

You can think of the Upstart daemon managing a set of jobs, much like the shell can manage background jobs. With the **start** and **stop** commands you can start and stop any job. Use status to find out the **status** of a job.

```
$ sudo stop tty1
tty1 (stop) running, process 5109
tty1 (stop) pre-stop, (main) process 5109
tty1 (stop) stopping, process 5109
tty1 (stop) killed, process 5109
tty1 (stop) post-stop
tty1 (stop) waiting
```

```
$ sudo start tty1
tty1 (start) waiting
tty1 (start) starting
tty1 (start) pre-start
tty1 (start) spawned, process 8457
tty1 (start) post-start, (main) process 8457
tty1 (start) running, process 8457
$ sudo status tty1
tty1 (start) running, process 8457
```

The **initctl** command with the **list** option will display a complete list of current Upstart jobs. You can add a pattern to search or a particular job. The initctl command also has **start, stop,** and **status** options form managing jobs.

```
sudo initctl list
```

You could also use the **emit** command to manually trigger an event that would run a certain job.

Upstart and Runlevels: event.d and init.d

Ubuntu still maintain SysVinit startup and shutdown scripts in the **/etc/init.d** directory which Upstart uses to start and stop services. You can run these scripts directly to start and stop a service. Upstart will also use the SysVinit links in runlevel directories (**/etc/rc/N.d**) to start and stop services. In effect, the supporting structure for runlevels remains the same, though in fact services are now handled by Upstart. SysVinit compatibility scripts, directory structure, and tools, like **telinit** and **runlevel** equivalents, are held in the **upstart-compat-sysv** package.

You can start up your system at different levels with certain capabilities. For example, you can run your system at an administrative level, locking out user access. Normal full operations are activated by simply running your system at a certain level of operational capability such as supporting multi-user access or graphical interfaces. These levels (also known as states or modes) are referred to as *runlevels,* the level of support that you are running your system at.

Note: You can select certain services to run and the runlevel at which to run them. Most services are servers like a web server or proxy server. Other services provide security, such as SSH or Kerberos. On Ubuntu you can **services-admin** to turn on and off services, specifying the runlevel. The default is runlevel 2.

Runlevels

Traditionally, a Linux system has several runlevels, numbered from 0 to 6. Support for these is now emulated by Upstart. When you power up your system, you enter the default runlevel. Runlevels 0, 1, and 6 are special runlevels that perform specific functions. Runlevel 0 is the power-down state and is invoked by the **halt** command to shut down the system. Runlevel 6 is the reboot state—it shuts down the system and reboots. Runlevel 1 is the single-user state, which allows access only to the superuser and does not run any network services. This enables you, as the administrator, to perform administrative actions without interference from others.

Other runlevels reflect how you want the system to be used. Ubuntu uses runlevel 2 for graphical logins and the remainder as user defined, also using graphical logins.

Tip: You can use the single-user runlevel (1) as a recovery mode state, allowing you to start up your system without running startup scripts for services like DNS. This is helpful if your system hangs when you try to start such services. Networking is disabled, as well as any multi-user access. You can also use `linux  -s` at the boot prompt to enter runlevel 1. If you want to enter the single-user state and also run the startup scripts, you can use the special s or s runlevel.

Runlevels in event.d directory

As noted, runlevels are managed by the Upstart service. Upstart service does not use runlevels. To maintain compatibility with System V compliant Linux and Unix applications, Upstart does provide a runlevel compatibility scripts in the **/etc/event.d** directory that emulate System V init. To start up a runlevel, it uses **telinit** with the runlevel number to. When your system starts up, it uses the default runlevel as specified by the **rc-default** script in the **/etc/event.d** directory. There are runlevel scripts for each runlevel in the **/etc/event.d** directory. The default runlevel is 2, which will run the **/etc/event.d/rc2** script ,which in turn invokes **telinit** with the argument **2**.

Using telinit

To change to another runlevel you can use **telinit** with the runlevel number. You can choose from runlevels 2 ,3, 4, and 5. These are all set up as standard multi-user graphical runlevels. The **single** runlevel (S) is reserved for recovery use. The **telinit** command just triggers a runlevel event for Upstart, which then uses the **/etc/init.d/rc** script to emulate a runlevel change. The **telinit** command is now just a wrapper for an Upstart runlevel event, not the **telinit** command used in previous releases with System V init.

The multi-user runlevels are initially all configured the same, though you could make changes in each, such as running different services at different runlevels (use services-admin, update-rc.d, or sysv-rc-conf to make these changes). You could then use **telinit** to start up at that runlevel.

```
sudo telinit 4
```

Formerly, you could also boot to a certain runlevel from the Grub boot menu by specifying the runlevel on the kernel line. With the Upstart emulation, you can now only boot directly to the **single** user runlevel from Grub menu. A recovery mode Grub boot entry is set up to do just that. For all other runlevels you have to login first as runlevel 2, the default, or S (single) and then use the **telinit** command to enter a new runlevel. Alternatively you could carefully edit the **rc-default** file to detect other runlevel numbers on the GRUB command line other than single, and invoke the corresponding runlevel with **telinit**. You could then make Grub entries for these runlevels or just edit the Grub kernel line to add the runlevel number. Editing **rc-default** is risky (back it up first), and requires an competency in shell programming.

default runlevel

The default runlevel is 2. You can change this default runlevel, to either 3, 4, or 5 if you wish. To actually change the default runlevel safely, you can create an **/etc/inittab** file and place and **initdefault** entry in it (use **vi** or **emacs** if editing from a command line interface).

```
gksu gedit /etc/inittab
```

This file would be just a dummy file used only by **rc-default** to read the default entry. A sample default entry is shown here, changing the default to runlevel 3. Your **/etc/inittab** file would have only this line.

```
id:3:initdefault:
```

Command line runlevel

On other distributions, like Fedora, some runlevels are designed for special behavior. On Fedora, runlevel 3 will run just the command line, without the graphical interface. This is not the case with Ubuntu. On Debian, Ubuntu, and similar distributions, the desktop version invokes the X server at all primary runlevels. To run the command line interface as the primary interface for a runlevel, you need to shut down the display managers (your login screen). To set up a particular runlevel to use just the command line, you would have to instruct its startup service for the X Server (**/etc/init.d/gdm**) to stop. To set up runlevel 3 to run just the command line interface when you start up your system, you would use the sysv-rc-conf, update-rc.d, or admin-users tool to have the GDM service to stop at runlevel 3, instead of start. This will put a stop link in the **/etc/rc3.d** directory for the GDM service, like K01gdm, replacing the start link, **S30gdm**. The **K01gdm** link would invoke the **gdm init.d** script with the **stop** option, shutting down the X server. You can then change to runlevel 3 with the telnet command and the argument 3. The screen will blank and start up the command line interface.

```
sudo telinit 3
```

Upon startup in runlevel 3, press ENTER display the login prompt (also from GRUB, remove splash option for kernel).

Tip: If you used **/etc/inittab** to change the default runlevel, and you want to change quickly back to using runlevel 2 as the default without having to edit the **/etc/inittab** file, you can just remove the **/etc/inittab** file. The **rc-start** script will start runlevel 2 if there is no **/etc/inittab** file, **sudo rm /etc/inittab**.

The runlevel Command

Use the `runlevel` command to see what state you are currently running in. It lists the previous state followed by the current one. If you have not changed states, the previous state will be listed as N, indicating no previous state. This is the case for the state you boot up in. In the next example, the system is running in state 3, with no previous state change:

```
runlevel
N 2
```

System Startup files and scripts

Each time you start your system, the Upstart init daemon starts up services defined in startup scripts. Currently most services still use the older System V init method for starting up services using runlevels. Upstart will use its event based init daemon to emulate the System V init structure, allowing many services to run as if they were using a System V init daemon. Eventually, service applications will be rewritten to use Upstart directly, without the need for a System V init emulation.

Upstart emulates the System V startup procedure by running a series of startup script from system service scripts located in your **/etc/init.d** directory. It uses links in directories with the name **rc*N*.d**, to determine what service scripts to run. The *N* in the name is a number from 1 to 6 indicating a runlevel, like **rc2.d** for runlevel 2. These initialization files are organized according to different tasks. You should not have to change any of these files (see Table 5-1).

File	Description
/etc/event.d	Upstart job files that actually start services and processes.
/etc/rc*N*.d	Directories that holds system startup and shutdown files, where *N* is the runlevel. The directories hold links to scripts in the **/etc/init.d** directory.
/etc/rc.local	Initialization file for your own commands; you can freely edit this file to add your own startup commands; this is the last startup file executed.
/etc/init.d	Directory that holds system service scripts
/etc/init.d/rc	Runlevel emulation by Upstart. Upstart runs this script to emulate runlevel changes.

Table 5-1: System Startup Files and Directories

rc.local

The **/etc/rc.local** file is the last initialization file executed. You can place commands of your own here. When you shut down your system, the system calls the **halt** file, which contains shutdown commands. The files in **init.d** are then called to shut down daemons, and the file systems are unmounted. **halt** is located in the **init.d** directory.

/etc/init.d

The **/etc/init.d** directory is designed primarily to hold scripts that start up and shut down different specialized daemons, such as network and printer daemons and those for font and web servers. These files perform double duty, starting a daemon when the system starts up and shutting down the daemon when the system shuts down. The files in **init.d** are designed in a way to make it easy to write scripts for starting up and shutting down specialized applications. Many of these files are set up for you automatically. You shouldn't need to change them. If you do change them, be sure you know how these files work first.

When your system starts up, several programs are automatically started and run continuously to provide services, such as a website or print servers. Depending on what kind of services you want your system to provide, you can add or remove items in a list of services to be started automatically. For example, the web server is run automatically when your system starts up. If you are not hosting a website, you have no need for the web server. You can prevent the service from starting, removing an extra task the system does not need to perform, freeing up resources, and possibly reducing potential security holes. Several of the servers and daemons perform necessary tasks. The **sendmail** server enables you to send messages across networks, and the **cupsd** server performs printing operations.

/etc/init.d/rc

The **/etc/init.d/rc** script is used by Upstart to emulate System V runlevel changes. The script takes as its argument a runlevel. I then checks the **/etc/rc***N***.d** links for the runlevel to determine what services to start or stop.

/etc/event.d

In the **/etc/event.d** directory, Upstart maintains event scripts for different runlevels, **rc***N*. For runlevel 2, there is an **rc2** script. This script simply run the **/etc/init.d/rc** script with the number 2 as its argument. The **/etc/init.d/rc** script will then search the **/etc/rc2.d** directory for links specifying which service script to start and which to stop.

When your system starts, the **/etc/event.d/rc.default** script is run which will start up with runlevel 2 or the runlevel specified in an **/etc/inittab** dummy file. For runlevel 2 it will invoke the **/etc/init.d/rc** script the argument 2. .

Service Script	Description
`networking`	Operations to start up or shut down your network connections
`xinetd`	Operations to start up or shut down the **xinetd** daemon
`cupsys`	The CUPS printer daemon (see Chapter 10)
`apache2`	Apache web server (see Chapter 8)
`innd`	Internet News service (see Chapter 9)
`nfs`	Network Filesystem (see Chapter 11)
`policykit`	Policy authentication tool
`postfix`	Postfix mail server (see Chapter 6)
`sendmail`	The Sendmail MTA daemon (see Chapter 6)
`samba`	Samba for Windows hosts (see Chapter 12)
`squid`	Squid proxy-cache server (see Chapter 14)
`vsftpd`	Very Secure FTP server (see Chapter 7)

Table 5-2: Selection of Service Scripts in /etc/init.d

Note: Keep in mind that the System V runlevel system does not exist on Ubuntu though its service management structure does. Instead, Upstart emulates System V runlevels using the **/etc/init.d/rc** script and the same service links and startup scripts in the **/etc/init.d** and **/etc/rc***N***.d** directories.

Service Scripts: /etc/init.d

You can manage the startup and shutdown of server daemons with special service scripts located in the **/etc/init.d** directory. These scripts often have the same name as the service's program. For example, for the **/usr/sbin/apache2** web server program, the corresponding script is called `/etc/init.d/apache2`. This script starts and stops the web server. This method of using **init.d** service scripts to start servers is called *SysV Init,* after the method used in Unix System V. Some of the more commonly used service scripts are listed in Table 5-2.

The service scripts in the **/etc/init.d** directory can be executed automatically whenever you boot your system. Be careful when accessing these scripts, however. These start essential programs, such as your network interface and your printer daemon. These init scripts are accessed from links in subdirectories set up in the **/etc** directory for each possible runlevel. These directories have names with the format **rc***n***.d**, where *n* is a number referring to a runlevel (see Table 5-3).

Runlevel	Directory	Description
0	**rc0.d**	Halts (shuts down) the system
1	**rc1.d**	Single-user mode (limited capabilities)
2	**rc2.d**	Multi-user mode with graphical login (full operation mode, X server started automatically)
3	**rc3.d**	User-defined
4	**rc4.d**	User-defined
5	**rc5.d**	User-defined
6	**rc6.d**	Reboots system
S	**rcS.d**	Single user mode

Table 5-3: Emulated System Runlevels for Ubuntu distributions

The **rc** script detects the runlevel in which the system was started and then executes only the service scripts specified in the subdirectory for that runlevel. When you start your system, the **rc** script executes the service scripts designated default start up directory like in **rc1.d** (graphical login for Debian and Ubuntu). The **rc***n***.d** directories hold symbolic links to certain service scripts in the **/etc/init.d** directory. Thus, the `apache2` script in the **/etc/init.d** directory is actually called through a symbolic link in an **rcn.d** directory. The symbolic link for the `/etc/init.d/apache2` script in the **rc3.d** directory is **S91apache2**. The *S* prefixing the link stands for "startup"; thus, the link calls the corresponding `init.d` script with the **start** option. The number indicates the order in which service scripts are run; lower numbers run first. **S91apache2** invokes `/etc/init.d/apache2` with the option **start**. If you change the name of the link to start with a *K,* the script is invoked with the **stop** option, stopping it. Such links are used in the runlevels 0 and 6 directories, **rc6.d** and **rc0.d**. Runlevel 0 halts the system, and runlevel 6 reboots it. You can use the **runlevel** command to find out what runlevel you are currently operating at. A listing of runlevels is shown in Table 5-3.

Services

A *service* is a daemon that runs concurrently with your other programs, continually looking for a request for its services, either from other users on your system or from remote users connecting to your system through a network. When a server receives a request from a user, it starts up a *session* to provide its services. For example, if users want to download a file from your system, they can use their own FTP client to connect to your FTP server and start up a session. In the session, they can access and download files from your system. Your server needs to be running for a user to access its services. For example, if you set up a website on your system with HTML files, you must have the **apache2** web server program running before users can access your website and display those files.

Managing Services Directly

You can use service scripts to start and stop your server manually. These scripts are located in the **/etc/init.d** directory and have the same names as the server programs. For example, the **/etc/init.d/apache2** script with the **start** option starts the web server. Using this script with the **stop** option stops it, and the **restart** option restarts it.. Instead of using the complete pathname for the script, you can use the **service** command and the script name, provided you have installed the **sysvconfig** package. Any of the service management tools will also work, like services-admin and rrconf. The services-admin tool in installed initially and is accessible from the System | Administration | Services menu. The following commands are equivalent:

```
sudo /etc/init.d/apache2 stop
sudo service apache2 stop
```

To see if your server is running, you can use the **status** option.

```
sudo /etc/init.d/apache2 status
sudo service apache2 status
```

Alternatively, you can use the **ps** command with the **-aux** option to list all currently running processes. You should see a process for the server program you started. To refine the list, you can add a **grep** operation with a pattern for the server name you want. The second command lists the process for the web server.

```
ps -aux
ps -aux | grep 'apache2'
```

You can just as easily check for the **apache2** process on the GNOME System Monitor.

Service Management: services-admin, rrconf, sysv-rc-conf, and update-rc.d

Instead of manually executing all the server programs each time you boot your system, you can have your system automatically start the servers for you. You can do this in two ways, depending on how you want to use a server. You can have a server running continuously from the time you start your system until you shut it down, or you can have the server start only when it receives a request from a user for its services. If a server is being used frequently, you may want to have it running all the time. If it is used rarely, you may want the server to start only when it receives a request. For example, if you are hosting a website, your web server is receiving requests all the time from remote users on the Internet. For an FTP site, however, you may receive requests infrequently, in which case you may want to have the FTP server start only when it receives a request. Of course, certain FTP sites receive frequent requests, which would warrant a continuously running FTP server.

A server that starts automatically and runs continuously is referred to as a *standalone* server. The SysV Init procedure can be used to start servers automatically whenever your system boots. This procedure uses service scripts for the servers located in the **/etc/init.d** directory. Most Linux systems configure the web server to start automatically and to run continuously by default. A script for it called **apache2** is in the **/etc/init.d** directory.

Though there is no distribution-independent tool for managing servers, most distributions use the **services-admin** (GNOME), **rcconf** (Debian), **sysv-rc-conf**, or **update-rc.d** tools. The **rcconf** and **update-rc.d** tools were developed by Debian and is used on Debian, Ubuntu, and similar distributions. The **sysv-rc-conf** tool is a generic tool that can be used on all distributions. The **services-admin** tool is part of GNOME system tools and is installed with Ubuntu

The tools provide simple interfaces you can use to choose what servers you want started up and how you want them to run. You use these tools to control any daemon you want started up, including system services such as **cron**, the print server, remote file servers for Samba and NFS, authentication servers for Kerberos, and, of course, Internet servers for FTP or HTTP. Such daemons are referred to as *services,* and you should think of these tools as managing these services. Any of these services can be set up to start or stop at different runlevels.

If you add a new service, **services-admin, rcconf,** or **sysv-rc-conf** can manage it. As described in the following section, services are started up at specific runlevels using service links in various runlevel directories. These links are connected to the service scripts in the **init.d** directory. Runlevel directories are numbered from 0 to 6 in the **/etc/** directory, such as **/etc/rc2.d** for runlevel 2 and **/etc/rc5.d** for runlevel 5. Removing a service from a runlevel only changes its link in the corresponding runlevel directory. It does not touch the service script in the **init.d** directory.

services-admin

GNOME's services-admin tool lets you turn services on or off as well as specify runlevels and the actions to take (see Figure 5-1). It provides a GUI interface on GNOME, usually accessible from the System | Administration menu as the Services entry. Every service has a checkbox. Those checked will be started at boot time, those unchecked will not. To turn on a service, scroll to its entry and click the checkbox next to it, if empty. To turn off a service, click its checkbox again.

Note: The Boot Up Manager (**bum**) provides a simple desktop interface for turning services on and off. Its features are similar to **rrconf**.

To turn a service on or off for a specific runlevel. right-click on the service to display a small pop-up menu with a Properties entry. Click on this entry to display a window with the runlevels listed and whether to the service will be started or stopped. To change or set a stop or start action for a runlevel, click and hold down on a specific runlevel. This displays a pop-up menu with start and stop options. Select the one you want.

Figure 5-1: services-admin tool, System | Administration | Service

rcconf and sysv-rc-conf

On Ubuntu, to turn services on or off for different runlevels, you can also use **rcconf** or **sysv-rc-conf**. Both tools are run from a terminal window on the command line. Both provide an easy cursor based interface for using arrow keys and the spacebar to turn services on or off. The **rcconf** tool is a more limited Debian tool that turns services on or all for the default runlevels, whereas sysv-rc-conf is more refined, allowing you to select specific runlevels.

The **sysv-rc-conf** tool displays a cursor-based screen where you can check which services to run or stop, and at which runlevel (see Figure 5-2). The runlevels will be listed from 0 to 6 and S. Use the arrow keys to position to the cell for your service and runlevel. Then use the spacebar to turn a service on or off. You can set the particular runlevel at which to start and stop services.

The sysv-rc-conf tool is part of the Universe repository. Once installed, you can start it up entering the following command in a terminal window. It is a cursor-based keyboard applications run entirely within the terminal window.

```
sudo sysv-rc-conf
```

```
┌──────────────────────────────────────────────────────────────────┐
│ ▣            richard@richard-desktop-u: ~              [_][□][✕]    │
│ File  Edit  View  Terminal  Tabs  Help                             │
│ ┌────────────────────────────────────────────────────────────────┐│
│ │SysV Runlevel Config   -: stop service  =/+: start service  h: help  q: quit││
│ │                                                                  ││
│ │ service      1     2     3     4     5     0     6     S         ││
│ │ ---------------------------------------------------------------  ││
│ │ acpi-supp$  [ ]   [X]   [X]   [X]   [X]   [ ]   [ ]   [ ]        ││
│ │ acpid       [ ]   [X]   [X]   [X]   [X]   [ ]   [ ]   [ ]        ││
│ │ alsa-utils  [ ]   [ ]   [ ]   [ ]   [ ]   [ ]   [ ]   [ ]        ││
│ │ anacron     [ ]   [X]   [X]   [X]   [X]   [ ]   [ ]   [ ]        ││
│ │ apache2     [ ]   [X]   [X]   [X]   [X]   [ ]   [ ]   [ ]        ││
│ │ apparmor    [ ]   [ ]   [ ]   [ ]   [ ]   [ ]   [ ]   [X]        ││
│ │ apport      [ ]   [X]   [X]   [X]   [X]   [ ]   [ ]   [ ]        ││
│ │ atd         [ ]   [X]   [X]   [X]   [X]   [ ]   [ ]   [ ]        ││
│ │ avahi-dae$  [ ]   [X]   [X]   [X]   [X]   [ ]   [ ]   [ ]        ││
│ │ backuppc    [ ]   [X]   [X]   [X]   [X]   [ ]   [ ]   [ ]        ││
│ │ bluetooth   [ ]   [X]   [X]   [X]   [X]   [ ]   [ ]   [ ]        ││
│ │ bootclean   [ ]   [ ]   [ ]   [ ]   [ ]   [ ]   [ ]   [ ]        ││
│ │ bootlogd    [ ]   [ ]   [ ]   [ ]   [ ]   [ ]   [ ]   [ ]        ││
│ │                                                                  ││
│ │                                                                  ││
│ │ Use the arrow keys or mouse to move around.    ^n: next pg    ^p: prev pg ││
│ │                  space: toggle service on / off                  ││
│ └────────────────────────────────────────────────────────────────┘│
└──────────────────────────────────────────────────────────────────┘
```

Figure 5-2: The sysv-rc-conf service management with runlevels

update-rc.d

The **update-rc.d** tool is a lower level tool that can install or remove runlevel links. It is usually used when installing service packages to create default runlevel links. You can use it to configure your own runlevels for a service, but requires detailed understanding of how runlevel links for services are configured.

The **update-rc.d** tool does not affect links that are already installed. It only works on links that are not already present in the runlevel directories. In this respect, it cannot turn a service on or off directly like **sysv-rc-conf** can. To turn off a service you would first have to remove all runlevel links in all the rc*n*.d directories using the **remove** option, and then add in the ones you want with the **start** or **stop** options. This makes turning services on an off using the **update-rc.d** tool much more complicated.

You use **start** and **stop** options along with the runlevel to set the runlevels at which to start or stop a service. You will need to provide a link number for ordering the sequence in which it will be run. You the enter the runlevel followed by a period. You can specify more than one runlevel. The following will start the web server on runlevel 5. The order number used for the link name is 91. The link name will be **S91apache**. Be sure to include the **sudo** command.

```
sudo update-rc.d apache start 91 5 .
```

The stop number is always 100 minus the start number. So the stop number for service with a start number of 91 would be 09.

```
sudo update-rc.d apache stop 09 6 .
```

The **start** and **stop** options can be combined.

```
update-rc.d apache 99 start 5 . stop 09 6 .
```

A **defaults** option will start and stop the service at predetermined runlevel. This option can be used to quickly set standard start and stop links for all runlevels. Startup links will be set in runlevels 2, 3, 4, and 5. Stop entries are set in runlevels 0, 1, and 6.

```
update-rc.d apache defaults
```

The following command performs the same operation with the stop and start options.

```
update-rc.d apache 99 start 2 3 4 5 . stop 09 0 1 6 .
```

The **multi-user** options will start entries at 2, 3, 4 , 5 and stop them at 1.

```
update-rc.d apache multiuser
```

To remove a service you use the remove option. The links will not be removed if the service script is still present in the **init.d** directory. Use the **-f** option to force removal of the links without having to remove the service script. The following removes all web service startup and shutdown entries from all runlevels.

```
update-rc.d -f apache  remove
```

To turn off a service at a given runlevel that is already turned on, you would have to first remove all its runlevel links and the add in the one's you want. So to turn off the apache server at runlevel 3, but still have it turned on at runlevels 2, 4, and 5 you would use the following commands.

```
update-rc.d -f apache remove
update-rc.d apache 99 start 2 4 5 . stop 09 0 1 3 6 .
```

Keep in mind that the **remove** option removes all stop links as well as start ones. So you have to restore the stop links for 0, 1, and 6.

Tip: On Debian and Ubuntu you can use file-rc instead of sysv-rc. The file-rc tool uses a single configuration file instead of links in separate runlevel directories.

Extended Internet Services Daemon (xinetd)

If your system averages only a few requests for a specific service, you don't need the server for that service running all the time. You need it only when a remote user is accessing its service. The Extended Internet Services Daemon (**xinetd**) manages Internet servers, invoking them only when your system receives a request for their services. **xinetd** checks continuously for any requests by remote users for a particular Internet service; when it receives a request, it then starts the appropriate server daemon.

The **xinetd** program is designed to be a replacement for **inetd**, providing security enhancements, logging support, and even user notifications. For example, with **xinetd** you can send banner notices to users when they are not able to access a service, telling them why. **xinetd** security capabilities can be used to prevent denial-of-service attacks, limiting remote hosts' simultaneous connections or restricting the rate of incoming connections. **xinetd** also incorporates TCP, providing TCP security without the need to invoke the **tcpd** daemon. Furthermore, you do not have to have a service listed in the **/etc/services** file. **xinetd** can be set up to start any kind of special-purpose server.

Some services on Ubuntu are still configured to use **inetd**, like the SWAT configuration tool for CUPS print servers. These will use the **openbsd-inetd** package. The **xinetd** and **openbsd-inetd** packages are incompatible. You must use one or the other. The inetd daemon will use a **/etc/inetd.conf** configuration file. Its init script will be **/etc/init.d/openbsd-inetd**.

xinetd and inetd Servers

To start the server only when a request for its services is received, you configure it using the **xinetd** or the older **inetd** daemons. If you add, change, or delete server entries in the **/etc/xinetd** files, you will have to restart the **xinetd** daemon for these changes to take effect. On distributions that support SysV Init scripts, you can restart the **xinetd** daemon using the `/etc/init.d/xinetd` script with the `restart` argument, as shown here:

```
sudo /etc/init.d/xinetd restart
```

You can also use the `xinetd` script to start and stop the **xinetd** daemon. Stopping effectively shuts down all the servers that the **xinetd** daemon manages (those listed in the **/etc/xinetd.conf** file or the **xinetd.d** directory).

```
sudo /etc/init.d/xinetd stop
sudo /etc/init.d/xinetd start
```

For **inetd** you would use the **openbsd-inetd** script.

```
sudo /etc/init.d/openbsd-inetd restart
```

You can also directly restart **xinetd** by stopping its process directly. To do this, you use the `killall` command with the `-HUP` signal and the name `xinetd`.

```
killall -HUP xinetd
```

xinetd Configuration: xinetd.conf

The xinetd.conf file contains settings for your xinetd server, such as logging and security attributes. This file can also contain server configuration entries, or they may be placed into separate configuration files located in the **/etc/xinetd.d** directory. The **includedir** attribute specifies this directory:

```
includedir /etc/xinetd.d
```

Logging xinetd Services

You can further add a variety of other attributes such as logging information about connections and server priority (`nice`). In the following example, the `log_on_success` attribute logs the duration (`DURATION`) and the user ID (`USERID`) for connections to a service, `log_on_failure` logs the users that failed to connect, and `nice` sets the priority of the service to 10.

```
log_on_success += DURATION USERID
log_on_failure += USERID
nice = 10
```

Attribute	Description
ids	Identifies a service. By default, the service ID is the same as the service name.
type	Type of service: RPC, INTERNAL (provided by **xinetd**), or UNLISTED (not listed in a standard system file).
flags	Possible flags include REUSE, INTERCEPT, NORETRY, IDONLY, NAMEINARGS (allows use of tcpd), NODELAY, and DISABLE (disable the service). See the **xinetd.conf** Man page for more details.
disable	Specify **yes** to disable the service.
socket_type	Specify **stream** for a stream-based service, **dgram** for a datagram-based service, **raw** for a service that requires direct access to IP, and **seqpacket** for reliable sequential datagram transmission.
protocol	Specifies a protocol for the service. The protocol must exist in **/etc/protocols**. If this attribute is not defined, the default protocol employed by the service will be used.
wait	Specifies whether the service is single-threaded or multithreaded (**yes** or **no**). If **yes**, the service is single-threaded, which means that **xinetd** will start the server and then stop handling requests for the service until the server stops. If **no**, the service is multithreaded and **xinetd** will continue to handle new requests for it.
user	Specifies the user ID (UID) for the server process. The username must exist in **/etc/passwd**.
group	Specifies the GID for the server process. The group name must exist in **/etc/group**.
instances	Specifies the number of server processes that can be simultaneously active for a service.
nice	Specifies the server priority.
server	Specifies the program to execute for this service.
server_args	Lists the arguments passed to the server. This does not include the server name.
only_from	Controls the remote hosts to which the particular service is available. Its value is a list of IP addresses. With no value, service is denied to all remote hosts.
no_access	Controls the remote hosts to which the particular service is unavailable.

Attribute	Description
`access_times`	Specifies the time intervals when the service is available. An interval has the form hour:min-hour:min.
`log_type`	Specifies where the output of the service log is sent, either the syslog facility (`SYSLOG`) or a file (`FILE`).
`log_on_success`	Specifies the information that is logged when a server starts and stops.
`log_on_failure`	Specifies the information that is logged when a server cannot be started. Inf
`rpc_version`	Specifies the RPC version for a RPC service.
`rpc_number`	Specifies the number for an UNLISTED RPC service.
`env`	Defines environment variables for a service.
`passenv`	The list of environment variables from **xinetd**'s environment that will be passed to the server.
`port`	Specifies the service port.
`redirect`	Allows a TCP service to be redirected to another host.
`bind`	Allows a service to be bound to a specific interface on the machine.
`interface`	Synonym for `bind`.
`banner`	The name of a file to be displayed for a remote host when a connection to that service is established.
`banner_success`	The name of a file to be displayed at the remote host when a connection to that service is granted.
`banner_fail`	The name of a file to be displayed at the remote host when a connection to that service is denied.
`groups`	Allows access to groups the service has access to (`yes` or `no`).
`enabled`	Specifies the list of service names to enable.
`include`	Inserts the contents of a specified file as part of the configuration file.
`includedir`	Takes a directory name in the form of `includedir /etc/xinetd.d`. Every file inside that directory will be read sequentially as an **xinetd** configuration file, combining to form the **xinetd** configuration.

Table 5-4: Attributes for xinetd

The default attributes defined in the defaults block often set global attributes such as default logging activity and security restrictions: `log_type` specifies where logging information is to be sent, such as to a specific file (`FILE`) or to the system logger (`SYSLOG`), `log_on_success` specifies information to be logged when connections are made, and `log_on_failure` specifies information to be logged when they fail.

```
log_type = SYSLOG daemon info
log_on_failure = HOST
log_on_success = PID HOST EXIT
```

xinetd Network Security

For security restrictions, you can use `only_from` to restrict access by certain remote hosts. The `no_access` attribute denies access from the listed hosts, but no others. These controls take IP addresses as their values. You can list individual IP addresses, a range of IP addresses, or a network, using the network address. The `instances` attribute limits the number of server processes that can be active at once for a particular service. The following examples restrict access to a local network 192.168.1.0 and the localhost, deny access from 192.168.1.15, and use the `instances` attribute to limit the number of server processes at one time to 60.

```
only_from = 192.168.1.0
only_from = localhost
no_access = 192.168.1.15
instances = 60
```

The **xinetd** program also provides several internal services, including **time**, **services**, **servers**, and **xadmin**: **services** provides a list of currently active services, and **servers** provides information about servers; **xadmin** provides **xinetd** administrative support.

xinetd Service Configuration Files: /etc/xinetd.d Directory

Instead of having one large **xinetd.conf** file for all services, the service configurations are split it into several configuration files, one for each service. The directory is specified in **xinetd.conf** file with an **includedir** option. In the following example, the **xinetd.d** directory holds **xinetd** configuration files for services like SWAT. This approach has the advantage of letting you add services by just creating a new configuration file for them. Modifying a service involves editing only its configuration file, not an entire **xinetd.conf** file.

Configuring Services: xinetd Attributes

Entries in an **xinetd** service file define the server to be activated when requested along with any options and security precautions. An entry consists of a block of attributes defined for different features, such as the name of the server program, the protocol used, and security restrictions. Each block for an Internet service such as a server is preceded by the keyword `service` and the name by which you want to identify the service. A pair of braces encloses the block of attributes. Each attribute entry begins with the attribute name, followed by an assignment operator, such as =, and then the value or values assigned. A special block specified by the keyword `default` contains default attributes for services. The syntax is shown here:

```
service <service_name>
{
<attribute> <assign_op> <value> <value> ...
 ...
}
```

Most attributes take a single value for which you use the standard assignment operator, =. Some attributes can take a list of values. You can assign values with the = operator, but you can also add or remove items from these lists with the =+ and =- operators. Use =+ to add values and =- to remove values. You often use the =+ and =- operators to add values to attributes that may have an initial value assigned in the default block.

Attributes are listed in Table 5-4. Certain attributes are required for a service. These include **socket_type** and **wait**. For a standard Internet service, you also need to provide the **user** (user ID for the service), the **server** (name of the server program), and the **protocol** (protocol used by the server). With **server_args**, you can also list any arguments you want passed to the server program (this does not include the server name). If **protocol** is not defined, the default protocol for the service is used.

Disabling and Enabling xinetd Services

You can turn services on or off manually by editing their **xinetd** configuration file. Services are turned on and off with the **disable** attribute in their configuration file. To enable a service, you set the disable attribute to **no**, as shown here:

```
disable = no
```

You then have to restart **xinetd** to start the service.

```
# /etc/init.d/xinetd restart
```

If you want to turn on a service that is off by default, you can set its **disable** attribute to **no** and restart **xinetd**. The entry for the TFTP FTP server, **tftpd**, is shown here. An initial comment tells you that it is off by default, but then the **disable** attribute turns it on:

```
service tftp
{
        socket_type     = dgram
        protocol        = udp
        wait            = yes
        user            = root
        server          = /usr/sbin/in.tftpd
        server_args     = -s /tftpboot
        disable         = yes
        per_source      = 11
        cps             = 100 2
        flags           = IPv4
}
```

Note: You can also use xinetd to implement SSH port forwarding, should your system be used to tunnel connections between hosts or services.

TCP Wrappers

TCP wrappers add another level of security to **xinetd**-managed servers. In effect, the server is wrapped with an intervening level of security, monitoring connections and controlling access. A server connection made through **xinetd** is monitored, verifying remote user identities and checking to make sure they are making valid requests. Connections are logged with the **syslogd** daemon and may be found in **syslogd** files such as **/var/log/secure**. With TCP wrappers, you can also restrict access to your system by remote hosts. Lists of hosts are kept in the **hosts.allow** and **hosts.deny** files. Entries in these files have the format `service:hostname:domain`. The domain is optional. For the service, you can specify a particular service, such as FTP, or you can enter `ALL` for all services. For the hostname, you can specify a particular host or use a wildcard to match several hosts. For example, `ALL` will match on all hosts. Table 5-5 lists the available wildcards. In the following example, the first entry allows access by all hosts to the web service, **http**. The second entry allows access to all services by the `pango1.train.com` host. The third and fourth entries allow FTP access to `rabbit.trek.com` and `sparrow.com`:

```
http:ALL
ALL:pango1.train.com
ftp:rabbit.trek.com
ftp:sparrow.com
```

Wildcard	Description
ALL	Matches all hosts or services.
LOCAL	Matches any host specified with just a hostname without a domain name. Used to match on hosts in the local domain.
UNKNOWN	Matches any user or host whose name or address is unknown.
KNOWN	Matches any user or host whose name or address is known.
PARANOID	Matches any host whose hostname does not match its IP address.
EXCEPT	An operator that lets you provide exceptions to matches. It takes the form of *list1* **EXCEPT** *list2* where those hosts matched in *list1* that are also matched in *list2* are excluded.

Table 5-5: TCP Wrapper Wildcards

The **hosts.allow** file holds hosts to which you allow access. If you want to allow access to all but a few specific hosts, you can specify `ALL` for a service in the **hosts.allow** file but list the ones you are denying access to in the **hosts.deny** file. Using IP addresses instead of hostnames is more secure because hostnames can be compromised through the DNS records by spoofing attacks where an attacker pretends to be another host.

When **xinetd** receives a request for an FTP service, a TCP wrapper monitors the connection and starts up the **in.ftpd** server program. By default, all requests are allowed. To allow all requests specifically for the FTP service, you enter the following in your **/etc/hosts.allow** file. The entry `ALL:ALL` opens your system to all hosts for all services:

```
ftp:ALL
```

Tip: Originally, TCP wrappers were managed by the **tcpd** daemon. However, **xinetd** has since integrated support for TCP wrappers into its own program. You can explicitly invoke the **tcpd** daemon to handle services if you wish. The **tcpd** Man pages (`man tcpd`) provide more detailed information about **tcpd**.

Network Time Protocol, NTP

For servers to run correctly, they need to always have the correct time. Internet time servers worldwide provide the time in the form of the Universal Time Coordinated (UTC). Local time is then calculated using the local systems local time zone. The time is obtained from Internet time servers from an Internet connection. You have the option of using a local hardware clock instead, though this may be much less accurate.

Normally, the time on a host machine is kept in a Time of Year chip (TOY) that maintains the time when the machine is off. Its time is used when the machine is rebooted. A host using the Network Time Protocol, then adjusts the time using the time obtained from an Internet time server. If there is a discrepancy of more than 1000 seconds (about 15 minutes), the system administrator is required to manually set the time. Time servers in the public network are organized in stratum levele, the the highest being 1. Time servers from a lower stratum obtain the time from those in the next higher level.

For servers on your local network, you may want to set up your own time server, insuring that all your servers are using a synchronized time. If all your servers are running on a single host system that is directly connected to the Internet and accessing an Internet time server, you will not need to set up a separate time server. You can use the **ntpdate** command to update directly from an Internet time server.

```
sudo ntpdate  ntp.ubuntu.com
```

If the servers are on different host systems, then you may want a time server to insure their times are synchronized. Alternatively, you could just use the **ntpdate** command to update those hosts directly at given intervals. You could set up a cron job to perform the **ntpdate** operation automatically.

There are packages on the Ubuntu repository for both the NTP server and its documentation.

```
ntp
ntp-docs
```

The documentation will be located in the /usr/share/doc/ntp-doc directory in Web page format.

```
/usr/share/doc/ntp-doc/html/index.html
```

The ntp server

The NTP server name is **ntpd** and is managed by the **/etc/init.d/ntp** script. Use the start, stop, and restart options to mange the server

```
sudo /etc/init.d/ntp start
```

Your host systems can then be configured to use NTP and access your NTP time server.

To check the status of your time server, you can use the **ntpq** command. With the **-p** option is displays the current status.

```
ntpq -p
```

The ntp.conf configuration file

The NTP server configuration file is **/etc/ntp.conf**. This file lists the Internet time servers that your own time server used to deterring the time. The default **ntp.conf** file is shown here. Check the **ntp.conf** Man page for a complete listing of the NTP server configuration directives.

```
#statsdir /var/log/ntpstats/

statistics loopstats peerstats clockstats
filegen loopstats file loopstats type day enable
filegen peerstats file peerstats type day enable
filegen clockstats file clockstats type day enable

# You do need to talk to an NTP server or two (or three).
server ntp.ubuntu.com

# Access control configuration; see
# /usr/share/doc/ntp-doc/html/accopt.html for
# details.  The web page
# <http://support.ntp.org/bin/view/Support/AccessRestrictions>
# might also be helpful.
#
# Note that "restrict" applies to both servers and clients, so a
# configuration that might be intended to block requests from certain
# clients could also end up blocking replies from your own upstream
# servers.

# By default, exchange time with everybody,
# but don't allow configuration.
restrict -4 default kod notrap nomodify nopeer noquery
restrict -6 default kod notrap nomodify nopeer noquery

# Local users may interrogate the ntp server more closely.
restrict 127.0.0.1
restrict ::1

# Clients from this (example!) subnet have unlimited access, but only if
# cryptographically authenticated.
#restrict 192.168.123.0 mask 255.255.255.0 notrust

# If you want to provide time to your local subnet, change the next
# line. (Again, the address is an example only.)
#broadcast 192.168.123.255

# If you want to listen to time broadcasts on your local subnet,
# de-comment the next lines. Please do this only if you trust everybody
# on the network!
#disable auth
#broadcastclient
```

The server directive specifies the Internet time server's Internet address that your NTP server uses to access the time. There is a default entry for the Ubuntu time server, but you can add more server entries for other time servers.

```
server ntp.ubuntu.com
```

NTP access controls

Access control to the NTP server is determined by the restrict directives. An NTP server is accessible from the Internet, anyone can access it. You can specify access options options and the addresses of hosts allowed access. The **default** option lets you specify the set of default options. The **noquery**, **notrust**, **nopeer**, and **nomodify** option deny all access. The notrust option will not trust hosts unless specifically allowed access. The nomodify option prevents any modification of the time server. The **noquery** option will not even allow queries from other hosts, unless specifically allowed.

```
restrict -4 default kod notrap nomodify nopeer noquery
```

Then the local user, users on the same host that is running the NTP server, are allowed to access the NTP server. Addresses are specified for both IPv4 and IPv6 local host, **127.0.0.1** and **::1**.

```
restrict 127.0.0.1
restrict ::1
```

To allow access from hosts on a private local network, you can use the restrict directive to specify the local network address and mask. The following allows access to a local network, 192.168.123, with a network mask of 255.255.255.0 to deterimine the range of allowable host addresses.

```
restrict 192.168.123.0 mask 255.255.255.0
```

If you want to require the use of encrypted keys for access, add the **notrust** option. Use **ntp-keygen** to generate the required public/private keys.

You can also run the time server in broadcast mode where the time is broadcasted to your network clients (this can involve security risks). Use the broadcast directive and your network's broadcast address. Your host systems need to have the **broadcastclient** setting set, which will listen for time broadcasts.

```
broadcast 192.168.123.255
```

NTP clock support

You can also list a reference to the local hardware clock, and have that clock used should your connection to the Internet time server fail. The hardware clock is references by the IP address that has the prefix 127.127 followed by the clock type and instance, as in 127.127.1.1. The type for the local clock is 1.

```
server 127.127.0.1
```

The **fudge** directive is used to specify the time for a hardware clock, passing time parameters for that clock's driver.

AppArmor security

Ubuntu installs AppArmor as its default security system, rather than SELinux. AppArmor (Application Armor) is designed as an alternative to SE-Linux. It is much less complicated, but makes use of the same kernel support provided for SE-Linux. AppArmor is a simple method for implementing mandatory access controls (MAC) for specified Linux applications. It is used primarily for servers like Samba, the Apache Web server, the CUPS print servers, or the time server. In this respect it is much more limited in scope than SELinux, which tries to cover every object. Instead of labeling each object, which SE-Linux does, AppArmor identifies an object by its path name. The object does not have to touched. Originally developed by Immunix and later supported for a time by Novell (OpenSUSE), AppArmor is available under the GNU Public License. You can find out more about AppArmor at **http://en.opensuse.org/Apparmor**.

AppArmor works by setting up a profile for supported applications. Essentially this is a security policy similar aim to SELinux policies. A profile defines what an application can access and use on the system. Ubuntu will install the apparmor and apparmor-utils packages (Ubuntu main repository). Also available are the **apparmor-profiles** and **apparmor-doc** packages (Universe repository).

AppArmor is started with the **/etc/init.d/apparmor** script, which you can use to start, stop, and restart AppArmor.

```
sudo /etc/init.d/apparmor
```

AppArmor utilities

The AppArmor utils packages installs several AppArmor tools including enforce which enables AppArmor and complain which instructs AppArmor to just issue warning messages (see Table 5-6). The unconfined tool will list applications that have no AppArmor profiles. The audit tool will turn on AppArmor message logging for an application (uses enforce mode). The **apparmor_status** tool will display current profile information. The **--complaining** options lists only those in complain mode, and **--enforced** for those in enforcing mode.

```
sudo apparmor_status
```

The logprof tool will analyze AppArmor logs to determine if any changes are needed in any of the application profile. Suggested changes will be presented and the user can allow (A) or deny them (D). In complain mode, allow is the default, and in enforce mode, deny is the default. You can also make your own changes with the new (N) option. Should you want the change applied to all files and directories in a suggested path, you can select the glob option (**G**), essentially replacing the last directory or file in a path with the b global file matching symbol.

The autodep tool will generate a basic AppArmor profile for a new or unconfined application. If you want a more effective profile, you can use genprof to analyze the applications use and generate profile controls accordingly.

The **genprof** tool will update or generate a detailed profile for a specified application. genprof will first set the profile to complain mode. You then starts up the application and uses it, generating complain mode log messages on that use. Then **genprof** prompts you to either scan the complain messages to further refine the profile (**S**), or to finish (**F**). When scanned, different violations are detected and the user is prompted to allow or deny recommended controls. You can then repeat the scan operation until you feel the profile is acceptable. Select finish (**F**) to finalize the profile and quit.

Utility	Description
apparmor_status	Status information about AppArmor policies.
audit applications	Enable logging for AppArmor messages for specified applications
complain	Set AppArmor to complain mode
enforce	Set AppArmor to enforce mode
autodep application	Generate a basic profile for new applications
logprof	Analyzes AppArmor complain messages for a profile, and suggests profile modifications.
genprof application	Generate profile for an application
unconfined	Lists applications not controlled by AppArmor (no profiles)

Table 5-6: AppArmor Utilities

AppArmor configuration

AppArmor configuration is located in the **/etc/apparmor** directory. Configurations for different profiles are located in the **/etc/apparmor.d** directory. Loaded profile configuration file have the name of their path, using periods instead of slashes to separate directory names. The profile file for the **smbd** (Samba) application is **usr.sbin.smbd**. For CUPS (**cupsd**) it is **usr.sbin.cupsd**.

Configuration rules for AppArmor profiles consist of a path and permissions allowable on that path. A detailed explanation of AppArmor rules and permissions can be found in the apparmor.d Man page, including a profile example. A path ending in a * matching symbol will select all the files in that directory. The ** selects all file in the parent directory. All file matching operations are supported (*, [], ?. Permissions include **r** (read), **w** (write), **x** (execute), and **l** (link). The u permission allows unconstrained access. The following entry allows all the files in the /var/log/samba directory with the prefix log. to be written to.

```
/var/log/samba/log.* w,
```

The abstractions subdirectory has files with profile rules that are common to different profiles. Rules from these files are read into actual profiles using the include directive. There are abstractions for applications like gnome, samba, and ftp. Some abstractions will include yet other more general abstractions, like those for the X server or GNOME. For example, the profile for the Samba smbd server, usr.sbin.smbd, will have a include directive for the samba abstraction. This abstraction holds rules common to both the smbd and nmbd servers, both used by the Samba service. The <> used in an include directive indicate the **/etc/arpparmor.d** directory. A list of abstraction files can be found in the apparmor.d Man page.

```
#include <abstractions/samba>
```

In some cases, like for the Web server profile, a profile may need access to some files in a directory that it normally should not have access to. In this case it may need to use a sub-profile to allow access. In effect, the application changes hats, taking on permissions is does not have in the original profile.

The armor-profiles package will provide profile default files for numerous applications in the **/usr/share/doc/apparmor-profiles/extras** directory. It will also activate several commonly used profiles, setting up profile files for them in the **/etc/apparmor.d** directory, like those for samba (**nmbd** and **smbd**), **avahi,** and the network time protocol daemon (**ntpd**).

6. Mail Servers

Mail servers provide Internet users with electronic mail services. They have their own TCP/IP protocols such as the Simple Mail Transfer Protocol (SMTP), the Post Office Protocol (POP), and the Internet Mail Access Protocol (IMAP). Messages are sent across the Internet through mail servers that service local domains. A *domain* can be seen as a subnet of the larger Internet, with its own server to handle mail messages sent from or received for users on that subnet. When a user mails a message, it is first sent from his or her host system to the mail server. The mail server then sends the message to another mail server on the Internet, the one servicing the subnet on which the recipient user is located. The receiving mail server then sends the message to the recipient's host system.

At each stage, a different type of operation takes place using different agents (programs). A mail user agent (MUA) is a mail client program, such as mail or Elm. With an MUA, a user composes a mail message and sends it. Then a mail transfer agent (MTA) transports the messages over the Internet. MTAs are mail servers that use SMTP to send messages across the Internet from one mail server to another, transporting them among subnets. On Ubuntu, the commonly used MTAs are Postfix Exim. These are mail server daemons that constantly checks for incoming messages from other mail servers and sends outgoing messages to appropriate servers (see Table 6-1). Incoming messages received by a mail server are distributed to a user with mail delivery agents (MDAs). Most Linux systems use procmail as their MDA, taking messages received by the mail server and delivering them to user accounts (see **procmail.org** for more information).

Mail Transport Agents

On Ubuntu you can install and configure either Exim, Postfix, or Sendmail. You can also set up your Linux system to run a POP server. POP servers hold users' mail until they log in to access their messages, instead of having mail sent to their hosts directly. The two recommended MTAs are Exim and Postfix, both in the main Ubuntu repository. Sendmail is also available from the Universe repository.

Courier is a fast, small, and secure MTA that maintains some compatibility with Sendmail. The Courier software package also includes POP, IMAP, and webmail servers along with mailing list services. It supports extensive authentication methods including shadow passwords, PAM, and LDAP.

Exim is a fast and flexible MTA similar to Sendmail. Developed at the University of Cambridge, it has a very different implementation than Sendmail.

Qmail is also a fast and secure MTA, but it has little compatibility with Sendmail. It has its own configuration and maintenance files. Like Postfix, it has a modular design, using a different program for each mail task. It also focuses on security, speed, and easy configuration.

Agent	Description
Sendmail	Sendmail mail transfer agent, supported by the Sendmail consortium **www.sendmail.org**
Postfix	Fast, easy-to-configure, and secure mail transfer agent compatible with Sendmail and designed to replace it **www.postfix.org**
Qmail	Fast, flexible, and secure MTA with its own implementation and competitive with Postfix **www.qmail.org**
Exim	MTA based on smail3 **www.exim.org**
Courier	Courier MTA **www.courier-major.org**

Table 6-1: Mail Transfer Agents

Postfix

Postfix is a fast, secure, and flexible MTA designed to replace Sendmail while maintaining as much compatibility as possible. Written by Wietse Venema and originally released as the IBM Secure Mailer, it is now available under the GNU license (**www.postfix.org**). Postfix was created with security in mind, treating all incoming mail as potential security risks. Postfix uses many of the same Sendmail directories and files and makes use of Sendmail wrappers, letting Sendmail clients interact seamlessly with Postfix servers. Postfix is also easier than Sendmail to configure, using its own configuration file.

Instead of one large program, Postfix is implemented as a collection of smaller programs, each designed to perform a specific mail-related task. A Postfix master daemon runs continuously and manages the use of the other Postfix daemons, running them only as needed. A **bounce** daemon handles undeliverable mail, a **trivial-rewrite** daemon redirects messages, and the **showq** daemon provides information on the print queues.

Postfix is available on the main Ubuntu repository. When you install Postfix, two configuration screens will appear to prompt you for the kind of installation you want. The first screen asks you select a standard configuration, with Internet site already selected as the default (see Figure 6-1). You can choose from Internet site, Internet with smarthost, Satellite system, Local, or No configuration.

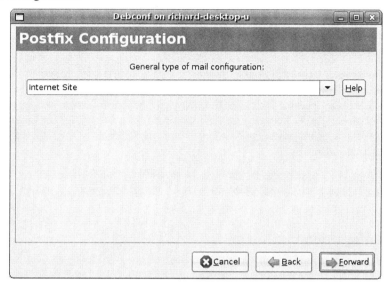

Figure 6-1: Postfix standard configuration selection

The following configuration screen will prompt you for your system mail name, displaying your computer host name as the default.

The options are as follows:

➢ **Internet site**: The default configuration. Mail server interacts directly with the Internet. Mail sent directly with SMTP

➢ **Internet site using smarthost**: Mail server for a local network that, in turn, uses an ISP mail server to interact with the Internet. Mail received and sent to and from the ISP mail server with mail server access tools like fetchmail. Mail can be received, but not sent, directly form the Internet.

➢ **Local delivery only**: System only mail server (no network access) for users on the mail server's system (host).

➢ **No configuration**: No configuration to standard configuration files (requires detailed configuration on your part)

➢ **Satellite system**: Outgoing forwarding mail server for sent mail only (no received mail)

Several other support packages are also available on the Ubuntu repository for Postfix. These include the Postfix documentation with examples (**postfix-doc**), LDAP (**postfix-ldap**), and MySQL (**postfix-mysql**), as well as Postfix greylisting support (**postgrey**).

Postfix Commands

Several Postfix commands allow you to manage your server tasks. The `sendmail` command sends messages. You use `mailq` to display the status of your mail queues. The `newaliases` command takes mail aliases listed in the aliases files and stores them in a database file that can be used by Postfix.

The `postmap` command is used to maintain various database files used by Postfix, such as the alias file for mail aliases and the access file that restricts messages received by the server. You can also implement these database files as SQL databases like MySQL, allowing for easier management. The **mysql_table** Man page provides detailed information on how to configure SQL database support (check **pgsql_table** for Postgresql database support). You could also use LDAP instead of SQL (**ldap_table**).

In addition, Postfix provides lower-level tools, all beginning with the term `post`, such as the `postalias` command, which maintains the alias database, and `postcat`, which displays print queue files.

Postfix Configuration: main.cf

Postfix configuration is handled by setting parameters in its configuration file, **main.cf**. In addition a **master.cf** file holds parameters for running Postfix services, and **dynamicmaps.cf** file for additional runtime capabilities.

A default **/etc/postfix/main.cf** file is installed with Postfix, with most of the essential configuration values already set. Parameter names tend to be user friendly. For example, directory locations are specified by parameters ending in the term `directory`, such as `queue_directory` for the location of Postfix queues and `daemon_directory` for the location of the Postfix daemons. Defaults are already implemented for most parameters. For example, defaults are set for particular resource controls, such as message size, time limits, and the number of allowed messages per queue. You can edit the **main.cf** file to change the parameter values to meet your own needs. After making any changes, you need only to reload the configuration using the `postfix reload` command:

```
postfix reload
```

Network Parameters

You will most likely need to set several network parameters. To ease this process, Postfix defines parameters that hold key network information, such as `myhostname`, which holds the hostname of your system, and `mydomain`, which holds the domain name of your network. For example, `myhostname` would be set to the host **turtle.mytrek.com**, whereas `mydomain` would be just **mytrek.com**. Parameters like `myhostname` and `mydomain` are themselves used as values assigned to other parameters. On Ubuntu, myhostname will be set to the system mail name you entered in the second configuration screen during the Postfix installation. In the next example, `myhostname` and `mydomain` are set to the host the mail server is running on and its network domain:

```
myhostname=turtle.mytrek.com
mydomain=mytrek.com
```

The `myorigin` parameter specifies the origin address for e-mail sent by the server. On Debian/Ubuntu this is commented your. You could set to the value of the parameter `myhostname`, as shown here. Note that a `$` precedes the `myhostname` variable to evaluate it.

```
myorigin=$myhostname
```

If you are using a single system directly attached to the Internet, you may want to keep this configuration, labeling mail as being sent by your host. However, if your system is operating as a gateway for a network, your mail server is sending out mail from different hosts on that network. You may wish to change the origin address to the domain name, so that mail is perceived as sent from the domain.

```
myorigin=$mydomain
```

Local Networks

The `mydestination` parameter holds the list of domains that your mail server will receive mail for. By default, these include **localhost** and your system's hostname.

```
mydestination = $myhostname localhost.$mydomain
```

If you want the mail server to receive mail for an entire local network, you need to also specify its domain name. That way, the server can receive mail addressed just to the domain, instead of your specific host.

```
mydestination = $myhostname localhost.$mydomain $mydomain
```

Also, if your host goes by other hostnames and there are DNS records identifying your host by those names, you need to specify those names as well. For example, your host could also be a web server to which mail could be directed. A host **turtle.mytrek.com** may also be identified as the website **mytrek.com**. Both names would have to be listed in the `mydestination` parameter.

```
mydestination = $myhostname localhost.$mydomain $mydomain www.$mydomain
```

If your system is a gateway for one or more local networks, you can specify them with the `mynetworks` parameter. This allows your mail server to relay mail addressed to those networks. Networks are specified using their IP addresses. The `relay_domains` parameter lets you specify domain addresses of networks for which you can relay messages. By default, this is set to `mydestination`:

```
mynetworks=192.168.0.0
relay_domains=$mydestination
```

Hosts within the local network connected to the Internet by a gateway need to know the identity of the relay host, the mail server. You set this with the `relayhost` parameter. Also, `myorigin` should be set to just `mydomain`. If there is a DNS server identifying the gateway as the mail server, you can just set `relayhost` to the value of `mydomain`. If not, then `relayhost` should be set to the specific hostname of the gateway/mail server. If your local network is not running a DNS server, be sure to set `disable_dns_lookups` to `yes`.

```
relay_host=$mydomain
```

Direct Connections

If your system is directly connected to the Internet and you use an ISP (Internet service provider) for receiving mail, you can configure Postfix as a null client to only send mail. Set the **relay_host** parameter to just your own domain name. Also, in the **master.cf** file, comment out the SMTP server and local delivery agent entries.

```
relayhost = $mydomain
```

Masquerading

If your mail server is operating on a gateway for a local network and you want to hide the hosts in that network, you can opt to masquerade the local hosts, letting it appear that all mail is coming from the domain in general, instead of a particular host. To set this option, you use the **masquerade_domains** parameter. In the following example, all mail sent by a local host such as **rabbit.mytrek.com** will be addressed as coming from **mytrek.com**. Thus a message sent by the user **chris@rabbit.mytrek.com** is sent out as coming from **chris@mytrek.com**:

```
masquerade_domains = $mydomain
```

Received mail is not masqueraded by default. This allows Postfix to still deliver received mail to particular hosts. If you want received mail to also be masqueraded, you have to add the **envelope_recipients** parameter to the list of values assigned to the **masquerade_class** parameter. In that case, Postfix will no longer be able to deliver received mail.

Virtual Domains and Virtual Accounts

If your network has implemented virtual domains, you will need to set up a virtual domain table and then specify that table with the **virtual_maps** option. Setting up a table is a simple matter of listing virtual names and their real addresses in a text file such as **/etc/postfix/virtual**. Then use the **postmap** command to create a Postfix table:

```
postmap /etc/postfix/virtual
```

In the **main.cf** file, specify the table with the **virtual_maps** parameter. Postfix will then use this table to look up virtual domains.

```
virtual_maps = hash:/etc/postfix/virtual
```

Note: See the Postfix FAQ at **postfix.org** for detailed information on how to set up Postfix for a gateway, a local workstation, or a host directly connected to the Internet (null server).

Instead of using mail accounts for actual users on a system, you can set up a virtual accounts. Virtual accounts can be managed either in standard Postfix text files, in SQL databases, or as LDAP entries. SQL databases are preferred for managing a large number of virtual accounts. For SQL support, you first create tables in a MySQL database for domains (the virtual domains), users (user accounts), and forwarding (aliases). Corresponding virtual domain configuration files will list information like the database, tables, and host to use, such as a **mysql_virt.cf** for SQL database access and **mysql_users.cf** for accessing the user table. Check the documentation at **www.postfix.org** for detailed information.

Postfix Greylisting Policy Server

Postfix also supports greylisting with the Postfix Greylisting Policy Server. Greylisting blocks spammers based on their mailing methods rather than content, relying on the fact that spammers will not attempt retries if rejected (**greylisting.org**). Messages from new previously unknown sources are rejected, whereupon a valid MTA will retry, whereas a spammer will not. To support the Greylisting Policy Server, Postfix is configured to delegate Policy access to a server. In the **/etc/postfix** directory you can use the postgrey_whitelist files to exclude email addresses from greylisting.

The Greylisting Policy Server is run as a standalone server, using its own startup script. The postgrey Man page provides detailed information about the server's options.

Controlling User and Host Access

With an access file, you can control access by certain users, hosts, and domains. The access file works much like the one used for Sendmail. Entries are made in a text file beginning with the user, host, or domain name or address, followed by an action to take. A user, host, or domain can be accepted, rejected with no message, or rejected with a message. Once entries are made, they can be installed in a Postfix database file with the **postmap** command:

```
postmap /etc/postfix/access
```

You can then use the access file in various Postfix operations to control clients, recipients, and senders.

Access can also be controlled by use of the Mail Abuse Prevention System (MAPS), which provides the RBL+ service, a collection of mail address DNS-based databases (**mail-abuse.com**). These databases, like the Realtime Blackhole List (RBL), list mail addresses that are known be used by mail abusers. A domain or host is matched against a list maintained by the service, which can be accessed on a local server or directly from an online site. Various Postfix operations let you use MAPS databases to control access by clients, recipients, or senders.

Header and Body Checks

With the **header_checks** parameter, you can specify a Postfix table where you can list criteria for rejecting messages. Check the **/etc/postfix/header_checks** file for details. The criteria are patterns that can match message headers. You can have matching messages rejected, rejected with a reply, simply deleted, or logged with a warning. You have the option of taking several actions, including REJECT, DISCARD, WARN, HOLD, and IGNORE.

```
header_checks = regexp:/etc/postfix/header_checks
```

The database, in this case **/etc/postfix/header_checks**, will have lines, each with a regular expression and a corresponding action. The regular expression can either be a standard regular expression as denoted by **regexp** in the **header_checks** parameter, or conform to a Perl Compatible Regular Expression, **prece**.

The **body_checks** parameter lets you check the body of text messages, line by line, using regular expressions and actions like those used for **header_checks** in an **/etc/postfix/body_checks** file.

Controlling Client, Senders, and Recipients

With the `smtpd_client_restrictions` parameter, you can restrict access to the mail server by certain clients. Restrictions you can apply include `reject_unknown_client_hostname`, which will reject any clients with unresolved addresses; `permit_mynetworks`, which allows access by any clients defined by `mynetworks`; and `check_client_access`, which will check an access database to see if a client should be accepted or rejected. The `reject_rbl_client` and `reject_rhsbl_client` parameters will reject clients from specified domains.

```
smtpd_client_restrictions = permit_mynetworks, \
          reject_unknown_client, check_client_access, reject_maps_rbl
```

The `reject_rbl_client` restriction rejects domain addresses according to a specified MAPS service. The site can be an online site or a local one set up to provide the service. The `reject_rhsbl_client` restriction rejects host addresses.

```
smtpd_client_restrictions = reject_rbl_client relays.mail-abuse.org
```

To implement restrictions from a access file, you can use the **hash** directive and the name of the file.

```
smtpd_client_restrictions = hash:/etc/postfix/access
```

The corresponding `smtpd_sender_restrictions` parameter works much the same way as its client counterpart but controls access from specific senders. It has many of the same restrictions but adds `reject_non_fqdn_sender`, which will reject any mail header without a fully qualified domain name, and `reject_sender_login_mismatch`, which will require sender verification. The `reject_rhsbl_sender` restriction rejects domain addresses according to a specified MAPS service.

The `smtpd_recipient_restrictions` parameter will restrict the recipients the server will accept mail for. Restrictions include `permit_auth_destination`, which allows authorized messages, and `reject_unauth_destination`, which rejects unauthorized messages. The `check_recipient_access` restriction will checks local networks for a recipient address. The `reject_unknown_recipient_domain` restriction rejects recipient addresses with no DNS entry. The `reject_rhsbl_recipient` restriction rejects domain addresses according to a specified MAPS service.

You can further refine restrictions with parameters such as `smtpd_helo_restrictions`, which requires a HELO command from a client. Restriction parameters include `reject_invalid_hostname`, which checks for faulty syntax, `reject_unknown_hostname`, for hosts with no DNS entry, and `reject_non_fqdn_hostname` for hosts whose names are not fully qualified. The `strict_rfc821_envelopes` parameter will implement strict envelope protocol compliance.

Note: Sendmail operates as a server to both receive and send mail messages. Sendmail listens for any mail messages received from other hosts and addressed to users on the network hosts it serves and, at the same time, handles messages users are sending out to remote users, determining what hosts to send them to. You can learn more about Sendmail at **sendmail.org**, including online documentation and current software packages. You can also obtain a commercial version from **sendmail.com**.

POP and IMAP Server: Dovecot

The protocols Internet Mail Access Protocol (IMAP) and Post Office Protocol (POP) allow a remote server to hold mail for users who can then fetch their mail from it when they are ready. Unlike procmail, which delivers mail messages directly to a user account on a Linux system, the IMAP and POP protocols hold mail until a user accesses an account on the IMAP or POP server. The servers then transfer any received messages to the user's local mailbox. Such servers are often used by ISPs to provide Internet mail services for users. Instead of being sent directly to a user's machine, the mail resides in the IMAP or POP server until it's retrieved. Ubuntu can install Dovecot as its IMAP and POP servers. Other popular IMAP and POP servers available are Qpopper, the Qmail POP server, the Washington University POP and IMAP servers, and the Courier POP and IMAP servers.

You can access the POP server from different hosts; however, when you do, all the messages are transferred to that host. They are not kept on the POP server (though you can set an option to keep them). The POP server simply forwards your messages on the requesting host. When you access your messages from a certain computer, they will be transferred to that computer and erased from the POP server. If you access your POP server again from a different computer, those previous messages will be gone.

The Internet Mail Access Protocol (IMAP) allows a remote server to hold mail for users who can then log in to access their mail. Unlike the POP servers, IMAP servers retain user mail messages. Users can even save their mail on the IMAP mail server. This has the advantage of keeping a user's mail in one centralized location accessible anywhere on the network. Users can log in to the mail server from any host on the network and read, send, and save their mail.

Unlike POP, IMAP allows users to set up multiple folders on their mail server in which they can organize their mail. IMAP also supports the use of shared folders to which several users can access mail on a given topic.

Dovecot

Dovecot is a combination IMAP and POP server. Using its own indexing methods, Dovecot is able to handle a great deal of e-mail traffic. It features support for SSL, along with numerous authentication methods. Password database support includes shadow passwords, LDAP, PAM, and MySQL. Dovecot is available in POP, IMAP, and common packages on the Ubuntu main repository. The **/etc/dovecot.conf** file is configured to use plain password authentication with PAM, using the **passwd** file.

Configuration options are placed in **/etc/dovecot.conf**. This file contains commented default settings with detail explanations for each. Option specific to **imap** and **pop3** are placed in their own sections. These are some basic settings to configure:

> ➤ **protocols**   This can be set to `imap` and `pop`, as well as `imaps` and `pops` for SSL-encrypted connections.

> ➤ **listen**   These can be set to IPv4 or IPv4 protocols; IPv6 is set by default. The listen option is set in the respective protocol sections, like `protocol imap` or `protocol pop3`.

> ➤ **auth default** section   This section holds your default authentication options.

> ➤ **mechanism** in **auth** section plain by default   digest-MD5 and cran-MD5 are supported, but they are not needed if you are using SSL.

> ➤ **passwd** in **auth** section**mail_location**   The default mail storage method and location.

Dovecot supports either mailbox or maildir (IMAP) storage formats. The mailbox format uses single large mailbox files to hold several mail messages. Updates can be time consuming. The maildir format uses a separate file for each message, making updates much more efficient. Dovecot will automatically detect the kind of storage use, referencing the MAIL environment variable. This will be the user's **mbox** file at **/var/mail**. You can configure Dovecot to use a maildir format by setting the `mail_location` option to use a maildir setting, specifying the directory to use. The `%u` symbol can be used to represent the user name, `%h` for the home directory. Messages will be stored in a user's **maildir** directory instead of an **mbox** file. Be sure to create the **maildir** directory and give it read, write, and execute access.

```
mail_location=maildir:/var/mail/%1u/%u/maildir
```

Other POP and IMAP Servers

Many distributions also include the Cyrus IMAP server, which you can install and use instead of Dovecot. In addition, several other IMAP and POP servers are available for use on Linux:

> ➤ The University of Washington POP and IMAP servers (**ftp.cac.washington.edu/imap**) are part of the University of Washington's **imap** package (Universe repository). The POP server daemons are called **ipop2d** and **ipop3d**. Your Linux system then runs as a POP2 and POP3 server for your network. These servers are run through **xinetd**. The POP3 server uses the **ipop3** file in the **/etc/xinetd.d**, and the IMAP uses **imap**.

> ➤ The Cyrus IMAP server (**cyrusimap.web.cmu.edu**) features security controls and authentication, using a private mailbox structure that is easily scalable (Universe repository). Designed to be run on dedicated mail servers, it is supported and maintained by Carnegie Mellon. The name of the Cyrus IMAP server daemon is **imapd**. There will be a file called **imap** in the **/etc/xinetd.d** directory..

> ➤ The Courier-IMAP server (**courier-mta.org**) is a small, fast IMAP server that provides extensive authentication support including LDAP and PAM (Universe repository).

> ➤ Qpopper is the Berkeley POP server (popper) (Universe repository). Qpopper is unsupported software, currently available from Qualcomm, makers of Eudora e-mail software. The Qpopper web page is located at the Eudora site archives (**eudora.com**).

Note: The IMAP and POP servers provide SSL encryption for secure e-mail transmissions. You can also run IMAP and POP servers using Stunnel to provide similar security. Stunnel is an SSL wrapper for daemons like **imapd**, **popd**, and even **pppd** (modem connections). In the service's **xinetd** script, you can invoke the server with the `stunnel` command instead of running the server directly.

Spam: SpamAssassin

With SpamAssassin, you can filter sent and received e-mail for spam. The filter examines both headers and content, drawing on rules designed to detect common spam messages. When they are detected, it then tags the message as spam, so that a mail client can then discard it. SpamAssassin will also report spam messages to spam detection databases. The version of SpamAssassin distributed for Linux is the open source version developed by the Apache project, located at **spamassassin.apache.org**. There you can find detailed documentation, FAQs, mailing lists, and even a listing of the tests that SpamAssassin performs.

SpamAssassin rule files are located at **/usr/share/spamassassin**. The files contain rules for running tests such as detecting the fake hello in the header. Configuration files for SpamAssassin are located at **/etc/mail/spamassassin**. The **local.cf** file lists system-wide SpamAssassin options such as how to rewrite headers. The **init.pre** file holds spam system configurations. The **spamassassin-spamc.rc** file will redirect all mail to the **spamc** client.

Users can set their own SpamAssassin option in their **.spamassassin/user_prefs** file. Common options include `required_scorei`, which sets a threshold for classifying a message as SPAM, numerous whitelist and blacklist options that accept and reject messages from certain users and domains, and tagging options that either rewrite or just add SPAM labels. Check the Mail::SpamAssassin::Conf Man page for details.

To configure procmail to use SpamAssassin, you need to have procmail run the **/etc/mail/spamassassin/spamassassin-spamc.rc** file. This will filter all mail through SpamAssassin. The **spamassassin-spamc.rc** file uses the **spamd** daemon, which means you have to have the SpamAssassin service running. The **spamassassin-default.rc** file runs a less efficient script to use SpamAssassin, instead of the daemon. If you want systemwide procmail filtering, you use the **/etc/procmailrc** file; whereas to implement filtering on a per-user basis, you use a **.procmail** file in the user's home directory. Within the respective procmail files, add the following at the top:

```
INCLUDERC=/etc/mail/spamassassin/spamassassin-spamc.rc
```

Configuring Postfix for use with SpamAssassin can be complicated. A helpful tool for this task is **amavisd-new**, an interface between a mail transport agent like Exim or Postfix and content checkers like SpamAssassin and virus checkers. Check **ijs.si/software/amavisd** for more details.

7. FTP

The File Transfer Protocol (FTP) is designed to transfer large files across a network from one system to another. Like most Internet operations, FTP works on a client/server model. FTP client programs can enable users to transfer files to and from a remote system running an FTP server program. Any Linux system can operate as an FTP server. It has to run only the server software—an FTP daemon with the appropriate configuration. Transfers are made between user accounts on client and server systems. A user on the remote system has to log in to an account on a server and can then transfer files to and from that account's directories only. A special kind of user account, named *ftp,* allows any user to log in to it with the username "anonymous." This account has its own set of directories and files that are considered public, available to anyone on the network who wants to download them. The numerous FTP sites on the Internet are FTP servers supporting FTP user accounts with anonymous login. Any Linux system can be configured to support anonymous FTP access, turning them into network FTP sites. Such sites can work on an intranet or on the Internet.

FTP Servers

FTP server software consists of an FTP daemon and configuration files. The *daemon* is a program that continuously checks for FTP requests from remote users. When a request is received, it manages a login, sets up the connection to the requested user account, and executes any FTP commands the remote user sends. For anonymous FTP access, the FTP daemon allows the remote user to log in to the FTP account using **anonymous** or **ftp** as the username. The user then has access to the directories and files set up for the FTP account. As a further security measure, however, the daemon changes the root directory for that session to be the FTP home directory. This hides the rest of the system from the remote user. Normally, any user on a system can move around to any directories open to him or her. A user logging in with anonymous FTP can see only the FTP home directory and its subdirectories. The remainder of the system is hidden from that user. This effect is achieved by the `chroot` operation (discussed later) that literally changes the system root directory for that user to that of the FTP directory. By default, the FTP server also requires a user be using a valid shell. It checks for a list of valid shells in the **/etc/shells** file. Most daemons have options for turning off this feature.

Available Servers

Several FTP servers are available for use on Linux systems (see Table 7-1). Three of the more common servers include **vsftpd**, **pureftpd**, and **proftpd**. The Very Secure FTP Server provides a simple and very secure FTP server. The Pure FTPD servers is a lightweight, fast, and secure FTP server, based upon Troll-FTPd. Documentation and the latest sources are available from **pureftpd.org**.

FTP Servers	Site
Very Secure FTP Server (vsftpd)	**vsftpd.beasts.org**
ProFTPD	**proftpd.org**
PureFTP	**pureftpd.org**
NcFTPd	**ncftpd.org**
SSH sftp-server	**openssh.org**
Washington University web server (WU-FTPD)	**wu-ftpd.org**
Tux	Web server with FTP capabilities
gssftpd	Kerberos FTP server

Table 7-1: FTP Servers

ProFTPD is a popular FTP daemon based on an Apache web server design. It features simplified configuration and support for virtual FTP hosts. The compressed archive of the most up-to-date version, along with documentation, is available at the ProFTPD website at **proftpd.org**. Another FTP daemon, NcFTPd, is a commercial product produced by the same programmers who did the NcFTP FTP client. NcFTPd is free for academic use and features a reduced fee for small networks. Check **ncftpd.org** for more information.

Several security-based FTP servers are also available, including SSLFTP and SSH **sftpd**, along with **gssftpd**. SSLFTP uses SSL (Secure Sockets Layer) to encrypt and authenticate transmissions, as well as MD5 digests to check the integrity of transmitted files. SSH **sftpd** is an FTP server that is now part of the Open SSH package, using SSH encryption and authentication to establish secure FTP connections. The **gssftpd** server is part of the Kerberos 5 package and provides Kerberos-level security for FTP operations.

FTP Users

Normal users with accounts on an FTP server can gain full FTP access simply by logging into their accounts. Such users can access and transfer files directly from their own accounts or any directories they may have access to. You can also create users, known as guest users that have restricted access to the FTP publicly accessible directories. This involves setting standard user restrictions, with the FTP public directory as their home directory. Users can also log in as anonymous users, allowing anyone on the network or Internet to access files on an FTP server.

Anonymous FTP: vsftpd

An anonymous FTP site is essentially a special kind of user on your system with publicly accessible directories and files in its home directory. Anyone can log in to this account and access its files. Because anyone can log in to an anonymous FTP account, you must be careful to restrict a remote FTP user to only the files on that anonymous FTP directory. Normally, a user's files are interconnected to the entire file structure of your system. Normal users have write access that lets them create or delete files and directories. The anonymous FTP files and directories can be configured in such a way that the rest of the file system is hidden from them and remote users are given only read access. In ProFTPD, this is achieved through configuration directives placed in its configuration file. An older approach implemented by the vsftpd package involves having copies of certain system configuration, command, and library files placed within subdirectories of the FTP home directory. Restrictions placed on those subdirectories then control access by other users. Within the FTP home directory, you then have a publicly accessible directory that holds the files you want to make available to remote users. This directory usually has the name **pub**, for public.

An FTP site is made up of an FTP user account, an FTP home directory, and certain copies of system directories containing selected configuration and support files. Newer FTP daemons, such as ProFTPD, do not need the system directories and support files. Most distributions have already set up an FTP user account when you installed your system.

The FTP User Account: anonymous

To allow anonymous FTP access by other users to your system, you must have a user account named *FTP*. Most distributions already create this account for you. If your system does not have such an account, you will have to create one. You can then place restrictions on the FTP account to keep any remote FTP users from accessing any other part of your system. The entry for this account in your **/etc/passwd** file must be set up to prevent normal user access to it. The following is the entry you find in your **/etc/passwd** file on Ubuntu that sets up an FTP login as an anonymous user:

```
ftp:x:117:65534::/home/ftp:
```

The **x** in the password field blocks the account, which prevents any other users from gaining access to it, thereby gaining control over its files or access to other parts of your system. The user ID, 14, is a unique ID. The comment field is FTP User. The login directory is **/home/ftp**. When FTP users log in to your system, they are placed in this directory. If a home directory has not been set up, create one and then change its ownership to the FTP user with the **chown** command.

FTP Group

The group ID is the ID of the **ftp** group, which is set up only for anonymous FTP users. You can set up restrictions on the **ftp** group, thereby restricting any anonymous FTP users. Here is the entry for the **ftp** group you find in the **/etc/group** file. If your system does not have one, you should add it:

```
ftp::117:
```

Creating New FTP Users

If you are creating virtual FTP hosts, you will need to create an FTP user for each one, along with its directories. For example, to create an FTP server for a host1-ftp host, you create a host1-ftp user with its own directory.

```
useradd -d /home/host1-ftp host1-ftp
```

This creates a user such with a password entry as that described here:

```
host1-ftp:x:118:50::/home/host1-ftp:
```

You also need to create the corresponding home directory, **/home/host1-ftp** in this example, and set its permissions to give users restricted access.

```
mkdir /home/host1-ftp
chmod 755 /home/host1-ftp
```

In addition, you need to make sure that the root user owns the directory, not the new FTP users. This gives control of the directory only to the root user, not to any user that logs in.

```
chown root.root /home/host1-ftp
```

Anonymous FTP Server Directories

As previously noted, the FTP home directory is named **ftp** and is placed in the **/var** directory. When users log in anonymously, they are placed in this directory. An important part of protecting your system is preventing remote users from using any commands or programs not in the restricted directories. For example, you would not let a user use your `ls` command to list filenames, because `ls` is located in your **/bin** directory. At the same time, you want to let the FTP user list filenames using an `ls` command. Newer FTP daemons such as **vsftpd** and ProFTPD solve this problem by creating secure access to needed system commands and files, while restricting remote users to only the FTP site's directories. In any event, make sure that the FTP home directory is owned by the root user, not by the FTP user. Use the `ls -d` command to check on the ownership of the FTP directory.

```
ls -d /home/ftp
```

To change a directory's ownership, you use the `chown` command, as shown in this example:

```
chown  root.root /home/ftp
```

Another, more traditional solution is to create copies of certain system directories and files needed by remote users and to place them in the **ftp** directory where users can access them. A **bin** directory is placed in the **ftp** directory and remote users are restricted to it, instead of the system's **bin** directory. Whenever they use the `ls` command, remote users are using the one in **ftp/bin**, not the one you use in **/bin**. If, for some reason, you set up the anonymous FTP directories yourself, you must use the `chmod` command to change the access permissions for the directories so that remote users cannot access the rest of your system. Create an **ftp** directory and use the `chmod` command with the permission 555 to turn off write access: `chmod 555 ftp`. Next, make a new **bin** directory in the **ftp** directory, and then make a copy of the `ls` command and place it in **ftp/bin**. Do this for any commands you want to make available to FTP users. Then create an **ftp/etc** directory to hold a copy of your **passwd** and **group** files. Again, the idea is to prevent any access to the original files in the **/etc** directory by FTP users. The **ftp/etc/passwd** file should be edited to remove any entries for regular users on your system. All other entries should have their passwords set to **x** to block access. For the **group** file, remove all user groups and set all passwords to **x**. Create an **ftp/lib** directory, and then make copies of the libraries you need to run the commands you placed in the **bin** directory.

Anonymous FTP Files

A directory named **pub**, located in the FTP home directory, usually holds the files you are making available for downloading by remote FTP users. When FTP users log in, they are placed in the FTP home directory (**/home/ftp**), and they can then change to the **pub** directory to start accessing those files (**/home/ftp/pub**). Within the **pub** directory, you can add as many files and directories as you want. You can even designate some directories as upload directories, enabling FTP users to transfer files to your system.

In each subdirectory set up under the **pub** directory to hold FTP files, you should create a **README** file and an **INDEX** file as a courtesy to FTP users. The **README** file contains a brief description of the kind of files held in this directory. The **INDEX** file contains a listing of the files and a description of what each one holds.

Using FTP with rsync

Many FTP servers also support rsync operations using **rsync** as a daemon. This allows intelligent incremental updates of files from an FTP server. You can update multiple files in a directory or a single file such as a large ISO image.

Accessing FTP Sites with rsync

To access the FTP server running an rsync server, you enter the **rsync** command, and following the hostname, you enter a double colon and then either the path of the directory you want to access or one of the FTP server's modules. In the following example, the user updates a local **myproject** directory from the one on the **mytrek.com** FTP site:

```
rsync ftp.mytrek.com::/home/ftp/pub/myproject  /home/myproject
```

To find out what directories are supported by rsync, you check for rsync modules on that site. These are defined by the site's **/etc/rsyncd.conf** configuration file. A *module* is just a directory with all its subdirectories. To find available modules, you enter the FTP site with a double colon only.

```
rsync ftp.mytrek.com::
ftp
```

This tell you that the **ftp.mytrek.com** site has an FTP module. To list the files and directories on the module, you can use the **rsync** command with the **-r** option.

```
rsync -r ftp.mytrek.com::ftp
```

Many sites that run the rsync server will have an rsync protocol that will already be set to access the available rsync module (directory). You can even use **rsync** to update just a single file, such as an ISO image that may have been changed.

Configuring an rsync Server

To configure your FTP server to let clients use rsync on your site, you need to first run rsync as server. Use **services-admin** or **sysv-rc-conf** to turn on the rsync daemon, commonly known as **rsyncd**. This will run the rsync daemon through **xinetd**, using an **rsync** script in **/etc/xinetd.d** to turn it on and set parameters.

When run as a daemon, rsync will read the **/etc/rsyncd.conf** file for its configuration options. Here you can specify FTP options such as the location for the FTP site files. The configuration file is segmented into modules, each with its own options. A module is a symbolic representation of a exported tree (a directory and its subdirectories). The module name is enclosed in brackets, for instance, **[ftp]** for an FTP module. You can then enter options for that module, as by using the path option to specify the location of your FTP site directories and files. The user and group IDs can be specified with the **uid** and **gid** options. The default is nobody. A sample FTP module for anonymous access is shown here:

```
[ftp]
        path = /var/ftp/pub
        comment = ftp site
```

For more restricted access, you can add an **auth users** option to specify authorized users; rsync will allow anonymous access to all users by default. The hosts allow or deny to control access control access from specific hosts. Access to areas on the FTP site by rsync can be further controlled using a secrets file, such as **/etc/rsyncd.secrets**. This is a colon-separated list of user names and passwords.

```
aleina:mypass3
larisa:yourp5
```

A corresponding module to the controlled area would look like this:

```
[specialftp]
     path = /var/projects/special
     command = restricted access
     auth users = aleina,larisa
     secrets file = /etc/rsyncd.secrets
```

If you are on your FTP server and want to see what modules will be made available, you can run **rsync** with the **localhost** option and nothing following the double colon.

```
$ rsync localhost::
ftp
specialftp
```

Remote users can find out what modules you have by entering your hostname and double colon only.

```
rsync ftp.mytrek.com::
```

rsync Mirroring

Some sites will allow you to use rsync to perform mirroring operations. With rsync you do not have to copy the entire site, just those files that have been changed. The following example mirrors the mytrek FTP site to the **/home/ftp/mirror/mytrek** directory on a local system:

```
rsync -a --delete ftp.mytrek.com::ftp /home/ftp/mirror/mytrek
```

The **-a** option is archive mode, which includes several other options, such as **-r** (recursive) to include all subdirectories, **-t** to preserves file times and dates, **-l** recreate symbolic links, and **-p** to preserve all permissions. In addition, the **--delete** option is added to delete files that don't exist on the sending side, removing obsolete files.

The Very Secure FTP Server

The Very Secure FTP Server (vsftpd) is small, fast, easy, and secure. It is designed to avoid the overhead of large FTP server applications like ProFTPD, while maintaining a very high level of security. It can also handle a very large workload, managing high traffic levels on an FTP site. It is perhaps best for sites where many anonymous and guest users will be downloading the same files. It replaced the Washington University FTP server, WU-FTPD, as the primary FTP server, and is available on the man Ubuntu repository.

The Very Secure FTP Server is inherently designed to provide as much security as possible, taking full advantage of Unix and Linux operating system features. The server is separated into privileged and unprivileged processes. The unprivileged process receives all FTP requests, interpreting them and then sending them over a socket to the privileged process, which then securely filters all requests. Even the privileged process does not run with full root capabilities, using only those that are necessary to perform its tasks. In addition, the Very Secure FTP Server uses its own version of directory commands like **ls**, instead of the system's versions.

Running vsftpd

The Very Secure FTP Server's daemon is named **vsftpd**. It is designed to be run as a standalone server, which can be started and stopped using the **/etc/init.d/vsftpd** server script. To have the server start automatically, you can turn it on or off with **services-admin** or sysv-rc-conf. If you previously enabled another FTP server such as ProFTPD, be sure to disable it first. Run time vsftpd files are maintained in the **/var/run/vsftpd** directory. FTP server files are located in the **/home/ftp** directory.

Alternatively, you can implement **vsftpd** to be run by **xinetd**, running the server only when a request is made by a user. The **xinetd** daemon will run an **xinetd** script file called **vsftpd** located in the **/etc/xinetd.d** directory. Initially, the server will be turned off.

Firewall access

To allow firewall access to the FTP port, usually port 21, you should enable access using a firewall configuration tool like Firestarter or ufw. On the Policy panel, select the Inbound menu item and then right-click on the Services pane to add a rule. On Add new inbound rule window, select FTP from the pop up menu for Name, and the 20-21 ports will be selected for you. Firestarter maintains its own set of IPtables files in **/etc/Firestarter**.

For the **ufw** default firewall, you would use the following command. The ufw firewall maintains its IPtables files in **/etc/ufw**.

```
ufw allow tcp/21
```

If you are managing your IPtables firewall directly, you could manage access directly by adding the following IPtables rule. This accepts input on port 21 for TCP/IP protocol packages.

```
iptables -A INPUT -p tcp --dport 21 -j ACCEPT
```

Configuring vsftpd

You configure **vsftpd** using one configuration file, **vsftpd.conf**. Configuration options are simple and kept to a minimum, making it less flexible than ProFTPD, but much faster (see Table 7-2). The **vsftpd.conf** file contains a set of directives where an option is assigned a value (there are no spaces around the = sign). Options can be on and off flags assigned a **YES** or **NO** value, features that take a numeric value, or ones that are assigned a string. A default **vsftpd.conf** file is installed in the **/etc** or **/etc/vsftpd** directory. This file lists some of the commonly used options available with detailed explanations for each. Those that not used are commented out with a preceding **#** character. Option names are very understandable. For example, `anon_upload_enable` allows anonymous users to upload files, whereas `anon_mkdir_write_enable` lets anonymous users create directories. The Man page for **vsftpd.conf** lists all options, providing a detailed explanation for each.

Enabling Standalone Access

To run **vsftpd** as a standalone server, you set the listen option to **YES**. This instructs **vsftpd** to continually listen on its assigned port for requests. You can specify the port it listens on with the `listen_port` option.

```
listen=YES
```

Enabling Login Access

In the following example taken from the **vsftpd.conf** file, anonymous FTP is enabled by assigning the **YES** value to the `anonymous_enable` option. The `local_enable` option allows local users on your system to use the FTP server.

```
# Allow anonymous FTP?
anonymous_enable=YES
#
# Uncomment this to allow local users to log in.
local_enable=YES
```

Should you want to let anonymous users log in without providing a password, you can set **no_anon_password** to YES.

Local User Permissions

A variety of user permissions control how local users can access files on the server. If you want to allow local users to create, rename, and delete files and directories on their account, you have to enable write access with the `write_enable` option. This way, any files they upload, they can also delete. Literally, the `write_enable` option activates a range of commands for changing the file system, including creating, renaming, and deleting both files and directories. With **user_config_dir** you can configure specific users.

```
write_enable=YES
```

Option	Description
`listen`	Set standalone mode.
`listen_port`	Specify port for standalone mode.
`anonymous_enable`	Enable anonymous user access.
`local_enable`	Enable access by local users.
`no_anon_password`	Specify whether anonymous users must submit a password.
`anon_upload_enable`	Enable uploading by anonymous users.
`anon_mkdir_write_enable`	Allow anonymous users to create directories.
`aonon_world_readable_only`	Make uploaded files read-only to all users.
`idle_session_timeout`	Set time limit in seconds for idle sessions.
`data_connection_timeouts`	Set time limit in seconds for failed connections.
`dirmessage_enable`	Display directory messages.
`ftpd_banner`	Display FTP login message.
`xferlog_enable`	Enable logging of transmission transactions.
`xferlog_file`	Specify log file.
`deny_email_enable`	Enable denying anonymous users, whose e-mail addresses are specified in **vsftpd.banned**.
`userlist_enable`	Deny access to users specified in the **vsftp.user_list** file.
`userlist_file`	Deny or allow users access depending on setting of `userlist_deny`.
`userlist_deny`	When set to **YES**, **userlist_file** deny list users access. When set to **NO**, **userlist_file** allow list users, and only those users, access.
`chroot_list_enable`	Restrict users to their home directories.
`chroot_list_file`	Allow users access to home directories. Unless `chroot_local_user` is set to **YES**, this file contains a list of users not allowed access to their home directories.
`chroot_local_user`	Allow access by all users to their home directories.
`pam_service_name`	Specify PAM script.
`ls_recurse_enable`	Enable recursive listing.
`user_config_dir`	Directory for user specific configurability

Table 7-2: Configuration Options for vsftpd.conf

You can further specify the permissions for uploaded files using the **local_umask** option (022 is the default set in **vsftpd.conf**, read and write for the owner and read-only for all other users, 644).

```
local_umask=022
```

Because ASCII uploads entail certain security risks, they are turned off by default. However, if you are uploading large text files, you may want to enable them in special cases. Use **ascii_upload_enable** to allow ASCII uploads.

Anonymous User Permissions

You can also allow anonymous users to upload and delete files, as well as create or remove directories. Uploading by anonymous users is enabled with the **anon_upload_enable** option. To let anonymous users also rename or delete their files, you set the **anon_other_write_enable** option. To let them create directories, you set the **anon_mkdir_write_enable** option.

```
anon_upload_enable=YES
anon_other_write_enable=YES
anon_mkdir_write_enable=YES
```

The **anon_world_readable_only** option will make uploaded files read-only (downloadable), restricting write access to the user that created them. Only the user that uploaded a file can delete it.

All uploaded files are owned by the anonymous FTP user. You can have the files owned by another user, adding greater possible security. In effect, the actual user owning the uploaded files becomes hidden from anonymous users. To enable this option, you use **chown_uploads** and specify the new user with **chown_username**. Never make the user an administrative user like **root**.

```
chown_uploads=YES
chown_username=myftpfiles
```

The upload directory itself should be given write permission by other users.

```
chmod 777 /var/ftp/upload
```

You can control the kind of access that users have to files with the **anon_mask** option, setting default read/write permissions for uploaded files. The default is 077, which gives read/write permission to the owner only (600). To allow all users read access, you set the umask to 022, where the 2 turns off write permission but sets read permission (644). The value 000 allows both read and write for all users.

Connection Time Limits

To more efficiently control the workload on a server, you can set time limits on idle users and failed transmissions. The **idle_session_timeout** option will cut off idle users after a specified time, and **data_connection_timeouts** will cut off failed data connections. The defaults are shown here:

```
idle_session_timeout=600
data_connection_timeout=120
```

Messages

The **dirmessage_enable** option allows a message held in a directory's **.message** file to be displayed whenever a user accesses that directory. The **ftpd_banner** option lets you set up your own FTP login message. The default is shown here:

```
ftpd_banner=Welcome to blah FTP service.
```

Logging

A set of **xferlog** options control logging. You can enable logging, as well as specify the format and the location of the file.

```
xferlog_enable=YES
```

Use **xferlog_file** option to specify the log file you want to use. The default is shown here:

```
xferlog_file=/var/log/vsftpd.log
```

vsftpd Access Controls

Certain options control access to the FTP site. As previously noted, the **anonymous_enable** option allows anonymous users access, and **local_enable** permits local users to log in to their accounts (If **/etc/vsftpd** exits, no **vsftpd.** prefix is used on files)..

Denying Access

The **deny_email_enable** option lets you deny access by anonymous users, and the **banned_email** file option designates the file (usually **vstfpd.banned**) that holds the e-mail addresses of those users. The **vsftpd.ftpusers** file lists those users that can never be accessed. These are usually system users like **root**, **mail**, and **nobody**. See Table 7-3 for a list of vsftpd files.

File	Description
vsftpd.ftpusers	Users always denied access
vsftpd.user_list	Specified users denied access (allowed access if **userlist_deny** is **NO**)
vsftpd.chroot_list	Local users allowed access (denied access if **chroot_local_user** is on)
/etc/vsftpd.conf	vsftpd configuration file
/etc/pam.d/vsftpd	PAM vsftpd script
/etc//init.d/vsftpd	Service vsftpd server script, standalone
/etc/xinetd.d/vsftpd	Xinetd vsftpd server script

Table 7-3: Files for vsftpd

User Access

The `userlist_enable` option controls access by users, denying access to those listed in the file designated by the `userlist_file` option (usually **vsftpd.user_list**). If, instead, you want to restrict access to just certain select users, you can change the meaning and usage of the **vsftpd.user_list** file to indicate only those users allowed access, instead of those denied access. To do this, you set the `userlist_deny` option to **NO** (its default is **YES**). Only users listed in the **vsftpd.user_list** file will be granted access to the FTP site.

User Restrictions

The `chroot_list_enable` option controls access by local users, letting them access only their home directories, while restricting system access. The `chroot_list_file` option designates the file (usually **vstfpd.chroot**) that lists those users allowed access. You can allow access by all local users with the `chroot_local_user` option.

```
chroot_local_users=YES
```

If this option is set, then the file designated by `chroot_list_file` will have an inverse meaning, listing those users not allowed access. In the following example, access by local users is limited to those listed in **vsftpd.chroot**:

```
chroot_list_enable=YES
chroot_list_file=/etc/vsftpd.chroot_list
```

On Ubuntu the **secure_chroot_dir** option is used to specify a non-user secure root directory.

```
secure_chroot_dir=/var/run/vsftpd
```

User Authentication

The **vsftpd** server makes use of the PAM service to authenticate local users that are remotely accessing their accounts through FTP. In the **vsftpd.conf** file, the PAM script used for the server is specified with the `pam_service_name` option.

```
pam_service_name=vsftpd
```

In the **etc/pam.d** directory, you will find a PAM file named **vsftpd** with entries for controlling access to the **vsftpd** server. PAM is currently set up to authenticate users with valid accounts, as well as deny access to users in the **/etc/vsftpd.ftpusers** file. The default **/etc/pam.d/vsftpd** file is shown here:

```
#%PAM-1.0
auth required pam_listfile.so item=user sense=deny
                file=/etc/vsftpd.ftpusers onerr=succeed
auth    required  pam_stack.so service=system-auth
auth    required  pam_shells.so
account required  pam_stack.so service=system-auth
session required  pam_stack.so service=system-auth
```

Command Access

Command usage is highly restricted by vsftpd. Most options for the `ls` command that lists files are not allowed. Only the asterisk file-matching operation is supported. To enable recursive listing of files in subdirectories, you have to enable the use of the -R option by setting the ls_recurse_enable option to **YES**. Some clients, such as **ncftp**, will assume that the recursive option is enabled.

vsftpd Virtual Hosts

Though the capability is not inherently built in to vsftpd, you can configure and set up the vsftpd server to support virtual hosts. *Virtual hosting* is where a single FTP server operates as if it has two or more IP addresses. Several IP addresses can then be used to access the same server. The server will then use a separate FTP user directory and files for each host. With vsftpd, this involves manually creating separate FTP users and directories for each virtual host, along with separate vsftpd configuration files for each virtual host in the **/etc/vsftpd** directory. **vsftpd** is configured to run as a standalone service. Its **/etc/init.d/vsftpd** startup script will automatically search for and read any configuration files listed in the **/etc/vsftpd** directory.

If, on the other hand, you wish to run **vsftpd** as a **xinetd** service, you have to create a separate **xinetd** service script for each host in the **/etc/xinetd.d** directory. In effect, you have several **vsftpd** services running in parallel for each separate virtual host. The following example uses two IP addresses for an FTP server:

1. Create an FTP user for each host. Create directories for each host (you can use the one already set up for one of the users). For example, for the first virtual host you could use **FTP-host1**. Be sure to set root ownership and the appropriate permissions.

    ```
    useradd -d /home/ftp-host1 FTP-host1
    chown root.root /var/ftp-host1
    chmod a+rx /home/ftp-host1
    umask 022
    mkdir /home/ftp-host1/pub
    ```

2. Set up two corresponding vsftpd service scripts in the **/etc/xinetd.d** directory. The **vsftpd** directory in **/usr/share/doc** has an **xinetd** example script, **vsftpd.xinetd**. Within each, enter a **bind** command to specify the IP address the server will respond to.

    ```
    bind  192.168.0.34
    ```

3. Within the same scripts, enter a **server_args** entry specifying the name of the configuration file to use.

    ```
    server_args = vsftpd-host1.conf
    ```

4. Within the **/etc/vsftpd** directory, create separate configuration files for each virtual host. Within each, specify the FTP user you created for each, using the **ftp_username** entry.

    ```
    ftp_username = FTP-host1
    ```

vsftpd Virtual Users

Virtual users can be implemented by making use of PAM to authenticate authorized users. In effect, you are allowing access to certain users, while not having to actually set up accounts for them on the FTP server system. First, create a PAM login database file to use along with a PAM file in the **/etc/pam.d** directory that will access the database. Then create a virtual FTP user along with corresponding directories that the virtual users will access (see the vsftpd documentation at **vsftpd.beasts.org** for more detailed information). Then, in the **vsftpd.conf** file, you can disable anonymous FTP:

```
anonymous_enable=NO
local_enable=YES
```

and then enable guest access:

```
guest_enable=YES
guest_username=virtual
```

Note: ProFTPD is based on the same design as the Apache web server, implementing a similar simplified configuration structure and supporting such flexible features as virtual hosting. ProFTPD is an open source project made available under a GPL license. You can download the current version from its website at **proftpd.org**. There you will also find detailed documentation including FAQs, user manuals, and sample configurations. Check the site for new releases and updates. The ProFTPD is available on the Universe repository.

8. Web Servers

The primary web server for Ubuntu is Apache, which has almost become the standard web server for all Linux distributions. It is a very powerful, stable, and fairly easy-to-configure system. Ubuntu provide default configuration for the Apache, making it usable as soon as they are installed. In additions, the Zope Application server for Web development is included on the main Ubuntu repository. Zope application server (**zope.org**) is an open source web server with integrated security, web-based administration and development, and database interface features. It was developed by the Zope Corporation, which also developed the Python programming language.

Apache Web Server

The Apache web server is a full-featured free HTTP (web) server developed and maintained by the Apache Server Project. The aim of the project is to provide a reliable, efficient, and easily extensible web server, with free open source code made available under its own Apache Software License. The server software includes the server daemon, configuration files, management tools, and documentation. The Apache Server Project is maintained by a core group of volunteer programmers and supported by a great many contributors worldwide. The Apache Server Project is one of several projects currently supported by the Apache Software Foundation (formerly known as the Apache Group). This nonprofit organization provides financial, legal, and organizational support for various Apache Open Source software projects, including the Apache HTTPD Server, Java Apache, Jakarta, and XML-Apache. The website for the Apache Software Foundation is **apache.org**. Table 8-1 lists various Apache-related websites.

Apache was originally based on the NCSA web server developed at the National Center for Supercomputing Applications, University of Illinois, Urbana-Champaign. Apache has since emerged as a server in its own right and become one of the most popular web servers in use. Although originally developed for Linux and Unix systems, Apache has become a cross-platform application with Windows and OS/2 versions. Apache provides online support and documentation for its web server at **httpd.apache.org**. An HTML-based manual is also provided with the server installation.

Website	Description
apache.org	Apache Software Foundation
httpd.apache.org	Apache HTTP Server Project
jakarta.apache.org	Jakarta Apache Project
apache-gui.com	Apache GUI Project
php.net	PHP Hypertext Preprocessor, embedded web page programming language
zope.org	Zope application server

Table 8-1: Apache-Related Websites

Java: Apache Jakarta Project

The Apache Jakarta Project supports the development of Open Source Java software; its website is located at **jakarta.apache.org**. Currently, the Jakarta supports numerous projects, including libraries, tools, frameworks, engines, and server applications. Tomcat is an open source implementation of the Java Servlet and JavaServer Pages specifications. Tomcat is designed for use in Apache servers. JMeter is a Java desktop tool to test performance of server resources, such as server lets and CGI scripts. Velocity is a template engine that provides easy access to Java objects. Watchdog is a tool that checks the compatibility of servlet containers. Struts, Cactus, and Tapestry are Java frameworks, established methods for developing Java web applications.

Linux Apache Installation

Your Linux distribution will normally provide you with the option of installing the Apache web server during your initial installation of your Linux system. All the necessary directories and configuration files are automatically generated for you. Then, whenever you run Linux, your system is already a fully functional website. Every time you start your system, the web server will also start up, running continuously. On Ubuntu, the directory reserved for your website data files is **/var/www**. Place your web pages in this directory or in any subdirectories. Your system is already configured to operate as a web server. All you need to do is perform any needed network server configurations, and then designate the files and directories open to remote users. You needn't do anything else. Once your website is connected to a network, remote users can access it.

The web server normally sets up your website in the **/var/www** directory. It also sets up several directories for managing the site. You can use your browser to examine it. Your web pages are to be placed in the **/var/www/** directory. A simple **index.html** test page is already to use to check if your Web server is working. Your configuration files are located in a different directory, **/etc/apache2**. Table 8-2 lists the various Apache web server directories and configuration files.

Apache manual is installed from the **apacha2-doc** package, and is placed in the **/usr/share/doc/apache2-doc/manual** directory in html format.

Directories and Files	Description
.htaccess	Directory-based configuration files; an .htaccess file holds directives to control access to files within the directory in which it is located
/var/www	Directory for Apache Web site HTML files, location of the default server HTML files. Virtual sites will be located here.
/etc/apache2	Directory for Apache web server configuration files
/etc/init.d/apache2	Apache Web server script for start up and shut down,
/etc/default/apache2	Apache Web start up configuration
/usr/sbin	Location of the Apache web server program file and utilities
/usr/share/doc/apache2	Apache web server documentation
/usr/share/doc/apach2-doc	Apache web server manual, apache2-doc package
/var/log/apache2	Location of Apache log files
/usr/lib/apache2	Directory holding Apache modules
/usr/lib/cgi-bin	Directory holding Web CGI scripts.
/var/cache/apache2	Directory holding Apache cache

Table 8-2: Apache Web Server Files and Directories

Apache also installs several management applications such as **apache2ctl** for starting and stopping the server, and **a2enmod** for enabling particular modules. The **/etc/init.d/apache2** script is designed to safely run **apache2ctl**, and should be used to actually start and stop the server manually. It is also used by **services-admin** to start and stop the Web server when your system starts up an shuts down. Table 8-3 lists the applications.

Application	Description
apache2ctl	Control start, stop, and restart the apache server
a2enmod	Enable an Apache module
a2dismod	Disable an Apache module
a2ensite	Enable a Web site, loading its configuration file
a2dissite	Disable an Apache Web site
/etc/init.d/apache2	Script designed for Ubuntu to start, stop, and restart server, invoked apache2ctl. Managed by services-admin, System	Administration	Services.

Table 8-3: Apache management tools

Apache Multiprocessing Modules: MPM

Apache now uses a architecture with multiprocessing modules (MPMs), which are designed to customize Apache to different operating systems, as well as handle certain multiprocessing operations. For the main MPM, a Linux system uses either the prefork or worker MPM, whereas Windows uses the mpm_winnt MPM. The prefork is a standard MPM module designed to be compatible with older Unix and Linux systems, particularly those that do not support threading. Currently Ubuntu uses the worker modules. You can configure the workload parameters for both in the Apache configuration file, **/etc/apache2/apache2.conf**.

Many directives that once resided in the Apache core are now placed in respective modules and MPMs. With this modular design, several directives have been dropped, such as ServerType. Configuration files for these module are located in the **/etc/apache2/conf.d** directory.

Starting and Stopping the Web Server

On Ubuntu, Apache is installed as a standalone server, continually running. On the Ubuntu desktop you can use the **admin-services** tool to determine whether to run Apache or not. Your system will use an init script to automatically start up the web server daemon, invoking it whenever you start your system. A init script for the web server called **apache2** is in the **/etc/init.d** directory. This script uses the **apache2ctl** tool to manage the apache server. With **apache2ctl**, you can also start, stop, and restart the server from the command line. The **apache2ctl** command takes several arguments: **start** to start the server, **stop** to stop it, restart to shut down and restart the server, and **graceful** to shut down and restart gracefully. In addition, you can use **apache2ctl** to check the syntax of your configuration files with the **config** argument.

To check your web server, start your web browser on the host that is running the Web server, and use localhost as the domain name. Your Web server will be providing access on port 80. You would enter **http://localhost/**. You can also just enter your host name, like **http://turtle**. If you already have an Internet domain name address already supported by DNS servers, you could use that instead. This should display the home page you placed in your web root directory. A test page **index.html** file is set up for you that will display the words, It Works. Your Web site will be located in the **/var/www** directory. Here you would place the Web pages for your Web site.

As you configure your Web site, you may need to restart the Web server. You can to this by invoking the **apache2** service script with the **restart** option. The **stop** and **start** options will start and stop the server.

```
sudo /etc/init.d/apahce2 restart
```

If you make changes to yoru configuration, you will need to reload your configuration settings, usng the reload option. You then have to restart the server.

```
sudo /etc/init.d/apahce2 reload
sudo /etc/init.d/apahce2 restart
```

Once you have your server running, you can check its performance with the **ab** benchmarking tool, also provided by Apache: **ab** shows you how many requests at a time your server can handle. Options include **-v**, which enables you to control the level of detail displayed; **-n**, which specifies the number of requests to handle (default is 1); and **-t**, which specifies a time limit.

Apache Configuration

Configuration directives are run from the **apache2.conf** configuration file. A documented version of the **apache2.conf** configuration file is installed automatically in **/etc/apache2/apache2.conf**. It contains detailed descriptions and default entries for global Apache directives. Though the **apache2.conf** file runs the entire configuration, it does so by including the contents of other configuration files. In effect, Apache configuration is distributed among other configuration files tailored for specific tasks. Configuration files for Apache are listed in Table 8-4.

File or Directory	Description
apache2.conf	Apache web server configuration file, will run all other configuration files
conf.d	Directory holding specialized and local configuration files
ports.conf	Directives for defining the port the Web server will use
envvars	Variable definitions used by apache2.conf and other scripts, defines user, groups, and pid for Apache.
sites-enabled	Active modules, links to their configuration files in mods-available. Read by apache2.conf
mods-enabled	Configuration files for particular modules, including their directives. Also includes modules.
mods-available	Configuration files for particular modules, including their directives. Also includes modules.
sites-available	Configuration files for particular sites, including Directory directives
sites-enabled	Active sites, links to their configuration files in sites-available. Read by apache2.conf
httpd.conf	User added configuration directives

Table 8-4: Apache configuration files in the /etc/apache2 directory.

The **/etc/apache2/ports.conf** file holds the port directives determining what port Apache will use (normally 80). User defined directives are to be placed in the **/etc/apache2/httpd.conf** file. The apache2.conf file is configured to include and runt all the directives in the **ports.conf**, **conf.d**, **httpd.conf**, all the configuration files linked to in the **/etc/apache2/mofd-enabled** directory, and all the configuration files linked to in the **/etc/apache2/sites-enabled** directory. The **/etc/apache2/envvars** file holds variable definitions used by Apache tools and scripts like apache2ctl. Currently these include user and group definitions for running Apache.

Any of the directives in the main configuration files can be overridden on a per-directory basis using an **.htaccess** file located within a directory. Although originally designed only for access directives, the **.htaccess** file can also hold any resource directives, enabling you to tailor how web pages are displayed in a particular directory. You can configure access to **.htaccess** files in the **apache2.conf** file.

In addition, default start up settings for **htcacheclean** are set up in the /etc/default/apache2 file for managing the Web server cache.

Module configuration files

Available Apache modules are located in the **/etc/apache2/mods-available** directory, and enabled modules are listed in the /**etc/apache2/mods-enabled** directory as links to their corresponding modules in the **mods-available** directory. A module is disabled by removing its link. Use the **a2enmod** command to enable a module, and the **a2dismod** command to disable a module. These command work by adding or removing links for available modules in the /etc/apache2/mods-enabled directory.

Modules will have both a **.conf** and **.load** configuration file. For example, the SSL module has both an **ssl.conf** and **ssl.load** file The **.conf** file holds directives for configuring the module, and the **.load** file holds the LoadModule directive for performing the actual load operation, specifying the location and name of the module. Both are included in the **apach2.conf** include directives.

In addition, some of the modules provided for Apache may have their own configuration files. These are places in the **/etc/apache2/conf.d** directory. Sometimes these are links to configuration files set up of other applications, as is the case with BackupPC.

Site configuration files

All sites on the Web server are configured as virtual hosts, with a special site called default for the main Web server. Normally you would create your site as a virtual host, reserving the default for administration. Virtual hosts can then be enabled or disabled, letting you turn access to a site on and off. You use the **dissite** and **ensite** commands to enable or disable sites.

The configuration files for sites you have set up on your sever are listed in the **/etc/apache2/sites-available** directory. Configuration files will contain Directory directives specifying the location of the site and controls and features you have set up for it. The default file holds directory directives locating the site at **/var/www**. To make a site accessible, a link to its configuration file must be created in the **/etc/apache2/sites-enabled** directory. Use the **ensite** command to create such a link. There will already be a link for the **default** site.

Apache Configuration Directives

Apache configuration operations take the form of directives entered into the Apache configuration files. With these directives, you can enter basic configuration information, such as your server name, or perform more complex operations, such as implementing virtual hosts. The design is flexible enough to enable you to define configuration features for particular directories and different virtual hosts. Apache has a variety of different directives performing operations as diverse as controlling directory access, assigning file icon formats, and creating log files. Most directives set values such as `DirectoryRoot`, which holds the root directory for the server's web pages, or `Port`, which holds the port on the system that the server listens on for requests. The syntax for a simple directive is shown here:

```
directive option option ...
```

Certain directives create blocks able to hold directives that apply to specific server components (also referred to as sectional directives). For example, the **Directory** directive is used to define a block within which you place directives that apply only to a particular directory. Block directives are entered in pairs: a beginning directive and a terminating directive. The terminating directive defines the end of the block and consists of the same name beginning with a slash. Block directives take an argument that specifies the particular object to which the directives apply. For the **Directory** block directive, you must specify a directory name to which it will apply. The `<Directory` *mydir*`>` block directive creates a block whose directives within it apply to the *mydir* directory. The block is terminated by a `</Directory>` directive. The `<VirtualHost` *hostaddress*`>` block directive is used to configure a specific virtual web server and must include the IP or domain name address used for that server. `</VirtualHost>` is its terminating directive. Any directives you place within this block are applied to that virtual web server. The `<Limit` *method*`>` directive specifies the kind of access method you want to limit, such as GET or POST. The access control directives located within the block list the controls you are placing on those methods. The syntax for a block directive is as follows:

```
<block-directive option ... >
 directive option ...
 directive option ...
</block-directive>
```

Global directives are placed in one of the main configuration files. Directives for particular sites are located in that sites configuration file in **/etc/apache2/sites-available** directory. Directory directives in those files can be used to configure a particular directory. However, Apache also makes use of directory-based configuration files. Any directory may have its own **.htaccess** file that holds directives to configure only that directory. If your site has many directories, or if any directories have special configuration needs, you can place their configuration directives in their **.htaccess** files, instead of filling the main configuration file with specific **Directory** directives for each one. You can control what directives in an **.htaccess** file take precedence over those in the main configuration files. If your site allows user- or client-controlled directories, you may want to carefully monitor or disable the use of **.htaccess** files in them. (It is possible for directives in an **.htaccess** file to override those in the standard configuration files unless disabled with AllowOverride directives.)

You can find a complete listing of Apache web configuration directives at the Apache website, **http://httpd.apache.org/docs/2.2/mod/directives.html**.

Global Configuration

The standard Apache configuration has three sections: global settings, server settings, and virtual hosts. The global settings control the basic operation and performance of the web server. Here you set configuration locations, process ID files, timing, settings for the MPM module used, and what Apache modules to load.

The **ServerTokens** directive prevents disclosure of any optional modules your server is using. The **ServerRoot** directive specifies where your web server configuration files and modules are kept. This server root directory is then used as a prefix to other directory entries.

```
ServerRoot /etc/apache2
```

The server's process ID (PID) file is set by **PidFile**. On Ubuntu the Process ID file is defined by APACHE_PID_FILE variable in the **/etc/apache2/envvars** file.

```
PidFile $(APACHE_PID_FILE)
```

Connection and request timing is handled by **Timeout, KeepAlive, MaxKeepAlive,** and **KeepAliveTimeout** directives. **Timeout** is the time in seconds that the web server times out a send or receive request. **KeepAlive** allows persistent connections, several requests from a client on the same connection. This is turned off by default. **KeepAliveRequests** sets the maximum number of requests on a persistent connection. **KeepAliveTimeout** is the time that a given connection to a client is kept open to receive more requests from that client.

The **Listen** directive will bind the server to a specific port or IP address. By default this is port 80. The Listen directive is not defined in **apache2.conf**, but in the **/etc/apache2/ports.conf** file.

```
Listen 80
```

MPM Configuration

Configuration settings for MPM prefork and worker modules let you tailor your Apache web server to your workload demands. Default entries will already be set for a standard web server operating under a light load. You can modify these settings for different demands.

Two MPM modules commonly available to Unix and Linux systems are prefork and worker. The prefork module supports one thread per process, which maintains compatibility with older systems and modules. The worker module supports multiple threads for each process, placing a much lower load on system resources. They share several of the same directives, such as **StartServer** and **MaxRequestPerChild**. Ubuntu, currently uses the worker modules.

Apache runs a single parent process with as many child processes as are needed to handle requests. Configuration for MPM modules focuses on the number of processes that should be available. The prefork module will list server numbers, as a process is started for each server; the worker module will control threads, since it uses threads for each process. The **StartServer** directives lists the number of server processes to start for both modules. This will normally be larger for the prefork than for the worker module.

In the prefork module you need to set minimum and maximum settings for spare servers. **MaxClients** sets the maximum number of servers that can be started, and **ServerLimit** sets the number of servers allowed. The **MaxRequestsPerChild** sets the maximum number of requests allowed for a server.

In the worker module, **MaxClients** also sets the maximum number of client threads, and **ThreadsPerChild** sets the number of threads for each server. **MaxRequestsPerChild** limits the maximum number of requests for a server. Spare thread limits are also configured.

The directives serve as a kind of throttle on the web server access, controlling processes to keep available and limit the resources that can be used. In the prefork configuration, the **StartServer** is set number to 8, and the spare minimum to 5, with the maximum spare as 20. This means that initially 8 server processes will be started up and will wait for requests, along with 5 spare processes. When server processes are no longer being used, they will be terminated until the number of these spare processes is less than 20. The maximum number of server processes that can be started is 256. The maximum number of connections per server process is set at 4,000.

In the worker MPM, only 2 server processes are initially started. Spare threads are set at 25 and 75. The maximum number of threads is set at 150, with the threads per child at 25.

Included files

The **apache2.conf** file will include all module, port, and site configuration files with the include directive. Specialized and user configurations will be located in the **conf.d** directory and in **httpd.conf** if it exits.

```
# Include module configuration:
Include /etc/apache2/mods-enabled/*.load
Include /etc/apache2/mods-enabled/*.conf

# Include all the user configurations:
Include /etc/apache2/httpd.conf

# Include ports listing
Include /etc/apache2/ports.conf
# Include generic snippets of statements
Include /etc/apache2/conf.d/

# Include the virtual host configurations:
Include /etc/apache2/sites-enabled/
```

Site-Level Configuration

Site specific information is kept in the site's configuration files in **/etc/apache2/sites-available** directory. The **default** site configuration file will hold directives for the main server. The site configuration files hold site specific information like Directory directives for their Web pages and server information like the administrator address. Authentication controls can be placed on particular directives. You can use the default configuration file as a partial model.

A site configuration begins with a **VirtualHost** directive. The directive can name a particular IP address to use of a site name or ***:80** for the main server. The directive block ends with a **</VirtualHost>** directive at the end of the file. Within the block will be placed your site specific directives like Directory directives. Keep in mind that all the site level configurations that are enabled will be read directly as if they were part of one large **apache2.conf** file.

```
<VirtualHost *:80>

</VirtualHost>
```

The following is an example of the **ServerAdmin** directive used to set the address where users can send mail for administrative issues. You replace the **you@your.address** entry with the address you want to use to receive system administration mail. By default, this is set to **root@localhost**.

```
# ServerAdmin: Your address, where problems should be e-mailed.
ServerAdmin you@your.address
```

The **ServerName** directive holds the hostname for your web server. Specifying a hostname is important to avoid unnecessary DNS lookup failures that can hang your server. Notice the entry is commented with a preceding **#**. Simply remove the **#** and type your web server's hostname in place of *new.host.name*. If you are using a different port than 80, be sure to specify it attached to the host name, as in **turtle.mytrek.com:80**. Here is the original default entry:

```
# ServerName allows you to set a hostname which is sent
# back to clients for your server if it's different than the
# one the program would get (i.e. use
# "www" instead of the host's real name).

#ServerName new.host.name:80
```

A modified **ServerName** entry would look like this:

```
ServerName turtle.mytrek.com
```

One of the most flexible aspects of Apache is its ability to configure individual directories. With the **Directory** directive, you can define a block of directives that apply only to a particular directory. Such a directive can be placed in the **apache2.conf** or **access.conf** configuration file. You can also use an **.htaccess** file within a particular directory to hold configuration directives. Those directives are then applied only to that directory. The name ".htaccess" is set with the **AccessFileName** directive. You can change this if you want.

```
AccessFileName .htaccess
```

A Directory block begins with a **<Directory** *pathname>* directive, where *pathname* is the directory to be configured. The ending directive uses the same **<>** symbols, but with a slash preceding the word "Directory": **</Directory>**. Directives placed within this block apply only to the specified directory. The following example denies access to only the **mypics** directory by requests from **www.myvids.com**.

```
<Directory /var/www/mypics>
 Order Deny,Allow
 Deny from www.myvids.com
</Directory>
```

With the **Options** directive, you can enable certain features in a directory, such as the use of symbolic links, automatic indexing, execution of CGI scripts, and content negotiation. The default is the **All** option, which turns on all features except content negotiation (**Multiviews**). The following example enables automatic indexing (**Indexes**), symbolic links (**FollowSymLinks**), and content negotiation (**Multiviews**).

```
Options Indexes FollowSymLinks Multiviews
```

Configurations made by directives in main configuration files or in upper-level directories are inherited by lower-level directories. Directives for a particular directory held in **.htaccess** files and Directory blocks can be allowed to override those configurations. This capability can be controlled by the **AllowOverride** directive. With the **all** argument, **.htaccess** files can override any previous configurations. The **none** argument disallows overrides, effectively disabling the **.htaccess** file. You can further control the override of specific groups of directives. **AuthConfig** enables use of authorization directives, **FileInfo** is for type directives, **Indexes** is for indexing directives, **Limit** is for access control directives, and **Options** is for the options directive.

```
AllowOverride all
```

With access control directives, such as **allow** and **deny**, you can control access to your website by remote users and hosts. The **allow** directive followed by a list of hostnames restricts access to only those hosts. The **deny** directive with a list of hostnames denies access by those systems. The argument `all` applies the directive to all hosts. The **order** directive specifies in what order the access control directives are to be applied. Other access control directives, such as **require**, can establish authentication controls, requiring users to log in. The access control directives can be used globally to control access to the entire site or placed within **Directory** directives to control access to individual directives. In the following example, all users are allowed access:

```
order allow,deny
allow from all
```

When given a URL for a directory instead of an HTML file, and when no default web page is in the directory, Apache creates a page on the fly and displays it. This is usually only a listing of the different files in the directory. In effect, Apache indexes the items in the directory for you. You can set several options for generating and displaying such an index. If **FancyIndexing** is turned on, web page items are displayed with icons and column headers that can be used to sort the listing.

```
FancyIndexing on
```

Your web server can also control access on a per-user or per-group basis to particular directories on your website. You can require various levels for authentication. Access can be limited to particular users and require passwords, or expanded to allow members of a group access. You can dispense with passwords altogether or set up an anonymous type of access, as used with FTP.

To apply authentication directives to a certain directory, you place those directives within either a **Directory** block or the directory's **.htaccess** file. You use the **require** directive to determine what users can access the directory. You can list particular users or groups. The **AuthName** directive provides the authentication realm to the user, the name used to identify the particular set of resources accessed by this authentication process. The **AuthType** directive specifies the type of authentication, such as basic or digest. A **require** directive requires also **AuthType**, **AuthName**, and directives specifying the locations of group and user authentication files. In the following example, only the users **george**, **robert**, and **mark** are allowed access to the **newpics** directory:

```
<Directory /var/www/newpics
    AuthType Basic
    AuthName Newpics
    AuthUserFile /web/users
    AuthGroupFile /web/groups
    <Limit GET POST>
        require users george robert mark
    </Limit>
</Directory>
```

To set up anonymous access for a directory, place the **Anonymous** directive with the user anonymous as its argument in the directory's Directory block or **.htaccess** file. You can also use the **Anonymous** directive to provide access to particular users without requiring passwords from them.

Apache maintains its own user and group authentication files specifying what users and groups are allowed access to which directories. These files are normally simple flat files, such as your system's password and group files. They can become large, however, possibly slowing down authentication lookups. As an alternative, many sites have used database management files in place of these flat files. Database methods are then used to access the files, providing a faster response time. Apache has directives for specifying the authentication files, depending on the type of file you are using. The **AuthUserfile** and **AuthGroupFile** directives are used to specify the location of authentication files that have a standard flat file format. The **AuthDBUserFile** and **AuthDBGroupFile** directives are used for DB database files, and the **AuthDBMGUserFIle** and **AuthDBMGGroupFile** are used for DBMG database files.

The programs htdigest, htpasswd, and dbmmanage are tools provided with the Apache software package for creating and maintaining *user authentication files,* which are user password files listing users who have access to specific directories or resources on your website. The htdigest and htpasswd programs manage a simple flat file of user authentication records, whereas dbmmanage uses a more complex database management format. If your user list is extensive, you may want to use a database file for fast lookups. htdigest takes as its arguments the authentication file, the realm, and the username, creating or updating the user entry. htpasswd can also employ encryption on the password. dbmmanage has an extensive set of options to add, delete, and update user entries. A variety of different database formats are used to set up such files. Three common ones are Berkeley DB2, NDBM, and GNU GBDM. dbmmanage looks for the system libraries for these formats in that order. Be careful to be consistent in using the same format for your authentication files.

Virtual Hosting on Apache

All sites are treated as virtual hosts configured by their site configuration files in **/etc/apashe2/sites-available** directory. In effect, the server can act as several servers, each hosted website appearing separate to outside users.

Apache supports both IP address–based and name-based virtual hosting. IP address–based virtual hosts use valid registered IP addresses, whereas name-based virtual hosts use fully qualified domain addresses. These domain addresses are provided by the host header from the requesting browser. The server can then determine the correct virtual host to use on the basis of the domain name alone. See **httpd.apache.org** for more information.

You can enable or disable virtual site with the **a2dissite** and **a2ensite** commands. Enabled and disable sites are listed as symbolic links in the **/etc/apache2/sites-enabled** directory.

Virtual Host for main server: default

To support virtual hosts, the main server must also have a virtual host configuration. This is set up by Ubuntu as the default configuration in the sites-available directory. To implement name-based virtual hosting, use a **VirtualHost** directive. For the main server, the **VirtualHost** directive uses an * as its name with its port, 80. The directive block begins with **<VirtualHost *:80>** and ends with **</VirtualHost>**. The ServerName directive should be the main server's host name.

Should you have an alias for your main host, you can specify that using an added Virtual host directive that also uses the *:80 name, but with the alias as the ServerName. The following example sets up the default for the main Web server host as well as an alias, **www.turtle.com** and **www.turtle.org**.

```
<VirtualHost *:80>
 ServerName www.turtle.com
 ServerAdmin webmaster@mail.turtle.com
 DocumentRoot /var/www/
 ...
</VirtualHost>

<VirtualHost 192.168.1.5>
 ServerName www.turtle.org
 ServerAdmin webmaster@mail.turtle.com
 DocumentRoot /var/www/
 ....
</VirtualHost>
```

You will want to modify the **/etc/apache2/sites-available/default** configuration file to reflect the server name and mail address you want to use for your site.

Name-Based Virtual Hosting

With name-based virtual hosting, you can support any number of virtual hosts using no additional IP addresses. With only a single IP address for your machine, you can still support an unlimited number of virtual hosts. Such a capability is made possible by the HTTP/1.1 protocol, which lets a server identify the name by which it is being accessed. This method requires the client, the remote user, to use a browser that supports the HTTP/1.1 protocol, as current browsers do (though older ones may not). A browser using such a protocol can send a host header specifying the particular host to use on a machine.

```
ServerName turtle.mytrek.com
NameVirtualHost 192.168.1.5

<VirtualHost 192.168.1.5>
 ServerName www.mypics.com
 ServerAdmin webmaster@mail.mypics.com
 DocumentRoot /var/www/mypics/html
 ErrorLog /var/www/mypics/logs/error_log
 ...
</VirtualHost>

<VirtualHost 192.168.1.5>
 ServerName www.myproj.org
 ServerAdmin webmaster@mail.myproj.org
 DocumentRoot /var/www/myproj/html
 ErrorLog /var/www/myproj/logs/error_log
 ....
</VirtualHost>
```

To implement name-based virtual hosting, use a **VirtualHost** directive for each host and a **NameVirtualHost** directive to specify the IP address you want to use for the virtual hosts. If your system has only one IP address, you need to use that address. Within the **VirtualHost** directives, you use the **ServerName** directive to specify the domain name you want to use for that host. Using **ServerName** to specify the domain name is important to avoid a DNS lookup. A DNS lookup failure disables the virtual host. The **VirtualHost** directives each take the same IP address specified in the **NameVirtualHost** directive as their argument. You use Apache directives within the **VirtualHost** blocks to configure each host separately. Name-based virtual hosting uses the domain name address specified in a host header to determine the virtual host to use. If no such information exists, the first host is used as the default. The following example implements two name-based virtual hosts. Here, **www.mypics.com** and **www.myproj.org** are implemented as name-based virtual hosts instead of IP-based hosts:

If your system has only one IP address, implementing virtual hosts prevents access to your main server with that address. You could no longer use your main server as a Web server directly; you could use it only indirectly to manage your virtual host. You could configure a virtual host to manage your main server's Web pages. You would then use your main server to support a set of virtual hosts that would function as Web sites, rather than the main server operating as one site directly. If your machine has two or more IP addresses, you can use one for the main server and the other for your virtual hosts. You can even mix IP-based virtual hosts and name-based virtual hosts on your server. You can also use separate IP addresses to support different sets of virtual hosts. You can further have several domain addresses access the same virtual host. To do so, place a **ServerAlias** directive listing the domain names within the selected **VirtualHost** block.

```
ServerAlias www.mypics.com www.greatpics.com
```

Dynamic Virtual Hosting

If you have implemented many virtual hosts on your server that have the same configuration, you can use a technique called dynamic virtual hosting to have these virtual hosts generated dynamically. The code for implementing your virtual hosts becomes much smaller, and as a result, your server accesses them faster. Adding yet more virtual hosts becomes a simple matter of creating appropriate directories and adding entries for them in the DNS server.

To make dynamic virtual hosting work, the server uses commands in the mod_vhost_alias module (supported in Apache version 1.3.6 and up) to rewrite both the server name and the document root to those of the appropriate virtual server (for older Apache versions before 1.3.6, you use the mod_rewrite module). Dynamic virtual hosting can be either name-based or IP-based. In either case, you have to set the **UseCanonicalName** directive in such a way as to allow the server to use the virtual hostname instead of the server's own name. For name-based hosting, you simply turn off **UseCanonicalName**. This allows your server to obtain the hostname from the host header of the user request. For IP-based hosting, you set the **UseCanonicalName** directive to DNS. This allows the server to look up the host in the DNS server.

```
UseCanonicalName Off
UseCanonicalName DNS
```

You then have to enable the server to locate the different document root directories and CGI bin directories for your various virtual hosts. You use the **VirtualDocumentRoot** directive to specify the template for virtual hosts' directories. For example, if you place the different host directories in the **/var/www/hosts** directory, you can then set the **VirtualDocumentRoot** directive accordingly.

```
VirtualDocumentRoot /var/www/hosts/%0/html
```

The %0 will be replaced with the virtual host's name when that virtual host is accessed. It is important that you create the dynamic virtual host's directory using that host's name. For example, for a dynamic virtual host called **www.mygolf.org**, you first create a directory named **/var/www/hosts/www.mygolf.org**, then create subdirectories for the document root and CGI programs, as in **/var/www/hosts/www.mygolf.org/html**. For the CGI directory, use the **VirtualScriptAlias** directive to specify the CGI subdirectory you use.

```
VirtualScriptAlias /var/www/hosts/%0/cgi-bin
```

A simple example of name-based dynamic virtual hosting directives follows:

```
UseCanonicalName Off
VirtualDocumentRoot /var/www/hosts/%0/html
VirtualScriptAlias /var/www/hosts/%0/cgi-bin
```

A request for **www.mygolf.com/html/mypage** evaluates to

```
/var/www/hosts/www.mygolf.com/html/mypage
```

A simple example of dynamic virtual hosting is shown here:

```
UseCanonicalName Off

NameVirtualHost 192.168.1.5

<VirtualHost 192.168.1.5>
 ServerName www.mygolf.com
 ServerAdmin webmaster@mail.mygolf.com
 VirtualDocumentRoot /var/www/hosts/%0/html
 VirtualScriptAlias /var/www/hosts/%0/cgi-bin
 ...
</VirtualHost>
```

To implement IP-based dynamic virtual hosting instead, set the **UseCanonicalName** to DNS instead of Off.

```
UseCanonicalName DNS
VirtualDocumentRoot /var/www/hosts/%0/html
VirtualScriptAlias /var/www/hosts/%0/cgi-bin
```

Interpolated Strings

The mod_vhost_alias module supports various interpolated strings, each beginning with a % symbol and followed by a number. As you have seen, %0 references the entire web address. %1 references only the first segment, %2 references the second, %-1 references the last part, and %2+ references from the second part on. For example, to use only the second part of a web address for the directory name, use the following directives:

```
VirtualDocumentRoot /var/www/hosts/%2/html
VirtualScriptAlias /var/www/hosts/%2/cgi-bin
```

In this case, a request made for **www.mygolf.com/html/mypage** uses only the second part of the web address. This would be "mygolf" in **www.mygolf.com**, and would evaluate to

```
/var/www/hosts/mygolf/html/mypage
```

If you used **%2+** instead, as in **/var/www/hosts/%2/html**, the request for **www.mygolf.com/html/mypage** would evaluate to

```
/var/www/hosts/mygolf.com/html/mypage
```

The same method works for IP addresses, where **%1** references the first IP address segment, **%2** references the second, and so on.

Logs for Virtual Hosts

One drawback of dynamic virtual hosting is that you can set up only one log for all your hosts. However, you can create your own shell program to simply cut out the entries for the different hosts in that log.

```
LogFormat "%V %h %l %u %t \"%r\" %s %b" vcommon
CustomLog logs/access_log vcommon
```

Note: Apache also supports IP address–based virtual hosting. Your server must have a different IP address for each virtual host. Your machine can have separate physical network connections for each one. You can configure Apache to run a separate daemon for each virtual host, separately listening for each IP address, or you can have a single daemon running that listens for requests for all the virtual hosts. To set up a single daemon to manage all virtual hosts, use **VirtualHost** directives. To set up a separate daemon for each host, also use the **Listen** directive.

9. News and Database Services

Newsgroup severs are more rare, used for setting up newsgroups for local networks or for supporting the Internet's Usenet News service. Database servers are becoming more common for managing large collections of data on local networks as well as for Internet services.

News Servers

News servers provide Internet users with Usenet news services. They have their own TCP/IP protocol, the Network News Transfer Protocol (NNTP). On most Linux systems, the InterNetNews (INN) news server provides news services (**isc.org**). In addition, servers exist that provide better access to Internet resources.

The InterNetNews (INN) news server accesses Usenet newsfeeds, providing news clients on your network with the full range of newsgroups and their articles. Newsgroup articles are transferred using NNTP, and servers that support this protocol are known as *NNTP servers*. INN was written by Rich Salz and is currently maintained and supported by the Internet Software Consortium (ISC). You can download current versions from its website at **isc.org**. INN is also included with most Linux distributions. The documentation directory for INN in **/usr/share/doc** contains extensive samples. The primary program for INN is the **innd** daemon.

There are two versions of INN, a smaller INN used for local networks, and a much more complex INN2 used for large networks. Normally Ubuntu uses INN.

INN also includes several support programs to provide maintenance and crash recovery and to perform statistical analysis on server performance and usage. cleanfeed implements spam protection, and innreport generates INN reports based on logs. INN also features a very strong filter system for screening unwanted articles.

Note: Leafnode is an NNTP news server designed for small networks that may have slow connections to the Internet. You can obtain the Leafnode software package along with documentation from its website at **leafnode.org**. Along with the Leafnode NNTP server, the software package includes several utilities such as Fetchnews, Texpire, and Newsq that send, delete, and display news articles. slrnpull is a simple single-user version of Leafnode that can be used only with the slrn newsreader.

Database Servers: MySQL and PostgreSQL

Two fully functional database servers are included with most Linux distributions, MySQL and PostgreSQL. MySQL is by far the more popular of the two, though PostgreSQL is noted for providing more features. Recently, the MySQL AB project added MaxDB, formerly SAP DB, which provides capabilities comparable to many professional-level database management systems. This chapter will cover how to set up and manage a MySQL database and will offer a brief introduction to PostgreSQL. You can learn more about these products through the sites listed in Table 9-1.

Database	Resource
MySQL	mysql.com
PostgreSQL	postgresql.org
MaxDB	mysql.com

Table 9-1: Database Resources

Relational Database Structure

MySQL and PostgreSQL both use a relational database structure. Essentially, this means data is placed in tables, with identifier fields used to relate the data to entries in other tables. Each row in the table is a record, each with a unique identifier, like a record number. The connections between records in different tables are implemented by special tables that associate the unique identifiers from records in one table with those of another. Relational database theory and implementation are subjects beyond the scope of this chapter.

A simple, single-table database has no need for a unique identifier. A simple address book listing names and addresses is an example of a single-table database. However, most databases access complex information of different types, related in various ways. Instead of having large records with repeated information, you divide the data in different tables, each holding the unique instance of the data. This way, data is not repeated; you have only one table that holds a single record for person's name, rather than repeating that person's name each time the data references him or her. The relational organization then takes on the task of relating one piece of data to another. This way, you can store a great deal of information using relatively small database files.

Though there are many ways to implement a relational database, a simple rule of thumb is to organize data into tables where you have a unique instance of each item of data. Each record is given a unique identifier, usually a number. To associate the records in one table with another, you create tables that associate their identifiers.

The SQL query language is the language used by most relational database management systems (RDBMSs), including both MySQL and PostgreSQL. Though many RDBMSs use administrative tools to manage databases, on Linux MySQL and PostgreSQL, you still have to use the SQL commands directly. The following command will create the database:

```
CREATE DATABASE myphotos
```

Before performing any operations on a database, you first access it with the USE command.

```
USE myphotos
```

The tables are created using the CREATE TABLE command; the fields for each table are listed within parentheses following the table name. For each field, you need to specify a name, data type, and other options, such as whether it can have a null value or not.

```
CREATE TABLE names (
    personid INT(5) UNSIGNED NOT NULL,
    name VARCHAR(20) NOT NULL,
    street VARCHAR(30) NOT NULL,
    phone CHAR(8)
    );
```

MySQL

MySQL is structured on a client/server model with a server daemon (**mysqld**) filling requests from client programs. MySQL is designed for speed, reliability, and ease of use. It is meant to be a fast database management system for large databases and, at the same time, a reliable one, suitable for intensive use. To create databases, you use the standard SQL language. User access can be controlled by assigning privileges.

On Ubuntu you can install MySQL server and client packages, along with numerous MySQL configuration packages for certain services like Postfix, Exim, and Apache . Packages to install are **mysql-client**, **mysql-common**, and **mysql-server**. Documentation is held in the **mysql-doc** package and installed at **/usr/share/doc/mysql-doc**.

MySQL Configuration

The MySQL supports three different configuration files, one for global settings, and another for server-specific settings, and an optional one for user-customized settings.

➢ The **/etc/mysql/my.cnf** configuration file is used for global settings applied to both clients and servers. The **/etc/mysql/my.cnf** file provides information such as the data directory (**/var/lib/mysql**) and log files (**/var/log/mysql**) locations, as well as the server base directory (**/var/lib**).

➢ The **/var/lib/mysql/my.cnf** file is used for server settings only.

➢ The **.my.cnf** file allows users to customize their access to MySQL. It is located in a user's home directory. Note that this is a dot file.

Sample configuration **my.cnf** files can be found in the **mysql-server** directory in **/usr/share/doc**. The **mysql-server** directory lists configurations for small, medium, large, and huge implementations. The administrative manual is located in the **mysql** directory for **/usr/share/doc**. It is in the info format. Use `info mysql` to start it and the arrow and ENTER keys to move through the menus. Here you can find more information about different options.

Global Configuration:/etc/mysql/my.cnf

MySQL specifies options according to different groups, usually the names of server tools. The options are arranged in group segments. The group name is placed within brackets, and options applied to it follow. The default **/etc/mysql/my.cnf** file is shown here:

```
[mysqld]
user=mysql
datadir=/var/lib/mysql
pid-file = /var/run/mysqld/mysqld.pid
socket = /var/run/mysqld/mysqld.sock
port = 3306
basedir = /usr
datadir = /var/lib/mysql
tmpdir = /tmp
language = /usr/share/mysql/English
```

MySQL global options are listed in the **/etc/mysql/my.cnf** file. Options are set up according to groups that control different behaviors of the MySQL server: **mysqld** for the daemon and **safe_mysqld** for the MySQL startup script. The **datadir** directory, **/var/lib/mysql**, is where your database files will be placed. Server tools and daemons are located in the **basedir** directory, **/usr**, and the user that MySQL will run as has the name **mysql**, as specified in the **user** option.

A client group will set up options to be sent to clients, such as the port and socket to use to access the MySQL database.

```
[client]
port=3306
socket=/var/lib/mysqld/mysqld.sock
```

To see what options are currently set for both client and server, you run **mysqld** directly with the **--help** option.

```
/usr/libexec/mysqld --help
```

User Configuration: .my.cnf

Users who access the database server will have their own configuration file in their home directory: **.my.cnf**. Here the user can specify connection options such as the password used to access the database and the connection timeouts.

```
[client]
password=mypassword

[mysql]
no-auto-rehash
set-variable = connect_timeout=2

[mysql-hotcopy]
interactive-timeout
```

MySQL Tools

MySQL provides a variety of tools (as shown in Table 9-2), including server, client, and administrative tools. Backups can be handled with the **mysldump** command. The **mysqlshow** command will display a database, just as issuing the SQL command SELECT *.* does, and mysqlimport can import text files, just like LOAD INFILE.

Command	Description
mysqld	MySQL server
mysql	MySQL client
mysqladmin	Creates and administers databases
mysqldump	Database backup
mysqlimport	Imports text files
mysqlshow	Displays databases

Table 9-2: MySQL Commands

MySQL Management with mysql and mysqladmin

To manage your MySQL database, you use mysql as the **root** user. The mysql client starts up the MySQL monitor. As the root user, you can enter administrative commands to create databases and database tables, add or remove entries, as well as carry out standard client tasks such as displaying data.

Log in as the root user and open a terminal window. Then enter the mysql command. This will start a MySQL monitor shell with a mysql> prompt. Be sure to end your commands with a semicolon; otherwise, the monitor will provide an indented arrow prompt waiting for added arguments. In the monitor, the semicolon, not the ENTER key, ends commands.

```
# mysql -u root -p
mysql>
```

If you have set up a MySQL root user, you can use the -u root with the -p option. You will be prompted for a password.

```
# mysql -u root -p
```

Once the mysql client has started, you can use the **status** command to check the status of your server and **show databases** to list current databases.

```
mysql> status;
mysql> show databases;
```

Initially two databases set up by MySQL for its own management are displayed: mysql and test. The mysql database holds MySQL user information, and the test database is used to test the server.

PostgreSQL

PostgreSQL is based on the POSTGRESQL database management system, though it uses SQL as its query language. POSTGRESQL is a next-generation research prototype developed at the University of California, Berkeley. You can find more information on it from the PostgreSQL website at **postgresql.org**. PostgreSQL is an open source project, developed under the GPL license.

PostgreSQL is often used to provide database support for Internet servers with heavy demands, such as web servers. With a few simple commands, you can create relational database tables. Use the `createuser` command to create a PostgreSQL user that you can then log in to the server with. You can then create a database with the `createdb` command and construct relational tables using the **create table** directive. With an `insert` command, you can add records and then view them with the `select` command. Access to the server by remote users is controlled by entries in the **pg_hba.conf** file located in PostgreSQL directory, usually **/var/lib/pgsql**.

Note: The search and indexing server ht://Dig enables document searches of web and FTP sites (**htdig.org**). With it, you can index documents and carry out complex search requests.

Part 3: Shared Resources

Print Services: CUPS
Network File System: NFS (Unix/Linux)
Samba (Windows)
Distributed File System: GFS (Linux)

10. Print Services

Print services have become an integrated part of every Linux system. They allow you to use any printer on your system or network..

Printer Services: CUPS

Once treated as devices attached to a system directly, printers are now treated as network resources managed by print servers. In the case of a single printer attached directly to a system, the networking features become transparent and the printer appears as just one more device. On the other hand, you could easily use a print server's networking capability to let several systems use the same printer. Although printer installation is almost automatic on most Linux distributions, it helps to understand the underlying process. Printing sites and resources are listed in Table 10-1.

The Common Unix Printing System (CUPS) provides printing services. It is freely available under the GNU Public License. Though it is now included with most distributions, you can also download the most recent source-code version of CUPS from **cups.org**, which provides detailed documentation on installing and managing printers. CUPS is based on the Internet Printing Protocol (IPP), which was designed to establish a printing standard for the Internet (for more information, see **pwg.org/ipp**). Whereas the older line printer (LPD)based printing systems focused primarily on line printers, an IPP-based system provides networking, PostScript, and web support. CUPS works like an Internet server and employs a configuration setup much like that of the Apache web server. Its network support lets clients directly access printers on remote servers, without having to configure the printers themselves. Configuration needs to be maintained only on the print servers.

Resource	Description
cups.org	Common Unix Printing System
pwg.org/ipp	Internet Printing Protocol
sourceforge.net/projects/lprng	LPRng print server (Universe repository)

Table 10-1: Print Resources

CUPS is the primary print server for most Linux distributions. With **libgnomecups**, GNOME now provides integrated support for CUPS, allowing GNOME-based applications to directly access CUPS printers.

Once you have installed your printers and configured your print server, you can print and manage your print queue using print clients. There are a variety of printer clients available for the CUPS server, GNOME print manager, the CUPS configuration tool, and various line printing tools like `lpq` and `lpc`. These are described in further detail later in this chapter. The CUPS configuration tool is a web-based configuration tool that can also manage printers and print jobs (open your browser and enter the URL **http://localhost:631**). A web page is displayed with entries for managing jobs, managing printers, and administrative tasks. Select the Manage Jobs entry to remove or reorder jobs you have submitted.

Note: Line Printer, Next Generation (LPRng) was the traditional print server for Linux and Unix systems, but it has since been dropped from many Linux distributions. You can find out more about LPRng at **sourceforge.net/projects/lprng**.

Printer Devices and Configuration

Before you can use any printer, you first have to install it on a Linux system on your network. A local printer is installed directly on your own system. This involves creating an entry for the printer in a printer configuration file that defines the kind of printer it is, along with other features such as the device file and spool directory it uses. On CUPS, the printer configuration file is **/etc/cups/printers.conf**. Installing a printer is fairly simple: determine which device file to use for the printer and the configuration entries for it.

Tip: If you cannot find the drivers for your printer, you may be able to download them from OpenPrinting database at **linux-foundation.org/en/OpenPrinting**. The site maintains an extensive listing of drivers.

Printer Device Files

Linux dynamically creates the device names for printers that are installed. For parallel printers, the device names will be **lp0**, **lp1**, and **lp2**, depending on how many parallel printers are connected. The number used in these names corresponds to a parallel port on your PC; **lp0** references the LPT1 parallel port and **lp1** references the LPT2 parallel port. Serial printers will use serial ports, referenced by the device files like **ttyS0**, **ttyS1**, **ttyS2**, and so on. USB-connected printers will have a Hardware Abstract Layer (HAL) device connection. HAL is designed for removable devices that can easily be attached to other connections and still be recognized.

Spool Directories

When your system prints a file, it makes use of special directories called *spool directories.* A *print job* is a file to be printed. When you send a file to a printer, a copy of it is made and placed in a spool directory set up for that printer. The location of the spool directory is obtained from the printer's entry in its configuration file. On Linux, the spool directory is located at **/var/spool/cups** under a directory with the name of the printer. For example, the spool directory for the `myepson` printer would be located at **/var/spool/cups/myepson**. The spool directory contains several files for managing print jobs. Some files use the name of the printer as their extension. For example, the

myepson printer has the files **control.myepson**, which provides printer queue control, and **active.myepson** for the active print job, as well as **log.myepson,** which is the log file.

Installing Printers

There are several tools available for installing CUPS printers. The easiest method is to use Ubuntu system-config-printer tool. Alternatively you can use the CUPS Web browser-based configuration tools, included with the CUPS software. Finally you can just edit the CUPS printer configuration files directly.

Configuring Printers on Ubuntu with system-config-printer

As noted in Chapter 3, any printer will be automatically detected when you first attached it. You are then prompted to confirm automatically selected model and drivers. The tool used to configure printers is system-config-printers, accessible from the System | Administration | Printing menu item. Though printers are automatically detected when attached, you can also modify your configuration as well as add access to remote printers on your network.

When you start up system-config-printer, you are presented with a window that displays two panes, one that lists your servers and their printers and the other for configuration panels for those printers (see Figure 10-1). To display the configuration for a particular printer, just click its entry in the Server Settings pane, where printers will be listed in an expandable tree under the servers that the printers are connected to. Printers connected directly to your computer will be listed under Local Printers. Clicking the Server Settings entry will display a pane for setting global printing options such as allowing users to cancel their own print jobs or sharing your printers on your network.

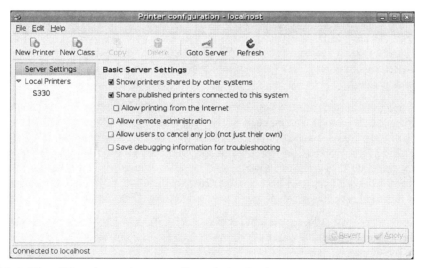

Figure 10-1: The Ubuntu system-config-printer tool

To add a new printer, click New Printer. To edit an installed printer, click its entry in the Server Settings pane to display its configuration panels. There are panels for Settings, Policies,

Access Control, Printer Options, and Job Control. Once you have made your changes, you can click Apply to save your changes and restart the printer daemon. If you have more than one printer on your system, you can make one the default by clicking Make Default Printer button in its Settings panel. The Delete button will remove a printer configuration. You can test your printer with a PostScript, A4, or ASCII test sheet selected from the Test menu.

You can connect to other CUPS print servers by click the Go To Server button. This opens a Connect to CUPS server window where you can enter the location of the server and your user name.

The New Class button lets you create a print class. This feature lets you select a group of printers to print a job instead of selecting just one. That way, if one printer is busy or down, another printer can be automatically selected to perform the job. Installed printers can be assigned to different classes. To create a class, click the New Class button to open the New Class window. Here you can enter the name for the class, any comments, and the location (your host name is entered by default). The next screen lists available printers on right side (Other printers) and the printers you assigned to the class on the left side (Printers in this class). Use the arrow button to add or remove printers to the class. Click Apply when finished. The class will appear under the Local Classes heading on the main system-config-printer window. Panels for a selected class are much the same as for a printer, with a members panel instead of a print control panel. In the Members panel you can change what printers belong to the class.

Adding a new printer manually

When you click New Printer, a series of dialog boxes are displayed where you can enter the printer name, its type, and its model. In the Printer Name dialog box, give the printer a name along with any particular description.

On the following Select Connection screen (see Figure 10-2), you select the appropriate printer connection information. Connected local printer brands will be listed by name, such as Canon, whereas for remote printers you specify the type of network connection, like Windows printers via Samba for printers connected to a Windows system, or Internet Printing Protocol (ipp) for printers connected to other Linux systems, or AppSocket/HP Direct for HP printers connected directly to your network.

For most connected printers, your connection is usually determined by the device hotplug services udev and HAL, which now manage all devices. This will be first entry in the list, and the description will show that it was detected by HAL. It is always preferable to use the HAL connection. With a HAL connection you can plug the printer into any USB port and HAL will automatically detect it. If, instead, you always want the USB printer to use a specific USB port, you can choose the USB-specific connection, such as Canon S330 USB #1. If for some reason your device is not detected, you can use the Other entry to enter the device name.

For an older local printer, you will need to specify the port the printer is connected to, such as LPT1 for the first parallel port used for older parallel printers, or Serial Port #1 for a printer connected to the first serial port.

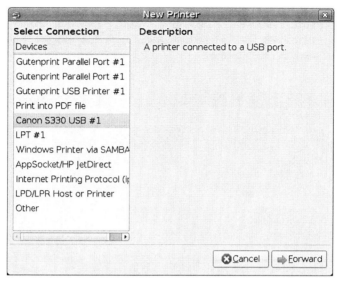

Figure 10-2: Printer type for new printers

On the next screen you select your printer manufacturer, choosing it from a printer database. Then, on the next screen you select that manufacturer's model along with its driver (see Figure 10-3). The selected drivers for your printer will be listed (on future versions of system-config-printer, you can find out more about the printer and driver by clicking the Printer and Driver buttons at the bottom of the screen). Then click the Forward button.

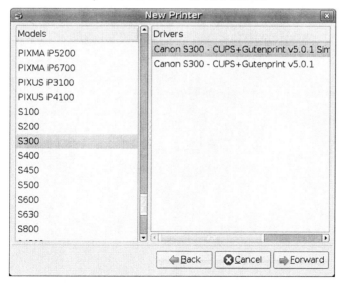

Figure 10-3: Printer Model and driver for new printers

On the next panel you can enter the printer name, description, and location (see Figure 10-4). A printer name and location will already be entered for you. You can change them if you wish. They are only labels to help users identify the printer. When you are finished, click the Apply button. You then see your printer listed in the system-config-printer window, with its configuration panel displayed. You are now ready to print.

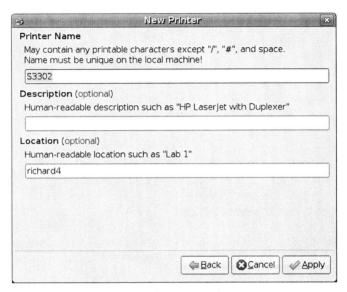

Figure 10-4: Printer name and location for new printers

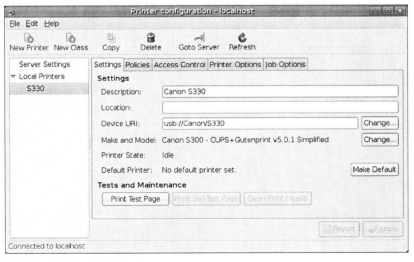

Figure 10-5: Modify installed printers

Modifying Printer Properties

You can also change a printer configuration by selecting its entry in the Printer configuration window. Once selected, a set of five tabbed panes for that printer are displayed: Settings, Policies, Access Control, Printer Options, and Job Options (see Figure 10-5). On the Settings panel you can change configuration settings like the driver and the printer name, enable or disable the printer, or specify whether to share it or not. You can also make it the default printer.

The Policies panel lets you specify a start and end banner, as well as an error policy which specifies whether to retry or abort the print job, or stop the printer should an error occur. The Access Control panel allows you to deny access to certain users. The Printer Options panel is where you set particular printing features like paper size and type, print quality, and the input tray to use (see Figure 10-6).

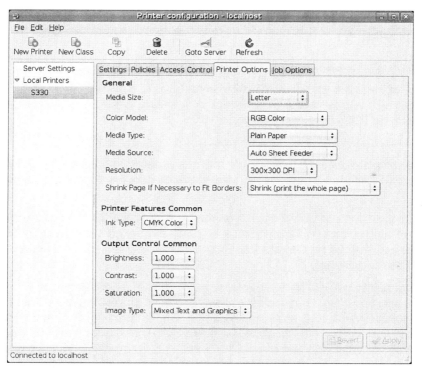

Figure 10-6: Printer Options panel

On the Job Options panel you can select default printing features. A pop-up menu provides a list of printing feature categories to choose from. You then click the Add button to add the category, selecting a particular feature from a pop-up menu. You can set such features as the number of copies (copies); letter, glossy, or A4-sized paper (media); the kind of document, for instance, text, PDF, PostScript, or image (document format); and single- or double-sided printing (sides).

Configuring Printers with KDE

KDE provides support for adding and configuring CUPS printers through the KDE Control Center. Select the Printers entry under Peripherals. The KDE Printer tool has the capability to perform many different kinds of printing such as sending faxes or saving to PDF files. USB printers that are automatically detected will be listed in the KDE Printer window. When you click on the printer entry, the Information, Jobs, Properties, and Instances panels let you manage your printer and its print jobs. The Properties panel has options for controlling user access, setting quotas, selecting a banner, and even changing your driver.

To change printer options like page size and resolution, you use select the Configure entry from the Printer menu. The Printer menu also lets you disable the printer or test it. The printer toolbar also provides buttons for these commonly performed tasks. The printer manager lets you configure general features like the fonts available, the previewer to use, or the printers to display. A pop-up menu for the printer system used will have CUPS selected by default. You could switch to LPRng if needed. Check the KDEPrint Handbook , accessible from the Documentation menu, for detailed information.

CUPS Web Browser-based configuration tool

One of the easiest way to configure and install printers with CUPS is to use the CUPS configuration tool, which is a web browser–based configuration tool.. To start the web interface, enter the following URL into your web browser:

```
http://localhost:631
```

This opens an administration screen where you can manage and add printers. You will first be asked to enter the administrator's username (usually **root**) and password (usually the root user's password).

With the CUPS configuration tool, you install a printer on CUPS through a series of web pages, each of which requests different information. To install a printer, click the Add Printer button to display a page where you enter the printer name and location. The location is the host to which the printer is connected.

Subsequent pages will prompt you to enter the model of the printer and driver, which you select from available listings. Once you have added the printer, you can configure it. Clicking the Manage Printers entry in the Administration page lists your installed printers. You can then click a printer to display a page that lets you control the printer. You can stop the printer, configure its printing, modify its installation, and even delete the printer. Clicking the Configure Printer button displays a page where you can configure how your printer prints, by specifying the resolution or paper size.

Configured information for a printer will be stored in the **/etc/cups/printers.conf** file. You can examine this file directly, even making changes. Here is an example of a printer configuration entry. The **DeviceURI** entry specifies the device used, in this case a USB printer managed by HAL. It is currently idle, with no jobs:

```
# Printer configuration file for CUPS
# Written by cupsd
<Printer mycannon>
Info Cannon s330
```

```
Location
DeviceURI
hal:///org/freedesktop/Hal/devices/usb_device_4a9_1074_300HCR_if0_printer_noseria
l
State Idle
StateTime 1166554036
Accepting Yes
Shared Yes
JobSheets none none
QuotaPeriod 0
PageLimit 0
KLimit 0
OpPolicy default
ErrorPolicy stop-printer
</Printer>
```

Note: You can perform all administrative tasks from the command line using the `lpadmin` command. See the CUPS documentation for more details.

Configuring Remote Printers on CUPS

To install a remote printer that is attached to a Windows system or another Linux system running CUPS, you specify its location using special URL protocols. For another CUPS printer on a remote host, the protocol used is **ipp**, for Internet Printing Protocol, whereas for a Windows printer, it would be **smb**. Older Unix or Linux systems using LPRng would use the **lpd** protocol.

Configuring Remote Printers with system-config-printers

You can also use system-config-printer to set up a remote printer on Linux, Unix, or Windows networks. Access system-config-printers form System | Administration | Printing menu. When you add a new printer or edit one, the New Printer/Select Connection dialog will list possible remote connection types (see Figure 10-7). When you select a remote connection entry, a panel will be displayed where you can enter configuration information. For a remote Linux or UNIX printer, select either Internet Printing Protocol (ipp), which is used for newer systems, or LPD/LPR Host or Printer, which is used for older systems. Both panels display entries for the Host name and the Printer name. For the Host name, enter the hostname for the system that controls the printer. For the Printer name, enter the device name on that host for the printer. The LPD/LPR dialog also has a probe button for detecting the printer.

A "Windows printer via Samba" is one located on a Windows network. You need to specify the Windows server (host name or IP address), the name of the share, the name of the printer's workgroup, and the username and password if required. The format of the printer SMB URL is shown on the SMP Printer panel. The SMB URL is the hostname and printer name in the smb URL format //workgroup/server/printername. The workgroup is the workgroup name for the Windows network. The server is the computer where the printer is located. The username and password can be for the printer resource itself, or for access by a particular user. The panel will display a box at the top where you can enter the share host and printer name as an smb URL.

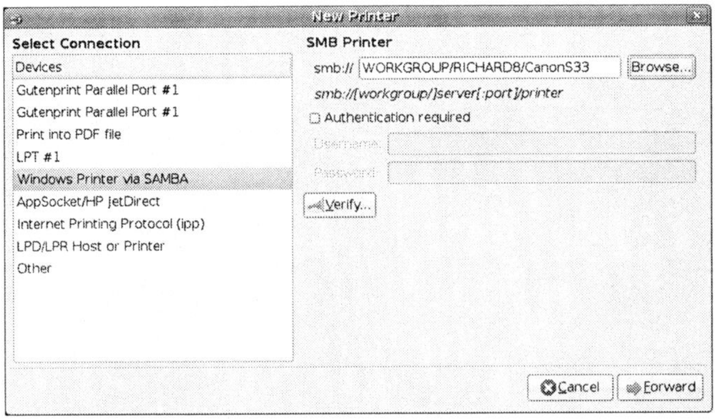

Figure 10-7: Windows Printer Connection Configuration

Instead of typing in the URL, you can Browse button to open a SMB Browser window, where you can select the printer from a listing of Windows hosts on your network (see Figure 10-8). For example, if your Windows network is WORKGROUP, then the entry WORKGROUP will be shown, which you can then expand to list all the Windows hosts on that network (if your network is MSHOME, then that is what will be listed). When you make your selection, the corresponding URL will show up in the smb:// box. If you are using the firestarter firewall, be sure to turn it off before browsing a Windows workgroup for a printer, unless already configured to allow Samba access.

Figure 10-8: Selecting a remote printer

Also on the panel, you can enter in any needed Samba authentication, if required, like user name or password. Check "Authentication required" to allow you to enter the Samba Username and Password.

You will still need the Linux drivers for that Windows printer. Click the Forward button to start the New Printer wizard, first selecting the manufacturer, and the model on the following screen. Then enter a name and location for the printer. Once you finish the wizard, the new printer will appear as an installed printer in system-config-printers.

To access an SMB shared remote printer, you need to install Samba and have the Server Message Block services enabled using the smb and nmb daemons. The Samba service will be enabled by default. The service is enabled by checking the Windows Folders entry in the Gnome Services tool (System | Administration | Services). Printer sharing must, in turn, be enabled on the Windows network.

Configuring remote printers manually

In the **cupsd.conf** file, for a remote printer, the DeviceURI entry, instead of listing the device, will have an Internet address, along with its protocol. For example, a remote printer on a CUPS server (**ipp**) would be indicated as shown here (a Windows printer would use an **smb** protocol):

```
DeviceURI ipp://mytsuff.com/printers/queue1
```

For a Windows printer, you first need to install, configure, and run Samba. (CUPS uses Samba to access Windows printers.) When you install the Windows printer on CUPS, you specify its location using the URL protocol **smb**. The user allowed to log in to the printer is entered before the hostname and separated from it by an @ sign. On most configurations, this is the **guest** user. The location entry for a Windows printer called **myhp** attached to a Windows host named **lizard** is shown here. Its Samba share reference would be **//lizard/myhp**:

```
DeviceURI smb://guest@lizard/myhp
```

To enable CUPS on Samba, you also have to set the printing option in the **/etc/samba/smb.conf** file to **cups**, as shown here:

```
printing = cups
printcap name = cups
```

To enable CUPS to work with Samba, you have to link the **smbspool** to the CUPS **smb** spool directory:

```
ln -s /usr/bin/smbspool   /usr/cups/backend/smb
```

Note: To configure a shared Linux printer for access by Windows hosts, you need to configure it as a SMB shared printer. You do this with Samba.

CUPS Printer Classes

CUPS features a way to let you select a group of printers to print a job instead of selecting just one. That way, if one printer is busy or down, another printer can be automatically selected to perform the job. Such groupings of printers are called *classes.* Once you have installed your printers, you can group them into different classes. For example, you may want to group all inkjet printers into one class and laser printers into another, or you may want to group printers connected to one specific printer server in their own class. To create a class, select Classes on the Administration page and enter the name of the class. You can then add printers to it.

CUPS Configuration files

CUPS configuration files are placed in the **/etc/cups** directory. These files are listed in Table 10-2. The **classes.conf**, **printers.conf**, and **client.conf** files can be managed by the web interface. The **printers.conf** file contains the configuration information for the different printers you have installed. Any of these files can be edited manually, if you wish.

Filename	Description
classes.conf	Contains configurations for different local printer classes
client.conf	Lists specific options for specified clients
cupsd.conf	Configures the CUPS server, **cupsd**
printers.conf	Contains printer configurations for available local printers

Table 10-2: CUPS Configuration Files

cupsd.conf

The CUPS server is configured with the **cupsd.conf** file located in **/etc/cups**. You must edit configuration options manually; the server is not configured with the web interface. Your installation of CUPS installs a commented version of the **cupsd.conf** file with each option listed, though most options will be commented out. Commented lines are preceded with a **#** symbol. Each option is documented in detail. The server configuration uses an Apache web server syntax consisting of a set of directives. As with Apache, several of these directives can group other directives into blocks.

CUPS Directives

Certain directives allow you to place access controls on specific locations. These can be printers or resources, such as the administrative tool or the spool directories. Location controls are implemented with the **Location** directive. **Allow From** and **Deny From** directives can permit or deny access from specific hosts. CUPS supports both Basic and Digest forms of authentication, specified in the **AuthType** directive. Basic authentication uses a user and password. For example, to use the web interface, you are prompted to enter the root user and the root user password. Digest authentication makes use of user and password information kept in the CUPS **/etc/cups/passwd.md5** file, using MD5 versions of a user and password for authentication. The **AuthClass** directive specifies the class allowed access. The **System** class includes the root, sys, and system users. The following example shows the **Location** directive for the **/admin** resource, the administrative tool:

```
<Location /admin>

AuthType Basic
AuthClass System

## Restrict access to local domain
Order Deny,Allow
Deny From All
Allow From 127.0.0.1

</Location>
```

CUPS Command Line Print Clients

Once a print job is placed on a print queue, you can use any of several print clients to manage the printing jobs on your printer or printers, such as Klpq, the GNOME Print Manager, and the CUPS Printer Configuration tool for CUPS. You can also use several command line print CUPS clients. These include the `lpr`, `lpc`, `lpq`, and `lprm` commands. With these clients, you can print documents, list a print queue, reorder it, and remove print jobs, effectively canceling them. For network connections, CUPS features an encryption option for its commands, `-E`, to encrypt print jobs and print information sent of a network. Table 10-3 shows various printer commands.

Note: The command line clients have the same name, and much the same syntax, as the older LPR and LPRng command line clients used in Unix and older Linux systems.

Printer Management	Description
GNOME Print Manager	GNOME print queue management tool (CUPS).
CUPS Configuration Tool	Prints, manages, and configures CUPS.
`lpr` *options file-list*	Prints a file, copies the file to the printer's spool directory, and places it on the print queue to be printed in turn. `-P` *printer* prints the file on the specified printer.
`lpq` *options*	Displays the print jobs in the print queue. `-P` *printer* prints the queue for the specified printer. `-1` prints a detailed listing.
`lpstat` *options*	Displays printer status.
`lprm` *options printjob-id* **or** *printer*	Removes a print job from the print queue. You identify a particular print job by its number as listed by `lpq`. `-P` *printer* removes all print jobs for the specified printer.
`lpc`	Manages your printers. At the `lpc>` prompt, you can enter commands to check the status of your printers and take other actions.

Table 10-3: CUPS Print Clients

lpr

The `lpr` client submits a job, and `lpd` then takes it in turn and places it on the appropriate print queue; `lpr` takes as its argument the name of a file. If no printer is specified, then the default printer is used. The `-P` option enables you to specify a particular printer. In the next example, the user first prints the file **preface** and then prints the file **report** to the printer with the name **myepson**:

```
$ lpr preface
$ lpr -P myepson report
```

lpc

You can use `lpc` to enable or disable printers, reorder their print queues, and re-execute configuration files. To use `lpc`, enter the command `lpc` at the shell prompt. You are then given an `lpc>` prompt at which you can enter `lpc` commands to manage your printers and reorder their jobs. The `status` command with the name of the printer displays whether the printer is ready, how many print jobs it has, and so on. The `stop` and `start` commands can stop a printer and start it back up. The printers shown depend on the printers configured for a particular print servers. A printer configured on CUPS will only show if you have switched to CUPS.

```
# lpc
lpc> status myepson
myepson:
 printer is on device 'hal' speed -1
 queuing is enabled
 printing is enabled
 1 entry in spool area
```

lpq and lpstat

You can manage the print queue using the `lpq` and `lprm` commands. The `lpq` command lists the printing jobs currently on the print queue. With the `-P` option and the printer name, you can list the jobs for a particular printer. If you specify a username, you can list the print jobs for that user. With the `-l` option, `lpq` displays detailed information about each job. If you want information on a specific job, simply use that job's ID number with `lpq`. To check the status of a printer, use `lpstat`.

```
# lpq
myepson is ready and printing
Rank    Owner  Jobs  File(s)        Total Size
active  chris  1     report         1024
```

lprm

The `lprm` command enables you to remove a print job from the queue, erasing the job before it can be printed. The `lprm` command takes many of the same options as `lpq`. To remove a specific job, use `lprm` with the job number. To remove all printing jobs for a particular printer, use the `-P` option with the printer name. `lprm` with no options removes the job printing currently. The following command removes the first print job in the queue (use `lpq` to obtain the job number):

```
# lprm 1
```

CUPS Command Line Administrative Tools

CUPS provides command line administrative tools like `lpadmin`, `lpoptions`, `lpinfo`, `enable`, `disable`, `accept`, and `reject`. The `enable` and `disable` commands start and stop print queues directly, whereas the `accept` and `reject` commands start and stop particular jobs. The `lpinfo` command provides information about printers, and `lpoptions` lets you set printing options. The `lpadmin` command lets you perform administrative tasks like adding printers and changing configurations. CUPS administrative tools are listed in Table 10-4.

Administration Tool	Description
lpadmin	CUPS printer configuration
lpoptions	Sets printing options
enable	Activates a printer
disable	Stops a printer
accept	Allows a printer to accept new jobs
reject	Prevents a printer from accepting print jobs
lpinfo	Lists CUPS devices available

Table 10-4: CUPS Administrative Tools

lpadmin

You can use the `lpadmin` command to either set the default printer or configure various options for a printer. You can use the `-d` option to specify a particular printer as the default destination. Here **myepson** is made the default printer:

```
lpadmin -d myepson
```

The `-p` option lets you designate a printer for which to set various options. The following example sets printer description information:

```
lpadmin -p myepson  -D  Epson550
```

Certain options let you control per-user quotas for print jobs. The `job-k-limit` option sets the size of a job allowed per user, `job-page-limit` sets the page limit for a job, and `job-quota-period` limits the number of jobs with a specified time frame. The following command set a page limit of 100 for each user:

```
lpadmin -p myepson  -o job-page-limit=100
```

User access control is determined with the `-u` option with an **allow** or **deny** list. Users allowed access are listed following the **allow**: entry, and those denied access are listed with a **deny**: entry. Here access is granted to **chris** but denied to **aleina** and **larisa**.

```
lpadmin -p myepson -u allow:chris  deny:aleina,larisa
```

Use **all** or **none** to permit or deny access to all or no users. You can create exceptions by using **all** or **none** in combination with user-specific access. The following example allows access to all users except **justin**:

```
lpadmin -p myepson  -u allow:all   deny:justin
```

lpoptions

The `lpoptions` command lets you set printing options and defaults that mostly govern how your print jobs will be printed. For example, you can set the color or page format to be used with a particular printer. Default settings for all users are maintained by the root user in the **/etc/cups/lpoptions** file, and each user can create their own configurations, which are saved in their

.lpoptions files. The -1 option lists current options for a printer, and the -p option designates a printer (you can also set the default printer to use with the -d option).

```
lpoptions -p myepson -l
```

Printer options are set using the -o option along with the option name and value, -o *option=value*. You can remove a printer option with the -r option. For example, to print on both sides of your sheets, you can set the **sides** option to **two-sided**:

```
lpoptions -p myepson -o sides=two-sided
```

To remove the option, use -r.

```
lpoptions -p myepson -r sides
```

To display a listing of available options, check the standard printing options in the CUPS Software Manual at **cups.org**.

enable and disable

The **enable** command starts a printer, and the **disable** command stops it. With the -c option, you can cancel all jobs on the printer's queue, and the -r option broadcasts a message explaining the shutdown.

```
disable myepson
```

accept and reject

The **accept** and **reject** commands let you control access to the printer queues for specific printers. The **reject** command prevents a printer from accepting jobs, whereas **accept** allows new print jobs.

```
reject myepson
```

lpinfo

The **lpinfo** command is a handy tool for letting you know what CUPS devices and drivers that are available on your system. Use the -v option for devices and the -m option for drivers.

```
lpinfo -m
```

11. Network File Systems: NFS

Linux provides several tools for accessing files on remote systems connected to a network. The Network File System (NFS) enables you to connect to and directly access resources such as files or devices like CD-ROMs that reside on another machine. The new version, NFS4, provides greater security, with access allowed by your firewall. The Network Information Service (NIS) maintains configuration files for all systems on a network.

Network File Systems: NFS and /etc/exports

NFS enables you to mount a file system on a remote computer as if it were local to your own system. You can then directly access any of the files on that remote file system. This has the advantage of allowing different systems on a network to access the same files directly, without each having to keep its own copy. Only one copy will be on a remote file system, which each computer can then access. You can find out more about NFS at its website at **nfs.sourceforge.net**.

NFS Daemons

NFS operates over a TCP/IP network. The remote computer that holds the file system makes it available to other computers on the network. It does so by exporting the file system, which entails making entries in an NFS configuration file called **/etc/exports**, as well as by running several daemons to support access by other systems. These include **rpc.mountd**, **rpc.nfsd**, and **rpc.portmapper**. Access to your NFS server can be controlled by the **/etc/hosts.allow** and **/etc/hosts.deny** files. The NFS daemons are listed here:

➤ **rpc.nfsd** Receives NFS requests from remote systems and translates them into requests for the local system.

➤ **rpc.mountd** Performs requested mount and unmount operations.

➤ **rpc.portmapper** Maps remote requests to the appropriate NFS daemon.

➤ **rpc.rquotad** Provides user disk quota management.

> ➢ **rpc.statd**   Provides locking services when a remote host reboots.

> ➢ **rpc.lockd**   Handles lock recovery for systems that have gone down.

Note: It is advisable to use NFS on a local secure network only. If used over the Internet, NFS opens your system up to nonsecure access.

The `nfs-kernel-server` service script will start up the **portmapper, nfsd, mountd**, and **rquotad** daemons. NFS locking provides for better recovery from interrupted operations that can occur from system crashes on remote hosts. You can use **services-admin** or **sysv-rc-conf** to have NFS start up automatically. On services-admin (System | Administration | Services), select the Folder Sharing Service (nfs-kernel-server) entry.

To see if NFS is actually running, you can use the `rpcinfo` command with the **-p** option. You should see entries for **mountd** and **nfs**. If not, NFS is not running.

Setting up NFS Directories with shared-admin: Shared Folders

You can set up and NFS shared folder easily using the **shares-admin** tool on the Ubuntu desktop. Enter shares-admin in a terminal window (see Figure 11-1). Do not use the **sudo** or **gksu** commands. Just enter **shares-admin** directly.

```
shares-admin
```

The Shared Folders window has three panels: Shared Folders, General Properties, and Users.

To use shares-admin to manage NFS directories, you first hae to unlock it, provoding you with administrative access. Click the Unlock button. A PolicyKit authorization dialog will appear, prompting you to enter your password. Upon entering your password, the Shared Unlock button on the Sahred Folders window will be grayed out and you can now add or modify NFS directories.

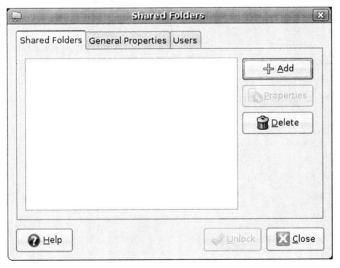

Figure 11-1: Share Folders tool

To add a new shared folder click on the Add button to open a Share Folder window (see Figure 11-2). On the Path pop-up menu select the folder you want to share. If the one you want is not listed, select Other to open a file browser for the entire system. You then select the server to share through. For NFS select Unix networks (NFS).

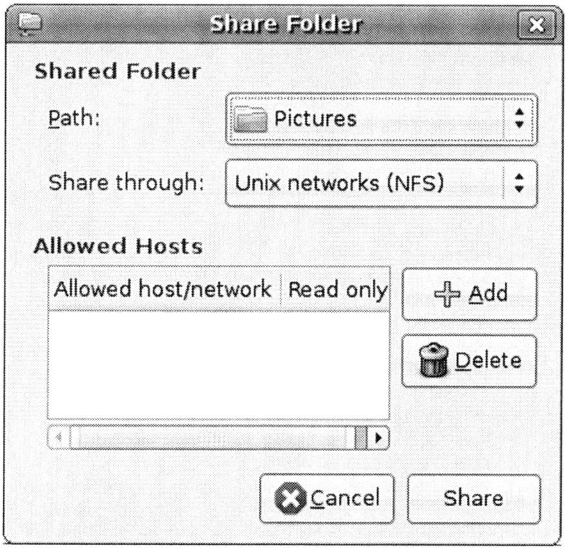

Figure 11-2: Adding a new shared folder

You then select the host or network to allow access to this folder(see Figure 11-3). Click Add to open the Add Allowed hosts window. Here you can select the a host name, IP address, or network address, and then enter the name or address. You can also specify read only, otherwise access is writeable.

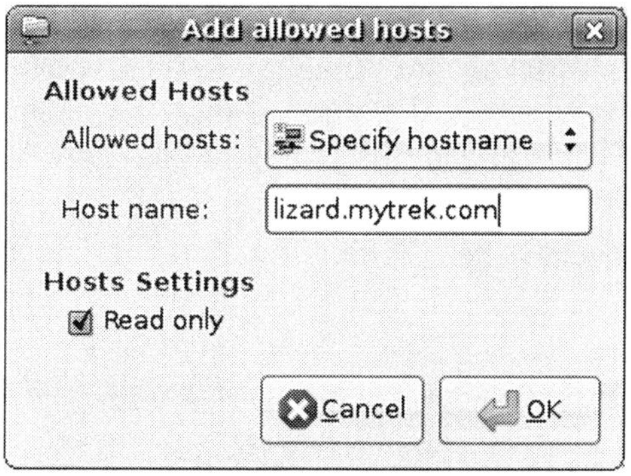

Figure 11-3: Specifying allowed hosts or networks

The allowed host will then show in the Share Folder window (see Figure 11-4). You can add more if you wish, or delete other to deny access. When finished click the Share button.

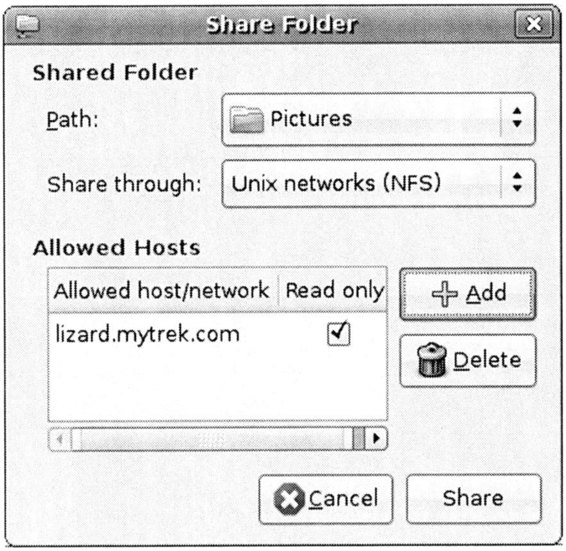

Figure 11-4: Share Folder with host access

The shared folder will then appear in the Shared Folders window.

NFS Configuration: /etc/exports

An entry in the **/etc/exports** file specifies the file system to be exported and the hosts on the network that can access it. For the file system, enter its *mountpoint,* the directory to which it was mounted on the host system. This is followed by a list of hosts that can access this file system along with options to control that access. A comma-separated list of export options placed within a set of parentheses may follow each host. For example, you might want to give one host read-only access and another read and write access. If the options are preceded by an * symbol, they are applied to any host. A list of options is provided in Table 11-1. The format of an entry in the **/etc/exports** file is shown here:

```
directory-pathname    host-designation(options)
```

NFS Host Entries

You can have several host entries for the same directory, each with access to that directory:

```
directory-pathname    host(options)  host(options)   host(options)
```

General Option	Description
secure	Requires that requests originate on secure ports, those less than 1024. This is on by default.
insecure	Turns off the secure option.
ro	Allows only read-only access. This is the default.
rw	Allows read/write access.
sync	Performs all writes when requested. This is the default.
async	Performs all writes when the server is ready.
no_wdelay	Performs writes immediately, not checking to see if they are related.
wdelay	Checks to see if writes are related, and if so, waits to perform them together. Can degrade performance. This is the default.
hide	Automatically hides an exported directory that is the subdirectory of another exported directory.
subtree_check	Checks parent directories in a file system to validate an exported subdirectory. This is the default.
no_subtree_check	Does not check parent directories in a file system to validate an exported subdirectory.
insecure_locks	Does not require authentication of locking requests. Used for older NFS versions.
User ID Mapping	**Description**
all_squash	Maps all UIDs and GIDs to the anonymous user. Useful for NFS-exported public FTP directories, news spool directories, and so forth.
no_all_squash	The opposite option to all_squash. This is the default setting.
root_squash	Maps requests from remote root user to the anonymous UID/GID. This is the default.
no_root_squash	Turns off root squashing. Allows the root user to access as the remote root.
anonuid	Sets explicitly the UID and GID of the anonymous account used for all_squash and root_squash options. The defaults are nobody and nogroup.

Table 11-1: The /etc/exports Options

You have a great deal of flexibility when specifying hosts. For hosts within your domain, you can just use the hostname, whereas for those outside, you need to use a fully qualified domain name. You can also use just the host's IP address. Instead of a single host, you can reference all the hosts within a specific domain, allowing access by an entire network. A simple way to do this is to use the * for the host segment, followed by the domain name for the network, such as ***.mytrek.com** for all the hosts in the **mytrek.com** network. Instead of domain names, you can use IP network addresses with a CNDR format where you specify the netmask to indicate a range of IP addresses. You can also use an NIS netgroup name to reference a collection of hosts. The NIS netgroup name is preceded by an @ sign.

```
directory      host(options)
directory      *(options)
directory      *.domain(options)
directory      192.168.1.0/255.255.255.0(options)
directory      @netgroup(options)
```

NFS Options

Options in **/etc/exports** operate as permissions to control access to exported directories. Read-only access is set with the `ro` option, and read/write with the `rw` option. The `sync` and `async` options specify whether a write operation is performed immediately (`sync`) or when the server is ready to handle it (`async`). By default, write requests are checked to see if they are related, and if so, they are written together (`wdelay`). This can degrade performance. You can override this default with `no_wdelay` and have writes executed as they are requested. If two directories are exported, where one is the subdirectory of another, the subdirectory is not accessible unless it is explicitly mounted (`hide`). In other words, mounting the parent directory does not make the subdirectory accessible. The subdirectory remains hidden until also mounted. You can overcome this restriction with the `no_hide` option (though this can cause problems with some file systems). If an exported directory is actually a subdirectory in a larger file system, its parent directories are checked to make sure that the subdirectory is the valid directory (`subtree_check`). This option works well with read-only file systems but can cause problems for write-enabled file systems, where filenames and directories can be changed. You can cancel this check with the `no_subtree_check` option.

NFS User-Level Access

Along with general options, there are also options that apply to user-level access. As a security measure, the client's root user is treated as an anonymous user by the NFS server. This is known as *squashing* the user. In the case of the client root user, squashing prevents the client from attempting to appear as the NFS server's root user. Should you want a particular client's root user to have root-level control over the NFS server, you can specify the `no_root_squash` option. To prevent any client user from attempting to appear as a user on the NFS server, you can classify them as anonymous users (the `all_squash` option). Such anonymous users only have access to directories and files that are part of the anonymous group.

Normally, if a user on a client system has a user account on the NFS server, that user can mount and access his or her files on the NFS server. However, NFS requires the User ID for the user be the same on both systems. If this is not the case, he or she is considered to be two different users. To overcome this problem, you can use an NIS service, maintaining User ID information in just one place, the NIS password file (see the following section for information on NIS).

NFS /etc/exports Example

Examples of entries in an **/etc/exports** file are shown here. Read-only access is given to all hosts to the file system mounted on the **/pub** directory, a common name used for public access. Users, however, are treated as anonymous users (`all_squash`). Read and write access is given to the **lizard.mytrek.com** computer for the file system mounted on the **/home/mypics** directory. The next entry allows access by **rabbit.mytrek.com** to the NFS server's CD-ROM, using only read access. The last entry allows anyone secure access to **/home/richlp**.

/etc/exports

```
/pub              *(ro,insecure,all_squash,sync)
/home/mypics      lizard.mytrek.com(rw,sync)
/media/cdrom      rabbit.mytrek.com(ro,sync)
/home/richlp      *(secure,sync)
```

Applying Changes

Each time your system starts up the NFS server (usually when the system starts up), the **/etc/exports** file will be read and those directories specified will be exported. When a directory is exported, an entry for it is made in the **/var/lib/nfs/xtab** file. It is this file that NFS reads and uses to perform the actual exports. Entries are read from **/etc/exports** and corresponding entries made in **/var/lib/nfs/xtab**. The **xtab** file maintains the list of actual exports.

If you want to export added entries in the **/etc/exports** file immediately, without rebooting, you can use the **exportfs** command with the **-a** option. It is helpful to add the **-v** option to display the actions that NFS is taking. Use the same options to effect any changes you make to the **/etc/exports** file.

```
exportfs -a -v
```

If you later make changes to the **/etc/exports** file, you can use the **-r** option to re-export its entries. The **-r** option will re-sync the **/var/lib/nfs/xtab** file with the **/etc/exports** entries, removing any other exports or any with different options.

```
exportfs -r -v
```

To both export added entries and re-export changed ones, you can combine the **-r** and **-a** options.

```
exportfs -r -a -v
```

Manually Exporting File Systems

You can also use the **exportfs** command to manually export file systems instead of using entries for them in the **/etc/exports** file. Export entries will be added to the **/var/lib/nfs/xtab** file directly. With the **-o** option, you can list various permissions and then follow them with the host and file system to export. The host and file system are separated by a colon. For example, to manually export the **/home/myprojects** directory to **golf.mytrek.com** with the permissions **ro** and **insecure**, you use the following:

```
exportfs -o rw,insecure golf.mytrek.com:/home/myprojects
```

You can also use **exportfs** to un-export a directory that has already be exported, either manually or by the **/etc/exports** file. Just use the **-u** option with the host and the directory exported. The entry for the export will be removed from the **/var/lib/nfs/xtab** file. The following example will un-export the **/home/foodstuff** directory that was exported to **lizard.mytrek.com**:

```
exportfs -u lizard.mytrek.com:/home/foodstuff
```

NFSv4

NFS version 4 is a new version of the NFS protocol with enhanced features like greater security, reliability, and speed. Most of the commands are the same with a few changes. For example, when you mount an NFSv4 file system, you need to specify the **nfs4** file type. Also, for NFSv4, in the **/etc/exports** file, you can use the **fsid=0** option to specify the root export location.

```
/home/richlp        *(fsid=0,ro,sync)
```

The preceding entry lets you mount the file system to the **/home/richlp** directory without having to specify it in the mount operation.

```
# mount -t nfs4  rabbit.mytrek.com:/  /home/dylan/projects
```

NFSv4 also supports the RPCSEC_GSS (Remote Procedure Call Security, Generic Security Services) security mechanism which provides for private/public keys, encryption, and authentication with support for Kerberos.

NFS File and Directory Security with NFS4 Access Lists

With NFS4 you can set up access control lists (ACL) for particular directories and files. You use the NFS4 ACL tools to manage these lists (nfs4-acl-tools package). The NFS4 file system ACL tools include **nfs4_getfacl**, **nfs4_setfacl**, and **nfs4_editfacl**. Check the Man page for each for detailed options and examples. **nfs4_getfacl** will list the access controls for a specified file or directory. **nfs4_setfacl** will create access controls for a directory or file, and **nfs4_editfacl** will let you change them. **nfs4_editfacl** simply invokes **nfs_setfacl** with the -e option. When editing access controls, you are placed in an editor where you can make your changes. For setting access controls you can read from a file, the standard input, or list the control entries on the command line.

The file and directory access controls are more refined that the standard permissions. The ACL entries follow the syntax described in detail on the **nfs4_acl** Man page. An ACL entry begins with an entry type such as an accept or deny entry (**A** or **D**); followed by an ACL flag, which can specify group or inheritance capability and then the principal to which the ACL is applied; and finally, the list of access options, such as **r** for read or **w** for write. The principal is usually a user URL that is to be permitted or denied access. You can also specify groups, but you need to set the **g** group flag. The special URLs OWNER@, GROUP@, and EVERYONE@ correspond to the owner, group, and other access used on standard permissions. The following example provides full access to the owner, but gives only read and execute access to the user **george@rabbit.com**. Group write and execute access is denied.

```
A::OWNER@:rwadtTnNcCy
A::george@rabbit.com:rxtncy
D:g:GROUP@:waxtc
```

In addition to read, write, and execute permissions (**r,w,x**), ACL lists also provide attribute reads (**t,n**) and attribute writes (**T,N**), as well as ACL read (**c**) and write (**C**) access. NFS read and write synchronization is enabled with the **y** option. The ability to delete files and directories is provided by the **d** option and for subdirectories with the **D** option. The **a** option lets you append data and create subdirectories. Keep in mind that **rtncy** are all read options, whereas **wadDTNC** are write options, while **x** remains the execute option. You will need **y** for any synchronized access. The **C** option in particular is very powerful as it allows the user to change the access controls (lowercase **c** allows only reading of the access controls).

Controlling Accessing to NFS Servers

You can use several methods to control access to your NFS server, such as using hosts.allow and hosts.deny to permit or deny access, as well as using your firewall to intercept access.

/etc/hosts.allow and /etc/hosts.deny

The **/etc/hosts.allow** and **/etc/hosts.deny** files are used to restrict access to services provided by your server to hosts on your network or on the Internet (if accessible). For example, you can use the **hosts.allow** file to permit access by certain hosts to your FTP server. Entries in the **hosts.deny** file explicitly deny access to certain hosts. For NFS, you can provide the same kind of security by controlling access to specific NFS daemons. The entries in the hosts.allow file are the same you specified in the **shares-admin** tool's Add Allow hosts window (Share Folder).

Portmapper Service

The first line of defense is to control access to the portmapper service. The portmapper tells hosts where the NFS services can be found on the system. Restricting access does not allow a remote host to even locate NFS. For a strong level of security, you should deny access to all hosts except those that are explicitly allowed. In the **hosts.deny** file, you place the following entry, denying access to all hosts by default. ALL is a special keyword denoting all hosts.

```
portmap:ALL
```

In the **hosts.allow** file, you then enter the hosts on your network, or any others that you want to permit access to your NFS server. Again, you specify the portmapper service and then list the IP addresses of the hosts you are permitting access. You can list specific IP addresses or a network range using a netmask. The following example allows access only by hosts in the local network, 192.168.0.0, and to the host 10.0.0.43. You can separate addresses with commas:

```
portmap: 192.168.0.0/255.255.255.0, 10.0.0.43
```

The portmapper is also used by other services such as NIS. If you close all access to the portmapper in **hosts.deny**, you will also need to allow access to NIS services in **hosts.allow**, if you are running them. These include ypbind and ypserver. In addition, you may have to add entries for remote commands like **ruptime** and **rusers**, if you are supporting them.

It is also advisable to add the same level of control for specific NFS services. In the **hosts.deny** file, you add entries for each service, as shown here:

```
mountd:ALL
rquotad:ALL
statd:ALL
lockd:ALL
```

Then, in the **hosts.allow** file, you can add entries for each service:

```
mountd:   192.168.0.0/255.255.255.0, 10.0.0.43
rquotad:  192.168.0.0/255.255.255.0, 10.0.0.43
statd:    192.168.0.0/255.255.255.0, 10.0.0.43
lockd:    192.168.0.0/255.255.255.0, 10.0.0.43
```

Netfilter Rules

You can further control access using Netfilter to check transmissions from certain hosts on the ports used by NFS services. portmapper uses port 111, and nfsd uses 2049. Netfilter is helpful if you have a private network that has an Internet connection and you want to protect it from the Internet. Usually a specific network device, such as an Ethernet card, is dedicated to the Internet connection. The following examples assume that device **eth1** is connected to the Internet. Any packets attempting access on port 111 or 2049 are refused.

```
iptables -A INPUT -i eth1 -p 111 -j DENY
iptables -A INPUT -i eth1 -p 2049 -j DENY
```

To enable NFS for your local network, you will have to allow packet fragments. Assuming that **eth0** is the device used for the local network, you could use the following example:

```
iptables -A INPUT -i eth0 -f -j ACCEPT
```

Mounting NFS File Systems: NFS Clients

Once NFS makes directories available to different hosts, those hosts can then mount those directories on their own systems and access them. The host needs to be able to operate as an NFS client. Current Linux kernels all have NFS client capability built in. This means that any NFS client can mount a remote NFS directory that it has access to by performing a simple mount operation.

Mounting NFS Automatically: /etc/fstab

You can mount an NFS directory either by an entry in the **/etc/fstab** file or by an explicit **mount** command. You have your NFS file systems mounted automatically by placing entries for them in the **/etc/fstab** file. An NFS entry in the **/etc/fstab** file has a mount type of NFS. An NFS file system name consists of the hostname of the computer it is located on, followed by the pathname of the directory where it is mounted. The two are separated by a colon. For example, **rabbit.trek.com:/home/project** specifies a file system mounted at **/home/project** on the **rabbit.trek.com** computer. The format for an NFS entry in the **/etc/fstab** file follows. The file type for NFS versions 1 through 3 is **nfs**, whereas for NFS version 4 it is **nfs4**.

```
host:remote-directory    local-directory    nfs    options    0   0
```

You can also include several NFS-specific mount options with your NFS entry. You can specify the size of datagrams sent back and forth and the amount of time your computer waits for a response from the host system. You can also specify whether a file system is to be hard-mounted or soft-mounted. For a *hard-mounted* file system, your computer continually tries to make contact if for some reason the remote system fails to respond. A *soft-mounted* file system, after a specified interval, gives up trying to make contact and issues an error message. A hard mount is the default. A system making a hard-mount attempt that continues to fail will stop responding to user input as it tries continually to achieve the mount. For this reason, soft mounts may be preferable, as they will simply stop attempting a mount that continually fails. Table 11-2 and the Man pages for **mount** contain a listing of these NFS client options. They differ from the NFS server options indicated previously.

Option	Description
rsize=*n*	The number of bytes NFS uses when reading files from an NFS server. The default is 1,024 bytes. A size of 8,192 can greatly improve performance.
wsize=*n*	The number of bytes NFS uses when writing files to an NFS server. The default is 1,024 bytes. A size of 8,192 can greatly improve performance.
timeo=*n*	The value in tenths of a second before sending the first retransmission after a timeout. The default value is seven-tenths of a second.
retry=*n*	The number of minutes to retry an NFS mount operation before giving up. The default is 10,000 minutes (one week).
retrans=*n*	The number of retransmissions or minor timeouts for an NFS mount operation before a major timeout (default is 3). At that time, the connection is canceled or a "server not responding" message is displayed.
soft	Mount system using soft mount.
hard	Mount system using hard mount. This is the default.
intr	Allows NFS to interrupt the file operation and return to the calling program. The default is not to allow file operations to be interrupted.
bg	If the first mount attempt times out, continues trying the mount in the background. The default is to fail without backgrounding.
tcp	Mounts the NFS file system using the TCP protocol, instead of the default UDP protocol.

Table 11-2: NFS Mount Options

An example of an NFS entry follows. The remote system is **rabbit.mytrek.com**, and the file system is mounted on **/home/projects**. This file system is to be mounted on the local system as the **/home/dylan/projects** directory. The **/home/dylan/projects** directory must already be created on the local system. The type of system is NFS, and the **timeo** option specifies the local system waits up to 20 tenths of a second (two seconds) for a response. The mount is a soft mount and can be interrupted by NFS.

```
rabbit.mytrek.com:/home/projects /home/dylan/projects nfs  soft,intr,timeo=20
```

Mounting NFS Manually: mount

You can also use the `mount` command with the `-t nfs` option to mount an NFS file system explicitly. For a NFSv4 file system you use `-t nfs4`. To mount the previous entry explicitly, use the following command:

```
# mount -t nfs -o soft,intr,timeo=20    \
        rabbit.mytrek.com:/home/projects    /home/dylan/projects
```

You can, of course, unmount an NFS directory with the `umount` command. You can specify either the local mountpoint or the remote host and directory, as shown here:

```
umount  /home/dylan/projects
umount  rabbit.mytrek.com:/home/projects
```

Mounting NFS on Demand: autofs

You can also mount NFS file systems using the automount service, autofs. This requires added configuration on the client's part. The autofs service will mount a file system only when you try to access it. A directory change operation (`cd`) to a specified directory will trigger the mount operation, mounting the remote file system at that time.

The autofs service is configured using a master file to list map files, which in turn lists the file systems to be mounted. The **/etc/auto.master** file is the autofs master file. The master file will list the root pathnames where file systems can be mounted along with a map file for each of those pathnames. The map file will then list a key (subdirectory), mount options, and the file systems that can be mounted in that root pathname directory. On some distributions, the **/auto** directory is already implemented as the root pathname for file systems automatically mounted. You can add your own file systems in the **/etc/auto.master** file along with your own map files, if you wish. You will find that the **/etc/auto.master** file contains the following entry for the **/auto** directory, listing **auto.misc** as its map file:

```
/auto   auto.misc   --timeout 60
```

Following the map file, you can add options, as shown in the preceding example. The `timeout` option specifies the number of seconds of inactivity to wait before trying to automatically unmount.

In the map file, you list the key, the mount options, and the file system to be mounted. The key will be the subdirectory on the local system where the file system is mounted. For example, to mount the **/home/projects** directory on the **rabbit.mytrek.com** host to the **/auto/projects** directory, you use the following entry:

```
projects  soft,intr,timeo=20  rabbit.mytrek.com:/home/projects
```

You can also create a new entry in the master file for an NFS file system, as shown here:

```
/myprojects   auto.myprojects   --timeout 60
```

You then create an **/etc/auto.myprojects** file and place entries in it for NFS files system mounts, like the following:

```
dylan    soft,intr,rw   rabbit.mytrek.com:/home/projects
newgame  soft,intr,ro   lizard.mytrek.com:/home/supergame
```

Network Information Service: NIS

On networks supporting NFS, many resources and devices are shared by the same systems. Normally, each system needs its own configuration files for each device or resource. Changes entail updating each system individually. However, NFS provides a special service called the Network Information System (NIS) that maintains such configuration files for the entire network. For changes, you need only to update the NIS files. NIS works for information required for most administrative tasks, such as those relating to users, network access, or devices. For example, you can maintain user and password information with an NIS service, having only to update those NIS password files. These are some standard entries:

```
passwd:      files nisplus
shadow:      files nisplus
group:       files nisplus

hosts:       files nisplus dns
bootparams:  nisplus [NOTFOUND=return] files

ethers:      files
netmasks:    files
networks:    files
protocols:   files nisplus
rpc:         files
services:    files nisplus
netgroup:    files nisplus
publickey:   nisplus
automount:   files nisplus
aliases:     files nisplus
```

Note: NIS+ is a more advanced form of NIS that provides support for encryption and authentication. However, it is more difficult to administer.

NIS was developed by Sun Microsystems and was originally known as Sun's Yellow Pages (YP). NIS files are kept on an NIS server (NIS servers are still sometimes referred to as YP servers). Individual systems on a network use NIS clients to make requests from the NIS server. The NIS server maintains its information on special database files called *maps*. Linux versions exist for both NIS clients and servers. Linux NIS clients easily connect to any network using NIS.

Note: Instead of NIS, many networks now use LDAP to manage user information and authentication.

The NIS client is installed as part of the initial installation on most Linux distributions. NIS client programs are ypbind (the NIS client daemon), ypwhich, ypcat, yppoll, ypmatch, yppasswd, and ypset. Each has its own Man page with details of its use. The NIS server programs are ypserv (the NIS server), ypinit, yppasswdd, yppush, ypxfr, and netgroup—each also with its own Man page.

To ensure that the client accesses the NIS server for a particular configuration file, you should specify **nisplus** in file's entry in the **/etc/nsswitch.conf** file. The **nisplus** option refers to the NIS version 3. The **nis** option refers to the older NIS version 2. The **/etc/nsswitch.conf** file specifies where a host should look for certain kinds of information. For example, the following entry says to check the local configuration files (`files`) first and then the NIS server (`nisplus`) for password data:

```
passwd:    files nisplus
```

The **files** designation says to first use the system's own files, those on the local host. **nis** says to look up entries in the NIS files, accessing the NIS server. **nisplus** says to use NIS+ files maintained by the NIS+ server. **dns** says to perform DNS lookups; it can only be used on files like **hosts** that contain hostnames.

12. Samba

With Samba, you can connect your Windows clients on a Microsoft Windows network to services such as shared files, systems, and printers controlled by the Linux Samba server and, at the same time, allow Linux systems to access shared files and printers on Windows systems. Samba is a collection of Linux tools that allow you to communicate with Windows systems over a Windows network. In effect, Samba allows a Linux system or network to act as if it were a Windows server, using the same protocols as used in a Windows network. Whereas most Unix and Linux systems use the TCP/IP protocol for networking, Microsoft networking with Windows uses a different protocol, called the Server Message Block (SMB) protocol that implements a local area network (LAN) of PCs running Windows. SMB makes use of a network interface called Network Basic Input Output System (NetBIOS) that allows Windows PCs to share resources, such as printers and disk space. One Windows PC on such a network can access part of another Windows PC's disk drive as if it were its own. SMB was originally designed for small LANs. To connect it to larger networks, including those with Unix systems, Microsoft developed the Common Internet File System (CIFS). CIFS still uses SMB and NetBIOS for Windows networking. Wanting to connect his Linux system to a Windows PC, Andrew Tridgell wrote a SMB client and server that he called Samba. Samba allows Unix and Linux systems to connect to such a Windows network; as if they were Windows PCs. Unix systems can share resources on Windows systems as if they were just another Windows PC. Windows PCs can also access resources on Unix systems as if they were Windows systems. Samba, in effect, has become a professional-level, open source, and free version of CIFS. It also runs much faster than CIFS. Samba effectively enables you to use a Linux or Unix server as a network server for a group of Windows machines operating on a Windows network. You can also use it to share files on your Linux system with other Windows PCs, or to access files on a Windows PC from your Linux system, as well as between Windows PCs. On Linux systems, a **cifs** file system enables you, in effect, to mount a remote SMB-shared directory on your own file system. You can then access it as if it were a directory on your local system.

You can obtain extensive documentation and current releases from the Samba Web and FTP sites at **www.samba.org** and **ftp.samba.org**. Samba HOW-TO documentation is also available at **www.tldp.org**. Other information can be obtained from the SMB newsgroup, **comp.protocols.smb**. Packages can be obtained from your distribution software repositories.

Extensive documentation is provided with the software package and installed on your system in the **/usr/share/doc/samba-doc** directory. Be sure to install the **samba-doc** package. The **htmldocs** subdirectory holds various documentation. All are in Web page format. Documentation includes the HOWTO, By Example, Using Samba, and Developers Guide. The examples include sample **smb.conf** files for different kinds of configuration. For PDF versions install the **samba-doc-pdf** package, **/usr/share/doc/samba-doc-pdf**.

On Ubuntu, Samba software is incorporated into several packages, with configuration tools such as SWAT and system-config-samba (see Table 12-1). By selecting the samba server package, needed supporting packages like smbclient and samba-common will be automatically selected. Documentation and configuration tools have to be selected manually.

Package name	Description
samba	The Samba server
samba-common	Samba Ubuntu configuration files and support tools
samba-doc	Documentation for Samba, including examples
system-config-samba	Samba GUI configuration tool from Red Hat
samba-doc-pdf	PDF versions for Samba documentation
swat	SWAT Samba Web interface for Samba configuration
smbclient	Samba clients for accessing Windows shares.
smbfs	Mount and unmount tools for Samba shares
kdenetwork-filesharing	Implements Samba file sharing by KDE
shares-admin	GNOME Samba file sharing support, installed with GNOME Desktop.

Table 12-1: Samba packages on Ubuntu

Samba Applications

The Samba software package consists of two server daemons and several utility programs (see Table 12-2). One daemon, **smbd**, provides file and printer services to SMB clients and other systems, such as Windows, that support SMB. The **nmbd** is a daemon that provides NetBIOS name resolution and service browser support. The **smbclient** tool provides FTP-like access by Linux clients to Samba services. **mount.cifs** and **umount.cifs** enable Linux clients to mount and unmount Samba shared directories (used by the `mount` command with the `-t samba` option). The smbstatus utility displays the current status of the SMB server and who is using it. You use **testparm** to test your Samba configuration. `smbtar` is a shell script that backs up SMB/CIFS-shared resources directly to a Unix tape drive. You use **nmblookup** to map the NetBIOS name of a Windows PC to its IP address. The primary Samba configuration tool for Ubuntu is system-config-samba, which enables you to use a GUI interface to create and maintain your Samba configuration file, **/etc/samba/smb.conf**. Alternatively, the Samba Web administration tool (SWAT) Samba to configure Samba. Configuration files are kept in the **/etc/samba** directory.

Samba provides four main services: file and printer services, authentication and authorization, name resolution, and service announcement. The SMB daemon, **smbd**, provides the file and printer services, as well as authentication and authorization for those services. This means users on the network can share files and printers. You can control access to these services by requiring users to provide a password. When users try to access a shared directory, they are prompted for a password. Control can be implemented in share mode or user mode. The *share* mode sets up one password for the shared resource and then enables any user who has that password to access it. The *user* mode provides a different password for each user. Samba maintains its own password file for this purpose: **/etc/samba/smbpasswd**.

Name resolution and service announcements are handled by the nmbd server. Name resolution essentially resolves NetBIOS names with IP addresses. Service announcements, also known as *browsing,* are the way a list of services available on the network is made known to the connected Windows PCs (and Linux PCs connected through Samba).

Application	Description
system-config-samba	Ubuntu Samba administration tool for configuring **smb.conf** with a GNOME GUI interface
SWAT	Samba Web administration tool for configuring **smb.conf** with a Web browser
smbd	Samba server daemon that provides file and printer services to SMB clients
nmbd	Samba daemon that provides NetBIOS name resolution and service browser support
winbindd	Uses authentication services provided by Windows domain
smbclient	Provides FTP-like access by Linux clients to Samba services
mount.cifs	Mounts Samba share directories on Linux clients (used by the `mount` command with the `-t cifs` option)
smbpasswd	Changes SMB-encrypted passwords on Samba servers
smbstatus	Displays the current status of the SMB network connections
smbrun	Interface program between **smbd** and external programs
testparm	Tests the Samba configuration file, **smb.conf**
smbtar	Backs up SMB/CIFS-shared resources directly to a Unix tape drive
nmblookup	Maps the NetBIOS name of a Windows PC to its IP address
/etc/init.d/samba	Samba init script to start, stop, and restart the Samba server.

Table 12-2: Samba Applications

Samba also includes the **winbindd** daemon, which allows Samba servers to use authentication services provided by a Windows domain. Instead of a Samba server maintaining its own set of users to allow access, it can make use of a Windows domain authentication service to authenticate users.

Setting Up Samba

To allow Windows to access a Linux system, as well as Linux to access a Windows system, you use the Samba server. First be sure that Samba is installed along with the system-config-samba or SWAT tools. Open the Synaptic Package Manager and do a search on samba. Be sure to install both the **samba** and **system-config-samba** packages.

Note: It is possible to set up Samba shared directories with the Shared Folders tool, shares-admin. However this tool does not provide for user level security which is now deprecated. It only provides very open share level access to any user.

Starting Samba

Once installed, Samba is normally configured to start up automatically. You can turn this option on or off using the GNOME Services Manager (System | Administration | Services). Make sure the Windows File Sharing entry with the Samba name is checked to start up Samba.

For a simple Samba setup, you can use Ubuntu system-config-samba or SWAT to configure your **/etc/samba/smb.conf** file. If you make changes, you must restart the Samba server to have the changes take effect. To restart Samba with your new configuration, use the **samba** init script with the **restart** option, **/etc/init.d/samba**. The start, stop, and restart options will start, stop, and restart the server. Run the following command from a terminal window to restart Samba.

```
sudo /etc/init.d/samba restart
```

Tip: The Samba server needs to run both the **nmb** and the **smbd** servers. Without the **nmbd** server, Windows cannot detect your Samba server. These are both started by the **samba** init script, **/etc/init.d/samba**.

Firewall access

The IPtables firewall prevents browsing Samba and Windows shares from your Linux desktop. To work around this restriction, you need to make sure your firewall treats Samba as a trusted service. To allow firewall access to the Samba ports, usually ports 137-139 and 445, you should enable access using a firewall configuration tool like Firestarter or ufw.

For Firestarter, on the Policy panel, select the Inbound menu item and then right-click on the Services pane to add a rule. On Add new inbound rule window, select Samba (SMB) from the pop up menu for Name, and the 137-139 and 445 ports will be selected for you. The Samba rule will show up in the Allow Service section of the Policy Inbound panel. Firestarter maintains its own set of IPtables files in **/etc/Firestarter**. Firestarter should show your Samba connection (Microsoft-ds)

For the **ufw** default firewall, you would use the following command. The ufw firewall maintains its IPtables files in **/etc/ufw**.

```
ufw allow 137/tcp
```

If you are managing your IPtables firewall directly, you could manage access directly by adding the following IPtables rule. This accepts input on port 21 for TCP/IP protocol packages.

```
iptables -A INPUT -p tcp --dport 137-139 -j ACCEPT
```

Setting Up Samba with system-config-samba

To set up simple file sharing on a Linux system, you first need to configure your Samba server. You can do this by directly editing the **/etc/samba/samba.conf** file or by using the configuration tools (see Figure 12-1). On Ubuntu can use the **system-config-samba** tool for configuring Samba from your desktop. The system-config-samba tool is not directly supported by Ubuntu, but is available on the Universe repository. Install the **system-config-samba** package using Synaptic.

. Due to a compatibility issue with Ubuntu, you may have to issue the following command in order to have the system-config-samba tool run correctly. You will only have to do this once.

```
sudo touch /etc/libuser.conf
```

Then you can use **system-config-samba** on Ubuntu.

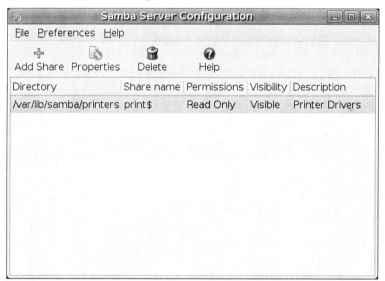

Figure 12-1: system-config-samba

Sever configuration

You will first have to configure the Samba server, designating users that can have access to shared resources like directories and printers. Open the system-config-samba tool by selecting System | Administration | Samba. Then under the Preferences menu, select Server Settings. On the Basic panel you enter the name of your Windows network workgroup (see Figure 12-2). The default names given by Windows are MSHOME or WORKGROUP. Use the name already given to your Windows network. For home networks, you can decide on your own. Just make sure all your computers use the same network name. Check your Windows Control Panel's System applet to make sure.

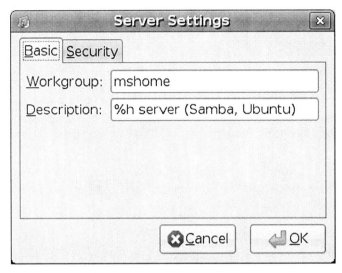

Figure 12-2: Samba Server Settings, Basic panel

On the Security panel you can select the kind of authentication you want to use. By default User security is used (see Figure 12-3). You could also use share or server security; these are more open, but both have been deprecated and may be dropped in later versions.

Figure 12-3: Samba Server Settings, Security panel

Samba Users

For user authentication you will have to associate a Windows user with a particular Linux account. Select Samba Users in the Preferences window (see Figure 12-4). Then select a Linux user to use. If you want to add a new Samba user, select Add User.

Figure 12-4: Samba Users

You should then edit the selected user, to enter the corresponding Windows user, and then a password that user can use to access Linux (see Figure 12-5). This is the Samba password for that user. Samba maintains its own set of passwords that users will need to access a Samba share. When a Windows user wants to access a Samba share, they will need their Samba password.

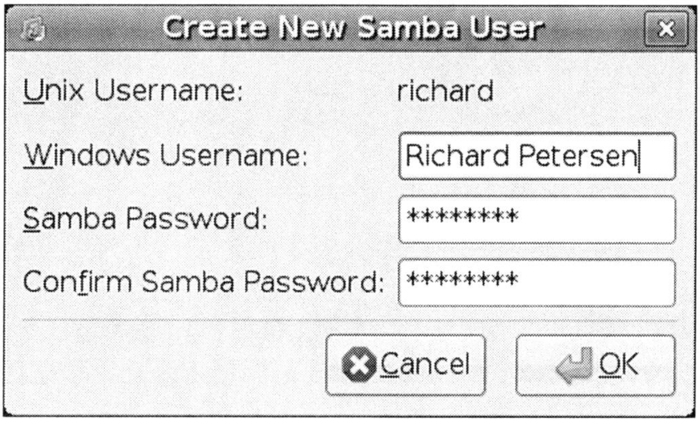

Figure 12-5: Create a new samba users

Samba Shares

To set up a simple share, click Add Share, which opens a Create Samba Share window (see Figure 12-6). On the Basic panel you select the Linux directory to share (click Browse to find it), and then specify whether it will be writable and visible.

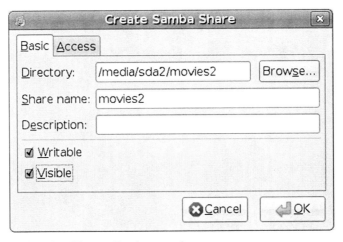

Figure 12-6: New Samba Share, Basic panel

On the Access panel you can choose to open the share to everyone, or just for specific users (see Figure 12-7).

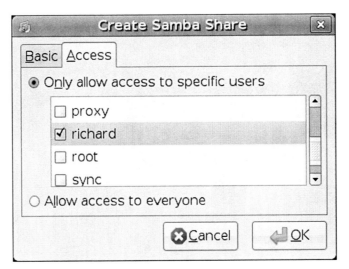

Figure 12-7: Samba share Access panel

Your new share will then be displayed in the Samba Server Configuration window (see Figure 12-8).

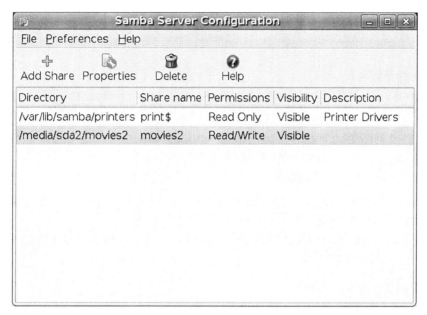

Figure 12-8: Samba with shares

SWAT

SWAT is a network-based Samba configuration tool that uses a Web page interface to enable you to configure your **smb.conf** file. Be sure you have installed the **swat** package from the Ubuntu main repository. SWAT is an easy way to configure your Samba server, providing the full range of configuration options. SWAT provides a simple-to-use Web page interface with buttons, menus, and text boxes for entering values. A simple button bar across the top enables you to select the sections you want to configure. A button bar is even there to add passwords. To see the contents of the **smb.conf** file as SWAT changes it, click View. The initial screen (HOME) displays the index for Samba documentation. One of SWAT's more helpful features is its context-sensitive help. For each parameter and option SWAT displays, you can click a Help button to display a detailed explanation of the option and examples of its use.

Activating SWAT

SWAT is installed as a separate package. SWAT is installed on Ubuntu as a inetd service, not an xinetd service. You will also have to install the inetd package to run SWAT. If you have installed xinetd (the enhanced version of xinetd), then xinetd will be removed to allow inetd to operate.   As an inetd service, it will be listed in the **/etc/services** and **/etc/inetd.conf** files. The SWAT program uses port 901, as designated in the **/etc/services** file and shown here:

```
swat 901/tcp # Samba Web Administration Tool
```

Before you use SWAT, back up your current **smb.conf** file. SWAT overwrites the original, replacing it with a shorter and more concise version of its own. The **smb.conf** file originally installed lists an extensive number of options with detailed explanations. This is a good learning tool, with excellent examples for creating various kinds of printer and directory sections. Simply make a backup copy:

```
cp /etc/samba/smb.conf /etc/samba/smb.bk
```

Accessing SWAT

You can start SWAT by opening your browser and enter the IP address 127.0.0.1 with port 901 to access SWAT.

```
http://127.0.0.1:901
```

Instead of 127.0.0.1 you can use **localhost.localdomain**.

```
http://localhost.localdomain:901
```

You can start SWAT from a remote locate by entering the address of the Samba server it is running on, along with its port (901), into a Web browser.

You are first asked to enter a username and a password. To configure Samba, you need to enter **root** and the root password.

SWAT Configuration Pages

The main SWAT page is displayed with a button bar, with buttons for links for HOME, GLOBAL, SHARES, PRINTERS, STATUS, VIEW, and PASSWORD (see Table 12-3). You can use STATUS to list your active SMB network connections.

Page	Description
HOME	SWAT home page listing documentation resources.
GLOBALS	Configures the global section for Samba.
SHARES	Selects and configures directories to be shared (shares).
PRINTERS	Sets up access to printers.
WIZARD	Quick server setup, rewrites original smb.conf file removing all comments and default values.
STATUS	Checks the status of the Samba server, both smbd and nmbd; lists clients currently active and the actions they are performing. You can restart, stop, or start the Samba server from this page.
VIEW	Displays the **smb.conf** configuration file.
PASSWORD	Sets up password access for the server and users that have access.

Table 12-3: SWAT Configuration Pages

For the various sections, SWAT can display either a basic or advanced version. The basic version shows only those entries needed for a simple configuration, whereas the advanced version shows all the possible entries for that type of section. Buttons labeled Advanced and Basic appear at the top of the section page for toggling between the advanced or basic versions . Section pages for printers and shares have added buttons and a menu for selecting the particular printer or share you want to configure. The term "share," as its used here, refers to directories you want to make available through Samba. When you click the SHARES button, you initially see only a few buttons displayed at the top of the SHARES page. You use these buttons to create new sections or to edit sections already set up for shares. To set up a new Share section, you enter its name in the box next to the Create Share button and then click that button. The new share name appears in the drop-down menu next to the Choose Share button. Initially, this menu is blank. Click its drop-down symbol to display the list of current Share sections. Select the one you want, and then click the Choose Share button. The page then displays the entries for configuring a share. For a new share, these are either blank or default values. For example, to select the Homes section that configures the default setting for user home directories, click the drop-down menu, where you find a Homes entry. Select it, and then click the Choose Share button. The entries for the Homes section are displayed. The same process works for the Printers page, where you can select either the Printers section or the Create sections for particular printers.

Note: For Samba to use a printer, it first has to be configured on your system as either a local or network printer. Keep in mind that a network printer could be a printer connected to a Windows system.

There is a Help link next to each entry. Such a link displays a Web page showing the Samba documentation for **smb.conf**, positioned at the appropriate entry.

When you finish working on a section, click the Commit Changes button on its page to save your changes. Do this for each separate page you work on, including the GLOBALS page. Clicking Commit Changes generates a new version of the **smb.conf** file. To have the Samba server read these changes, you then have to restart it. You can do this by clicking the Restart SMB button on the Status page.

Configuring Samba Access from Windows

To set up a connection for a Windows client, you need to specify the Windows workgroup name and configure the password. The workgroup name is the name that appears in the My Network Places on Windows 2000, NT, and XP (the Entire Network window in the Network Neighborhood on earlier Windows versions). On Vista, this is simply called network. To set the workgroup name on Windows XP, open System on the Control Panel, and on the Computer Name panel, click the Change button for the Rename Or Change Domain Entry. This opens a dialog window with a setting for the Workgroup, where you can enter the workgroup name. The default may be WORKGROUP or MSHOME. You can set up your own workgroup name, but all your computers would have to be configured to use that name.

On your Ubuntu Samba server, you specify the network name in the Sever Settings window on system-config-samba. Alternatively, you can manually enter it in the **smb.conf** file, you specify the workgroup name in the **workgroup=** entry in the **global** section. The workgroup name should be uppercase and contain no spaces. The default name used on Windows XP systems is simple WORKGROUP. The **smb.conf workgroup** entry would then look like this:

```
workgroup = WORKGROUP
```

Accessing Samba Shares from Windows

On a Windows client, you see the Samba server listed when you select View Workgroups Computers from My Network Places (network on Vista). On older Windows versions, use the Entire Network folder in your Network Neighborhood. The Samba server will have as a name the description you gave it in your Samba configuration. Opening the icon will display a window with all the configured shares and printers on that Samba server.

When a Windows user wants to access a new share on the Linux system, they open their My Network Places (network on Vista) and then "Add a network place" to add a network place entry for the share, or View workgroup computers to see computers on your Windows network. Selecting the Linux Samba server will display your Samba shares. To access the share, the user will be required to enter in the user name and the Samba password. You have the option of having the username and password remembered for automatic access.

You will also need to make sure that your Windows system has enabled TCP/IP networking. This may already be the case if your Windows client is connected to a Microsoft network. If you need to connect a Windows system directly to a TCP/IP network that your Linux Samba server is running on, you should check that TCP/IP networking is enabled on that Windows system. This involves making sure that the Microsoft Network client and the TCP/IP protocol are installed, and that your network interface card (NIC adapter) is configured to use TCP/IP. The procedures differ slightly on Windows 2000 and XP, and Windows 95, 98, and ME.

Sharing Windows Directories and Printers with Samba Clients

To manage directory shares, open the Computer Management tool in the Administrative window in the Control Panel. Click Shared Folders and there you can see the Shares, Sessions, and Open folders. To add a new share, click the Shares folder and then click the Action menu and select New File Share. The Sessions and Open folders' Action menus let you disconnect active sessions and folders.

Sharing Windows Directories

To share a directory, right-click the directory and select Sharing from the pop-up menu (Sharing And Security on Windows XP). Click Share This Folder and then enter the share name, the name by which the directory will be known by Samba. You can specify whether you want to allow others to change files on the share. You can also specify a user limit (maximum allowed is the default). You can further click the Permissions button to control access by users. Here, you can specify which users will have access, as well as the type of access. For example, you could allow only read access to the directory.

Sharing Windows Printers

To share a printer, locate the printer in the Printers window and right-click it, selecting the Sharing As option. This opens the Sharing panel, where you can click the Shared As button and enter the name under which the printer will be known by other hosts. For example, on the Windows client named lizard, to have a printer called Epson Stylus Color shared as myepson, the Sharing panel for this printer would have the Shared As button selected and the name myepson entered. Then when the user double-clicks the lizard icon in the Computers Near Me window, the printer icon labeled myepson will appear.

For a Linux system to use this printer, it will have be first configured as a remote Windows printer on that Linux system. You can do this easily with the **system-config-printer** tool (see Chapter 10).

User Level Security

Samba primarily provides user level security, requiring users on remote systems to login using Samba registered passwords. Samba still provides share and server level access, but these methods have been deprecated and are not recommended. User level security requires the use of Windows encrypted passwords. Windows uses its own methods of encryption. For Samba to handle such passwords, it has to maintain its own Windows compatible password database. It cannot use the Linux password databases. Windows also uses additional information for the login process like where the user logged in.

User level security requires that each user that wants to login to a Samba share from a Windows system has to have a corresponding user account on the Samba server. These are the users listed in the system-config-samba Samba Users window (see Figure 12-4). In addition, for this account, has to have a separate Samba password with which to login to the Samba share. In effect they become Samba users.

The account on the Samba server does not have to have the same name as the one on the Windows system. A Windows user name can be specified for a Samba user. On system-config-samba, the Create New Samba User window lets you enter a Windows user name in the Windows Username entry (see Figure 12-5). This mapping of windows users to Samba (Linux) users is listed in the **/etc/smbusers file**. The following maps the Windows user **rpetersen** to the Samba (Linux) user **richard**.

```
richard = rpetersen
```

When the Windows user in Windows tries to access the Samba share, the user will be prompt to login. The Windows user would then enter **rpetersen** as the user name and the Samba password that was set up for **richard**. On system-config-samba, this is the Samba password entered in the Samba Password entries in the Create New Samba Users window (see Figure 12-5)

User level security is managed by password backend databases. By default the **tdbsam** back end database is used. This is a **tdb** database file (trivial data base) that stores Samba passwords along with Windows extended information. The tdbsam database is designed for small networks. For systems using LDAP to manage users, you can use the LDAP enabled back end, **ldbsam**. The **ldbsam** database is designed for larger networks. The **smbpasswd** file previously used, is still available, but included only for backward compatibility. The default configuration entries for user access in the **smb.conf file** are shown here.

```
security = user
passdb backend = tdbsam
```

The **username map** option specifies the file used to associate Windows and Linux users. Windows users can use the Windows user name to login as the associated user. The username map file is usually **/etc/samba/smbusers**.

```
username map = /etc/samba/smbusers
```

If you are using an LDAP enabled Samba database, ldbsam, you would use special LDAP Samba tools to manage users. These are provided in the smbldap-tools package. They are prefixed with the term smbldap. There are tools for adding, modifying, and deleting users and groups like **smbldap-useradd**, **smbldap-userdelete**, and **smbldap-groupmod**. You use the **sbmldap-passwd** command to manage Samba passwords with LDAP. The **smdbldap-userinfo** to obtain information about a user. You configure your LDAP Samba tools support using the **/etc/smbldap-tools/smbldap.conf** file.

Samba also provides its own Samba password PAM module, **pam_smbpass.o**. With this module, you provide PAM authentication support for Samba passwords, enabling the use of Windows hosts on a PAM-controlled network. The module could be used for authentication and password management in your PAM **samba** file. The following entries in the PAM **samba** file would implement PAM authentication and passwords using the Samba password database:

```
auth required pam_smbpass.so nodelay
password required pam_smbpass.so nodelay
```

Be sure to enable PAM in the **smb.conf** file:

```
obey pam restrictions = yes
```

Samba Passwords: smbpasswd

With user-level security, access to Samba server resources by a Windows client is allowed only to users on that client. A The User name and Samba password used to access the Samba server has to be registered in the Samba password database.

Note: If you are using the older smbpasswd file, you can use the `mksmbpasswd.sh` script to generate an smbpasswd file made up of all the users listed in your **/etc/passwd** file. You pipe the contents of the passwd file to `mksmbpasswd.sh` and then use redirection (>) to create the file.

You can use either system-config-samba or the smbpasswd tool to manage Samba passwords. On system-config-samba you use the Samba Users window (Preferences | Samba Users) to add or edit passwords (see Figure 12-4). Alternatively, you can use the `smbpasswd` command in a terminal window to add, or later change, passwords. To add or change a password for a particular user, you use the `smbpasswd` command with the username:

```
# smbpasswd dylan
New SMB Password: new-password
Repeat New SMB Password: new-password
```

Users can use `smbpasswd` to change their own password. The following example shows how you would use `smbpasswd` to change your Samba password. If the user has no Samba password, that user can just press the ENTER key.

```
$ smbpasswd
Old SMB password: old-password
New SMB Password: new-password
Repeat New SMB Password: new-password
```

Should you want to use no passwords, you can use smbpasswd with the **-n** option. The **smb.conf** file will have to have the **null passwords** option set to yes. Note: If you are using the older smbpasswords file, be sure that Samba is configured to use encrypted passwords. Set the **encrypt passwords** option to **yes** and specify the SMB password file.

Managing Samba Users: smbasswd and pdbedit

To manage users you can either use the **smbpasswd** command or the **pdbedit** tool, as well as system-config-samba. The **smbpasswd** command with the **-a** option with add a user and the **-x** option will remove one. To enable or disable users you would use the **-e** and **-d** options.

```
smbpasswd -a aleina
```

The smbpasswd command will operate on either the older smbasswd file or the newer tdbsam backend database files. For just the **tdbsam** backend database files you can use **pdbedit** instead. To add a user you would use the **-a** option and to remove a user you use the **-x** option.

```
pdbedit -a larisa
```

This is a command line tool with options for adding and removing users, as well as features like changing password and setting the home directory. You can also import or export the user entries to or from other backend databases.

The **pdbedit** command lets you display more information about users. To display users from the backend database you could use the **-L** option. Add the **-v** option for detailed information. For a particular user add the user name.

```
pdbedit -Lv richard
```

For domain policies like minimum password length or retries, you use the -P option.

```
pdbedit -P
```

You use the **-i** and **-e** options to import and export database entries. The following will import entries from the old **smbpasswd** file to the new **tdbsam** backend database.

```
pdbedit -i smbpasswd -e tdbsam
```

If your system is using LDAP enabled Samba database, then use the smbldap tools to manage users and groups.

The Samba smb.conf Configuration File

Samba configuration is held in the **smb.conf** file located in the **/etc/samba** directory. Samba configuration tools like system-config-samba and SWAT, will maintain this file for you. Alternatively, you can manually edit the file directly, creating your own Samba configuration. You may have to do this if your Samba configuration proves to be very complex. Direct editing can provide more refined control over your shares.

You use the testparm command to check the syntax of any changes you have made to the **/etc/samba/smb.conf** file. Run the following in a terminal window.

```
testparm
```

The file is separated into two basic parts: one for global options and the other for shared services. A shared service, also known as *shares,* can either be file space services (used by clients as an extension of their native file systems) or printable services (used by clients to access print services on the host running the server). The file space service is a directory to which clients are given access; they can use the space in it as an extension of their local file system. A printable service provides access by clients to print services, such as printers managed by the Samba server.

The **/etc/samba/smb.conf** file holds the configuration for the various shared resources, as well as global options that apply to all resources. Linux installs an **smb.conf** file in your **/etc/samba** directory. The file contains default settings used for your distribution. You can edit the file to customize your configuration to your own needs. Many entries are commented with either a semicolon or a # sign, and you can remove the initial comment symbol to make them effective. For a complete listing of the Samba configuration parameters, check the Man page for **smb.conf**. An extensive set of sample **smb.conf** files is located in the **/usr/share/doc/samba*** directory in the **examples** subdirectory.

In the **smb.conf** file, global options are set first, followed by each shared resource's configuration. The basic organizing component of the **smb.conf** file is called a *section*. Each resource has its own section that holds its service name and definitions of its attributes. Even global options are placed in a section of their own, labeled `global`. For example, each section for a file space share consists of the directory and the access rights allowed to users of the file space. The section of each share is labeled with the name of the shared resource. Special sections, called `printers` and `homes`, provide default descriptions for user directories and printers accessible on the Samba server. Following the special sections, sections are entered for specific services, namely access to specific directories or printers.

A section begins with a section label consisting of the name of the shared resource encased in brackets. Other than the special sections, the section label can be any name you want to give it. Following the section label, on separate lines, different parameters for this service are entered. The parameters define the access rights to be granted to the user of the service. For example, for a directory, you may want it to be browsable, but read-only, and to use a certain printer. Parameters are entered in the format *parameter name = value*. You can enter a comment by placing a semicolon at the beginning of the comment line.

A simple example of a section configuration follows. The section label is encased in brackets and followed by two parameter entries. The `path` parameter specifies the directory to which access is allowed. The `writeable` parameter specifies whether the user has write access to this directory and its file space.

```
[mysection]
path = /home/chris
writeable = true
```

A printer service has the same format but requires certain other parameters. The path parameter specifies the location of the printer spool directory. The **read-only** and **printable** parameters are set to **true**, indicating the service is read-only and printable. **public** indicates anyone can access it.

```
[myprinter]
path = /var/spool/samba
read only = true
printable = true
public = true
```

Parameter entries are often synonymous but different entries that have the same meaning. For example, `read only = no`, `writeable = yes`, and `write ok = yes` all mean the same thing, providing write access to the user.

Hint: The **writeable** option is an alias for the inverse of the **read only** option. The **writeable = yes** entry is the same as **read only = no** entry.

Global Section

The Global section determines configuration for the entire server, as well as specifying default entries to be used in the home and directory segments. In this section, you find entries for the workgroup name, password configuration, and directory settings. Several of the more important entries are discussed here. .

The Workgroup entry specifies the workgroup name you want to give to your network. This is the workgroup name that appears on the Windows client's Network window. The default Workgroup entry in the **smb.conf** file is shown here:

```
[global]

# workgroup = NT-Domain-Name or Workgroup-Name
 workgroup = WORKGROUP
```

The workgroup name has to be the same for each Windows client that the Samba server supports. On a Windows client, the workgroup name is usually found on the Network Identification or General panel in the System tool located in the Control Panel window. On many clients, this is defaulted to WORKGROUP. If you want to keep this name, you have to change the Workgroup entry in the **smb.conf** file accordingly. The Workgroup entry and the workgroup name on each Windows client have to be the same. In this example the workgroup name is **mygroup**.

```
workgroup = mygroup
```

The server string entry holds the descriptive name you want displayed for the server on the client systems. On Windows systems, this is the name displayed on the Samba server icon. The default is Samba Server, but you can change this to any name you want.

```
# server string is the equivalent of the NT Description field
   server string = %h server (Samba, Ubuntu)
```

Note: You can also configure Samba to be a Primary Domain Controller (PDC) for Windows NT networks. As a PDC, Samba sets up the Windows domain that other systems will use, instead of participating in an already established workgroup.

Name service resolution is normally provided by the WINS server (Windows NetBIOS Name Service, nmbd), which is started by the **samba** init script. If your local network already has a WINS server, you can specify that instead. The commented default entry is shown here. Replace w.x.y.z with your network's WINS server name.

```
;   wins server = w.x.y.z
```

WINS server support by your Samba **nmbd** server would have to be turned off, turning your Samba name resolution server into just a client. The commented entry to turn off WINDS support is shown here.

```
;   wins support = no
```

If you network also has its own DNS server that it wants to use for name resolution, you can enable that instead. By default this is turned off as shown here. Change the no to yes to allow use of your network's DNS server for Windows name resolution. Also, WINS server support would have to be turned off.

```
dns proxy = no
```

Also name resolution can be instructed to check the **lmhosts** and **/etc/hosts** files first. The commented default entry is shown here.

```
;   name resolve order = lmhosts host wins bcast
```

Samba resources are normally accessed with either share or user-level security. On a share level, any user can access the resource without having to log in to the server. On a user level, each user has to log in, using a password. Furthermore, Windows 98, ME, NT, and XP clients use encrypted passwords for the login process. . Passwords are encrypted by default and managed by the password database, as noted previously

```
security = user
passdb backend = tdbsam
```

If you want share-level security, specify **share** as the security option. However this option is deprecated. User level security is considered the standard:

```
security = share
```

As a security measure, you can restrict access to SMB services to certain specified local networks. On the host's network, type the network addresses of the local networks for which you want to permit access. To deny access to everyone in a network except a few particular hosts, you can use the EXCEPT option after the network address with the IP addresses of those hosts. The localhost (127) is always automatically included. The next example allows access to two local networks:

```
hosts allow = 192.168.1. 192.168.2.
```

To enable printing, specify the load printer configurations.

```
load printers = yes
```

Other options like **printing** let you specify a different printing server (CUPS is the default).

```
printing = cups
```

You can use a guest user login to make resources available to anyone without requiring a password. A guest user login would handle any users who log in without a specific account. On Linux systems, by default Samba will use the **nobody** user as the guest user. Alternatively, you can set up and designate a specific user to use as the guest user. You designate the guest user with the Guest Account entry in the **smb.conf** file. The commented **smb.conf** file provided with Samba currently lists a commented entry for setting up a guest user called **nobody**. You can make this the user you want to be used as the guest user. Be sure to add the guest user to the password file:

```
guest account = nobody
```

Homes Section

The Homes section specifies default controls for accessing a user home directory through the SMB protocols by remote users. Setting the **browseable** entry to **no** prevents the client from listing the files in a file browser. The **writeable** entry specifies whether users have read and write control over files in their home directories. The **create mode** and **directory mode** set default permissions for new files and directories. The **valid users** entry uses the %S macro to map to the current service.

```
[homes]
 comment = Home Directories
 browseable = no
 read only = no
 valid users = %S
 create mode = yes
 directory mask = 775
```

The printer and print$ Sections

The printers section specifies the default controls for accessing printers. These are used for printers for which no specific sections exist. Setting **browseable** to **no** simply hides the Printers section from the client, not the printers. The **path** entry specifies the location of the spool directory Samba will use for printer files. To enable printing at all, the **printable** entry must be set to yes. To allow guest users to print, set the **guest ok** entry to **yes**. If you can't print, be sure to check the Default Print entry. This specifies the command the server actually uses to print documents. The standard implementation of the Printers section is shown here:

```
[printers]
 comment = All Printers
 path = /var/spool/samba
 browseable = no
 guest ok = yes
 writable = no
 printable = yes
 read only = yes
 create mask = 0700
```

The print$ section specifies where a Windows client can find a print driver on your Samba server. The printer drivers are located in the **/var/lib/samba/printers** directory and are read only.

```
# Windows clients look for this share name as a source of downloadable
# printer drivers
[print$]
   comment = Printer Drivers
   path = /var/lib/samba/printers
   browseable = yes
   read only = yes
   guest ok = no
```

Shares

Sections for specific shared resources, such as directories on your system, are usually placed after the Homes and Printers sections. For a section defining a shared directory, enter a label for the system. Then, on separate lines, enter options for its pathname and the different permissions you want to set. In the `path` = *option,* specify the full pathname for the directory. The `comment` = *option* holds the label to be given the share. You can make a directory writable, public, or read-only. You can control access to the directory with the Valid Users entry. With this entry, you can list those users permitted access. For those options not set, the defaults entered in the Global, Homes, and Printers segments are used.

The following example is the **myprojects** share. Here the **/myprojects** directory is defined as a share resource that is open to any user with guest access.

```
[myprojects]
    comment = Great Project Ideas
    path = /myprojects
    read only = no
    guest ok = yes
```

To limit access to certain users, you can list a set of valid users. Setting the **guest ok** option to **no** closes it off from access by others.

```
[mynewmusic]
comment =  New Music
path = /home/specialprojects
valid users = mark
guest ok = no
read only = no
```

To allow complete public access, set the **guest ok** entry to **yes**, with no valid user's entry.

```
[newdocs]
comment =  New Documents
path = /home/newdocs
guest ok = yes
read only = no
```

To set up a directory that can be shared by more than one user, where each user has control of the files he or she creates, simply list the users in the Valid Users entry. Permissions for any created files are specified in the Advanced mode by the Create Mask entry (same as create mode). In this example, the permissions are set to 765, which provides read/write/execute access to owners, read/write access to members of the group, and only read/execute access to all others (the default is 744, read-only for group and other permission):

```
[myshare]
comment = Writer's projects
path = /usr/local/drafts
valid users = justin chris dylan
guest ok = no
read only = no
create mask = 0765
```

For more examples, check those in the original **smb.conf** file that shows a Shares section for a directory **fredsdir**.

Printers

Access to specific printers is defined in the Printers section of the **smb.conf** file. For a printer, you need to include the Printer and Printable entries, as well as specify the type of Printing server used. With the Printer entry, you name the printer, and by setting the Printable entry to yes, you allow it to print. You can control access to specific users with the valid users entry and by setting the Public entry to no. For public access, set the Public entry to yes. For the CUPS server, set the printing option cups.

The following example sets up a printer accessible to guest users. This opens the printer to use by any user on the network. Users need to have write access to the printer's spool directory, located in **/var/spool/samba**. Keep in mind that any printer has to first be installed on your system. The following printer was already installed as myhp and has an **/etc/printcap** entry with that name. You use the CUPS administrative tool to set up printers for the CUPS server. The Printing option can be inherited from general Printers share.

```
[myhp]
     path = /var/spool/samba
     read only = no
     guest ok = yes
     printable = yes
     printer = myhp
     oplocks = no
     share modes = no
     printing = cups
```

As with shares, you can restrict printer use to certain users, denying it to public access. The following example sets up a printer accessible only by the users **larisa** and **aleina** (you could add other users if you want). Users need to have write access to the printer's spool directory.

```
[larisalaser]
     path = /var/spool/samba
     read only = no
     valid users = larisa aleina
     guest ok = no
     printable = yes
     printing = cups
     printer = larisalaser
     oplocks = no
     share modes = no
```

Variable Substitutions

For string values assigned to parameters, you can incorporate substitution operators. This provides greater flexibility in designating values that may be context-dependent, such as usernames. For example, suppose a service needs to use a separate directory for each user who logs in. The path for such directories could be specified using the `%u` variable that substitutes in the name of the current user. The string `path = /tmp/%u` would become `path = /tmp/justin` for the **justin** user and `/tmp/dylan` for the **dylan** user. Table 12-4 lists several of the more common substitution variables.

Variable   **Description**

Variable	Description
%S	Name of the current service
%P	Root directory of the current service
%u	Username of the current service
%H	Home directory of the user
%h	Internet hostname on which Samba is running
%m	NetBIOS name of the client machine
%L	NetBIOS name of the server
%M	Internet name of the client machine
%I	IP address of the client machine

Table 12-4: Samba Substitution Variables

Testing the Samba Configuration

After you make your changes to the **smb.conf** file, you can then use the testparm program to see if the entries are correctly entered. testparm checks the syntax and validity of Samba entries. By default, testparm checks the **/etc/samba/smb.conf** file. If you are using a different file as your configuration file, you can specify it as an argument to testparm. You can also have testparm check to see if a particular host has access to the service set up by the configuration file.

With SWAT, the Status page will list your connections and shares. From the command line, you can use the `smbstatus` command to check on current Samba connections on your network.

To check the real-time operation of your Samba server, you can log in to a user account on the Linux system running the Samba server and connect to the server.

Domain Logons

Samba also supports domain logons whereby a user can log on to the network. Logon scripts can be set up for individual users. To configure such netlogon capability, you need to set up a **netlogon** share in the **smb.conf** file. The following sample is taken from the original **smb.conf** file. This share holds the `netlogon` scripts—in this case, the **/var/lib/samba/netlogon** directory— which should not be writable but should be accessible by all users (Guest OK):

```
[netlogon]
 comment = Network Logon Service
 path = /var/lib/samba/netlogon
 guest ok = yes
 writeable = no
 share modes = no
```

The Global section would have the following parameters enabled:

```
domain logons = yes
```

With netlogon, you can configure Samba as an authentication server for both Linux and Windows hosts. A Samba username and password need to be set up for each host. In the Global section of the **smb.conf** file, be sure to enable encrypted passwords, user-level security, and domain logons, as well as a operating system level of 33 or more:

```
[global]
 encrypt passwords = yes
 security = user
 domain logons = yes
 os level = 33
```

Accessing Samba Services with Clients

Client systems connected to the SMB network can access the shared services provided by the Samba server. Windows clients should be able to access shared directories and services automatically through the Network Neighborhood and the Entire Network icons on a Windows desktop. For Linux systems connected to the same network, Samba services can be accessed using the GNOME Nautilus file manager and KDE file manager, as well as special Samba client programs.

With the Samba smbclient, a command line client, a local Linux system can connect to a shared directory on the Samba server and transfer files, as well as run shell programs. Using the **mount** command with the **-t cifs** option,, directories on the Samba server can be mounted to local directories on the Linux client. The **cifs** option invokes **mount.cifs** to mount the directory.

Accessing Windows Samba Shares from GNOME

You can use Nautilus (the GNOME file manager) to access your Samba shares. You can open the My Computer icon and then the Network icon. This will display the icons for your network. The Windows Network icon will hold the Windows workgroups that your Windows hosts are part of. Opening up the Windows Network icon will list your Windows network groups, like WORKGROUP. Opening up the Windows group icon will list the hosts in that group. These will show host icon for your shared Windows hosts. Clicking a host icon will list all the shared resources on it.

Alternatively, you can start Nautilus in browser mode and enter the **smb:** protocol to display all the Samba and Windows networks, from which you can access the Samba and Windows shares.

smbclient

The smbclient utility operates like FTP to access systems using the SMB protocols. Whereas with an FTP client you can access other FTP servers or Unix systems, with smbclient you can access SMB-shared services, either on the Samba server or on Windows systems. Many smbclient commands are similar to FTP, such as **mget** to transfer a file or **del** to delete a file. The smbclient program has several options for querying a remote system, as well as connecting to it. See the **smbclient** Man page for a complete list of options and commands. The smbclient program takes as its argument a server name and the service you want to access on that server. A double slash precedes the server name, and a single slash separates it from the service. The service can be any shared resource, such as a directory or a printer. The server name is its NetBIOS name, which may or may not be the same as its IP name. For example, to specify the **myreports** shared directory on the server named **turtle.mytrek.com**, use **//turtle.mytrek.com/myreports**. If you must specify a pathname, use backslashes for Windows files and forward slashes for Unix/Linux files:

```
//server-name/service
```

You can also supply the password for accessing the service. Enter it as an argument following the service name. If you do not supply the password, you are prompted to enter it.

You can then add several options to access shares, such as the remote username or the list of services available. With the -I option, you can specify the system using its IP address. You use the -U option and a login name for the remote login name you want to use on the remote system. Attach % with the password if a password is required. With the -L option, you can obtain a list of the services provided on a server, such as shared directories or printers. The following command will list the shares available on the host **turtle.mytrek.com**:

```
smbclient -L turtle.mytrek.com
```

To access a particular directory on a remote system, enter the directory as an argument to the `smbclient` command, followed by any options. For Windows files, you use backslashes for the pathnames, and for Unix/Linux files, you use forward slashes. Once connected, an SMB prompt is displayed and you can use smbclient commands such as `get` and `put` to transfer files. The `quit` or `exit` commands quit the smbclient program. In the following example, smbclient accesses the directory **myreports** on the **turtle.mytrek.com** system, using the **dylan** login name:

```
smbclient //turtle.mytrek.com/myreports -I 192.168.0.1 -U dylan
```

In most cases, you can simply use the server name to reference the server, as shown here:

```
smbclient //turtle.mytrek.com/myreports -U dylan
```

If you are accessing the home directory of a particular account on the Samba server, you can simply specify the **homes** service. In the next example, the user accesses the home directory of the **aleina** account on the Samba server, after being prompted to enter that account's password:

```
smbclient //turtle.mytrek.com/homes -U aleina
```

You can also use smbclient to access shared resources located on Windows clients. Specify the computer name of the Windows client along with its shared folder. In the next example, the user accesses the **windata** folder on the Windows client named **lizard**. The folder is configured to allow access by anyone, so the user just presses the ENTER key at the password prompt.

```
$ smbclient //lizard/windata
```

Once logged in, you can execute smbclient commands to manage files and change directories. Shell commands can be executed with the ! operator. To transfer files, you can use the `mget` and `mput` commands, much as they are used in the FTP program. The `recurse` command enables you to turn on recursion to copy whole subdirectories at a time. You can use file-matching operators, referred to here as *masks,* to select a certain collection of files. The file-matching (mask) operators are *, [], and ? (see Chapter 17). The default mask is *, which matches everything. The following example uses `mget` to copy all files with a .c suffix, as in **myprog.c**:

```
smb> mget *.c
```

mount.cifs: mount -t cifs

Using the `mount` command with the `-t cifs` option., a Linux or Unix client can mount a shared directory onto its local system. The `cifs` option invokes the `mount.cifs` command to perform the mount operation. The syntax for the `mount.cifs` command is similar to that for the `smbclient` command, with many corresponding options. The `mount.cifs` command takes as its arguments the Samba server and shared directory, followed by the local directory where you want to mount the directory. The following example mounts the **myreports** directory onto the **/mnt/myreps** directory on the local system:

Instead of using `mount.cifs` explicitly, you use the `mount` command with the file system type **cifs**. `mount` will then run the `/sbin/mount.cifs` command, which will invoke **smbclient** to mount the file system:

```
mount -t cifs //turtle.mytrek.com/myreports /mnt/myreps -U dylan
```

To unmount the directory, use the `cifs.umount` command with the local directory name, as shown here:

```
umount /mnt/myreps
```

To mount the home directory of a particular user on the server, specify the **homes** service and the user's login name. The following example mounts the home directory of the user **larisa** to the **/home/chris/larisastuff** directory on the local system:

```
mount -t samba //turtle.mytrek.com/homes /home/chris/larisastuff -U larisa
```

You can also mount shared folders on Windows clients. Just specify the computer name of the Windows client along with its folder. If the folder name contains spaces, enclose it in single quotes. In the following example, the user mounts the **windata** folder on **lizard** as the **/mylinux** directory. For a folder with access to anyone, just press ENTER at the password prompt:

```
$ mount -t cifs //lizard/windata  /mylinux
Password:
$ ls /mylinux
_hi_mynewdoc.doc_myreport.txt
```

To unmount the shared folder when you are finished with it, use the `cifs.umount` command.

```
umount /mylinux
```

You could also specify a username and password as options, if user-level access is required:

```
mount -t cifs -o username=chris passwd=mypass //lizard/windata /mylinux
```

You can also use the cifs type in an **/etc/fstab** entry to have a Samba file system mounted automatically:

```
//lizard/windata /mylinux cifs defaults 0 0
```

13. Distributed Network File Systems

For very large distributed systems like Linux clusters, Linux also supports distributed network file systems, such as Oracle Cluster File System for Linux (OCFS2), Intermezzo, and Red Hat Global File System (GFS and GFS 2). These systems build on the basic concept of NFS as well as RAID techniques to create a file system implemented on multiple hosts across a large network, in effect, distributing the same file system among different hosts at a very low level (see Table 13-1). You can think of it as a kind of RAID array implemented across network hosts instead of just a single system. Instead of each host relying on its own file systems on its own hard drive, they all share the same distributed file system that uses hard drives collected on different distributed servers. This provides far more efficient use of storage available to the hosts, as well as providing for more centralized management of file system use.

Website	Name
fedoraproject.org/wiki/Tools/GFS	Fedora GFS resources and links
oss.oracle.com/projects/ocfs2/	OCFS2, Oracle Cluster File System for Linux
sourceware.org/gfs	Global File System
inter-mezzo.org	Intermezzo (open source)
clusterfs.com	Lustre

Table 13-1: Distributed File Systems

Note: The Parallel Virtual File System (PVFS) implements a distributed network file system using a management server that manages the files system on different I/O servers. Management servers maintain the file system information, including access permissions, directory structure, and metadata information, **pvfs.org**.

Red Hat Global File System (GFS and GFS 2)

Red Hat has released its Global File System (GFS) as an open source freely available distributed network file system. The original GFS version has been replaced with the new version of GFS, GFS 2, which uses a similar set of configuration and management tools, as well as native kernel support. Instead of a variety of seemingly unrelated packages, GFS 2 is implemented with just three: **gfs2-utils**, **cman**, and **clvm**. Native kernel support for GFS 2 provides much of the kernel-level operations.

To configure GFS you can use **system-config-cluster**, the Red Hat GUI configuration tool for GFS. It is now available for Ubuntu from the Ubuntu main repository. Access it from Administration | System Tools | Cluster Management.

A distributed network file system builds on the basic concept of NFS as well as RAID techniques to create a file system implemented on multiple hosts across a large network, in effect, distributing the same file system among different hosts at a very low level. You can think of it as a kind of RAID array implemented across network hosts instead of just a single system. That is, instead of each host relying on its own file systems on its own hard drive, they all share the same distributed file system that uses hard drives collected on different distributed servers. This provides far greater efficient use of storage available to the hosts and provides for more centralized management of file system use. GFS can be run either directly connected to a SAN (storage area network) or using GNBD (Global Network Block Device) storage connected over a LAN. The best performance is obtained from a SAN connection, whereas a GNBD format can be implemented easily using the storage on LAN (Ethernet)–connected systems. As with RAID devices, mirroring, failover, and redundancy can help protect and recover data.

GFS separates the physical implementation from the logical format. A GFS appears as a set of logical volumes on one seamless logical device that can be mounted easily to any directory on your Linux file system. The logical volumes are created and managed by the Cluster Logical Volume Manager (CLVM), which is a cluster-enabled LVM. Physically, the file system is constructed from different storage resources, known as cluster nodes, distributed across your network. The administrator manages these nodes, providing needed mirroring or storage expansion. Should a node fail, GFS can fence a system off until it has recovered the node. Setting up a GFS requires planning. You have to determine ahead of time different settings like the number and names of your Global File Systems, the nodes that will be able to mount the file systems, fencing methods, and the partitions and disks to use.

For detailed information check the Cluster Project Page site at **sourceware.org/cluster**. Listed are the packages used in both GFS (Cluster Components—Old) and GFS 2 (Cluster Components—New). Here you will find links for documentation like the clustering FAQ. The Red Hat GFS Administrators Guide can be helpful but may be dated. The guide can be found on the Red Hat documentation page located at **redhat.com**. (Bear in mind that GFS now uses logical volumes instead of pools to set up physical volumes.)

Website	Name
redhat.com/software/gfs	Global File System (Red Hat commercial version)
redhat.com/docs/manuals/csgfs/	Global File System Red Hat manuals (Red Hat Enterprise implementation)
sourceware.org/cluster	Cluster Project website, which includes links for GFS documentation
/etc/cluster/cluster.conf	GFS cluster configuration file (css)
system-config-cluster	Red Hat GUI configuration tool for GFS (Ubuntu main repository), Administration	System Tools	Cluster Management

GFS 2 Packages

The original GFS, GFS 1, used a variety of separate packages for cluster servers and management tools, which did not appear related just by their names. With GFS 2, these packages have been combined into the **cman** and **gfs2-tools** packages. Here you will find tools such as fence, cman cluster manager, dlm locking control, and **ccs** cluster configuration. Cluster configuration is supported by the Cluster Configuration System, **ccs**. Fencing is used to isolate failed resources. It is supported by in the fence server. LVM cluster support is located in a separate package, **clvm** .

To run a cluster, you need both a cluster manager and locking mechanism. **cman** with the Distributed Lock Manager (**dlm**) implements cluster management and locking. **cman** manages connections between cluster devices and services, using **dlm** to provide locking. The **dlm** locking mechanism operates as a daemon with supporting libraries.

All these services are invoked by the cman script, which checks the **/etc/cluster/cluster.conf** file for cluster configuration.

GFS 2 Service Scripts

To start the GFS file system, you run the cman script to start the needed daemon and implement your configuration. The cman script will run the **ccsd** to start up configuration detection, **fenced** for fencing support, **dlm_controld** for cluster management **dlm** locking, and **cman** for cluster management. The script will check for any GFS configuration settings in **/etc/cluster/cluster.conf**. You the use the gfs2-tools script to mount your GFS 2 file systems. To shut down the GFS file system service, you use the cman script with the **stop** option.

```
sudo /etc/init.d/cman start
sudo /etc/init.d/gfs2-tools start
```

The gfs2-tools service script will mount GFS file systems to the locations specified in the **/etc/fstab** file. You will need entries for all the GFS file systems you want to mount in **/etc/fstab**. The stop option will unmount the file systems.

The gfs2-tools script can be started automatically with the admin-services tool (System | Administration | Services). Select Cluster Management Tools (gfs2-tools).

Implementing a GFS 2 File System

To set up a GFS 2 file system, you first need to create cluster devices using the physical volumes and organizing them into logical volumes. You use the CLVM (Clustering Logical Volume Manager) to set up logical volumes from physical partitions (in the past you used a volume manager called pool to do this). You can then install GFS file systems on these logical volumes directly. CLVM operates like LVM, using the same commands. It works over a distributed network and requires that the **clvmd** server be running.

You then configure your system with the Cluster Configuration System. Create a **/etc/cluster/cluster.conf** file and set up your configuration. The configuration will include information like the nodes used, the fencing methods, and the locking method used. Consult the **cluster.conf** Man page for configuration details. Test the configuration with the **ccs_test** tool.

```
ccs_test mygfs
```

You then use the **ccs_tool** to create **cluster.ccs**, **fence.ccs**, and **node.ccs** configuration files. These files are organized into a CCS archive that is placed on each node and cluster device.

On each node, start the **ccsd** configuration, the **fenced** fencing server, and the locking method you want to use, such as **dlm**. Check the respective Man pages for details on the locking servers. You can start the servers with their service scripts as noted previously.

To create new file systems on the cluster devices, you use the `gfs2_mkfs` command and mount them with the `-t gfs2` option. The following command creates a GFS file system on the **/dev/gv0/mgfs** and then mounts it to the **/mygfs** directory. For `gfs2_mkfs`, the `-t` option indicates the lock table used and the `-p` option specifies the lock protocol. The `-j` option specifies the number of journals.

```
gfs2_mkfs  -t mycluster:mygfs  -p lock_dlm  -j 2   /dev/vg0/mgfs
mount -t gfs /dev/vg0/mgfs /gfs1
```

To have the `gfs` service script mount the GFS file system for you, you need to place an entry for it in the **/etc/fstab** file. If you do not want the file system automatically mounted, add the `noauto` option.

```
/dev/vg0/mgfs   /mygfs    gfs2   noauto,defaults   0   0
```

With GFS **/etc/fstab** entries, you can then use the `gfs2` script to mount the GFS file system.

```
service gfs2-tools start
```

Command	Description
`ccs`	CCS service script to start Cluster Configuration Service server
`ccs_tool`	CCS configuration update tool
`ccs_test`	CCS diagnostic tool to test CCS configuration files
`ccsd`	Daemon run on nodes to provide CCS configuration data to cluster software

`clvmd`	Cluster Logical Volume Manager daemon, needed to create and manage LVM cluster devices, also a service script to start **clvmd**
`cman`	The Cluster Manager, `cman`, startup script, uses dlm for locking (`cman` is run as a kernel module directly)
`cman_tool`	Manages cluster nodes, requires `cman`
`dlm`	Distributed Lock Manager, implemented as a kernel module, invoked by the `cman` script
`fence`	Fence overview
`fenced`	Fencing daemon, also a service script for starting the fenced daemon
`fence_tool`	Manages the **fenced** daemon
`fence_node`	Invokes a fence agent
fencing agents	Numerous fencing agents available for different kinds of connections, see **fence** Man page
`fence_manual`	Fence agent for manual interaction
`fence_ack_manual`	User interface for fence_manual
`gfs2`	GFS 2 service script to mount GFS 2 file systems, also a Man page overview
`gfs2_mount`	Invoked by mount; use **-t gfs2** mount option
`gfs2_fsck`	The GFS 2 file system checker
`gfs2_grow`	Grows a GFS 2 file system
`gfs2_jadd`	Adds a journal to a GFS 2 file system
`mkfs.gfs2`	Makes a GFS 2 file system
`gfs2_quota`	Manipulates GFS 2 disk quotas
`gfs2_tool`	Manages a GFS 2 file system
`getfacl`	Gets the ACL permissions for a file or directory
`setfacl`	Sets access control (ACL) for a file or directory
`rmanager`	Resource Group Manager, manage user services
`system-config-cluster`	GUI configuration tool for GFS

Table 13-2: GFS Tools, Daemons, and Service Scripts

GFS Tools

GFS has several commands in different categories, such as those that deal with fencing, like `fence_tool`; `gulm_tool` to manage gulm locking; and those used for configuration, like `cman_tool`. The GFS commands for managing GFS file systems are listed in Table 13-2. Check their respective Man pages for detailed descriptions.

GFS File System Operations

. Several GFS commands manage the file system, such as `gfs2_mount` for mounting file systems, `gfs2_mkfs` to make a GFS file system, `gfs2_fsck` to check and repair, and `gfs2_grow` to expand a file system. Check their respective Man pages for detailed descriptions.

Note: For GFS 1, you use the same names for the GFS tools without the number 2; that is, `gfs` instead of `gfs2`.

To mount a GFS file system, you use the **mount** command specifying `gfs2` as the mount type, as in

```
mount -t gfs2 /dev/vg0/mgfs /mygfs
```

This will invoke the `gfs2_mount` tool to perform the mount operation. Several GFS-specific mount options are also available, specified with the `-o` option, such as `lockproto` to specify a different lock protocol and `acl` to enable ACL support .

To check the status of a file system, you can use `gfs2_fsck`. This tool operates much like fsck, checking for corrupt systems and attempting repairs. You must first unmount the file system before you can use `gfs2_fsck` on it.

Should you add available space to the device on which a GFS file system resides, you can use `gfs2_grow` to expand the file system to that available space. It can be run on just one node to expand the entire cluster. If you want journaling, you first have to add journal files with the `gfs2_jadd` tool. `gfs2_grow` can only be run on a mounted GFS file system.

Journal files for GFS are installed in space outside of the GFS file system, but on the same device. After creating a GFS file system, you can run `gfs2_add` to add the journal files for it. If you are expanding a current GFS file system, you need to run `gfs2_add` first. Like `gfs2_grow`, `gfs2_add` can only be run on mounted file systems. With the `setfacl` command you can set permissions for files and directories.

As noted previously, to create a GFS file system you use the `gfs2_mkfs` command. The `-t` option specifies the lock table to use, the `-j` options indicates the number of journals to create, and the `-p` option specifies the lock protocol to use.

The Resource Group Manager, **rgmanager**, provides a command line interface for managing user services and resources on a GFS file system, letting you perform basic administrative tasks like setting user quotas, shutting down the system (**clushutdown**), and getting statistics on GFS use (**clustat**). The primary administrative tool is **clusterfs**. Options can be set in the **/etc/sysconfig/cluster** file. You start up **rgmanager** with the `rgmanager` script. This starts up the **clurgmgrd** daemon, providing access to the GFS system.

GFS also supports access controls. You can restrict access by users or groups to certain files or directories, specifying read or write permissions. With the `setfacl` command you can set permissions for files and directories. You use the **-m** option to modify an ACL permission and **-x** to delete it. The **getfacl** obtains the current permissions for file or directory. The following sets read access by the user **dylan** to **myfile**.

```
setfacl -m u:dylan:r myfile
```

GFS 1

GFS 1, the first version of GFS, implements GFS with a series of separate packages, seemingly unrelated. To use GFS 1, you have to install a number of different packages that include the GFS 1 tools, the locking method you want to use, and configuration tools. The GFS 1 tools and locking methods also have several corresponding kernel module and header packages. See **sourceware.org/cluster** under the heading "Cluster Components—Old" for a listing of GFS 1 tools. There were kernel module packages for the different types of kernels: i586, i686, SMP, and Xen.

ubuntu

Part 4: Network Support

Proxy Servers
Domain Name System
Network Autoconfiguration: IPv6 and DHCP
Firewalls

14. Proxy Servers: Squid

Proxy servers operate as an intermediary between a local network and services available on a larger one such as the Internet. Requests from local clients for web services can be handled by the proxy server, speeding transactions as well as controlling access. Proxy servers maintain current copies of commonly accessed web pages, speeding web access times by eliminating the need to access the original site constantly. They also perform security functions, protecting servers from unauthorized access.

Protocol	Description and Port
HTTP	Web pages, port 3128
FTP	FTP transfers through websites, port 3128
ICP	Internet Caching Protocol, port 3130
HTCP	Hypertext Caching Protocol, port 4827
CARP	Cache Array Routing Protocol
SNMP	Simple Network Management Protocol, port 3401
SSL	Secure Socket Layer

Table 14-1: Protocols Supported by Squid

Squid is a free, open source, proxy-caching server for web clients, designed to speed Internet access and provide security controls for web servers. It implements a proxy-caching service for web clients that caches web pages as users make requests. Copies of web pages accessed by users are kept in the Squid cache, and as requests are made, Squid checks to see if it has a current copy. If Squid does have a current copy, it returns the copy from its cache instead of querying the original site. If it does not have a current copy, it will retrieve one from the original site. Replacement algorithms periodically replace old objects in the cache. In this way, web browsers can then use the local Squid cache as a proxy HTTP server. Squid currently handles web pages supporting the HTTP, FTP, and SSL protocols (Squid cannot be used with FTP clients), each with an associated default port (see Table 14-1). It also supports ICP (Internet Cache Protocol), HTCP (Hypertext Caching Protocol) for web caching, and SNMP (Simple Network Management Protocol) for providing status information.

You can find out more about Squid at **squid-cache.org**. For detailed information, check the Squid FAQ and the user manual located at their website. The FAQ is also installed in your **/usr/share/doc** under the **squid** directory.

As a proxy, Squid does more that just cache web objects. It operates as an intermediary between the web browsers (clients) and the servers they access. Instead of connections being made directly to the server, a client connects to the proxy server. The proxy then relays requests to the web server. This is useful for situations where a web server is placed behind a firewall server, protecting it from outside access. The proxy is accessible on the firewall, which can then transfer requests and responses back and forth between the client and the web server. The design is often used to allow web servers to operate on protected local networks and still be accessible on the Internet. You can also use a Squid proxy to provide web access to the Internet by local hosts. Instead of using a gateway providing complete access to the Internet, local hosts can use a proxy to allow them just web access. You can also combine the two, allowing gateway access, but using the proxy server to provide more control for web access. In addition, the caching capabilities of Squid can provide local hosts with faster web access.

Technically, you could use a proxy server to simply manage traffic between a web server and the clients that want to communicate with it, without doing caching at all. Squid combines both capabilities as a proxy-caching server.

Squid also provides security capabilities that let you exercise control over hosts accessing your web server. You can deny access by certain hosts and allow access by others. Squid also supports the use of encrypted protocols such as SSL. Encrypted communications are tunneled (passed through without reading) through the Squid server directly to the web server.

Squid is supported and distributed under a GNU Public License by the National Laboratory for Applied Network Research (NLANR) at the University of California, San Diego. The work is based on the Harvest Project to create a web indexing system that includes a high-performance cache daemon called **cached**. You can obtain current source code versions and online documentation from the Squid home page at **squid-cache.org**. The Squid software package consists of the Squid server, several support scripts for services like LDAP and HTTP, and a cache manager script called `cachemgr.cgi`. The `cachemgr.cgi` lets you view statistics for the Squid server as it runs. You can set the Squid server to start up automatically using **services-admin** or **sysv-rc-conf**. Squid is available on the main Ubuntu repository.

Configuring Client Browsers

Squid supports both standard proxy caches and transparent caches. With a standard proxy cache, users will need to configure their browsers to specifically access the Squid server. A transparent cache, on the other hand, requires no browser configuration by users. The cache is transparent, allowing access as if it were a normal website. Transparent caches are implemented by IPtables using net filtering to intercept requests and direct them to the proxy cache.

With a standard proxy cache, users need to specify their proxy server in their web browser configuration. For this they will need the IP address of the host running the Squid proxy server as well as the port it is using. Proxies usually make use of port 3128. To configure use of a proxy server running on the private network, you enter the following. The proxy server is running on **turtle.mytrek.com** (192.168.0.1) and using port 3128.

```
192.168.0.1 3128
```

On Firefox, Mozilla, and Netscape, the user on the sample local network first selects the Proxy panel located in Preferences under the Edit menu. Then, in the Manual proxy configuration's View panel, you enter the previous information. The user will see entries for FTP, HTTP, and security proxies. For standard web access, enter the IP address in the FTP and web boxes. For their port boxes, enter **3128**.

For GNOME, select Network Proxy in Preferences menu or window, and for Konqueror on the KDE Desktop, select the Proxies panel on the Preferences | Web Browsing menu window. Here, you can enter the proxy server address and port numbers. If your local host is using Internet Explorer (as a Windows system does), you set the proxy entries in the Local Area Network settings accessible from the Internet Options window.

On Linux or Unix systems, local hosts can set the **http_proxy** and **ftp_proxy** shell variables to configure access by Linux-supported web browsers such as Lynx. You can place these definitions in your **.bash_profile** or **/etc/profile** file to have them automatically defined whenever you log in.

```
http_proxy=192.168.0.1:3128
ftp_proxy=192.168.0.1:3128
export http_proxy ftp_proxy
```

Alternatively, you can use the proxy's URL.

```
http_proxy=http://turtle.mytrek.com:3128
```

For the Elinks browser, you can specify a proxy in its configuration file, **/etc/elinks.conf**. Set both FTP and web proxy host options, as in:

```
protocol.http.proxy.host   turtle.mytrek.com:3128
protocol.ftp.proxy.host    turtle.mytrek.com:3128
```

Before a client on a local host can use the proxy server, access permission has to be given to it in the server's **squid.conf** file, described in the later section "Security." Access can easily be provided to an entire network. For the sample network used here, you would have to place the following entries in the **squid.conf** file. These are explained in detail in the following sections.

```
acl mylan src 192.168.0.0/255.255.255.0
http_access allow mylan
```

Tip: Web clients that need to access your Squid server as a standard proxy cache will need to know the server's address and the port for Squid's HTTP services, by default 3128.

The squid.conf File

The Squid configuration file is **squid.conf**, located in the **/etc/squid** directory. In the **/etc/squid/squid.conf** file, you set general options such as ports used, security options controlling access to the server, and cache options for configuring caching operations. You can use a backup version called **/etc/squid/squid.conf.default** to restore your original defaults. The default version of **squid.conf** provided with Squid software includes detailed explanations of all standard entries, along with commented default entries. Entries consist of tags that specify different attributes. For example, **maximum_object_size** and **maximum_object** set limits on objects transferred.

```
maximum_object_size 4096 KB
```

Options	Description
src *ip-address/netmask*	Client's IP address
src *addr1-addr2/netmask*	Range of addresses
dst *ip-address/netmask*	Destination IP address
myip *ip-address/netmask*	Local socket IP address
srcdomain *domain*	Reverse lookup, client IP
dstdomain *domain*	Destination server from URL; for **dstdomain** and **dstdom_regex**, a reverse lookup is tried if an IP-based URL is used
srcdom_regex **[-i]** *expression*	Regular expression matching client name
dstdom_regex **[-i]** *expression*	Regular expression matching destination
time *[day-abbrevs] [h1:m1-h2:m2]*	Time as specified by day, hour, and minutes. Day abbreviations: S = Sunday, M = Monday, T = Tuesday, W = Wednesday, H = Thursday, F = Friday, A = Saturday
url_regex **[-i]** *expression*	Regular expression matching on whole URL
urlpath_regex **[-i]** *expression*	Regular expression matching on URL path
port *ports*	A specific port or range of ports
proto *protocol*	A specific protocol, such as HTTP or FTP
method *method*	Specific methods, such as GET and POST
browser **[-i]** *regexp*	Pattern match on user-agent header
ident *username*	String match on **ident** output
src_as *number*	Used for routing of requests to specific caches
dst_as *number*	Used for routing of requests to specific caches
proxy_auth *username*	List of valid usernames
snmp_community *string*	A community string to limit access to your SNMP agent

Table 14-2: Squid ACL Options

As a proxy, Squid will use certain ports for specific services, such as port 3128 for HTTP services like web browsers. Default port numbers are already set for Squid. Should you need to use other ports, you can set them in the **/etc/squid/squid.conf** file. The following entry shows how you set the web browser port:

```
http_port 3128
```

Note: Squid uses the Simple Network Management Protocol (SNMP) to provide status information and statistics to SNMP agents managing your network. You can control SNMP with the **snmp access** and **port** configurations in the **squid.conf** file.

Proxy Security

Squid can use its role as an intermediary between web clients and a web server to implement access controls, determining who can access the web server and how. Squid does this by checking access control lists (ACLs) of hosts and domains that have had controls placed on them. When it finds a web client from one of those hosts attempting to connect to the web server, it executes the control. Squid supports a number of controls with which it can deny or allow access to the web server by the remote host's web client (see Table 14-2). In effect, Squid sets up a firewall just for the web server.

The first step in configuring Squid security is to create ACLs. These are lists of hosts and domains for which you want to set up controls. You define ACLs using the **acl** command, creating a label for the systems on which you are setting controls. You then use commands such as **http_access** to define these controls. You can define a system, or a group of systems, by use of several **acl** options, such as the source IP address, the domain name, or even the time and date. For example, the **src** option is used to define a system or group of systems with a certain source address. To define a **mylan acl** entry for systems in a local network with the addresses 192.168.0.0 through 192.168.0.255, use the following ACL definition:

```
acl mylan src 192.168.0.0/255.255.255.0
```

Once it is defined, you can use an ACL definition in a Squid option to specify a control you want to place on those systems. For example, to allow access by the mylan group of local systems to the web through the proxy, use an **http_access** option with the **allow** action specifying **mylan** as the **acl** definition to use, as shown here:

```
http_access allow mylan
```

By defining ACLs and using them in Squid options, you can tailor your website with the kind of security you want. The following example allows access to the web through the proxy by only the **mylan** group of local systems, denying access to all others. Two **acl** entries are set up: one for the local system and one for all others; **http_access** options first allow access to the local system and then deny access to all others.

```
acl mylan src 192.168.0.0/255.255.255.0
acl all src 0.0.0.0/0.0.0.0
http_access allow mylan
http_access deny all
```

The default entries that you will find in your **squid.conf** file, along with an entry for the **mylan** sample network, are shown here. You will find these entries in the ACCESS CONTROLS section of the **squid.conf** file.

```
acl all src 0.0.0.0/0.0.0.0
acl manager proto cache_object
acl localhost src 127.0.0.1/255.255.255.255
acl mylan src 192.168.0.0/255.255.255.0
acl SSL_ports port 443 563
```

The order of the `http_access` options is important. Squid starts from the first and works its way down, stopping at the first `http_access` option with an ACL entry that matches. In the preceding example, local systems that match the first `http_access` command are allowed, whereas others fall through to the second `http_access` command and are denied.

For systems using the proxy, you can also control what sites they can access. For a destination address, you create an `acl` entry with the `dst` qualifier. The `dst` qualifier takes as its argument the site address. Then you can create an `http_access` option to control access to that address. The following example denies access by anyone using the proxy to the destination site **rabbit.mytrek.com**. If you have a local network accessing the web through the proxy, you can use such commands to restrict access to certain sites.

```
acl myrabbit dst rabbit.mytrek.com
http_access deny myrabbit
```

The `http_access` entries already defined in the **squid.conf** file, along with an entry for the **mylan** network, are shown here. Access to outside users is denied, whereas access by hosts on the local network and the local host (Squid server host) is allowed.

```
http_access allow localhost
http_access allow mylan
http_access deny all
```

Proxy Caches

Squid primarily uses the Internet Cache Protocol (ICP) to communicate with other web caches. It also provides support for the more experimental Hypertext Cache Protocol (HTCP) and the Cache Array Routing Protocol (CARP).

Using the ICP protocols, your Squid cache can connect to other Squid caches or other cache servers, such as Microsoft proxy server, Netscape proxy server, and Novell BorderManager. This way, if your network's Squid cache does not have a copy of a requested web page, it can contact another cache to see if it is there instead of accessing the original site. You can configure Squid to connect to other Squid caches by connecting it to a cache hierarchy. Squid supports a hierarchy of caches denoted by the terms *child, sibling,* and *parent.* Sibling and child caches are accessible on the same level and are automatically queried whenever a request cannot be located in your own Squid's cache. If these queries fail, a parent cache is queried, which then searches its own child and sibling caches—or its own parent cache, if needed—and so on.

You can set up a cache hierarchy to connect to the main NLANR server by registering your cache using the following entries in your **squid.conf** file:

```
cache_announce 24
announce_to sd.cache.nlanr.net:3131
```

Use `cache_peer` to set up parent, sibling, and child connections to other caches. This option has five fields. The first two consist of the hostname or IP address of the queried cache and the cache type (parent, child, or sibling). The third and fourth are the HTTP and the ICP ports of that cache, usually 3128 and 3130. The last is used for cache_peer options such as proxy-only to not save fetched objects locally, no-query for those caches that do not support ICP, and weight, which assigns priority to a parent cache. The following example sets up a connection to a parent cache:

```
cache_peer sd.cache.nlanr.net parent 3128 3130
```

Squid provides several options for configuring cache memory. The `cache_mem` option sets the memory allocated primarily for objects currently in use (objects in transit). If available, the space can also be used for frequently accessed objects (hot objects) and failed requests (negative-cache objects). The default is 8MB. The following example sets it to 256MB:

```
cache_mem 256 MB
```

Logs

Squid keeps several logs detailing access, cache performance, and error messages.

➢ **access.log** holds requests sent to your proxy.

➢ **cache.log** holds Squid server messages such as errors and startup messages.

➢ **store.log** holds information about the Squid cache such as objects added or removed.

You can use the cache manager (**cachemgr.cgi**) to manage the cache and view statistics on the cache manager as it runs. To run the cache manager, use your browser to execute the **cachemgr.cgi** script (this script should be placed in your web server's **cgi-bin** directory).

15. Domain Name System

The Domain Name System (DNS) is an Internet service that locates and translates domain names into their corresponding Internet Protocol (IP) addresses. As you may recall, all computers connected to the Internet are addressed using an IP address. As a normal user on a network might have to access many different hosts, keeping track of the IP addresses needed quickly became a problem. It was much easier to label hosts with names and use the names to access them. Names were associated with IP addresses. When a user used a name to access a host, the corresponding IP address was looked up first and then used to provide access.

With the changeover from IPv4 to IPv6 address, DNS servers will have some configuration differences. Both are covered here, though some topics will use IPv4 addressing for better clarity, as they are easier to represent.

DNS Address Translations

The process of translating IP addresses into associated names is fairly straightforward. Small networks can be set up easily, with just the basic configuration. The task becomes much more complex when you deal with larger networks and with the Internet. The sheer size of the task can make DNS configuration a complex operation.

Fully Qualified Domain Names

IP addresses were associated with corresponding names, called fully qualified domain names. A *fully qualified domain name* is composed of three or more segments. The first segment is the name that identifies the host, and the remaining segments are for the network in which the host is located. The network segments of a fully qualified domain name are usually referred to simply as the domain name, while the host part is referred to as the hostname (though this is also used to refer to the complete fully qualified domain name). In effect, subnets are referred to as domains. The fully qualified domain name **www.linux.org** could have an IPv4 address 198.182.196.56, where 198.182.196 is the network address and 56 is the host ID. Computers can be accessed only with an IP address, so a fully qualified domain name must first be translated into its corresponding IP address to be of any use. The parts of the IP address that make up the domain name and the hosts can vary.

IPv4 Addresses

The IP address may be implemented in either the newer IPv6 (Internet Protocol Version 6) format or the older and more common IPv4 (Internet Protocol Version 4) format. Since the IPv4 addressing is much easier to read, that format will be used in these examples. In the older IPv4 format, the IP address consists of a number composed of four segments separated by periods. Depending on the type of network, several of the first segments are used for the network address and one or more of the last segments are used for the host address. In a standard class C network used in smaller networks, the first three segments are the computer's network address and the last segment is the computer's host ID (as used in these examples). For example, in the address 192.168.0.2, 192.168.0 is the network address and 2 is the computer's host ID within that network. Together, they make up an IP address by which the computer can be addressed from anywhere on the Internet. IP addresses, though, are difficult to remember and easy to get wrong.

IPv6 Addressing

IPv6 addressing uses a very different approach designed to provide more flexibility and support for very large address spaces. There are three different types of IPv6 addresses, unicast, multicast, and anycast, of which unicast is the most commonly used. A unicast address is directed to a particular interface. There are several kinds of unicast addresses, depending on how the address is used. For example, you can have a global unicast address for access through the Internet or a site-level unicast address for private networks.

Though consisting of 128 bits in eight segments (16 bits, 2 bytes, per segment), an IPv6 address is made up of several fields that conform roughly to the segments and capabilities of an IPv4 address, networking information, subnet information, and the interface identifier (host ID). The network information includes a format prefix indicating the type of network connection. In addition, a subnet identifier can be used to specify a local subnet. The network information take up the first several segments; the remainder are used for the interface ID. The interface ID is an 64-bit (four-segment) Extended Unique Identifier (EUI-64) generated from a network device's Media Access Control (MAC) address. IP addresses are written in hexadecimal numbers, making them difficult to use. Each segment is separated from the next by a colon, and a set of consecutive segments with zero values like the reserved segment can be left empty.

Manual Translations: /etc/hosts

Any computer on the Internet can maintain a file that manually associates IP addresses with domain names. On Linux and Unix systems, this file is called the **/etc/hosts** file. Here, you can enter the IP addresses and domain names of computers you commonly access. Using this method, however, each computer needs a complete listing of all other computers on the Internet, and that listing must be updated constantly. Early on, this became clearly impractical for the Internet, though it is still feasible for small, isolated networks as well as simple home networks.

DNS Servers

The Domain Name System has been implemented to deal with the task of translating the domain name of any computer on the Internet to its IP address. The task is carried out by interconnecting servers that manage the Domain Name System (also referred to as DNS servers or name servers). These DNS servers keep lists of fully qualified domain names and their IP addresses, matching one up with the other. This service that they provide to a network is referred to as the Domain Name System. The Internet is composed of many connected subnets called *domains,* each with its own Domain Name System (DNS) servers that keep track of all the fully qualified domain names and IP addresses for all the computers on its network. DNS servers are hierarchically linked to root servers, which, in turn, connect to other root servers and the DNS servers on their subnets throughout the Internet. The section of a network for which a given DNS server is responsible is called a *zone.* Although a zone may correspond to a domain, many zones may, in fact, be within a domain, each with its own name server. This is true for large domains where too many systems exist for one name server to manage.

DNS Operation

When a user enters a fully qualified domain name to access a remote host, a resolver program queries the local network's DNS server requesting the corresponding IP address for that remote host. With the IP address, the user can then access the remote host. In Figure 15-1, the user at **rabbit.mytrek.com** wants to connect to the remote host **lizard.mytrek.com**. **rabbit.mytrek.com** first sends a request to the network's DNS server—in this case, **turtle.mytrek.com**—to look up the name **lizard.mytrek.com** and find its IP address. **turtle.mytrek.com** then returns the IP address for **lizard.mytrek.com**, 192.168.0.3, to the requesting host, **rabbit.mytrek.com**. With the IP address, the user at **rabbit.mytrek.com** can then connect to **lizard.mytrek.com**.

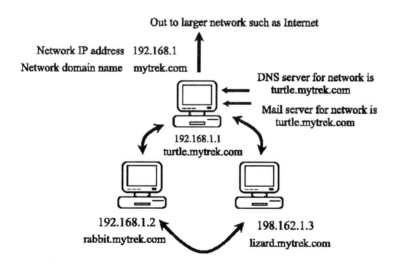

Figure 15-1: DNS server operation

DNS Clients: Resolvers

The names of the DNS servers that service a host's network are kept in the host's **/etc/resolv.conf** file. When setting up an Internet connection, the name servers provided by your Internet service provider (ISP) were placed in this file. These name servers resolve any fully qualified domain names that you use when you access different Internet sites. For example, when you enter a Web site name in your browser, the name is looked up by the name servers and the name's associated IP address is then used to access the site.

/etc/resolv.conf

```
search mytrek.com   mytrain.com
nameserver  192.168.0.1
nameserver  192.168.0.3
```

Local Area Network Addressing

If you are setting up a DNS server for a local area network (LAN) that is not connected to the Internet, you should use a special set of IP numbers reserved for such local networks (also known as *private networks* or *intranets*). This is especially true if you are implementing IP masquerading, where only a gateway machine has an Internet address, and the others make use of that one address to connect to the Internet. Though structurally the same, IPv4 and IPv6 use different addressing formats for local addresses. Many local and home networks still use the IPv4 format, and this is the format used in the following local addressing example.

Address	Networks
10.0.0.0	Class A network
172.16.0.0–172.31.255.255	Class B network
192.168.0.0	Class C network
127.0.0.0	Loopback network (for system self-communication)

Table 15-1: Non-Internet Private Network IP Addresses

IPv4 Private Networks

IPv4 provides a range of private addresses for the three classes supported by IPv4. As you have seen, class C IPv4 network numbers have the special network number 192.168. Numbers are also reserved for class A and class B non-Internet local networks. Table 15-1 lists these addresses. The possible addresses available span from 0 to 255 in the host segment of the address. For example, class B network addresses range from 172.16.0.0 to 172.16.255.255, giving you a total of 65,534 possible hosts. The class C network ranges from 192.168.0.0 to 192.168.255.255, giving you 254 possible subnetworks, each with 254 possible hosts. The number 127.0.0.0 is reserved for a system's loopback interface, which allows it to communicate with itself, as it enables users on the same system to send messages to each other.

These numbers were originally designed for class-based addressing. However, they can just as easily be used for Classless Interdomain Routing (CIDR) addressing, where you can create subnetworks with a smaller number of hosts. For example, the 254 hosts addressed in a class C network could be split into two subnetworks, each with 125 hosts.

IPv6 Private Networks

IPv6 supports private networks with site-local addresses that provide the same functionality of IPv4 private addresses. The site-local addresses have no public routing information. They cannot access the Internet. They are restricted to the site they are used on. The site-local addresses use only three fields: a format prefix, subnet identifier, and interface identifier. A site-level address has the format prefix **fec0**. If you have no subnets, it will be set to 0. This will give you a network prefix of **fec0:0:0:0**. You can drop the set of empty zeros to give you **fec0::**. The interface ID field will hold the interface identification information, similar to the host ID information in IPv4.

```
fec0::          IPv6 site-local prefix
```

The loopback device will have special address of **::1**, also known as localhost.

```
::1             IPv6 loopback network
```

Rather than using a special set of reserved addresses as IPv4 does, with IPv6 you only use the site-local prefix, **fec0**, and the special loopback address, **::1**.

Tip: Once your network is set up, you can use ping6 or ping to see if it is working. The ping6 tool is designed for Ipv6 addresses, whereas ping is used for IPv4.

Local Network Address Example Using IPv4

If you are setting up a LAN, such as a small business or home network, you are free to use class C IPv4 network (254 hosts or less), that have the special network number 192.168, as used in these examples. These are numbers for your local machines. You can set up a private network, such as an intranet, using network cards such as Ethernet cards and Ethernet hubs, and then configure your machines with IP addresses starting from 192.168.0.1. The host segment can range from 1 to 254, where 255 is used for the broadcast address. If you have three machines on your home network, you can give them the addresses 192.168.0.1, 192.168.0.2, and 192.168.0.3. You can then set up domain name system services for your network by running a DNS server on one of the machines. This machine becomes your network's DNS server. You can then give your machines fully qualified domain names and configure your DNS server to translate the names to their corresponding IP addresses. As shown in Figure 15-1, for example, you could give the machine 192.168.0.1 the name **turtle.mytrek.com** and the machine 192.168.0.2 the name **rabbit.mytrek.com**. You can also implement Internet services on your network such as FTP, Web, and mail services by setting up servers for them on your machines. You can then configure your DNS server to let users access those services using fully qualified domain names. For example, for the **mytrek.com** network, the Web server could be accessed using the name **www.mytrek.com**. Instead of a Domain Name System, you could have the **/etc/hosts** files in each machine contain the entire list of IP addresses and domain names for all the machines in your network. But for any changes, you would have to update each machine's **/etc/hosts** file.

BIND

The DNS server software currently in use on Linux systems is Berkeley Internet Name Domain (BIND). BIND was originally developed at the University of California, Berkeley, and is currently maintained and supported by the Internet Software Consortium (ISC). You can obtain BIND information and current software releases from its Web site at **www.isc.org**. Web page documentation and manuals are included with the software package. At the site you can also access the BIND Administration Manual for detailed configuration information. RPM packages are available at distribution FTP sites. The BIND directory in **/usr/share/doc** contains extensive documentation, including Web page manuals and examples. The Linux HOW-TO for the Domain Name System, DNS-HOWTO, provides detailed examples. Documentation, news, and DNS tools can be obtained from the DNS Resource Directory (DNSRD) at **www.dns.net/dnsrd**. The site includes extensive links and online documentation, including the *BIND Operations Guide (BOG)*.

The DNS server packages on Ubuntu are

```
bind9
bind9-doc
```

Alternative DNS Servers

Several alternative DNS servers are now available. These include djbdns, noted for its security features, CustomDNS, a dynamic server implemented in Java (**customdns.sourceforge.net**), and Yaku-NS, an embedded server. The djbdns server (**cr.yp.to/djbdns.html**), written by D.J. Bernstein, is designed specifically with security in mind, providing a set of small server daemons, each performing specialized tasks. In particular, djbdns separates the name server, caching server, and zone transfer tasks into separate programs: tinydns (tinydns.org) implements the authoritative name server for a network, whereas dnscache implements a caching server that will resolve requests from DNS clients such as Web browsers. In effect, dnscache operates as the name server that your applications will use to resolve addresses. dnscache will then query tinydns to resolve addresses on your local network. Zone transfers are handled separately by axfrdns and asfget.

BIND Servers and Tools

The BIND DNS server software consists of a name server daemon, several sample configuration files, and resolver libraries. As of 1998, a new version of BIND, beginning with the series number 8.*x,* implemented a new configuration file using a new syntax. Version 9.0 adds new security features and support for IPv6. Older versions, which begin with the number 4.*x,* use a different configuration file with an older syntax. Most distributions currently install the newer 9.*x* version of BIND.

The name of the BIND name server daemon is **named**. To operate your machine as a name server, simply run the **named** daemon with the appropriate configuration. The **named** daemon listens for resolution requests and provides the correct IP address for the requested hostname. You can use the Remote Name Daemon Controller utility, `rndc`, provided with BIND to start, stop, restart, and check the status of the server as you test its configuration. `rndc` with the `stop` command stops **named** and, with the `start` command, starts it again, reading your **named.conf** file. `rndc` with the `help` command provides a list of all `rndc` commands. Configuration is set in the **/etc/rndc.conf** file. Once your name server is running, you can test it using the `dig` or `nslookup` utility, which queries a name server, providing information about hosts and domains. If you start `dig` with no arguments, it enters an interactive mode where you can issue different `dig` commands to refine your queries.

To check the syntax of your DNS server configuration and zone files, BIND provides the `named-checkconfig` and `named-checkzone` tools: `named-checkconfig` will check the syntax of

DNS configuration file, **named.conf**, and `named-checkzone` will check a zone file's syntax. Other syntax checking tools are also available, such as `nslint`, which operates like the programming tool `lint`.

Numerous other DNS tools are also available. Check the DNS Resource Directory at **www.dns.net/dnsrd** for a listing. Table 15-2 lists several DNS administrative tools.

Tool	Description
`dig` *domain*	Domain Information Groper, tool to obtain information on a DNS server. Preferred over `nslookup`
`host` *hostname*	Simple lookup of hosts
`nslookup` *domain*	Tool to query DNS servers for information about domains and hosts
`named-checkconf`	BIND tool to check the syntax of your DNS configuration file, **/etc/named.conf**
`named-checkzone`	BIND tool to check the syntax of your DNS zone files
`nslint`	Tool to check the syntax of your DNS configuration and zone files
`rndc` *command*	Remote Name Daemon Controller, an administrative tool for managing a DNS server (version 9.*x*)
`ndc`	Name Daemon Controller (version 8.*x*)

Table 15-2: BIND Diagnostic and Administrative Tools

On most distributions, **named** runs as a stand-alone daemon, starting up when the system boots and constantly running. If you don't want **named** to start up automatically, you can use `services-admin` to change its status.

Domain Name System Configuration

You configure a DNS server using a configuration file, several zone files, and a cache file. The part of a network for which the name server is responsible is called a *zone*. A zone is not the same as a domain, because in a large domain you could have several zones, each with its own name server. You could also have one name server service several zones. In this case, each zone has its own zone file.

DNS Zones

The zone files hold resource records that provide hostname and IP address associations for computers on the network for which the DNS server is responsible. Zone files exist for the server's network and the local machine. Zone entries are defined in the **named.conf** file. Here, you place zone entries for your master, slave, and forward DNS servers. The most commonly used zone types are described here:

➤ **Master zone**   This is the primary zone file for the network supported by the DNS server. It holds the mappings from domain names to IP addresses for all the hosts on that network.

> **Slave zone**   These are references to other DNS servers for your network. Your network can have a master DNS server and several slave DNS servers to help carry the workload. A slave DNS server automatically copies its configuration files, including all zone files, from the master DNS server. Any changes to the master configuration files trigger an automatic download of these files to the slave servers. In effect, you only have to manage the configuration files for the master DNS server, as they are automatically copied to the slave servers.

> **Forward zone**   The forward zone lists name servers outside your network that should be searched if your network's name server fails to resolve an address.

> **IN-ADDR.ARPA zone**   DNS can also provide reverse resolutions, where an IP address is used to determine the associated domain name address. Such lookups are provided by **IN-ADDR.ARPA** zone files. Each master zone file usually has a corresponding **IN-ADDR.ARPA** zone file to provide reverse resolution for that zone. For each master zone entry, a corresponding reverse mapping zone entry named **IN-ADDR.ARPA** also exists, as well as one for the localhost. This entry performs reverse mapping from an IP address to its domain name. The name of the zone entry uses the domain IP address, which is the IP address with segments listed starting from the host, instead of the network. So for the IP address 192.168.0.4, where 4 is the host address, the corresponding domain IP address is 4.0.168.192, listing the segments in reverse order. The reverse mapping for the localhost is 1.0.0.127.

> **IP6.ARPA zone**   This is the IPv6 equivalent of the **IN-ADDR.ARPA** zone, providing reverse resolution for that zone. The IP6.ARPA zone uses bit labels the provide a bit-level format that is easier to write, requiring no reverse calculation on the part of the DNS administrator.

> **IP6.INT zone**   This is the older form of the IPv6 IP6.ARPA zone, which is the equivalent of the IPv4 **IN-ADDR.ARPA** zone, providing reverse resolution for a zone. IP6.INT is meant to be used with the older AAAA IPv6 address records. IP6.INT uses a nibble format to specify a reverse zone. In this format, a hexadecimal IPv6 address is segmented into each of its 32 hexadecimal numbers and listed in reverse order, each segment separated by a period.

> **Hint zone**   A hint zone specifies the root name servers and is denoted by a period (.). A DNS server is normally connected to a larger network, such as the Internet, which has its own DNS servers. DNS servers are connected this way hierarchically, with each server having its root servers to which it can send resolution queries. The root servers are designated in the hint zone.

DNS Servers Types

There are several kinds of DNS servers, each designed to perform a different type of task under the Domain Name System. The basic kind of DNS server is the *master* server. Each network must have at least one master server that is responsible for resolving names on the network. Large networks may need several DNS servers. Some of these can be slave servers that can be updated directly from a master server. Others may be *alternative master* servers that hosts in a network can use. Both are commonly referred to as *secondary* servers. For DNS requests a DNS server cannot resolve, the request can be forwarded to specific DNS servers outside the network, such as on the

Internet. DNS servers in a network can be set up to perform this task and are referred to as *forwarder* servers. To help bear the workload, local DNS servers can be set up within a network that operate as caching servers. Such a server merely collects DNS lookups from previous requests it sent to the main DNS server. Any repeated requests can then be answered by the caching server.

A server that can answer DNS queries for a given zone with authority is known as an *authoritative* server. An authoritative server holds the DNS configuration records for hosts in a zone that will associate each host's DNS name with an IP address. For example, a master server is an authoritative server. So are slave and stealth servers (see the list that follows). A caching server is not authoritative. It only holds whatever associations it picked up from other servers and cannot guarantee that the associations are valid.

> **Master server**   This is the primary DNS server for a zone.

> **Slave server**   A DNS server that receives zone information from the master server.

> **Forwarder server**   A server that forwards unresolved DNS requests to outside DNS servers. Can be used to keep other servers on a local network hidden from the Internet.

> **Caching only server**   Caches DNS information it receives from DNS servers and uses it to resolve local requests.

> **Stealth server**   A DNS server for a zone not listed as a name server by the master DNS server.

Location of Bind Server Files: /etc/bind/

Both the configuration and zone files used by BIND are placed in a the **/etc/bind** directory. Zone files begin with the prefix db, as in **db.127** for the localhost zone file.

```
/etc/bind/named.conf        BIND configuration file
/etc/bind/db.*              BIND zone files
```

named.conf

The configuration file for the **named** daemon is **named.conf**. A link to it is located in the **/etc** directory, with the original file located in the **/var/named/chroot/etc** directory. It uses a flexible syntax similar to C programs. The format enables easy configuration of selected zones, enabling features such as access control lists and categorized logging. The **named.conf** file consists of BIND configuration statements with attached blocks within which specific options are listed. A configuration statement is followed by arguments and a block that is delimited with braces. Within the block are lines of option and feature entries. Each entry is terminated with a semicolon. Comments can use the C, C++, or Shell/Perl syntax: enclosing /* */, preceding //, or preceding #. The following example shows a `zone` statement followed by the zone name and a block of options that begin with an opening brace ({). Each option entry ends with a semicolon. The entire block ends with a closing brace, also followed by a semicolon. The format for a **named.conf** entry is show here, along with the different kinds of comments allowed. Tables 35-5, 35-6, and 35-7 list several commonly used statements and options.

```
// comments
/* comments */
# comments

statements {
 options and features; //comments
};
```

The following example shows a simple caching server entry:

```
// a caching only nameserver config
//
zone "." {
      type hint;
      file "named.ca";
      };
```

Once you have created your configuration file, you should check its syntax with the **named-checkconfig** tool. Enter the command on a shell command line. If you do not specify a configuration file, it will default to **/etc/named.conf**.

```
named-checkconfig
```

The zone Statement

The **zone** statement is used to specify the domains the name server will service. You enter the keyword **zone**, followed by the name of the domain placed within double quotes. Do not place a period at the end of the domain name. In the following example, a period is within the domain name, but not at the end, "**mytrek.com**"; this differs from the zone file, which requires a period at the end of a complete domain name.

After the zone name, you can specify the class **in**, which stands for Internet. You can also leave it out, in which case **in** is assumed (there are only a few other esoteric classes that are rarely used). Within the zone block, you can place several options (see Table 15-3). Two essential options are **type** and **file**. The **type** option is used to specify the zone's type. The **file** option is used to specify the name of the zone file to be used for this zone. You can choose from several types of zones: master, slave, stub, forward, and hint. *Master* specifies that the zone holds master information and is authorized to act on it. A master server was called a primary server in the older 4.*x* BIND configuration. *Slave* indicates that the zone needs to update its data periodically from a specified master name server. You use this entry if your name server is operating as a secondary server for another primary (master) DNS server. A *stub zone* copies only other name server entries, instead of the entire zone. A *forward zone* directs all queries to name servers specified in a **forwarders** statement. A *hint zone* specifies the set of root name servers used by all Internet DNS servers. You can also specify several options that can override any global options set with the **options** statement. Table 15-3 lists the BIND zone types. The following example shows a simple **zone** statement for the **mytrek.com** domain. Its class is Internet (in), and its type is master. The name of its zone file is usually the same as the zone name, in this case, "**mytrek.com**."

```
zone "mytrek.com" in {
      type master;
      file "mytrek.com";
      };
```

Type	Description
master	Primary DNS zone
slave	Slave DNS server; controlled by a master DNS server
hint	Set of root DNS Internet servers
forward	Forwards any queries in it to other servers
stub	Like a slave zone, but holds only names of DNS servers

Table 15-3: DNS BIND Zone Types

Statement	Description
/* *comment* */	BIND comment in C syntax.
// *comment*	BIND comment in C++ syntax.
# *comment*	BIND comment in Unix shell and Perl syntax.
acl	Defines a named IP address matching list.
include	Includes a file, interpreting it as part of the **named.conf** file.
key	Specifies key information for use in authentication and authorization.
logging	Specifies what the server logs and where the log messages are sent.
options	Global server configuration options and defaults for other statements.
controls	Declares control channels to be used by the ndc utility.
server	Sets certain configuration options for the specified server basis.
sortlists	Gives preference to specified networks according to a queries source.
trusted-keys	Defines DNSSEC keys preconfigured into the server and implicitly trusted.
zone	Defines a zone.
view	Defines a view.

Table 15-4: BIND Configuration Statements

Configuration Statements

Other statements, such as **acl**, **server**, **options**, and **logging**, enable you to configure different features for your name server (see Table 15-4). The **server** statement defines the characteristics to be associated with a remote name server, such as the transfer method and key ID for transaction security. The **control** statement defines special control channels. The **key** statement defines a key ID to be used in a **server** statement that associates an authentication method with a particular name server (see "DNSSEC" later in this chapter). The **logging** statement is used to configure logging options for the name server, such as the maximum size of the log file and a severity level for messages. Table 15-5 lists the BIND statements. The **sortlists** statement lets you specify preferences to be used when a query returns multiple responses. For example, you could give preference to your localhost network or to a private local network such a 192.168.0.0.

Option	Description
type	Specifies a zone type.
file	Specifies the zone file for the zone.
directory	Specifies a directory for zone files.
forwarders	Lists hosts for DNS servers where requests are to be forwarded.
masters	Lists hosts for DNS master servers for a slave server.
notify	Allows master servers to notify their slave servers when the master zone data changes and updates are needed.
allow-transfer	Specifies which hosts are allowed to receive zone transfers.
allow-query	Specifies hosts that are allowed to make queries.
allow-recursion	Specifies hosts that are allowed to perform recursive queries on the server.

Table 15-5: Zone Options

The options Statement

The **options** statement defines global options and can be used only once in the configuration file. An extensive number of options cover such components as forwarding, name checking, directory path names, access control, and zone transfers, among others (see Table 15-6). A complete listing can be found in the BIND documentation.

The directory Option

A critically important option found in most configuration files is the **directory** option, which holds the location of the name server's zone and cache files on your system. The following example is taken from the **/etc/named.conf** file. This example specifies the zone files are located in the **/var/named** directory. In this directory, you can find your zone files, including those used for your local system. The example uses IPv4 addresses.

```
options {
        directory "/var/named";
        forwarders { 192.168.0.34;
                192.168.0.47;
                };
    };
```

The forwarders Option

Another commonly used global option is the **forwarders** option. With the **forwarders** option, you can list several DNS servers to which queries can be forwarded if they cannot be resolved by the local DNS server. This is helpful for local networks that may need to use a DNS server connected to the Internet. The **forwarders** option can also be placed in forward zone entries.

Option	Description
sortlist	Gives preference to specified networks according to a queries source.
directory	Specifies a directory for zone files.
forwarders	Lists hosts for DNS servers where requests are to be forwarded.
allow-transfer	Specifies which hosts are allowed to receive zone transfers.
allow-query	Specifies hosts that are allowed to make queries.
allow-recursion	Specifies hosts that are allowed to perform recursive queries on the server.
notify	Allows master servers to notify their slave servers when the master zone data changes and updates are needed.
blackhole	Option to eliminate denial response by **allow-query**.

Table 15-6: Bind Options for the options Statement

The notify Option

With the **notify** option turned on, the master zone DNS servers send messages to any slave DNS servers whenever their configuration has changed. The slave servers can then perform zone transfers in which they download the changed configuration files. Slave servers always use the DNS configuration files copied from their master DNS servers. The **notify** option takes one argument, **yes** or **no**, where **yes** is the default. With the **no** argument, you can have the master server not send out any messages to the slave servers, in effect preventing any zone transfers.

The named configuration files

BIND configuration uses three named configuration files for your zones and server options.

➢ **named.conf** The primary BIND configuration file. This file will read in the named.conf.local and the named.conf.options files. The DNS server actually only looks for the named.conf file.

➢ **named.conf.options** This file includes global options for your DNS server.

➢ **named.conf.local** Here you add your own zone configuration entries.

The named.conf configuration file

The named.conf configuration file will first read in any global options from the named.conf.options file, using the include directive.

A one statements is configured the localhost network addresses (localhost). The localhost and 127 `zone` statements define a zone and reverse mapping zone for the loopback interface, the method used by the system to address itself and enable communication between local users on the system. The zone file for local host is **db.local**, and its reverse lookup file is **db.127**. Two revers lookup zones are then setup for the broadcast zone, 0 and 255, in the **db0** and **db.255** zone files. Both reference the localhost.

```
// This is the primary configuration file for the BIND DNS server named.
//
// Please read /usr/share/doc/bind9/README.Debian.gz for information on the
// structure of BIND configuration files in Debian, *BEFORE* you customize
// this configuration file.
//
// If you are just adding zones, please do that in /etc/bind/named.conf.local

include "/etc/bind/named.conf.options";

// prime the server with knowledge of the root servers
zone "." {
    type hint;
    file "/etc/bind/db.root";
};

// be authoritative for the localhost forward and reverse zones, and for
// broadcast zones as per RFC 1912

zone "localhost" {
    type master;
    file "/etc/bind/db.local";
};

zone "127.in-addr.arpa" {
    type master;
    file "/etc/bind/db.127";
};

zone "0.in-addr.arpa" {
    type master;
    file "/etc/bind/db.0";
};

zone "255.in-addr.arpa" {
    type master;
    file "/etc/bind/db.255";
};

include "/etc/bind/named.conf.local";
```

The "." zone is set up for accessing the root DNS servers, the db.root zone file.

The last entry will read in any zone statements you add in the named.conf.local file.

You should not have to modify the named.conf file. Any options you can specify in the named.conf.options file and your network's zone entreis can be placed in the named.conf.local file.

The **named.conf** file installed by the BIND server package to the **/etc/bind** directory is shown above. The file begins with comments using C++ syntax, **//**.

The named.conf.options configuration file

The named.conf.options file contains an options statement with global options listed. The directory option sets the directory for the zone and cache files to **/var/cache/bind**. Here, you find links to your zone files and reverse mapping files, along with the cache file, **named.ca**. The original files will be located in **/var/bind**.

The commented query-source directive is used for firewall access. The forwarders option can be used for your ISP DNS servers.

```
options {
    directory "/var/cache/bind";

// If there is a firewall between you and nameservers you want
// to talk to, you might need to uncomment the query-source
// directive below.  Previous versions of BIND always asked
// questions using port 53, but BIND 8.1 and later use an
// unprivileged port by default.

// query-source address * port 53;

// If your ISP provided one or more IP addresses for stable
// nameservers, you probably want to use them as forwarders.
// Uncomment the following block, and insert the addresses
// replacing the all-0's placeholder.

    // forwarders {
    //      0.0.0.0;
    // };

    auth-nxdomain no;    # conform to RFC1035
    listen-on-v6 { any; };
};
```

The named.conf.local configuration file

In the named.conf.local file you add the zone statements for your particular DNS server. Initially this file will be empty.

A sample named.conf.local file is shown here.

The first **zone** statement defines a zone for the **mytrek.com** domain. Its type is master, and its zone file is named "**mytrek.com**." The next zone is used for reverse IP mapping of the previous zone. Its name is made up of a reverse listing of the **mytrek.com** domain's IP address with the term **IN-ADDR.ARPA** appended. The domain address for **mytrek.com** is 192.168.0, so the reverse is 1.168.192. The **IN-ADDR.ARPA** domain is a special domain that supports gateway location and Internet address–to–host mapping.

```
//
// A simple BIND  configuration
//


zone "mytrek.com" {
                            type master;
                            file "mytrek.com";
                            };
zone "1.168.192.IN-ADDR.ARPA" {
                            type master;
                            file "192.168.0";
                            };
```

An IPv6 named.conf Example

The IPv6 version for the preceding **named.conf.local** file appears much the same, except that the IN-ADDR.ARPA domain is replaced by the IP6.ARPA domain in the reverse zone entries. IP6.ARPA uses bit labels providing bit-level specification for the address. This is simply the full hexadecimal address, including zeros, without intervening colons. You need to use IP6.ARPA format of the IPv6 address for both the **mytrek.com** domain and the localhost domain..

```
named.conf

//
// A simple BIND 9 configuration
//

zone "mytrek.com" {
                            type master;
                            file "mytrek.com";
                            };
zone "\[xFEC0000000000000/64].IP6.ARPA" {
                            type master;
                            file "fec.ip6.arpa";
                            };
```

Resource Records for Zone Files

Your name server holds domain name information about the hosts on your network in resource records placed in zone and reverse mapping files. Resource records are used to associate IP addresses with fully qualified domain names. You need a record for every computer in the zone that the name server services. A record takes up one line, though you can use parentheses to use several lines for a record, as is usually the case with SOA records. A resource record uses the Standard Resource Record Format as shown here:

name [*<ttl>*] [*<class>*] *<type> <rdata>* [*<comment>*]

Here, *name* is the name for this record. It can be a domain name or a hostname (fully qualified domain name). If you specify only the hostname, the default domain is appended. If no name entry exists, the last specific name is used. If the @ symbol is used, the name server's domain name is used. *ttl* (time to live) is an optional entry that specifies how long the record is to be cached ($TTL directive sets default). *class* is the class of the record. The class used in most resource record entries is IN, for Internet. By default, it is the same as that specified for the domain in the **named.conf** file. *type* is the type of the record. *rdata* is the resource record data. The following is an example of a resource record entry. The name is **rabbit.mytrek.com**, the class is Internet (IN), the type is a host address record (A), and the data is the IP address 192.168.0.2.

```
rabbit.mytrek.com.     IN   A    192.168.0.2
```

Resource Record Types

Different types of resource records exist for different kinds of hosts and name server operations (see Table 15-7 for a listing of resource record types). A, NS, MX, PTR, and CNAME are the types commonly used. A is used for host address records that match domain names with IP addresses. NS is used to reference a name server. MX specifies the host address of the mail server that services this zone. The name server has mail messages sent to that host. The PTR type is used for records that point to other resource records and is used for reverse mapping. CNAME is used to identify an alias for a host on your system.

Type	Description
A	An IPv4 host address, maps hostname to IPv4 address
A6	An IPv6 host address
NS	Authoritative name server for this zone
CNAME	Canonical name, used to define an alias for a hostname
SOA	Start of Authority, starts DNS entries in zone file, specifies name server for domain, and other features such as server contact and serial number
WKS	Well-known service description
PTR	Pointer record, for performing reverse domain name lookups, maps IP address to hostname
RP	Text string that contains contact information about a host
HINFO	Host information
MINFO	Mailbox or mail list information
MX	Mail exchanger, informs remote site of your zone's mail server
TXT	Text strings, usually information about a host
KEY	Domain private key
SIG	Resource record signature
NXT	Next resource record

Table 15-7: Domain Name System Resource Record Types

Time To Live Directive and Field: $TTL

All zone files begin with a Time To Live directive, which specifies the time that a client should keep the provided DNS information before refreshing the information again from the DNS server. Realistically this should be at least a day, though if changes in the server are scheduled sooner, you can temporarily shorten the time, later restoring it. Each record, in fact, has a Time To Live value that can be explicitly indicated with the TTL field. This is the second field in a resource record. If no TTL field is specified in the record, then the default as defined by the $TLL directive can be used. The $TTL directive is placed at the beginning of each zone file. By default it will list the time in seconds, usually 86400, 24 hours.

```
$TTL 86400
```

You can also specify the time in days (d), hours (h), or minutes (m), as in

```
$TTL 2d3h
```

When used as a field, the TTL will be a time specified as the second field. In the following example, the turtle resource record can be cached for three days. This will override the default time in the TTL time directive:

```
turtle    3d    IN   A    192.168.0.1
```

Start of Authority: SOA

A zone or reverse mapping file always begins with a special resource record called the Start of Authority (SOA) record. This record specifies that all the following records are authoritative for this domain. It also holds information about the name server's domain, which is to be given to other name servers. An SOA record has the same format as other resource records, though its data segment is arranged differently. The format for an SOA record follows:

```
name {ttl} class SOA Origin Person-in-charge (
                          Serial number
                          Refresh
                          Retry
                          Expire
                          Minimum )
```

Each zone has its own SOA record. The SOA begins with the zone name specified in the **named.conf** zone entry. This is usually a domain name. An @ symbol is usually used for the name and acts like a macro expanding to the domain name. The *class* is usually the Internet class, IN. *SOA* is the type. *Origin* is the machine that is the origin of the records, usually the machine running your name server daemon. The *person-in-charge* is the e-mail address for the person managing the name server (use dots, not @, for the e-mail address, as this symbol is used for the domain name). Several configuration entries are placed in a block delimited with braces. The first is the *serial number*. You change the serial number when you add or change records, so that it is updated by other servers. The serial number can be any number, as long as it is incremented each time a change is made to any record in the zone. A common practice is to use the year-month-day-number for the serial number, where number is the number of changes in that day. For example, 1999120403 would be the year 1999, December 4, for the third change. Be sure to update it when making changes.

Refresh specifies the time interval for refreshing SOA information. *Retry* is the frequency for trying to contact an authoritative server. *Expire* is the length of time a secondary name server keeps information about a zone without updating it. *Minimum* is the length of time records in a zone live. The times are specified in the number of seconds.

The following example shows an SOA record. The machine running the name server is **turtle.mytrek.com,** and the e-mail address of the person responsible for the server is **hostmaster.turtle.mytrek.com**. Notice the periods at the ends of these names. For names with no periods, the domain name is appended. **turtle** would be the same as **turtle.mytrek.com**. When entering full hostnames, be sure to add the period so that the domain is not appended.

```
@ IN SOA turtle.mytrek.com. hostmaster.turtle.mytrek.com. (
                        1997022700 ; Serial
                        28800 ; Refresh
                        14400 ; Retry
                        3600000 ; Expire
                        86400 ) ; Minimum
```

Name Server: NS

The name server record specifies the name of the name server for this zone. These have a resource record type of NS. If you have more than one name server, list them in NS records. These records usually follow the SOA record. As they usually apply to the same domain as the SOA record, their name field is often left blank to inherit the server's domain name specified by the @ symbol in the previous SOA record.

```
        IN    NS       turtle.mytrek.com.
```

You can, if you wish, enter the domain name explicitly as shown here:

```
mytrek.com.  IN   NS       turtle.mytrek.com.
```

Address Record: A and A6

Resource records of type A are address records that associate a fully qualified domain name with an IP address. Often, only their hostname is specified. Any domain names without a terminating period automatically have the domain appended to them. Given the domain **mytrek.com**, the **turtle** name in the following example is expanded to **turtle.mytrek.com**:

```
rabbit.mytrek.com. IN    A      192.168.0.2
turtle             IN    A      192.168.0.1
```

BIND supports IPv6 addresses. IPv6 IP addresses have a very different format from that of the IPv4 addresses commonly used. Instead of the numerals arranged in four segments, IPv6 uses hexadecimal numbers arranged in seven segments. In the following example, **turtle.mytrek.com** is associated with a site-local IPv6 address: **fec0::.** Recall that there are only three fields in a site-local address: format prefix, subnet identifier, and interface identifier. The empty segments of the subnet identifier can be represented by an empty colon pair (::). The interface identifier follows, **8:800:200C:417A**.

```
turtle.mytrek.com. IN    A6     FEC0::8:800:200C:417A
```

IPv6 also supports the use of IPv4 addresses as an interface identifier, instead of the MAC-derived identifier. The network information part of the IPv6 address would use IPv6 notation, and the remaining interface (host) identifier would use the full IPv4 address. These are known as mixed addresses. In the next example, **lizard.mytrek.com** is given a mixed address using IPv6 network information and IPv4 interface information. The IPv6 network information is for an IPv6 site-local address.

```
lizard.mytrek.com. IN      A6      fec0::192.168.0.3
```

The AAAA record is an older and deprecated version of an IPv6 record. It is still in use in many networks. An AAAA record operates much like a standard A address record, requiring a full IPv6 address. You can do the same with an A6 record. An A6 record, though, can be more flexible, in that it does not require a full address. Instead you chain A6 records together, specifying just part of the address in each. For example, you could specify just an interface identifier for a host, letting the network information be provided by another IPv6 record. In the next example, the first A6 record lists only the address for the interface identifier for the host **divit**. Following the address is the domain name, **mytrek.com**, whose address is to be used to complete **divit**'s address, providing network information. The next A6 record provides the network address information for **mytrek.com**.

```
divit.mygolf.com. IN    A6    0:0:0:0:1234:5678:3466:af1f  mytrek.com.
mytrek.com.       IN    A6    3ffe:8050:201:1860::
```

Mail Exchanger: MX

The Mail Exchanger record, MX, specifies the mail server that is used for this zone or for a particular host. The mail exchanger is the server to which mail for the host is sent. In the following example, the mail server is specified as **turtle.mytrek.com**. Any mail sent to the address for any machines in that zone will be sent to the mail server, which in turn will send it to the specific machines. For example, mail sent to a user on **rabbit.mytrek.com** will first be sent to **turtle.mytrek.com**, which will then send it on to **rabbit.mytrek.com**. In the following example, the host 192.168.0.1 (**turtle.mytrek.com**) is defined as the mail server for the **mytrek.com** domain:

```
mytrek.com. IN      MX    10    turtle.mytrek.com.
```

You could also inherit the domain name from the SOA record, leaving the domain name entry blank.

```
            IN      MX    turtle.mytrek.com.
```

You could use the IP address instead, but in larger networks, the domain name may be needed to search for and resolve the IP address of a particular machine, which could change.

```
mytrek.com. IN      MX    10    192.168.0.1
```

An MX record recognizes an additional field that specifies the ranking for a mail exchanger. If your zone has several mail servers, you can assign them different rankings in their MX records. The smaller number has a higher ranking. This way, if mail cannot reach the first mail server, it can be routed to an alternate server to reach the host. In the following example, mail for hosts on the **mytrek.com** domain is first routed to the mail server at 192.168.0.1 (**turtle.mytrek.com**), and if that fails, it is routed to the mail server at 192.168.0.2 (**rabbit.mytrek.com**).

```
mytrek.com. IN MX 10 turtle.mytrek.com.
            IN MX 20 rabbit.mytrek.com.
```

You can also specify a mail server for a particular host. In the following example, the mail server for **lizard.mytrek.com** is specified as **rabbit.mytrek.com**:

```
lizard.mytrek.com. IN      A        192.168.0.3
                   IN      MX  10   rabbit.mytrek.com.
```

Aliases: CNAME

Resource records of type CNAME are used to specify alias names for a host in the zone. Aliases are often used for machines running several different types of servers, such as both Web and FTP servers. They are also used to locate a host when it changes its name. The old name becomes an alias for the new name. In the following example, **ftp.mytrek.com** is an alias for a machine actually called **turtle.mytrek.com**:

```
ftp.mytrek.com. IN CNAME turtle.mytrek.com.
```

The term CNAME stands for canonical name. The canonical name is the actual name of the host. In the preceding example, the canonical name is **turtle.mytrek.com**. The alias, also known as the CNAME, is **ftp.mytrek.com**. In a CNAME entry, the alias points to the canonical name. Aliases cannot be used for NS (name server) or MX (mail server) entries. For those records, you need to use the original domain name or IP address.

A more stable way to implement aliases is simply to create another address record for a host or domain. You can have as many hostnames for the same IP address as you want, provided they are certified. For example, to make **www.mytrek.com** an alias for **turtle.mytrek.com**, you only have to add another address record for it, giving it the same IP address as **turtle.mytrek.com**.

```
turtle.mytrek.com. IN A 192.168.0.1
www.mytrek.com. IN A 192.168.0.1
```

Pointer Record: PTR

A PTR record is used to perform reverse mapping from an IP address to a host. PTR records are used in the reverse mapping files. The name entry holds a reversed IP address, and the data entry holds the name of the host. The following example maps the IP address 192.168.0.1 to **turtle.mytrek.com**:

```
1.1.168.192 IN PTR turtle.mytrek.com.
```

In a PTR record, you can specify just that last number segment of the address (the host address) and let DNS fill in the domain part of the address. In the next example, 1 has the domain address, 1.168.192, automatically added to give 1.1.168.192:

```
1 IN PTR turtle.mytrek.com.
```

Host Information: HINFO, RP, MINFO, and TXT

The HINFO, RP, MINFO, and TXT records are used to provide information about the host. The RP record enables you to specify the person responsible for a certain host. The HINFO record provides basic hardware and operating system identification. The TXT record is used to enter any text you want. MINFO provides a host's mail and mailbox information. These are used sparingly, as they may give too much information out about the server.

Zone Files

A DNS server uses several zone files covering different components of the DNS. Each zone uses two zone files: the principal zone file and a reverse mapping zone file. The *zone file* contains the resource records for hosts in the zone. A *reverse mapping file* contains records that provide reverse mapping of your domain name entries, enabling you to map from IP addresses to domain names. The name of the file used for the zone file can technically be any name, but on the Ubuntu server zone files use the prefix **db**, as in **db.local** for the localhost zone. The name of the file is specified in the `zone` statement's file entry in the **named.conf** and **named.conf.local** files. If your server supports several zones, you may want to use a name that denotes the specific zone. Most systems use the domain name as the name of the zone file. For example, the zone **mytrek.com** would have a zone file with the same name and the prefix **db**, as in **db.mytrek.com**. The zone file used in the following example is called **db.mytrek.com**. The reverse mapping file can also be any name, though it is usually the reverse IP address domain specified in its corresponding zone file. For example, in the case of **mytrek.com.zone** zone file, the reverse mapping file might be called **db.192.168.0**, the IP address of the **mytrek.com** domain defined in the **db.mytrek.com.** zone file. This file would contain reverse mapping of all the host addresses in the domain, allowing their hostname addresses to be mapped to their corresponding IP addresses. In addition, BIND sets up a cache file and a reverse mapping file for the localhost. The cache file holds the resource records for the root name servers to which your name server connects. The cache file can be any name, although it is usually called **db.root**. The localhost reverse mapping file holds reverse IP resource records for the local loopback interface, localhost. Although localhost can be any name, it usually has the name **db.local**. The IPv6 version could be **db.ip6.local**.

Once you have created your zone files, you should check their syntax with the `named-checkzone` tool. This tool requires that you specify both a zone and a zone file. In the following example, in the **/etc/bind** directory, the zone **mytrek.com** in the zone file **db,mytrek.com** is checked:

```
named-checkzone  mytrek.com db.mytrek.com
```

Zone Files for Internet Zones

A zone file holds resource records that follow a certain format. The file begins with general directives to define default domains or to include other resource record files. These are followed by a single SOA record, name server and domain resource records, and then resource records for the different hosts. Comments begin with a semicolon and can be placed throughout the file. The @ symbol operates like a special macro, representing the domain name of the zone to which the records apply. The @ symbol is used in the first field of a resource or SOA record as the zone's domain name. Multiple names can be specified using the * matching character. The first field in a resource record is the name of the domain to which it applies. If the name is left blank, the previous explicit name entry in another resource record is automatically used. This way, you can list several entries that apply to the same host without having to repeat the hostname. Any host or domain name used throughout this file that is not terminated with a period has the zone's domain appended to it. For example, if the zone's domain is **mytrek.com** and a resource record has only the name **rabbit** with no trailing period, the zone's domain is automatically appended to it, giving you **rabbit.mytrek.com.**. Be sure to include the trailing period whenever you enter the complete fully qualified domain name, **turtle.mytrek.com.**, for example.

Directives

You can also use several directives to set global attributes. $ORIGIN sets a default domain name to append to address names that do not end in a period. $INCLUDE includes a file. $GENERATE can generate records whose domain or IP addresses differ only by an iterated number. The $ORIGIN directive is often used to specify the root domain to use in address records. Be sure to include the trailing period. The following example sets the domain origin to **mytrek.com** and will be automatically appended to the **lizard** host name that follows:

```
$ORIGIN  mytrek.com.
lizard   IN   A    192.168.0.2
```

SOA Record

A zone file begins with an SOA record specifying the machine the name server is running on, among other specifications. The @ symbol is used for the name of the SOA record, denoting the zone's domain name. After the SOA, the name server resource records (NS) are listed. Just below the name server records are resource records for the domain itself. Resource records for host addresses (A), aliases (CNAME), and mail exchangers (MX) follow. The following example shows a sample zone file, which begins with an SOA record and is followed by an NS record, resource records for the domain, and then resource records for individual hosts:

```
; Authoritative data for turle.mytrek.com
;
$TTL 86400
@ IN SOA turtle.mytrek.com. hostmaster.turtle.mytrek.com.(
                          93071200 ; Serial number
                             10800 ; Refresh 3 hours
                              3600 ; Retry 1 hour
                           3600000 ; Expire 1000 hours
                             86400 ) ; Minimum 24 hours

            IN        NS          turtle.mytrek.com.
            IN        A           192.168.0.1
            IN        MX    10    turtle.mytrek.com.
            IN        MX    15    rabbit.mytrek.com.

turtle      IN        A           192.168.0.1
            IN        HINFO       PC-686 LINUX
ftp         IN        CNAME       turtle.mytrek.com.
www         IN        A           192.168.0.1

rabbit      IN        A           192.168.0.2

lizard      IN        A           192.168.0.3
            IN        HINFO       MAC MACOS
localhost   IN        A           127.0.0.1
```

The first two lines are comments about the server for which this zone file is used. Notice that the first two lines begin with a semicolon. The class for each of the resource records in this file is IN, indicating these are Internet records. The SOA record begins with an @ symbol that stands for the zone's domain. In this example, it is **mytrek.com**. Any host or domain name used throughout this file that is not terminated with a period has this domain appended to it. For example, in the following resource record, **turtle** has no period, so it automatically expands to **turtle.mytrek.com**. The same happens for **rabbit** and **lizard**. These are read as **rabbit.mytrek.com** and **lizard.mytrek.com**. Also, in the SOA, notice that the e-mail address for hostmaster uses a period instead of an @ symbol; @ is a special symbol in zone files and cannot be used for any other purpose.

Nameserver Record

The next resource record specifies the name server for this zone. Here, it is **mytrek.com.**. Notice the name for this resource record is blank. If the name is blank, a resource record inherits the name from the previous record. In this case, the NS record inherits the value of @ in the SOA record, its previous record. This is the zone's domain, and the NS record specifies **turtle.mytrek.com** as the name server for this zone.

```
         IN   NS    turtle.mytrek.com.
```

Here the domain name is inherited. The entry can be read as the following. Notice the trailing period at the end of the domain name:

```
mytrek.com. IN   NS    turtle.mytrek.com.
```

Address Record

The following address records set up an address for the domain itself. This is often the same as the name server, in this case 192.168.0.1 (the IP address of **turtle.mytrek.com**). This enables users to reference the domain itself, rather than a particular host in it. A mail exchanger record follows that routes mail for the domain to the name server. Users can send mail to the **mytrek.com** domain and it will be routed to **turtle.mytrek.com**.

```
         IN   A     192.168.0.1
```

Here the domain name is inherited. The entry can be read as the following:

```
mytrek.com. IN   A     192.168.0.1
```

Mail Exchanger Record

The next records are mail exchanger (MX) records listing **turtle.mytrek.com** and **fast.mytrek.com** as holding the mail servers for this zone. You can have more than one mail exchanger record for a host. More than one host may exist through which mail can be routed. These can be listed in mail exchanger records for which you can set priority rankings (a smaller number ranks higher). In this example, if **turtle.mytrek.com** cannot be reached, its mail is routed through **rabbit.mytrek.com**, which has been set up also to handle mail for the **mytrek.com** domain:

```
         IN   MX    100   turtle.mytrek.com.
         IN   MX    150   rabbit.mytrek.com.
```

Again the domain name is inherited. The entries can be read as the following:

```
mytrek.com.   IN   MX 100   turtle.mytrek.com.
mytrek.com.   IN   MX 150   rabbit.mytrek.com.
```

Address Record with Host Name

The following resource record is an address record (A) that associates an IP address with the fully qualified domain name **turtle.mytrek.com**. The resource record name holds only **turtle** with no trailing period, so it is automatically expanded to **turtle.mytrek.com**. This record provides the IP address to which **turtle.mytrek.com** can be mapped.

```
turtle   IN   A      192.168.0.1
```

Inherited Names

Several resource records immediately follow that have blank names. These inherit their names from the preceding full record—in this case, **turtle.mytrek.com**. In effect, these records also apply to that host. Using blank names is an easy way to list additional resource records for the same host (notice that an apparent indent occurs). The first record is an information record, providing the hardware and operating system for the machine.

```
         IN   HINFO    PC-686 LINUX
```

Alias Records

If you are using the same machine to run several different servers, such as Web and FTP,servers, you may want to assign aliases to these servers to make accessing them easier for users. Instead of using the actual domain name, such as **turtle.mytrek.com**, to access the Web server running on it, users may find using the following is easier: for the Web server, **www.mytrek.com**; and for the FTP server, **ftp.mytrek.com**. In the DNS, you can implement such a feature using alias records. In the example zone file, one CNAME alias records exist for the **turtle.mytrek.com** machine: FTP. The next record implements an alias for **www** using another address record for the same machine. None of the name entries ends in a period, so they are appended automatically with the domain name **mytrek.com**. **www.mytrek.com** and **ftp.mytrek.com** are aliases for **turtle.mytrek.com**. Users entering those URLs automatically access the respective servers on the **turtle.mytrek.com** machine.

Loopback Record

Address and mail exchanger records are then listed for the two other machines in this zone: **rabbit.mytrek.com** and **lizard.mytrek.com**. You could add HINFO, TXT, MINFO, or alias records for these entries. The file ends with an entry for localhost, the special loopback interface that allows your system to address itself.

IPv6 Zone File Example

This is the same zone file using IPv6 addresses. The addresses are site-local (FEC0), instead of global (3), providing private network addressing. The loopback device is represented by the IPv6 address `::1`. The A6 IPv6 address records are used.

Reverse Mapping File

Reverse name lookups are enabled using a reverse mapping file. *Reverse mapping* files map fully qualified domain names to IP addresses. This reverse lookup capability is unnecessary, but it is convenient to have. With reverse mapping, when users access remote hosts, their domain name addresses can be used to identify their own host, instead of only the IP address. The name of the file can be anything you want. On most current distributions, it is the zone's domain address (the network part of a zone's IP address). For example, the reverse mapping file for a zone with the IP address of 192.168.0.1 is 192.168.0. Its full pathname would be something like

/var/named/192.168.0. On some systems using older implementations of BIND, the reverse mapping filename may consist of the root name of the zone file with the extension **.rev**. For example, if the zone file is called **mytrek.com**, the reverse mapping file would be called something like **mytrek.rev**.

```
; Authoritative data for turle.mytrek.com, IPv6 version
;
$TTL 1d
@ IN SOA turtle.mytrek.com. hostmaster.turtle.mytrek.com. (
                          93071200 ; Serial number
                            10800 ; Refresh 3 hours
                             3600 ; Retry 1 hour
                          3600000 ; Expire 1000 hours
                            86400 ) ; Minimum 24 hours


               IN     NS        turtle.mytrek.com.
               IN     A6        FEC0::8:800:200C:417A
               IN     MX   10   turtle.mytrek.com.
               IN     MX   15   rabbit.mytrek.com.

turtle         IN     A6        FEC0::8:800:200C:417A
               IN     HINFO     PC-686 LINUX
ftp            IN     CNAME     turtle.mytrek.com.
www            IN     A6        FEC0::8:800:200C:417A

rabbit         IN     A6        FEC0::FEDC:BA98:7654:3210

lizard         IN     A6        FEC0::E0:18F7:3466:7D
               IN     HINFO     MAC MACOS
localhost      IN     A6        ::1
```

IPv4 IN-ADDR.ARPA Reverse Mapping Format

In IPv4, the zone entry for a reverse mapping in the **named.conf** and **named.conf.local** files use a special domain name consisting of the IP address in reverse, with an **in-addr.arpa** extension. This reverse IP address becomes the zone domain referenced by the @ symbol in the reverse mapping file. For example, the reverse mapping zone name for a domain with the IP address of **192.168.43** would be **43.168.192.in-addr.arpa**. In the following example, the reverse domain name for the domain address **192.168.0** is **1.168.192.in-addr.arpa**:

```
zone "1.168.192.in-addr.arpa" in {
        type master;
        file "db.192.168.0";
        };
```

A reverse mapping file begins with an SOA record, which is the same as that used in a forward mapping file. Resource records for each machine defined in the forward mapping file then follow. These resource records are PTR records that point to hosts in the zone. These must be actual hosts, not aliases defined with CNAME records. Records for reverse mapping begin with a reversed IP address. Each segment in the IP address is sequentially reversed. Each segment begins with the host ID, followed by reversed network numbers. If you list only the host ID with no trailing period, the zone domain is automatically attached. In the case of a reverse mapping file, the zone domain as specified in the **zone** statement is the domain IP address backward. The 1 expands to 1.1.168.192. In the following example, **turtle** and **lizard** inherit the domain IP address, whereas **rabbit** has its address explicitly entered:

```
; reverse mapping of domain names 1.168.192.IN-ADDR.ARPA
;
$TTL 86400
@ IN SOA turtle.mytrek.com. hostmaster.turtle.mytrek.com.(
                        92050300 ; Serial (yymmddxx format)
                        10800 ; Refresh 3hHours
                        3600 ; Retry 1 hour
                        3600000 ; Expire 1000 hours
                        86400 ) ; Minimum 24 hours


@             IN    NS    turtle.mytrek.com.
1             IN    PTR   turtle.mytrek.com.
2.1.168.192   IN    PTR   rabbit.mytrek.com.
3             IN    PTR   lizard.mytrek.com.
```

IPv6 IP6.ARPA Reverse Mapping Format

In IPv6, reverse mapping can be handled either with the current IP6.ARPA domain format, or with the older IP6.INT format. With IP6.ARPA, the address is represented by a bit-level representation that places the hexadecimal address within brackets. The first bracket is preceded by a backslash. The address must be preceded by an *x* indicating that it is a hexadecimal address. Following the address is a number indicating the number of bits referenced. In a 128-bit address, usually the first 64 bits reference the network address and the last 64 bits are for the interface address. The following example shows the network and interface addresses for lizard.

```
FEC0:0000:0000:0000:00E0:18F7:3466:007D   lizard IPv6 address
\[xFEC0000000000000/64]                   lizard network address
\[x00E018F73466007D/64]                   lizard interface address
```

The zone entry for a reverse mapping in the **named.conf** file with an **IP6.ARPA** extension would use the bit-level representation for the network address.

```
zone "\[xfec0000000000000/64].IP6.ARPA" in {
        type master;
        file "fec.ip6.arpa";
        };
```

A reverse mapping file then uses the same bit-level format for the interface addresses.

```
$TTL 1d
@ IN SOA turtle.mytrek.com. hostmaster.turtle.mytrek.com.(
                        92050300 ; Serial (yymmddxx format)
                        10800 ; Refresh 3hHours
                        3600 ; Retry 1 hour
                        3600000 ; Expire 1000 hours
                        86400 ) ; Minimum 24 hours


@                             IN    NS    turtle.mytrek.com.
\[x00080800200C417A/64]       IN    PTR   turtle.mytrek.com.
\[xFEDCBA9876543210/64]       IN    PTR   rabbit.mytrek.com.
\[x00E018F73466007D/64]       IN    PTR   lizard.mytrek.com.
```

Localhost Reverse Mapping

A localhost reverse mapping file implements reverse mapping for the local loopback interface known as *localhost,* whose network address is 127.0.0.1. This file can be any name. localhost is given the name **named.local** for IPv4 and **named.ip6.local** for IPv6 addressing. On other systems, localhost may use the network part of the IP address, 127.0.0. This file allows mapping the domain name localhost to the localhost IP address, which is always 127.0.0.1 on every machine. The address 127.0.0.1 is a special address that functions as the local address for your machine. It allows a machine to address itself. In the `zone` statement for this file, the name of the zone is **127.in-addr.arpa**. The domain part of the IP address is entered in reverse order, with **in-addr.arpa** appended to it, **127.in-addr.arpa**. The **named.conf** entry is shown here:

```
zone "127.in-addr.arpa" {
        type master;
        file " /etc/bind/db.127";
        };
```

IPv4 Locahost

The name of the file used for the localhost reverse mapping file is usually **db.local**, though it can be any name. The NS record specifies the name server localhost should use. This file has a PTR record that maps the IP address to the localhost. The 1 used as the name expands to append the zone domain—in this case, giving you 1.0.0.127, a reverse IP address. The contents of the **db.local** file are shown here. Notice the trailing periods for localhost:

```
;
; BIND reverse data file for local loopback interface
;
$TTL    604800
@      IN     SOA     localhost. root.localhost. (
                                 1         ; Serial
                            604800         ; Refresh
                             86400         ; Retry
                           2419200         ; Expire
                            604800 )       ; Negative Cache TTL
;
        IN     NS      turtle.mytrek.com.
@       IN     NS      localhost.
1.0.0   IN     PTR     localhost.
```

IPv6 Locahost

In IPv6, localhost reverse mapping is specified using the reverse of the IPv6 localhost address. This address consists of 31 zeros and a 1, which can be written in shorthand as **::1**, where :: represents the sequence of 31 zeros. With IPv6 IP6.ARPA format, these can be written in a bit-level format, where the first 64 bits consist of a network address of all zeros, and the interface address has the value 1.

```
0000:0000:0000:0000:0000:0000:0000:0001   locahost IPv6 address
\[x00000000000000000000000000000001/128]   localhost address
```

In the **named.conf** file, the IP6.ARPA localhost entry would look like this:

```
zone "\[x0000000000000000000000000000001/64].IP6.ARPA" in {
        type master;
        file "named.ip6.local";
        };
```

In the localhost reverse mapping file, the localhost entry would appear like this:

```
\[x0000000000000001/64]       IN      PTR    localhost.
```

Subdomains and Slaves

Adding a subdomain to a DNS server is a simple matter of creating an additional master entry in the **named.conf** file, and then placing name server and authority entries for that subdomain in your primary DNS server's zone file. The subdomain, in turn, has its own zone file with its SOA record and entries listing hosts, which are part of its subdomain, including any of its own mail and news servers.

Subdomain Zones

The name for the subdomain could be a different name altogether or a name with the same suffix as the primary domain. In the following example, the subdomain is called **beach.mytrek.com**. It could just as easily be called **mybeach.com**. The name server to that domain is on the host **crab.beach.mytrek.com**, in this example. Its IP address is 192.168.0.33, and its zone file is **db.beach.mytrek.com**. The **beach.mytrek.com** zone file holds DNS entries for all the hosts being serviced by this name server. The following example shows zone entries for its **named.conf**:

```
zone "beach.mytrek.com" {
        type master;
        file "db.beach.mytrek.com";
        };

zone "1.168.192.IN-ADDR.ARPA" {
        type master;
        file "192.168.0";
        };
```

Subdomain Records

On the primary DNS server, in the example **turtle.mytrek.com**, you would place entries in the master zone file to identify the subdomain server's host and designate it as a name server. Such entries are also known as *glue records*. In this example, you would place the following entries in the **mytrek.com** zone file on **turtle.mytrek.com**:

```
beach.mytrek.com.    IN    NS    beach.mytrek.com.
beach.mytrek.com.    IN    A     192.168.0.33.
```

URL references to hosts serviced by **beach.mytrek.com** can now be reached from any host serviced by **mytrek.com**, which does not need to maintain any information about the **beach.mytrek.com** hosts. It simply refers such URL references to the **beach.mytrek.com** name server.

Slave Servers

A slave DNS server is tied directly to a master DNS server and periodically receives DNS information from it. You use a master DNS server to configure its slave DNS servers automatically. Any changes you make to the master server are automatically transferred to its slave servers. This transfer of information is called a *zone transfer*. Zone transfers are automatically initiated whenever the slave zone's refresh time is reached or the slave server receives a notify message from the master. The *refresh time* is the second argument in the zone's SOA entry. A notify message is automatically sent by the master whenever changes are made to the master zone's configuration files and the **named** daemon is restarted. In effect, slave zones are automatically configured by the master zone, receiving the master zone's zone files and making them their own.

Slave Zones

Using the previous examples, suppose you want to set up a slave server on **rabbit.mytrek.com**. Zone entries, as shown in the following example, are set up in the **named.conf** configuration file for the slave DNS server on **rabbit.mytrek.com**. The slave server is operating in the same domain as the master, and so it has the same zone name, **mytrek.com**. Its SOA file is named **slave.mytrek.com**. The term "slave" in the filename is merely a convention that helps identify it as a slave server configuration file. The **masters** statement lists its master DNS server—in this case, 192.168.0.1. Whenever the slave needs to make a zone transfer, it transfers data from that master DNS server. The entry for the reverse mapping file for this slave server lists its reverse mapping file as **slave.192.168.0**.

```
zone "mytrek.com" {
        type slave;
        file "slave.mytrek.com";
        masters { 192.168.0.1;
        };

zone "1.168.192.IN-ADDR.ARPA" {
        type slave;
        file "slave.192.168.0";
        masters { 192.168.0.1;
        };
```

Slave Records

On the master DNS server, the master SOA zone file has entries in it to identify the host that holds the slave DNS server and to designate it as a DNS server. In this example, you would place the following in the **mytrek.com** zone file:

```
        IN      NS      192.168.0.2
```

You would also place an entry for this name server in the **mytrek.com** reverse mapping file:

```
        IN      NS      192.168.0.2
```

Controlling Transfers

The master DNS server can control which slave servers can transfer zone information from it using the **allow-transfer** statement. Place the statement with the list of IP addresses for the slave servers to which you want to allow access. Also, the master DNS server should be sure its **notify** option is not disabled. The **notify** option is disabled by a "notify no" statement in the options or zone **named.conf** entries. Simply erase the "no" argument to enable notify.

Incremental Zone Transfers

With BIND versions 8.2.2 and 9.0, BIND now supports incremental zone transfers (IXFR). Previously, all the zone data would be replaced in an update, rather than changes such as the addition of a few resource records simply being edited in. With incremental zone transfers, a database of changes is maintained by the master zone. Then only the changes are transferred to the slave zone, which uses this information to update its own zone files. To implement incremental zone transfers, you have to turn on the **maintain-ixfr-base** option in the options section.

```
maintain-ixfr-base yes;
```

You can then use the **ixfr-base** option in a zone section specify a particular database file to hold changes.

```
ixfr-base "db.mytrek.com.ixfr";
```

IP Virtual Domains

IP-based virtual hosting allows more than one IP address to be used for a single machine.

```
zone "sail.com" in {
        type master;
        file "sail.com";
        };

; Authoritative data for sail.com
;
$TTL 1d
@ IN SOA turtle.mytrek.com. hostmaster.turtle.mytrek.com. (
                            93071200 ; Serial (yymmddxx)
                               10800 ; Refresh 3 hours
                                3600 ; Retry 1 hour
                             3600000 ; Expire 1000 hours
                               86400 ) ; Minimum 24 hours

        IN      NS          turtle.mytrek.com.
        IN      MX    10    turtle.mytrek.com.
        IN      A           192.168.0.42 ;address of the sail.com domain

jib     IN      A           192.168.0.42
www     IN      A           jib.sail.com.
ftp     IN      CNAME       jib.sail.com.
```

In your reverse mapping file (**/var/named/1.168.192**), add PTR records for any virtual domains.

```
42.1.168.192      IN      PTR     sail.com.
42.1.168.192      IN      PTR     jib.sail.com.
```

If a machine has two registered IP addresses, either one can be used to address the machine. If you want to treat the extra IP address as another host in your domain, you need only create an address record for it in your domain's zone file. The domain name for the host would be the same as your domain name. If you want to use a different domain name for the extra IP, however, you have to set up a virtual domain for it. This entails creating a new **zone** statement for it with its own zone file. For example, if the extra IP address is 192.168.0.42 and you want to give it the domain name **sail.com**, you must create a new **zone** statement for it in your **named.conf** file with a new zone file. The **zone** statement would look something like this. The zone file is called **sail.com**:

In the **sail.com** file, the name server name is **turtle.mytrek.com** and the e-mail address is **hostmaster@turtle.mytrek.com**. In the name server (NS) record, the name server is **turtle.mytrek.com.** This is the same machine using the original address that the name server is running as. **turtle.mytrek.com** is also the host that handles mail addressed to **sail.com** (MX). An address record then associates the extra IP address 192.168.0.42 with the **sail.com** domain name. A virtual host on this domain is then defined as **jib.sail.com**. Also, **www** and **ftp** aliases are created for that host, creating **www.sail.com** and **ftp.sail.com** virtual hosts.

You also have to configure your network connection to listen for both IP addresses on your machine.

Cache File

The *cache file* is used to connect the DNS server to root servers on the Internet. The file can be any name. On many systems, the cache file is called **named.ca**. Other systems may call the cache file **named.cache** or **roots.hints**. The cache file is usually a standard file installed by your BIND software, which lists resource records for designated root servers for the Internet. You can obtain a current version of the **named.ca** file from the **rs.internic.net** FTP site. The following example shows sample entries taken from the **named.ca** file:

```
; formerly NS.INTERNIC.NET
;
. 3600000 IN NS A.ROOT-SERVERS.NET.
A.ROOT-SERVERS.NET. 3600000 A 198.41.0.4
;
; formerly NS1.ISI.EDU
;
. 3600000 NS B.ROOT-SERVERS.NET.
B.ROOT-SERVERS.NET. 3600000 A 128.9.0.107
```

If you are creating an isolated intranet, you need to create your own root DNS server until you connect to the Internet. In effect, you are creating a fake root server. This can be another server on your system pretending to be the root or the same name server.

Dynamic Update: DHCP and Journal Files

There are situations where you will need to have zones updated dynamically. Instead of your manually editing a zone file to make changes in a zone, an outside process updates the zone, making changes and saving the file automatically. Dynamic updates are carried out both by master zones updating slave zones and by DHCP servers providing IP addresses they generated for hosts to the DNS server.

A journal file is maintained recording all the changes made to a zone, having a **.jnl** extension. Should a system crash occur, this file is read to implement the most current changes. Should you want to manually update a dynamically updated zone, you will need to erase its journal file first; otherwise, your changes would be overwritten by the journal file entries.

You allow a zone to be automatically updated by specifying the **allow-update** option. This option indicates the host that can perform the update.

```
allow-update {turtle.mytrek.com;};
```

Alternatively, for master zones, you can create a more refined set of access rules using the **update-policy** statement. With the **update-policy** statement, you can list several grant and deny rules for different hosts and types of hosts.

TSIG Signatures and Updates

With BIND 9.*x*, TSIG signature names can be used instead of host names or IP addresses for both **allow-update** and **update-policy** statements (see the following sections on TSIG). Use of TSIG signatures implements an authentication of a host performing a dynamic update, providing a much greater level of security. For example, to allow a DHCP server to update a zone file, you would place an **allow-update** entry in the zone statement listed in the **named.conf** file.

The TSIG key is defined in a key statement, naming the key previously created by the **dnssec-keygen** command. The algorithm is HMAC-MD5, and the secret is the encryption key listed in the **.private** file generated by **dnssec-keygen**.

```
key mydhcpserver {
algorithm HMAC-MD5;
secret "ONQAfbBLnvWU9H8hRqq/WA==";
};
```

The key name can then be used in an **allow-update** or **allow-policy** statement to specify a TSIG key.

```
allow-update { key mydhcpserver;};
```

Manual Updates: nsupdate

You can use the update procedure to perform any kind of update you want. You can perform updates manually or automatically using a script. For DHCP updates, the DHCP server is designed to perform dynamic updates of the DNS server. You will need to configure the DHCP server appropriately, specifying the TSIG key to use and the zones to update.

You can manually perform an update using the **nsupdate** command, specifying the file holding the key with the **-k** option.

```
nsupdate -k myserver.private
```

At the prompt, you can use **nsupdate** commands to implement changes. You match on a record using its full or partial entry. To update a record, you would first delete the old one and then add the changed version, as shown here:

```
update delete rabbit.mytrek.com. A 192.168.0.2
update add rabbit.mytrek.com. A 192.168.0.44
```

DNS Security: Access Control Lists, TSIG, and DNSSEC

DNS security currently allows you to control specific access by hosts to the DNS server, as well as providing encrypted communications between servers and authentication of DNS servers. With access control lists, you can determine who will have access to your DNS server. The DNS Security Extensions (DNSSEC), included with BIND 9.*x,* provide private/public key–encrypted authentication and transmissions. TSIGs (transaction signatures) use shared private keys to provide authentication of servers to secure actions such as dynamic updates between a DNS server and a DHCP server.

Access Control Lists

To control access by other hosts, you use access control lists, implemented with the `acl` statement. `allow` and `deny` options with access control host lists enable you to deny or allow access by specified hosts to the name server. With `allow-query`, you can restrict queries to specified hosts or networks. Normally this will result in a response saying that access is denied. You can further eliminate this response by using the `blackhole` option in the `options` statement.

You define an ACL with the `acl` statement followed by the label you want to give the list and then the list of addresses. Addresses can be IP addresses, network addresses, or a range of addresses based on CNDR notation. You can also use an ACL as defined earlier. The following example defines an ACL called **mynet**:

```
acl mynet { 192.168.0.1; 192.168.0.2; };
```

If you are specifying a range, such as a network, you also add exceptions to the list by preceding such addresses with an exclamation point (!). In the following example, the mynetx ACL lists all those hosts in the 192.168.0.0 network, except for 192.168.0.3:

```
acl myexceptions {192.168.0.0; !192.168.0.3; };
```

Four default ACLs are already defined for you. You can use them wherever an option uses a list of addresses as an argument. These are **any** for all hosts, **none** for no hosts, **localhost** for all local IP addresses, and **localnet** for all hosts on local networks served by the DNS server.

```
acl mynet { 192.168.0.0; };
acl myrejects { 10.0.0.44; 10.0.0.93; };

zone "mytrek.com" {
        type master;
        file "mytrek.com";
        allow-query { mynet; };
        allow-recursion { mynet; };
        allow-transfer { none; };
        blackhole {myrejects};
        };
```

Once a list is defined, you can then use it with the `allow-query`, `allow-transfer`, `allow-recursion`, and `blackhole` options in a `zone` statement to control access to a zone. `allow-query` specifies hosts that can query the DNS server. `allow-transfer` is used for master/slave zones, designating whether update transfers are allowed. `allow-recursion` specifies those hosts that can perform recursive queries on the server. The `blackhole` option will deny contact from any hosts in its list, without sending a denial response. In the next example, an ACL of mynet is created. Then in the **mytrek.com** zone, only these hosts are allowed to query the server. As the server has no slave DNS serves, zone transfers are disabled entirely. The `blackhole` option denies access from the myrejects list, without sending any rejection notice.

Secret Keys

Different security measures will use encryption keys generated with the `dnssec-keygen` command. You can use `dnssec-keygen` to create different types of keys, including zone (ZONE), host (HOST), and user (USER) keys. You specify the type of key with the `-n` option. A zone key will require the name ZONE and the name of the zone's domain name. A zone key is used in DNSSEC operations. The following example creates a zone key for the **mytrek.com** zone:

```
dnssec-keygen -n ZONE mytrek.com.
```

To create a host key, you would use the HOST type. HOST keys are often used in TSIG operations.

```
dnssec-keygen -n HOST turtle.mytrek.com.
```

You can further designate an encryption algorithm (`-a`) and key size (`-b`). Use the `-h` option to obtain a listing of the `dnssec-keygen` options. Currently you can choose from RSA, DSA, HMAC-MD5, and DH algorithms. The bit range will vary according to the algorithm. RSA ranges from 512 to 4096, and HMAC-MD5 ranges from 1 to 512. The following example creates a zone key using a 768-bit key and the DSA encryption algorithm:

```
dnssec-keygen -a DSA -b 768 -n ZONE mytrek.com.
```

The `dnssec-keygen` command will create public and private keys, each in corresponding files with the suffixes **.private** and **.key**. The **.key** file is a KEY resource record holding the public key. For DNSSEC, the private key is used to generate signatures for the zone, and the public key is used to verify the signatures. For TSIG, a shared private key generated by the HMAC-MD5 algorithm is used instead of a public/private key pair.

DNSSEC

DNSSEC provides encrypted authentication to DNS. With DNSSEC, you can create a signed zone that is securely identified with an encrypted signature. This form of security is used primarily to secure the connections between master and slave DNS servers, so that a master server transfers update records only to authorized slave servers and does so with a secure encrypted communication. Two servers that establish such a secure connection do so using a pair of public and private keys. In effect, you have a parent zone that can securely authenticate child zones, using encrypted transmissions. This involves creating zone keys for each child and having those keys used by the parent zone to authenticate the child zones.

Zone Keys

You generate a zone key using the `dnssec-keygen` command and specifying the zone type, ZONE, with the `-n` option. For the key name, you use the zone's domain name. The following example creates a zone key for the **mytrek.com** zone:

```
dnssec-keygen -n ZONE mytrek.com.
```

You can further designate an encryption algorithm (**-a**) and a key size (**-b**). Use the **-h** option to obtain a listing of the **dnssec-keygen** options. Since you are setting up a public/private key pair, you should choose either the RSA or DSA algorithm. The bit range will vary according to the algorithm. RSA ranges from 512 to 4096, and DSA ranges from 512 to 1024. The following example creates a zone key using a 768-bit key and the DSA encryption algorithm:

```
dnssec-keygen -a DSA -b 768 -n ZONE mytrek.com.
```

The **dnssec-keygen** command will create public and private keys, each in corresponding files with the suffixes **.private** and **.key**. The private key is used to generate signatures for the zone, and the public key is used to verify the signatures. The **.key** file is a KEY resource record holding the public key. This is used to decrypt signatures generated by the corresponding private key. You add the public key to the DNS configuration file, **named.conf**, using the **$INCLUDE** statement to include the **.key** file.

DNSSEC Resource Records

In the zone file, you then use three DNSSEC DNS resource records to implement secure communications for a given zone: KEY, SIG, and NXT. In these records, you use the signed keys for the zones you have already generated. The KEY record holds public keys associated with zones, hosts, or users. The SIG record stores digital signatures and expiration dates for a set of resource records. The NXT record is used to determine that a resource record for a domain does not exist. In addition, several utilities let you manage DNS encryption. With the **dnskeygen** utility, you generated the public and private keys used for encryption. **dnssigner** signs a zone using the zone's private key, setting up authentication.

To secure a DNS zone with DNSSEC, you first use **dnskeygen** to create public and private keys for the DNS zone. Then use **dnssigner** to create an authentication key. In the DNS zone file, you enter a KEY resource record in which you include the public key. The public key will appear as a lengthy string of random characters. For the KEY record, you enter in the domain name followed by the KEY and then the public key.

```
mytrek.com. KEY 0x4101 3 3 (
AvqyXgKk/uguxkJF/hbRpYzxZFG3x8EfNX389l7GX6w7rlLy
BJ14TqvrDvXr84XsShg+OFcUJafNr84U4ER2dg6NrlRAmZA1
jFfV0UpWDWcHBR2jJnvgV9zJB2ULMGJheDHeyztM1KGd2oGk
Aensm74NlfUqKzy/3KZ9KnQmEpj/EEBr48vAsgAT9kMjN+V3
NgAwfoqgS0dwj5OiRJoIR4+cdRt+s32OUKsclAODFZTdtxRn
vXF3qYV0S8oewMbEwh3trXi1c7nDMQC3RmoY8RVGt5U6LMAQ
KITDyHU3VmRJ36vn77QqSzbeUPz8zEnbpik8kHPykJZFkcyj
jZoHT1xkJ1tk )
```

For authentication, you can sign particular resource records for a given domain or host. Enter the domain or host followed by the term **SIG** and then the resource record's signature.

```
mytrek.com. SIG KEY 3 86400 19990321010705 19990218010705 4932 com. (
Am3tWJzEDzfU1xwg7hzkiJ0+8UQaPtlJhUpQx1snKpDUqZxm
igMZEVk= )
```

The NXT record lets you negatively answer queries.

```
mytrek.com. NXT ftp.mytrek.com. A NS SOA MX SIG KEY NXT
```

Signing Keys

To set up secure communications between a parent (master) DNS server and a child (slave) DNS server, the public key then needs to be sent to the parent zone. There, the key can be signed by the parent. As you may have more than zone key, you create a keyset using the **dnssec-makekeyset** command. This generates a file with the extension **.keyset** that is then sent to the parent. The parent zone then uses the **dnssec-signkey** command to sign a child's keyset. This generates a file with the prefix **signedkey-**. This is sent back to the child and now contains both the child's keyset and the parent's signatures. Once the child has the **signedkey-** files, the **dnssec-signedzone** command can be used to sign the zone. The **dnssec-signedzone** command will generate a file with the extension **.signed**. This file is then included in the **named.conf** file with the INCLUDE operation. The **trusted-keys** statement needs to list the public key for the parent zone.

TSIG Keys

TSIG (transaction signatures) also provide secure DNS communications, but they share the private key instead of a private/public key pair. They are usually used for communications between two local DNS servers, and to provide authentication for dynamic updates such as those between a DNS server and a DHCP server.

Note: For BIND 8.0, you use **dnskeygen** instead of **dnssec-keygen**.

Generating TSIG keys

To create a TSIG key for your DNS server, you use the **dnssec-keygen** command as described earlier. Instead of using the same keys you use for DNSSEC, you create a new set to use for transaction signatures. For TSIG, a shared private key is used instead of a public/private key pair. For a TSIG key you would use an HMAC-MD5 algorithm that generates the same key in the both the **.key** and **.private** files. Use the **-a** option to specify the HMAC-MD5 algorithm to use and the **-b** option for the bit size. (HMAC-MD5 ranges from 1 to 512.) Use the **-n** option to specify the key type, in this case HOST for the host name. The bit range will vary according to the algorithm. The following example creates a host key using a 128-bit key and the HMAC-MD5 encryption algorithm:

```
dnssec-keygen -a HMAC-MD5 -b 128 -n HOST turtle.mytrek.com
```

This creates a private key and a public key, located in the **.key** and **.private** files. In a TSIG scheme, both hosts would use the same private key for authentication. For example, to enable a DHCP server to update a DNS server, both would need the private (secret) key for a TSIG authentication. The HMAC-MD5 key is used as a shared private key, generating both the same private and public keys in the **.key** and **.private** files.

The Key Statement

You then specify a key in the **named.conf** file with the **key** statement. For the algorithm option, you list the HMAC-MD5 algorithm, and for the secret option, you list the private key. This key will be listed in both the **.private** and **.key** files. The preceding example would generate key and private files called **Kturtle.mytrek.com.+157.43080.key** and **Kturtle.mytrek.com.+157.43080.private**. The contents of the **.key** file consist of a resource record shown here:

```
turtle.mytrek.com. IN KEY 512 3 157 ONQAfbBLnvWU9H8hRqq/WA==
```

The contents of the private file show the same key along with the algorithm:

```
Private-key-format: v1.2
Algorithm: 157 (HMAC_MD5)
Key: ONQAfbBLnvWU9H8hRqq/WA==
```

Within the **named.conf** file, you then name the key using a **key** statement:

```
key myserver {
algorithm HMAC-MD5;
secret "ONQAfbBLnvWU9H8hRqq/WA==";
};
```

The key's name can then be used to reference the key in other named statements, such as **allow-update** statements:

```
allow-update myserver;
```

The DNS server or DHCP server with which you are setting up communication will also have to have the same key. See the earlier section "Dynamic Update: DHCP and Journal Files". For communication between two DNS servers, each would have to have a server statement specifying the shared key. In the following example, the **named.conf** file for the DNS server on 192.168.0.1 would have to have the following server statement to communicate with the DNS server on 10.0.0.1, using the shared myserver key. The **named.conf** file on the 10.0.0.1 DNS server would have to have a corresponding server statement for the 192.168.0.1 server.

```
server 10.0.0.1 { keys {myserver;}; };
```

Split DNS: Views

BIND 9.*x* allows you to divide DNS space into internal and external views. This organization into separate views is referred to as split DNS. Such a configuration is helpful to manage a local network that is connected to a larger network, such as the Internet. Your internal view would include DNS information on hosts in the local network, whereas an external view would show only the part of the DNS space that is accessible to other networks. DNS views are often used when you have a local network that you want to protect from a larger network such as the Internet. In effect, you protect DNS information for hosts on a local network from a larger external network such as the Internet.

Internal and External Views

To implement a split DNS space, you need to set up different DNS servers for the internal and external views. The internal DNS servers will hold DNS information about local hosts. The external DNS server maintains connections to the Internet through a gateway as well as manages DNS information about any local hosts that allow external access, such as FTP or Web sites. The gateways and Internet-accessible sites make up the external view of hosts on the network. The internal servers handle all queries to the local hosts or subdomains. Queries to external hosts such as Internet sites are sent to the external servers, which then forward them on to the Internet. Queries sent to those local hosts that operate external servers such as Internet FTP and Web sites are sent to the external DNS servers for processing. Mail sent to local hosts from the Internet is handled first by the external servers, which then forward messages on to the internal servers. With a split DNS configuration, local hosts can access other local hosts, Internet sites, and local hosts maintaining Internet servers. Internet users, on the other hand, can access only those hosts open to the Internet (served by external servers) such as those with Internet servers like FTP and HTTP. Internet users can, however, send mail messages to any of the local hosts, internal and external.

You can also use DNS views to manage connections between a private network that may use only one Internet address to connect its hosts to the Internet. In this case, the internal view holds the private addresses (192.168...), and the external view connects a gateway host with an Internet address to the Internet. This adds another level of security, providing a result similar to IP masquerading.

Configuring Views

DNS views are configured with the allow statements such as `allow-query` and `allow-transfer`. With these statements, you can specify the hosts that a zone can send and receive queries and transfers to and from. For example, the internal zone could accept queries from other local hosts, but not from local hosts with external access such as Internet servers. The local Internet servers, though, can accept queries from the local hosts. All Internet queries are forwarded to the gateway. In the external configuration, the local Internet servers can accept queries from anywhere. The gateways receive queries from both the local hosts and the local Internet servers.

In the following example, a network of three internal hosts and one external host is set up into a split view. There are two DNS servers: one for the internal network and one for external access, based on the external host. In reality these make up one network but they are split into two views. The internal view is known as **mygolf.com**, and the external as **greatgolf.com**. In each configuration, the internal hosts are designated in ACL-labeled internals, and the external host is designated in ACL-labeled externals. Should you want to designate an entire IP address range as internal, you could simply use the network address, as in 192.168.0.0/24. In the options section, `allow-query`, `allow-recursion`, and `allow-transfers` restrict access within the network.

Split View Example

The following example shows only the configuration entries needed to implement an internal view (see next page). In the **mygolf.com** zone, queries and transfers are allowed only among internal hosts. The global `allow-recursion` option allows recursion among internals.

Internal DNS server

```
acl internals { 192.168.0.1; 192.168.0.2; 192.168.0.3; };
acl externals {10.0.0.1;};
options {
          forward only;
          forwarders {10.0.0.1;}; // forward to external servers
          allow-transfer { none; }; // allow-transfer to no one by default
          allow-query { internals; externals; };// restrict query access
          allow-recursion { internals; }; // restrict recursion to internals
          }
zone "mygolf.com" {
          type master;
          file "mygolf";
          forwarders { };
          allow-query { internals; };
          allow-transfer { internals; }
          };
```

In the configuration for the external DNS server, the same ACLs are set up for internals and externals. In the **options** statement, recursion is now allowed for both externals and internals. In the **mygolf.com** zone, queries are allowed from anywhere, and recursion is allowed for externals and internals. Transfers are not allowed at all.

External DNS server

```
acl internals { 192.168.0.1; 192.168.0.2; 192.168.0.3; };
acl externals {10.0.0.1;};
options {
          allow-transfer { none; }; // allow-transfer to no one
          allow-query { internals; externals; };// restrict query access
          allow-recursion { internals; externals }; // restrict recursion
          };

zone "greatgolf.com" {
          type master;
          file "greatgolf";
          allow-query { any; };
          allow-transfer { internals; externals; };
};
```

16. Network Auto-configuration with IPv6, DHCPv6, and DHCP

Many networks now provide either IPv6 autoconfiguration or the DHCP (Dynamic Host Configuration Protocol) service, which automatically provides network configuration for all connected hosts. Autoconfiguration can be either stateless, as in the case of IPv6, or stateful, as with DHCP. Stateless IPv6 autoconfiguration requires no independent server or source to connect to a network. It is a direct plug-and-play operation, where the hardware network interfaces and routers can directly determine the correct addresses. DCHP is an older method that requires a separate server to manage and assign all addresses. Should this server ever fail, hosts cannot connect.

With the DHCP protocol, an administrator uses a pool of IP addresses from which the administrator can assign an IP address to a host as needed. The protocol can also be used to provide all necessary network connection information such as the gateway address for the network or the netmask. Instead of having to configure each host separately, network configuration can be handled by a central DHCP server. The length of time that an address can be used can be controlled by means of leases, making effective use of available addresses. If your network is configuring your systems with DHCP, you will not have to configure it.

There are currently two versions of DHCP, one for the original IPv4 protocol and another, known as DHCPv6, for the IPv6 protocol. The IPv6 protocol includes information for dynamic configuration that the IPv4 protocol lacks. In this respect, the IPv4 protocol is much more dependent on DHCP than IPv6 is.

IPv6 Stateless Autoconfiguration

In an IPv6 network, the IPv6 protocol includes information that can directly configure a host. With IPv4 you either had to manually configure each host or rely on a DHCP server to provide configuration information. With IPv6, configuration information is integrated into the Internet protocol directly. IPv6 address autoconfiguration is described in detail in RFC 2462.

IPv6 autoconfiguration capabilities are known as stateless, meaning that it can directly configure a host without recourse of an external server. Alternatively, DHCP, including DHCPv6, is stateful, where the host relies on an external DHCP server to provide configuration information. Stateless autoconfiguration has the advantage of hosts not having to rely on a DHCP server to maintain connections to a network. Networks can even become mobile, hooking into one subnet or another, automatically generating addresses as needed. Hosts are no longer tied to a particular DHCP server.

Generating the Local Address

To autoconfigure hosts on a local network, IPv6 makes use of the each network device's hardware MAC address. This address is used to generate a temporary address, with which the host can be queried and configured.

The MAC address is used to create a link-local address, one with a link-local prefix, **FE80::0**, followed by an interface identifier. The link-local prefix is used for physically connected hosts such as those on a small local network.

A uniqueness test is then performed on the generated address. Using the Neighbor Discovery Protocol (NDP), other hosts on the network are checked to see if another host is already using the generated link-local address. If no other host is using the address, then the address is assigned for that local network. At this point the host has only a local address valid within the local physical network. Link-local addresses cannot be routed to a larger network.

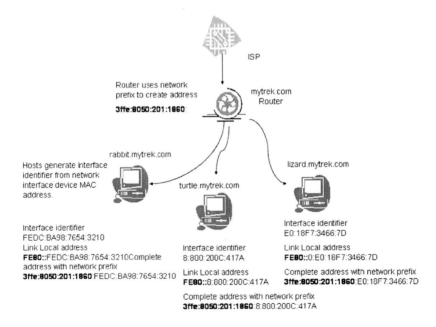

Figure 16-1: Stateless IPv6 address autoconfiguration

Generating the Full Address: Router Advertisements

Once the link-local address has been determined, the router for the network is queried for additional configuration information. The information can be either stateful or stateless, or both. For stateless configuration, information such as the network address is provided directly, whereas for stateful configuration, the host is referred to a DHCPv6 server where it can obtain configuration information. The two can work together. Often the stateless method is used for addresses, and the stateful DHCPv6 server is used to provide other configuration information such as DNS server addresses.

In the case of stateless addresses, the router provides the larger network address, such as the network's Internet address. This address is then added to the local address, replacing the original link-local prefix, giving either a complete global Internet address or, in the case of private networks, site-local addresses. Routers will routinely advertise this address information, though it can also be specifically requested. The NDP is used to query the information. Before the address is officially assigned, a duplicate address detection procedure checks to see if the address is already in use. The process depends on the router's providing the appropriate addressing information in the form of router advertisements. If there is no router, or there are no route advertisements, then a stateful method like DHCPv6 or manual configuration must be used to provide the addresses.

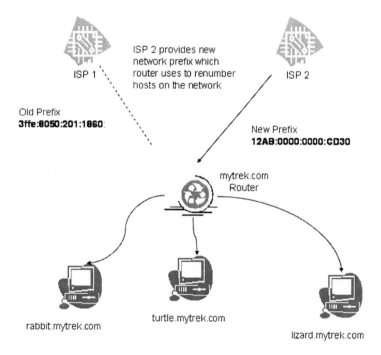

IPv6 Router Renumbering

Figure 16-2: Router renumbering with IPv6 autoconfiguration

Figure 16-1 shows a network that is configured with stateless address autoconfiguration. Each host first determines its interface identifier using its own MAC hardware address to create a temporary link-local address for each host using the **FE80::0** prefix. This allows initial communication with the network's router. The router then uses its network prefix to create full Internet addresses, replacing the link-local prefix.

Router Renumbering

With IPv6, routers have the ability to renumber the addresses on their networks by changing the network prefix. Renumbering is carried out through the Router Renumbering (RR) Protocol. (See RFC 2894 for a description of router renumbering.) Renumbering is often used when a network changes ISP providers and requires that the net address for all hosts be changed (see Figure 16-2). It can also be used for mobile networks where a network can be plugged in to different larger networks, renumbering each time.

With renumbering, routers place a time limit on addresses, similar to the lease time in DHCP, by specifying an expiration limit for the network prefix when the address is generated. To ease transition, interfaces still keep their old addresses as deprecated addresses, while the new one are first being used. The new ones will be the preferred addresses used for any new connections, while deprecated ones are used for older connections. In effect, a host can have two addresses, one deprecated and one preferred. This regeneration of addresses effectively renumbers the hosts.

IPv6 Stateful Autoconfiguration: DHCPv6

The IPv6 version of DHCP (DHCPv6) provides stateful autoconfiguration to those networks that still want a DHCP-like service on IPv6 networks. DHCP IPv6 provides configuration information from a server, just like DHCP, but it is a completely different protocol from the IPv4 version, with different options and capabilities. As a stateful configuration process, information is provided by an independent server. A version of the DHCP IPv6 server and client are available from the Wide project and located in the Ubuntu Universe repository. You can file out more about the Wide project at wide-dhcpv6.sourceforge.net. The server requires its own Wide DHCPv6 clients.

As with IPv6 autoconfiguration, the host identifier for a local address is first automatically generated. This is a local-link address containing a host identifier address generated from the host interface's MAC address.

Once the local-link address is determined, the router is queried for the DHCPv6 server. This information is provided in router advertisements that are broadcast regularly. At this point the two different kinds of stateful information can be provided by the server: addresses and other configuration information. The host is notified which kinds of stateful information are provided. If address information is not given by the DHCPv6 server, then addresses will be determined using the stateless autoconfiguration method described in the preceding section. If address information is provided, then an address will be obtained from the server instead of being directly generated. Before leasing an address, the server will run a duplicate address detection procedure to make sure the address is unique.

Linux as an IPv6 Router: radvd

For a Linux system that operates as a router, you use the **radvd** (Router ADVertisement Daemon) to advertise addresses, specifying a network prefix in the **/etc/radvd.conf** file (Ubuntu main repository). The **radvd** daemon will detect router network address requests from hosts, known as router solicitations, and provide them with a network address using a router advertisement. These router advertisements will also be broadcast to provide the network address to any hosts that do not send in requests. For **radvd** to work, you will have to turn on IPv6 forwarding. Use **sysctl** and set **net.ipv6.conf.all.forwarding** to 1. To start up the **radvd** daemon, you use the radvd startup script. To check the router addresses **radvd** is sending, you can use radvdump.

You will have to configure the **radvd** daemon yourself, specifying the network address to broadcast. Configuration, though, is very simple, as the full address will be automatically generated using the host's hardware address. A configuration consists of interface entries, which in turn lists interface options, prefix definitions, and options, along with router definitions if needed. The configuration is placed in the **/etc/radvd.conf** file, which will look something like this:

```
interface eth0 {
    AdvSendAdvert on;
        prefix fec0:0:0:0::/64
        {
        AdvOnLink on;
        AdvAutonomous on;
        };
};
```

This assumes one interface is used for the local network, **eth0**. This interface configuration lists an interface option (AdvSendAdvert) and a prefix definition, along with two prefix options (AdvOnLink and AdvAutonomous). To specify prefix options for a specific prefix, add them within parentheses following the prefix definition. The prefix definition specifies your IPv6 network address. If a local area network has its own network address, you will need to provide its IPv6 network prefix address. For a private network, such as a home network, you can use the site-local IPv6 prefix, which operates like the IPv4 private network addresses, 192.168.0. The preceding example uses a site-local address that is used for private IPv6 networks, fec0:0:0:0::, which has a length of 64 bits.

The AdvSendAdvert interface option turns on network address advertising to the hosts. The AdvAutonomous network prefix option provides automatic address configuration, and AdvOnLink simply means that host requests can be received on the specified network interface.

A second network interface is then used to connect the Linux system to an ISP or larger network. If the ISP supports IPv6, this is simply a matter of sending a router solicitation to the ISP router. This automatically generates your Internet address using the hardware address of the network interface that connects to the Internet and the ISP router's advertised network address. In Figure 16-2, shown earlier, the **eth0** network interface connects to the local network, whereas **eth1** connects to the Internet.

DHCP for IPv4

DHCP provides configuration information to systems connected to a IPv4 TCP/IP network, whether the Internet or an intranet. The machines on the network operate as DHCP clients, obtaining their network configuration information from a DHCP server on their network. A machine on the network runs a DHCP client daemon that automatically receives its network configuration information from its network's DHCP server. The information includes its IP address, along with the network's name server, gateway, and proxy addresses, including the netmask. Nothing has to be configured manually on the local system, except to specify the DHCP server it should get its network configuration from. This has the added advantage of centralizing control over network configuration for the different systems on the network. A network administrator can manage the network configurations for all the systems on the network from the DHCP server.

A DHCP server also supports several methods for IP address allocation: automatic, dynamic, and manual. Automatic allocation assigns a permanent IP address for a host. Manual allocation assigns an IP address designated by the network administrator. With dynamic allocation, a DHCP server can allocate an IP address to a host on the network only when the host actually needs to use it. Dynamic allocation takes addresses from a pool of IP addresses that hosts can use when needed and release when they are finished.

The current version of DHCP now supports the DHCP failover protocol, in which two DHCP servers support the same address pool. Should one fail, the other can continue to provide DHCP services for a network. Both servers are in sync and have the same copy of network support information for each host on the network. Primary and secondary servers in this scheme are designated with the primary and secondary statements.

A variety of DHCP servers and clients are available for different operating systems. The Ubuntu main repository provides DHCP version 3 software from the Internet Software Consortium (ISC) at **isc.org**. The software available includes a DHCP server, a client, and a relay agent. The DHCP client is called **dhclient**, and the IPv4 server is called **dhcpd**.

Configuring DHCP IPv4 Client Hosts

Configuring hosts to use a DHCP server is a simple matter of setting options for the host's network interface device, such as an Ethernet card. For a Linux host, you can use a distribution network tool to set the host to automatically access a DHCP server for network information. On a network tool's panel for configuring the Internet connection, you will normally find a check box for selecting DHCP. Clicking this box will enable DHCP.

Client support is carried out by the dhclient tool. When your network starts up, it uses dhclient to set up your DHCP connection. Though defaults are usually adequate, you can further configure the DHCP client using the **/etc/dhclient.conf** file. Consult the **dhclient.conf** Man page for a detailed list of configuration options. dhclient keeps lease information on the DCHP connection in the **/var/lib/dhcp/dhclient.leases** file. You can also directly run dhclient to configure DHCP connections.

dhclient

Configuring the DHCP IPv4 Server

You can stop and start the DHCP server using the `dhcp3-server` script in the **/etc/rc.d/init.d** directory. Use the services-admin tool or the `dhcp3-server` script with the `start`, `restart`, and `stop` options. The following example starts the DHCP server. Use the `stop` option to shut it down and `restart` to restart it.

```
sudo /etc/init.d/dhcp3-server start
```

Dynamically allocated IP addresses, known as *leases,* will be assigned for a given time. When a lease expires, it can be extended or a new one generated. Current leases are listed in the **dhcpd.leases** file located in the **/var/lib/dhcp** directory. A lease entry will specify the IP address and the start and end times of the lease along with the client's hostname.

GNOME DHCPD Configuration, GDHCPD

You can also use the GNOME DHCPD configuration tool (**GDHCPD** package, Universe repository) to configure DHCP server graphically. Though still in early development, the GDHCPD too provides an easy to use method of setting up your server. The package will be installed on the Administration | System Tools menu. You may need to use gsku to start it.

```
gksu gdhcpd
```

On the Scopes panel you enter the network connection, IP address for that connection and the netmask. Then click Add. In the Range from boxes, enter a range of addresses to allocate, then click Add.

The single hosts panel lets you specify static IP addresses to assign to particular hosts. These are normally used for systems like servers whose IP addresses do not usually change.

Click the Settings button to see your server configuration settings like the configuration and leases files used, and whether to allow DNS updates.

/etc/dhcp3/dhcpd.conf

The configuration file for the DHCP server is **/etc/dhcp3/dhcpd.conf**, where you specify parameters and declarations that define how different DHCP clients on your network are accessed by the DHCP server, along with options that define information passed to the clients by the DHCP server. These parameters, declarations, and options can be defined globally for certain subnetworks or for specific hosts. Global parameters, declarations, and options apply to all clients, unless overridden by corresponding declarations and options in subnet or host declarations. Technically, all entries in a **dhcpd.conf** file are statements that can be either declarations or parameters. All statements end with a semicolon. Options are specified in `options` parameter statements. Parameters differ from declarations in that they define if and how to perform tasks, such as how long a lease is allocated. Declarations describe network features such as the range of addresses to allocate or the networks that are accessible. See Table 16-1 for a listing of commonly used declarations and options.

Entries	Description
Declarations	
`shared-network` *name*	Indicates if some subnets share the same physical network.
`subnet` *subnet-number netmask*	References an entire subnet of addresses.
`range` [*dynamic-bootp*] *low-address* [*high-address*] ;	Provides the highest and lowest dynamically allocated IP addresses.
`host` *hostname*	References a particular host.
`group`	Lets you label a group of parameters and declarations and then use the label to apply them to subnets and hosts.
`allow unknown-clients;` `deny unknown-clients;`	Does not dynamically assign addresses to unknown clients.
`allow bootp; deny bootp;`	Determines whether to respond to `bootp` queries.
`allow booting; deny booting;`	Determines whether to respond to client queries.
Parameters	
`default-lease-time` *time;*	Assigns length in seconds to a lease.
`max-lease-time` *time;*	Assigns maximum length of lease.
`hardware` *hardware-type hardware-address;*	Specifies network hardware type (Ethernet or token ring) and address.
`filename` "*filename*";	Specifies name of the initial boot file.
`server-name` "*name*";	Specifies name of the server from which a client is booting.
`next-server` *server-name;*	Specifies server that loads the initial boot file specified in the filename.
`fixed-address` *address* [, *address* ...] ;	Assigns a fixed address to a client.
`get-lease-hostnames` *flag;*	Determines whether to look up and use IP addresses of clients.
`authoritative;` `not authoritative;`	Denies invalid address requests.
`server-identifier hostname;`	Specifies the server.
Options	

`option` **`subnet-mask`** *ip-address*`;`	Specifies client's subnet mask.
`option` **`routers`** *ip-address* `[,` *ip-address...* `]`;	Specifies list of router IP addresses on client's subnet.
`option` **`domain-name-servers`** *ip-address* `[,` *ip-address...* `]`;	Specifies list of domain name servers used by the client.
`option` **`log-servers`** *ip-address* `[,` *ip-address...* `]`;	Specifies list of log servers used by the client.
`option` **`host-name`** *string*`;`	Specifies client's hostname.
`option` **`domain-name`** *string*`;`	Specifies client's domain name.
`option` **`broadcast-address`** *ip-address*`;`	Specifies client's broadcast address.
`option` **`nis-domain`** *string*`;`	Specifies client's Network Information Service domain.
`option` **`nis-servers`** *ip-address* `[,` *ip-address...* `]`;	Specifies NIS servers the client can use.
`option` **`smtp-server`** *ip-address* `[,` *ip-address...* `]`;	Lists SMTP servers used by the client.
`option` **`pop-server`** *ip-address* `[,` *ip-address...* `]`;	Lists POP servers used by the client.
`option` **`nntp-server`** *ip-address* `[,` *ip-address...* `]`;	Lists NNTP servers used by the client.
`option` **`www-server`** *ip-address* `[,` *ip-address...* `]`;	Lists web servers used by the client.

Table 16-1: DHCP Declarations, Parameters, and Options

Declarations provide information for the DHCP server or designate actions it is to perform. For example, the **`range`** declaration is used to specify the range of IP addresses to be dynamically allocated to hosts:

```
range 192.168.0.5 192.168.0.128;
```

With parameters, you can specify how the server is to treat clients. For example, the **`default-lease-time`** declaration sets the number of seconds a lease is assigned to a client. The **`filename`** declaration specifies the boot file to be used by the client. The **`server-name`** declaration informs the client of the host from which it is booting. The **`fixed-address`** declaration can be used to assign a static IP address to a client. See the Man page for **dhcpd.conf** for a complete listing.

Options provide information to clients that they may need to access network services, such as the domain name of the network, the domain name servers that clients use, or the broadcast address. See the Man page for **dhcp-options** for a complete listing. This information is provided by **`option`** parameters as shown here:

```
option broadcast-address 192.168.0.255;
option domain-name-servers 192.168.0.1, 192.168.0.4;
option domain-name "mytrek.com";
```

Your **dhcpd.conf** file will usually begin with declarations, parameters, and options that you define for your network serviced by the DHCP server. The following example provides router (gateway), netmask, domain name, and DNS server information to clients. Additional parameters define the default and maximum lease times for dynamically allocated IP addresses.

```
option routers 192.168.0.1;
option subnet-mask 255.255.255.0;
option domain-name "mytrek.com ";
option domain-name-servers 192.168.0.1;
default-lease-time 21600;
max-lease-time 43200;
```

With the subnet, host, and group declarations, you can reference clients in a specific network, particular clients, or different groupings of clients across networks. Within these declarations, you can enter parameters, declarations, or options that will apply only to those clients. Scoped declarations, parameters, and options are enclosed in braces. For example, to define a declaration for a particular host, you use the **host** declaration as shown here:

```
host rabbit {
       declarations, parameters, or options;
       }
```

You can collect different subnet, global, and host declaration into groups using the **group** declaration. In this case, the global declarations are applied only to those subnets and hosts declared within the group.

Dynamic IPv4 Addresses for DHCP

Your DHCP server can be configured to select IP addresses from a given range and assign them to different clients. Given a situation where you have many clients that may not always be connected to the network, you can effectively service them with a smaller pool of IP addresses. IP addresses are assigned only when they are needed. With the **range** declaration, you specify a range of addresses that can be dynamically allocated to clients. The declaration takes two arguments, the first and last addresses in the range.

```
range 192.168.1.5 192.168.1.128;
```

For example, if you are setting up your own small home network, you would use a network address beginning with 192.168. The range would specify possible IP addresses with that network. So, for a network with the address 192.168.0.0, you place a **range** declaration along with any other information you want to give to your client hosts. In the following example, a range of IP addresses extending from 192.168.0.1 to 192.168.0.128 can be allocated to the hosts on that network:

```
range 192.168.0.5 192.168.0.128;
```

You should also define your lease times, both a default and a maximum:

```
default-lease-time 21600;
max-lease-time 43200;
```

For a small, simple home network, you just need to list the **range** declaration along with any global options as shown here. If your DHCP server is managing several subnetworks, you will have to use the **subnet** declarations.

In order to assign dynamic addresses to a network, the DHCP server will require that your network topology be mapped. This means it needs to know what network addresses belong to a given network. Even if you use only one network, you will need to specify the address space for it. You define a network with the **subnet** declaration. Within this **subnet** declaration, you can specify any parameters, declarations, or options to use for that network. The **subnet** declaration informs the DHCP server of the possible IP addresses encompassed by a given subnet. This is determined by the network IP address and the netmask for that network. The next example defines a local network with address spaces from 192.168.0.0 to 192.168.0.255. The **range** declaration allows addresses to be allocated from 192.168.0.5 to 192.168.0.128.

```
subnet 192.168.1.0 netmask 255.255.255.0 {
        range 192.168.0.5 192.168.0.128;
 }
```

Versions of DHCP prior to 3.0 required that you even map connected network interfaces that are not being served by DHCP. Thus each network interface has to have a corresponding **subnet** declaration. Those not being serviced by DHCP don't have a **not authoritative** parameter as shown here (192.168.2.0 being a network not to be serviced by DHCP). In version 3.0 and later, DHCP simply ignores unmapped network interfaces:

```
subnet 192.168.2.0 netmask 255.255.255.0 {
      not authoritative;
}
```

The implementation of a very simple DHCP server for dynamic addresses is shown in the sample **dhcpd.conf** file that follows:

/etc/dhcp3/dhcpd.conf

```
option routers 192.168.0.1;
 option subnet-mask 255.255.255.0;
 option domain-name "mytrek.com ";
 option domain-name-servers 192.168.0.1;

subnet 192.168.1.0 netmask 255.255.255.0 {
        range 192.168.0.5 192.168.0.128;
        default-lease-time 21600;
        max-lease-time 43200;
        }
```

DHCP Dynamic DNS Updates

For networks that also support a Domain Name Server, dynamic allocation of IP addresses currently needs to address one major constraint: DHCP needs to sync with a DNS server. A DNS server associates hostnames with particular IP addresses, whereas in the case of dynamic allocation, the DHCP server randomly assigns its own IP addresses to different hosts. These may or may not be the same as the IP addresses that the DNS server expects to associate with a hostname. A solution to this problem is being developed, called Dynamic DNS. With Dynamic DNS, the DHCP server is able to automatically update the DNS server with the IP addresses the DHCP server has assigned to different hosts.

Note: Alternatively, if you want to statically synchronize your DHCP and DNS servers with fixed addresses, you configure DHCP to assign those fixed addresses to hosts.

You can then have the DHCP server perform a DNS lookup to obtain the IP address it should assign, or you can manually assign the same IP address in the DHCP configuration file. Performing a DNS lookup has the advantage of specifying the IP address in one place, the DNS server.

The DHCP server has the ability to dynamically update BIND DNS server zone configuration files. You enable dynamic updates on a DNS server for a zone file by specifying the `allow-update` option for it in the **named.conf** file. Furthermore, it is strongly encouraged that you use TSIG signature keys to reference and authenticate the BIND and DHCP servers. Currently, DHCP uses the Interim DNS Update Scheme to perform dynamic DNS updates, replacing an earlier Ad-Hoc DNS Update Scheme. A finalized version will be implemented in future DHCP releases. You can find detailed information about dynamic DNS in the **dhcpd.conf** Man page.

Enabling the use of a TSIG key involves syncing configurations for both your DHCP and DNS servers. Both have to be configured to use the same key for the same domains. First you need to create a shared secret TSIG signature key using `dnssec-keygen`,. In the DNS server, you place TSIG key declarations and `allow-update` entries in the server's **named.conf** file, as shown in this example:

```
key mydhcpserver {
algorithm HMAC-MD5;
secret "ONQAfbBLnvWU9H8hRqq/WA==";
};



zone "mytrek.com" {
      type master;
      file "mytrek.com";
      allow-update {key mydhcpserver;};
 };

zone "1.168.192.IN-ADDR.ARPA" {
      type master;
      file "192.168.0";
      allow-update {key mydhcpserver;};
};
```

In the DHCP server, you place a corresponding TSIG key declaration and `allow-update` entries in the server's **dhcpd.conf** file, as shown in this example. The `key` declaration has the same syntax as the DNS server. DHCP `zone` statements are then used to specify the IP address of the domain and the TSIG key to use. The domain names and IP addresses need to match exactly in the configuration files for both the DNS and DHCP servers. Unlike in the **named.conf** file, there are no quotes around the domain name or IP addresses in the **dhcpd.conf** file. In the **dhcpd.conf** file, the domain names and IP addresses used in the `zone` statement also need to end with a period, as they do in the DNS zone files. The `key` statement lists the key to use. Though the DHCP server will try to determine the DNS servers to update, it is recommended that you explicitly identify them with a primary statement in a `zone` entry.

```
key mydhcpserver {
    algorithm HMAC-MD5;
    secret "ONQAfbBLnvWU9H8hRqq/WA==";
    };

zone mytrek.com. {               #DNS domain zone to update
    primary 192.168.0.1;         #address of DNS server
    key mydhcpserver;            #TSIG signature key
};

zone 1.168.192.IN-ADDR.ARPA. {   #domain PTR zone to update
    primary 192.168.0.1;         #address of DNS server
    key mydhcpserver;            # TSIG signature key
};
```

To generate a fully qualified hostname to use in a DNS update, the DHCP server will normally use its own domain name and the hostname provided by a DHCP client (see the **dhcpd.conf** Man page for exceptions). Should you want to assign a specific hostname to a host, you can use the **ddns-hostname** statement to specify it in the host's hardware section. The domain name is specified in the **domain-name** option:

```
option domain-name "mytrek.com"
```

The DNS update capability can be turned on or off for all domains with the **ddns-update-style** statement. It is on by default. To turn off DNS updates for particular domains, you can use the **ddns-updates** statement. This is also on by default.

DHCP Subnetworks

If you are dividing your network space into several subnetworks, you can use a single DHCP server to manage them. In that case, you will have a **subnet** declaration for each subnetwork. If you are setting up your own small network, you use a network address beginning with 192.168. The range specifies possible IP addresses within that network so, for a network with the address 192.168.0.0, you create a **subnet** declaration with the netmask 255.255.255.0. Within this declaration, you place a **range** declaration along with any other information you want to give to your client hosts. In the following example, a range of IP addresses extending from 192.168.0.1 to 192.168.0.75 can be allocated to the hosts on that network:

```
subnet 192.168.0.0 netmask 255.255.255.0 {
 range 192.168.0.5 192.168.0.75;
}
```

You may want to specify different policies for each subnetwork, such as different lease times. Any entries in a **subnet** declaration will override global settings. So if you already have a global lease time set, a lease setting in a **subnet** declaration will override it for that subnet. The next example sets different lease times for different subnets, as well as different address allocations. The lease times for the first subnet are taken from the global lease time settings, whereas the second subnet defines its own lease times:

```
default-lease-time 21600;
max-lease-time 43200;

subnet 192.168.1.0 netmask 255.255.255.0 {
      range 192.168.0.5 192.168.0.75;
      }
subnet 192.168.1.128 netmask 255.255.255.252 {
      range 192.168.0.129 192.168.0.215;
      default-lease-time 56000;
      max-lease-time 62000;
      }
```

If your subnetworks are part of the same physical network, you need to inform the server of this fact by declaring them as shared networks. You do this by placing subnet declarations within a **shared-network** declaration, specifying the shared network's name. The name can be any descriptive name, though you can use the domain name. Any options specified within the **shared-network** declaration and outside the subnet declarations will be global to those subnets. In the next example, the subnets are part of the same physical network and so are placed within a **shared-network** declaration:

```
shared-network mytrek.com
{
default-lease-time 21600;
max-lease-time 43200;
subnet 192.168.1.0 netmask 255.255.255.0 {
      range 192.168.0.5 192.168.0.75;
      }
subnet 192.168.1.128 netmask 255.255.255.252 {
      range 192.168.0.129 192.168.0.215;
      default-lease-time 56000;
      max-lease-time 62000;
      }
}
```

DHCP Fixed Addresses

Instead of using a pool of possible IP addresses for your hosts, you may want to give each one a specific addresses. Using the DHCP server still gives you control over which address will be assigned to a given host. However, to assign an address to a particular host, you need to know the hardware address for that host's network interface card (NIC). In effect, you have to inform the DHCP server that it has to associate a particular network connection device with a specified IP address. To do that, the DHCP server needs to know which network device you are referring to. You can identify a network device by its hardware address, known as its MAC address. To find out a client's hardware address, you log in to the client and use the **ifconfig** command to find out information about your network devices. To list all network devices, use the **-a** option. If you know your network device name, you can use that. The next example will list all information about the first Ethernet device, **eth0**:

```
ifconfig eth0
```

This will list information on all the client's network connection devices. The entry (usually the first) with the term **HWaddr** will display the MAC address. Once you have the MAC address, you can use it on the DHCP server to assign a specific IP address to that device.

In the **dhcpd.conf** file, you use a `host` declaration to set up a fixed address for a client. Within the `host` declaration, you place a `hardware` option in which you list the type of network connection device and its MAC address. Then you use the `fixed-address` parameter to specify the IP address to be assigned to that device. In the following example, the client's network device with a MAC address of 08:00:2b:4c:29:32 is given the IP address 192.168.0.2:

```
host rabbit {
        option host-name "rabbit.mytrek.com"
        hardware ethernet 08:00:2b:4c:29:32;
        fixed-address 192.168.0.2;
        }
```

You can also have the DHCP server perform a DNS lookup to obtain the host's IP address. This has the advantage of letting you manage IP addresses in only one place, the DNS server. Of course, this requires that the DNS server be operating so that the DHCP server can determine the IP address. For example, a proxy server connection (which can provide direct web access) needs just an IP address, not a DNS hostname, to operate. If the DNS server were down, the preceding example would still assign an IP address to the host, whereas the following example would not:

```
host rabbit {
        option host-name "rabbit.mytrek.com"
        hardware ethernet 08:00:2b:4c:29:32;
        fixed-address rabbit.mytrek.com;
        }
```

You can also use the `host` declaration to define network information for a diskless workstation or terminal. In this case, you add a `filename` parameter specifying the boot file to use for that workstation or terminal. Here the terminal called **myterm** obtains boot information from the server **turtle.mytrek.com**:

```
host myterm {
        option host-name "myterm.mytrek.com"
        filename "/boot/vmlinuz";
        hardware ethernet 08:00:2b:4c:29:32;
        server-name "turtle.mytrek.com";
        }
```

A common candidate for a fixed address is the DNS server for a network. Usually, you want the DNS server located at the same IP address, so that it can be directly accessed. The DHCP server can then provide this IP address to its clients.

17. Firewalls

Most systems currently connected to the Internet are open to attempts by outside users to gain unauthorized access. Outside users can try to gain access directly by setting up an illegal connection, by intercepting valid communications from users remotely connected to the system, or by pretending to be a valid user. Firewalls, encryption, and authentication procedures are ways of protecting against such attacks. A *firewall* prevents any direct unauthorized attempts at access, *encryption* protects transmissions from authorized remote users, and *authentication* verifies that a user requesting access has the right to do so. The current Linux kernel incorporates support for firewalls using the Netfilter (IPtables) packet filtering package (the previous version, IP Chains, is used on older kernel versions). To implement a firewall, you simply provide a series of rules to govern what kind of access you want to allow on your system. If that system is also a gateway for a private network, the system's firewall capability can effectively help protect the network from outside attacks.

Web Site	Security Application
www.netfilter.org	Netfilter project, Iptables, and NAT
www.netfilter.org/ipchains	IP Chains firewall
www.openssh.org	Secure Shell encryption
www.squid-cache.org	Squid Web Proxy server
web.mit.edu/Kerberos	Kerberos network authentication

Table 17-1: Network Security Applications

To provide protection for remote communications, transmission can be simply encrypted. For Linux systems, you can use the Secure Shell (SSH) suite of programs to encrypt any transmissions, preventing them from being read by anyone else. Kerberos authentication provides another level of security whereby individual services can be protected, allowing use of a service only to users who are cleared for access. Outside users may also try to gain unauthorized access through any Internet services you may be hosting, such as a Web site. In such a case, you can set up a proxy to protect your site from attack. For Linux systems, use Squid proxy software to set up a proxy to protect your Web server. Table 17-1 lists several network security applications commonly used on Linux.

Firewalls management tools

You can choose from several different popular firewall management tools (see Table 17-2). Ubuntu now provides its own firewall configuration tool called the Uncomplicated Firewall (ufw). IPtables and ufw are on the Ubuntu main repository, all others are in the Universe repository. You can also choose to use other popular management tools like Firestarter or Fwbuilder. Firestarter provides a desktop interface whereas ufw is command line only. Both ufw and Firestarter are covered in this chapter, along with the underlying IPTables firewall application. Search Synaptic Package Manager for firewall to see a more complete listing.

Firewall	Description
IPTables	IPTables: netfilter, NAT, and mangle. **netfilter.org** (Main repository)
ufw	Uncomplicated Firewall, ufw. **wiki.ubuntu.com/UbuntuFirewall** (Ubuntu Main repository), also see Ubuntu Server Guide at **doc.ubuntu.com**.
Firestarter	Firestarter firewall configuration tool, **www.fs-secruity.com** (Universe repository)
Fwbuilder	Firewall configuration tool, allow for more complex configuration **www.fwbuilder.org** (Universe repository)
Lokkit, Gnome-Lokkit	Basic firewall configuration **www.shorewall.net** (Universe repository)
Shorewall	Shoreline firewall (Universie repository)
guarddog	KDE firewall configuration tool **www.simonzone.com/software/guarddog** (Universe repository)

Table 17-2: Ubuntu Firewall configuration tools

Setting Up Your Firewall with Firestarter

Ubuntu provides the Firestarter firewall configuration tool with which you can set up your firewall. Select Firewall from the System | Administration menu. Much of the configuration is automatic. If you are using a local home or work network, you may have to add rules for services like Samba Windows network access or the network address of your local network.

The first time you start up Firestarter the Firewall Wizard starts up which will prompt you for your network device and Internet connection sharing information (see Figure 17-1). After the Welcome screen, the Network device setup panel lets you select your network device, like an Ethernet connection or modem, as well as whether to use DHCP to detect your address information

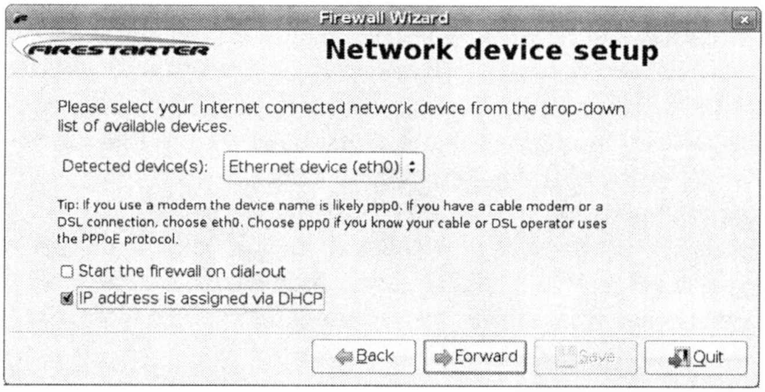

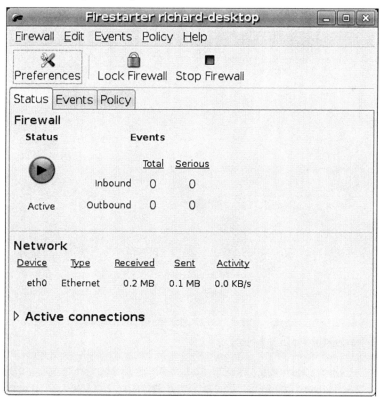

Figure 17-1: Firestarter setup wizard

The Internet connection sharing setup panel is rarely used. You will most likely just skip it. It is used only for local networks where your computer is being used as a gateway to the Internet, letting other computer on your local network to access the Internet through your computer. There is usually a second Ethernet device connected to the local network as well as a local DHCP server controlling local network addressing. Again, this is rarely used, as most Internet gateways are now handled by dedicated routers, not computers.

Figure 17-2: Firestarter Firewall

Firestarter will then start up with a window titled with your computer name. There are three panels: Status, Events, and Policy (see Figure 17-2). The toolbar entries will change with each panel selected. The Status panel lets you start and stop your firewall using the Stop/Start Firewall button in the toolbar. Its status is shown as a play or stop icon in the Status segment of the Status panel. The Events segment of this panel shows inbound and outbound traffic, and the Network segment lists your network devices along with device information like the number of packets received, sent, and average activity. Usually there will be only one device listed (a computer functioning as a gateway will have several). An expansion list will show Active connections. Here you can see what kind of connection is active, like Samba or Internet connections.

The Events panel will list any rejected connections, Blocked Connections. The Save, Clear, and Reload buttons on the toolbar let you save the event log, clear it, or reload to see the latest events.

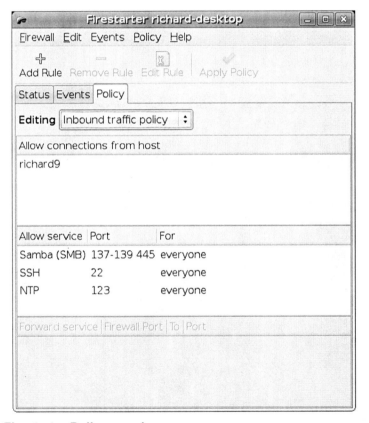

Figure 17-3: Firestarter Policy panel

The Policy panel shows rules for allowing host and service connections (see Figure 17-3). A pop-up menu lets you show Inbound traffic or Outbound traffic policies. On this panel you can add your own simplified rules for inbound or outbound hosts. The toolbar shows Add Rule, Remove Rule, Edit Rule, and Apply Rule buttons.

For Inbound Traffic, when you can set up rules for connections, services, or forwarding. There will be segments for each. Click on the segment first, and then click on the Add Rule button. The dialog is different depending on the type of rule you are setting up. For a connection, the Add Rule dialog will let you enter the host, IP address, or network from which you can receive connections.

For a service, you can select the service to allow from a pop-up menu, along with the port, as well as whether to allow access by anyone or from a specific host or network (see Figure 17-4). By default all inbound traffic is denied, unless explicitly allowed by a rule. If you are setting up a firewall for just your personal computer connected to a network, you would enter a rule for the local network address. You could also set up rules to allow access by services like Samba or BitTorrent.

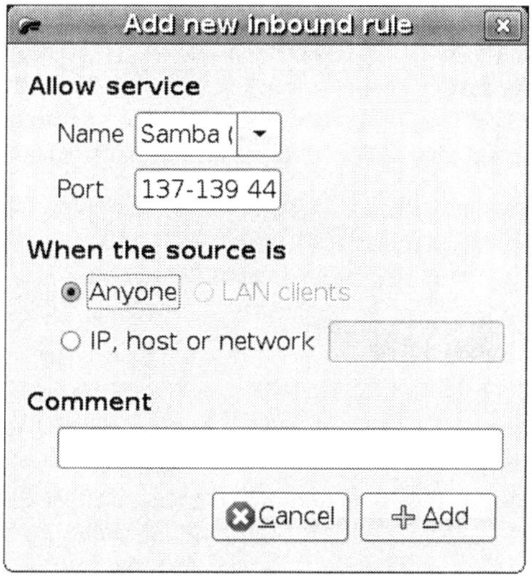

Figure 17-4: Firestarter, choosing a service to permit

The Outbound Traffic is more complex. Here you can set either a permissive or restrictive policy. There are entries for each to select which. The permissive is selected by default. The permissive entry will still reject blacklisted hosts and services, and the restrictive entry will allow white listed hosts and services. Each has both a connection and service segment, just like the Inbound connections, with the same options.

If permissive is selected, you will allow all outbound traffic, except those you specifically deny. For this configuration, you can create Deny rules for certain hosts and services. When setting up a Deny rule for a service you can choose a service from a pop-up menu, and specify its port. You can then reject either anyone using this service, or specify a particular host or network. For a connection, you simply specify the host, IP address, or network that can connect. The connection rules act like your own blacklist, listing hosts or network you will not allow yourself or others on your network to connect to.

If restrictive, you deny all outbound traffic, except those you specifically allow. In this case, you can set up Allow rules to allow connections by certain hosts and services, rejecting everything else. The restrictive option is not normally used, as it would cut off any connections from your computer to the Internet, unless you added a rule to permit the connection.

To configure your Firestarter firewall, click on the Preferences button. This opens a Preference window where you can set either Interface or Firewall settings.

For the Interface settings you can set either the Events logged or the Policy. The Events panel lets you eliminate logging of unwanted events, like redundant events or events from specific hosts or ports. The Policy panel has an option to let you apply changes immediately.

For Firewall Settings, you have panels for Network Settings, ICMP Filtering, ToS Filtering, and Advanced Options. Network Settings just selects your network device. Here you could change your network device between Ethernet, wireless, or modem. The ICMP filtering panel blocks ICMP packet attacks. Options allow certain ICMP packets through, like Unreachable to notify you of an unknown site. The Type of Service panel lets you prioritize your packets by both the kind of service and maximized efficiency.. For the kind of service you can choose either workstations, servers, or the X Window System. For maximized efficiency you can choose reliability, throughput, or interactivity. Workstations and throughput are selected by default.

The Advanced options panel lets you select the drop method (silent or error reported), the Broadcast traffic rejection policy for internal and external connections (External broadcasts are blocked by default), and traffic validation block reserved addresses

Setting up a firewall with ufw

The Uncomplicated Firewall, ufw, is now the official firewall application for Ubuntu. It provides a simple firewall that can be managed with a few command-line operations. Like all firewall applications, ufw uses IPTables to define rules and run the firewall. The ufw applications is just a management interface for IPtables. Default IPtables rules are kept in before and after files, with added rules in user files. The IPtables rule files are held in the **/etc/ufw** directory. Firewall configuration for certain packages will be placed in the **/usr/share/ufw.d** directory. The ufw firewall is started up at boot using the **/etc/init.d/ufw** script. You can find out more about ufw at the Ubuntu Firewall site at **wiki.ubuntu.com/UbuntuFirewall**. and at the Ubuntu firewall section in the Ubuntu Server Guide at **doc.ubuntu.com**. The Server Guide also shows information on how to implement IP Masquerading on ufw.

IPtables firewall rules are set up using **ufw** commands entered on a command line in a Terminal window. Most users may only need to use **ufw** commands to allow or deny access by services like the Web server or Samba server. To check the current firewall status, listing those services allowed or blocked, use the status command.

```
sudo ufw status
```

If the firewall is not enabled, you will have to first enable it with the enable command.

```
sudo ufw enable
```

You can restart the firewall, reloading your rules, using the /etc/init.d/ufw command.

```
sudo /etc/init.d/ufw restart
```

You can then add rules using the allow and deny command and their options as listed in Table 17-3. To allow a service, use the allow command and the service name. This is the name for the service listed in the /etc/services file. The following allows the ftp service.

```
sudo ufw allow ftp
```

If the service you want is not listed in /etc/services, and you know the port and protocol it uses, can specify the port and protocol directly. For example, the Samba service uses port 137 and protocol tcp.

```
sudo ufw allow 137/tcp
```

The status operation will then show what services are allowed.

```
sudo ufw status
To                  Action          From
21:tcp              ALLOW           Anywhere
21:udp              ALLOW           Anywhere
137:tcp             ALLOW           Anywhere
```

To remove a rule, prefix it with the **delete** command.

```
sudo ufw delete allow 137/tcp
```

More detailed rules can be specified using address, port, and protocol commands. These are very similar to the actual IPTables commands. Packets to and from particular networks, hosts, and ports can be controlled. The following denies ssh access (port 22) from host 192.168.03.

```
sudo ufw deny proto tcp from 192.168.03 to any port 22
```

The rules you add are placed in the **/var/lib/ufw/user.rules** file as IPTables rules. ufw is just a front end for **iptables-restore** which will read this file and set up the firewall using **iptables** commands. **ufw** will also have **iptables-restore** read the **before.rules** and **after.rules** files in the **/etc/ufw** directory. These files are considered administrative files that include needed supporting rules for your IPTables firewall. Administrators can add their own IPTables rules to these files for system specific features like IP Masquerading.

The **before.rules** file will specify a table with the * symbol, as in ***filter** for the netfilter table. For the NAT table you would use ***nat**. At the end of each table segment, a COMMIT command is needed to instruct ufw to apply the rules. Rules use **-A** for allow and **-D** for deny, assuming the **iptables** command. The following would implement IP Forwarding when placed at the end of the **before.rules** file (see Ubuntu firewall server documentation). This particular rule works on the first Ethernet device (eth0) for a local network (192.168.0.0/24).

```
# nat Table rules
*nat
:POSTROUTING ACCEPT [0:0]
# Forward traffic from eth1 through eth0.
-A POSTROUTING -s 192.168.0.0/24 -o eth0 -j MASQUERADE
# don't delete the 'COMMIT' line or these nat table rules won't be processed
COMMIT
```

Commands	Description
enable | disable	Turn the firewall on or off
status	Display status along with services allowed or denied.
logging on | off	Turn logging on or off
default allow | deny	Set the default policy, allow is open, whereas deny is restrictive
allow *service*	Allow access by a service. Services are defined in **/etc/services** which specifies the ports for that service.
allow *port-number/protocol*	Allow access on a particular port using specified protocol. The protocol is optional.
deny *service*	Deny access by a service
delete *rule*	Delete an installed rule, use **allow** or **deny** and include rule specifics.
proto *protocol*	Specify protocol in **allow** or **deny** rule
from *address*	Specify source address in **allow** or **deny** rule
to *address*	Specify destination address in **allow** or **deny** rule
port *port*	Specify port in **allow** or **deny** rule for **from** and **to** address operations

Table 17-3: UFW firewall operations

Default settings for ufw are placed in **/etc/defaults/ufw**. Here you will find the default INPUT, OUTPUT, and FORWARD policies. A **default deny** command will set the default INPUT to DROP and OUTPUT to ACCEPT, whereas a **default allow** will set both INPUT and OUTPUT defaults to ACCEPT. FORWARD will always be drop. To allow IP Masquerading, FORWARD would have to be set to ACCEPT. Any user rules you have set up would not be affected. You would have to change these manually.

IPtables, NAT, Mangle, and ip6tables

A good foundation for your network's security is to set up a Linux system to operate as a firewall for your network, protecting it from unauthorized access. You can use a firewall to implement either packet filtering or proxies. *Packet filtering* is simply the process of deciding whether a packet received by the firewall host should be passed on into the local network. The packet-filtering software checks the source and destination addresses of the packet and sends the packet on, if it's allowed. Even if your system is not part of a network but connects directly to the Internet, you can still use the firewall feature to control access to your system. Of course, this also provides you with much more security.

With proxies, you can control access to specific services, such as Web or FTP servers. You need a proxy for each service you want to control. The Web server has its own Web proxy, while an FTP server has an FTP proxy. Proxies can also be used to cache commonly used data, such as Web pages, so that users needn't constantly access the originating site. The proxy software commonly used on Linux systems is Squid.

An additional task performed by firewalls is network address translation (NAT). Network address translation redirects packets to appropriate destinations. It performs tasks such as redirecting packets to certain hosts, forwarding packets to other networks, and changing the host source of packets to implement IP masquerading.

Note: The IP Chains package is the precursor to IPtables that was used on Linux systems running the 2.2 kernel. It is still in use on many Linux systems. The Linux Web site for IP Chains, which is the successor to ipfwadm used on older versions of Linux, is currently **www.netfilter.org/ipchains**. IP Chains is no longer included with many Linux distributions.

The Netfilter software package implements both packet filtering and NAT tasks for the Linux 2.4 kernel and above. The Netfilter software is developed by the Netfilter Project, which you can find out more about at **www.netfilter.org**.

IPtables

The command used to execute packet filtering and NAT tasks is `iptables`, and the software is commonly referred to as simply IPtables. However, Netfilter implements packet filtering and NAT tasks separately using different tables and commands. A table will hold the set of commands for its application. This approach streamlines the packet-filtering task, letting IPtables perform packet-filtering checks without the overhead of also having to do address translations. NAT operations are also freed from being mixed in with packet-filtering checks. You use the `iptables` command for both packet filtering and NAT tasks, but for NAT you add the `-nat` option. The IPtables software can be built directly into the kernel or loaded as a kernel module, **iptable_filter.o**.

ip6tables

The ip6tables package provides support for IPv6 addressing. It is identical to IPtables except that it allows the use of IPv6 addresses instead of IPv4 addresses. Both filter and mangle tables are supported in ip6tables, but not NAT tables. The filter tables support the same options and commands as in IPtables. The mangle tables will allow specialized packet changes like those for IPtables, using PREROUTING, INPUT, OUTPUT, FORWARD, and POSTROUTING rules. Some extensions have ipv6 labels for their names, such as ipv6-icmp, which corresponds to the IPtables icmp extension. The ipv6headers extension is used to select IPv6 headers.

Modules

Unlike its predecessor, IP Chains, Netfilter is designed to be modularized and extensible. Capabilities can be added in the form of modules such as the state module, which adds connection tracking. Most modules are loaded as part of the IPtables service. Others are optional; you can elect to load them before installing rules. The IPtables modules are located at /usr/lib/*kernel-version*/kernel/net/ipv4/netfilter, where *kernel-version* is your kernel number. For IPv6 modules, check the **ipv6/netfilter** directory. Modules that load automatically will have an **ipt_** prefix, and optional ones have just an **ip_** prefix. If you are writing you own iptables script, you would have to add **modpobe** commands to load optional modules directly.

Packet Filtering

Netfilter is essentially a framework for packet management that can check packets for particular network protocols and notify parts of the kernel listening for them. Built on the Netfilter framework is the packet selection system implemented by IPtables. With IPtables, different tables of rules can be set up to select packets according to differing criteria. Netfilter currently supports three tables: filter, nat, and mangle. Packet filtering is implemented using a filter table that holds rules for dropping or accepting packets. Network address translation operations such as IP masquerading are implemented using the NAT table that holds IP masquerading rules. The mangle table is used for specialized packet changes. Changes can be made to packets before they are sent out, when they are received, or as they are being forwarded. This structure is extensible in that new modules can define their own tables with their own rules. It also greatly improves efficiency. Instead of all packets checking one large table, they access only the table of rules they need to.

IP table rules are managed using the **iptables** command. For this command, you will need to specify the table you want to manage. The default is the filter table, which need not be specified. You can list the rules you have added at any time with the **-L** and **-n** options, as shown here. The **-n** option says to use only numeric output for both IP addresses and ports, avoiding a DNS lookup for hostnames. You could, however, just use the **-L** option to see the port labels and hostnames:

```
iptables -L -n
```

Chains

Rules are combined into different chains. The kernel uses chains to manage packets it receives and sends out. A *chain* is simply a checklist of rules. These rules specify what action to take for packets containing certain headers. The rules operate with an if-then-else structure. If a packet does not match the first rule, the next rule is then checked, and so on. If the packet does not match any rules, the kernel consults chain policy. Usually, at this point the packet is rejected. If the packet does match a rule, it is passed to its target, which determines what to do with the packet. The standard targets are listed in Table 17-4. If a packet does not match any of the rules, it is passed to the chain's default target.

Targets

A *target* could, in turn, be another chain of rules, even a chain of user-defined rules. A packet could be passed through several chains before finally reaching a target. In the case of user-defined chains, the default target is always the next rule in the chains from which it was called. This sets up a procedure- or function call–like flow of control found in programming languages. When a rule has a user-defined chain as its target, when activated, that user-defined chain is executed. If no rules are matched, execution returns to the next rule in the originating chain.

Tip: Specialized targets and options can be added by means of kernel patches provided by the Netfilter site. For example, the SAME patch returns the same address for all connections. A patch-o-matic option for the Netfilter make file will patch your kernel source code, adding support for the new target and options. You can then rebuild and install your kernel.

Target	Function
ACCEPT	Allow packet to pass through the firewall.
DROP	Deny access by the packet.
REJECT	Deny access and notify the sender.
QUEUE	Send packets to user space.
RETURN	Jump to the end of the chain and let the default target process it.

Table 17-4: IPtables Targets

Firewall and NAT Chains

The kernel uses three firewall chains: INPUT, OUTPUT, and FORWARD. When a packet is received through an interface, the INPUT chain is used to determine what to do with it. The kernel then uses its routing information to decide where to send it. If the kernel sends the packet to another host, the FORWARD chain is checked. Before the packet is actually sent, the OUTPUT chain is also checked. In addition, two NAT table chains, POSTROUTING and PREROUTING, are implemented to handle masquerading and packet address modifications. The built-in Netfilter chains are listed in Table 17-5.

Chain	Description
INPUT	Rules for incoming packets
OUTPUT	Rules for outgoing packets
FORWARD	Rules for forwarded packets
PREROUTING	Rules for redirecting or modifying incoming packets, NAT table only
POSTROUTING	Rules for redirecting or modifying outgoing packets, NAT table only

Table 17-5: Netfilter Built-in Chains

Adding and Changing Rules

You add and modify chain rules using the `iptables` commands. An `iptables` command consists of the command `iptables`, followed by an argument denoting the command to execute (see Table 17-6). For example, `iptables -A` is the command to add a new rule, whereas `iptables -D` is the command to delete a rule. The `iptables` commands are listed in Table 17-4. The following command simply lists the chains along with their rules currently defined for your system. The output shows the default values created by `iptables` commands.

```
iptables -L -n
Chain input (policy ACCEPT):
Chain forward (policy ACCEPT):
Chain output (policy ACCEPT):
```

To add a new rule to a chain, you use **-A**. Use **-D** to remove it, and **-R** to replace it. Following the command, list the chain to which the rule applies, such as the INPUT, OUTPUT, or FORWARD chain, or a user-defined chain. Next, you list different options that specify the actions you want taken (most are the same as those used for IP Chains, with a few exceptions). The **-s** option specifies the source address attached to the packet, **-d** specifies the destination address, and the **-j** option specifies the target of the rule. The ACCEPT target will allow a packet to pass. The **-i** option now indicates the input device and can be used only with the INPUT and FORWARD chains. The **-o** option indicates the output device and can be used only for OUTPUT and FORWARD chains. Table 17-5 lists several basic options.

Option	Function
-A *chain*	Appends a rule to a chain.
-D *chain* [*rulenum*]	Deletes matching rules from a chain. Deletes rule *rulenum* (1 = first) from *chain.*
-I *chain* [*rulenum*]	Inserts in *chain* as *rulenum* (default 1 = first).
-R *chain rulenum*	Replaces rule *rulenum* (1 = first) in *chain.*
-L [*chain*]	Lists the rules in *chain* or all chains.
-E [*chain*]	Renames a chain.
-F [*chain*]	Deletes (flushes) all rules in *chain* or all chains.
-R *chain*	Replaces a rule; rules are numbered from 1.
-Z [*chain*]	Zero counters in *chain* or all chains.
-N *chain*	Creates a new user-defined chain.
-X *chain*	Deletes a user-defined chain.
-P *chain target*	Changes policy on *chain* to *target.*

Table 17-6: IPtables Commands

IPtables Options

The IPtables package is designed to be extensible, and there are number of options with selection criteria that can be included with IPtables (see Table 17-7). For example, the TCP extension includes the **--syn** option that checks for SYN packets. The ICMP extension provides the **--icmp-type** option for specifying ICMP packets as those used in ping operations. The limit extension includes the **--limit** option, with which you can limit the maximum number of matching packets in a specified time period, such as a second.

Note: In IPtables commands, chain names have to be entered in uppercase, as with the chain names INPUT, OUTPUT, and FORWARD.

In the following example, the user adds a rule to the INPUT chain to accept all packets originating from the address 192.168.0.55. Any packets that are received (`INPUT`) whose source address (`-s`) matches 192.168.0.55 are accepted and passed through (`-j ACCEPT`):

```
iptables -A INPUT -s 192.168.0.55 -j ACCEPT
```

Accepting and Denying Packets: DROP and ACCEPT

There are two built-in targets, DROP and ACCEPT. Other targets can be either user-defined chains or extensions added on, such as REJECT. Two special targets are used to manage chains, RETURN and QUEUE. RETURN indicates the end of a chain and returns to the chain it started from. QUEUE is used to send packets to user space.

```
iptables -A INPUT -s www.myjunk.com -j DROP
```

You can turn a rule into its inverse with an `!` symbol. For example, to accept all incoming packets except those from a specific address, place an `!` symbol before the `-s` option and that address. The following example will accept all packets except those from the IP address 192.168.0.45:

```
iptables -A INPUT -j ACCEPT ! -s 192.168.0.45
```

You can specify an individual address using its domain name or its IP number. For a range of addresses, you can use the IP number of their network and the network IP mask. The IP mask can be an IP number or simply the number of bits making up the mask. For example, all of the addresses in network 192.168.0 can be represented by 192.168.0.0/225.255.255.0 or by 192.168.0.0/24. To specify any address, you can use 0.0.0.0/0.0.0.0 or simply 0/0. By default, rules reference any address if no `-s` or `-d` specification exists. The following example accepts messages coming in that are from (source) any host in the 192.168.0.0 network and that are going (destination) anywhere at all (the `-d` option is left out or could be written as `-d 0/0`):

```
iptables -A INPUT -s 192.168.0.0/24  -j ACCEPT
```

The IPtables rules are usually applied to a specific network interface such as the Ethernet interface used to connect to the Internet. For a single system connected to the Internet, you will have two interfaces, one that is your Internet connection and a loopback interface (**lo**) for internal connections between users on your system. The network interface for the Internet is referenced using the device name for the interface. For example, an Ethernet card with the device name **/dev/eth0** would be referenced by the name **eth0**. A modem using PPP protocols with the device name **/dev/ppp0** would have the name **ppp0**. In IPtables rules, you use the `-i` option to indicate the input device; it can be used only with the INPUT and FORWARD chains. The `-o` option indicates the output device and can be used only for OUTPUT and FORWARD chains. Rules can then be applied to packets arriving and leaving on particular network devices. In the following examples, the first rule references the Ethernet device **eth0**, and the second, the localhost:

```
iptables -A INPUT -j DROP -i eth0 -s 192.168.0.45
iptables -A INPUT -j ACCEPT  -i lo
```

User-Defined Chains

With IPtables, the FORWARD and INPUT chains are evaluated separately. One does not feed into the other. This means that if you want to completely block certain addresses from passing through your system, you will need to add both a FORWARD rule and an INPUT rule for them.

```
iptables -A INPUT -j DROP -i eth0 -s 192.168.0.45
iptables -A FORWARD -j DROP -i eth0 -s 192.168.0.45
```

A common method for reducing repeated INPUT and FORWARD rules is to create a user chain that both the INPUT and FORWARD chains feed into. You define a user chain with the **-N** option. The next example shows the basic format for this arrangement. A new chain is created called incoming (it can be any name you choose). The rules you would define for your FORWARD and INPUT chains are now defined for the incoming chain. The INPUT and FORWARD chains then use the incoming chain as a target, jumping directly to it and using its rules to process any packets they receive.

```
iptables -N incoming

iptables -A incoming -j DROP -i eth0 -s 192.168.0.45
iptables -A incoming -j ACCEPT  -i lo

iptables -A FORWARD -j incoming
iptables -A INPUT -j incoming
```

Option	Function
-p [!] *proto*	Specifies a protocol, such as TCP, UDP, ICMP, or ALL.
-s [!] *address*[*/mask*] [!] [*port*[:*port*]]	Source address to match. With the *port* argument, you can specify the port.
--sport [!] [*port*[:*port*]]	Source port specification. You can specify a range of ports using the colon, *port:port.*
-d [!] *address*[*/mask*] [!] [*port*[:*port*]]	Destination address to match. With the *port* argument, you can specify the port.
--dport [!] [*port*[:*port*]]	Destination port specification.
--icmp-type [!] *typename*	Specifies ICMP type.
-i [!] *name*[+]	Specifies an input network interface using its name (for example, **eth0**). The + symbol functions as a wildcard. The + attached to the end of the name matches all interfaces with that prefix (**eth+** matches all Ethernet interfaces). Can be used only with the INPUT chain.
-j *target* [**port**]	Specifies the target for a rule (specify [**port**] for REDIRECT target).
--to-source < *ipaddr*>[-< *ipaddr*>][: *port-*	Used with the SNAT target, rewrites packets

port]	with new source IP address.
--to-destination < *ipaddr*>[-< *ipaddr*>] [: *port*- *port*]	Used with the DNAT target, rewrites packets with new destination IP address.
-n	Numeric output of addresses and ports, used with **-L**.
-o [!] *name*[+]	Specifies an output network interface using its name (for example, **eth0**). Can be used only with FORWARD and OUTPUT chains.
-t *table*	Specifies a table to use, as in **-t nat** for the NAT table.
-v	Verbose mode, shows rule details, used with **-L**.
-x	Expands numbers (displays exact values), used with **-L**.
[!] **-f**	Matches second through last fragments of a fragmented packet.
[!] **-V**	Prints package version.
!	Negates an option or address.
-m	Specifies a module to use, such as state.
--state	Specifies options for the state module such as NEW, INVALID, RELATED, and ESTABLISHED. Used to detect packet's state. NEW references SYN packets (new connections).
--syn	SYN packets, new connections.
--tcp-flags	TCP flags: SYN, ACK, FIN, RST, URG, PS, and ALL for all flags.
--limit	Option for the limit module (**-m limit**). Used to control the rate of matches, matching a given number of times per second.
--limit-burst	Option for the limit module (**-m limit**). Specifies maximum burst before the limit kicks in. Used to control denial-of-service attacks.

Table 17-7: IPtables Options

ICMP Packets

Firewalls often block certain Internet Control Message Protocol (ICMP) messages. ICMP redirect messages, in particular, can take control of your routing tasks. You need to enable some ICMP messages, however, such as those needed for ping, traceroute, and particularly destination-unreachable operations. In most cases, you always need to make sure destination-unreachable packets are allowed; otherwise, domain name queries could hang. Some of the more common ICMP packet types are listed in Table 17-8. You can enable an ICMP type of packet with the -- `icmp-type` option, which takes as its argument a number or a name representing the message. The following examples enable the use of echo-reply, echo-request, and destination-unreachable messages, which have the numbers 0, 8, and 3:

```
iptables -A INPUT -j ACCEPT  -p icmp -i eth0 --icmp -type  echo-reply -d 10.0.0.1
iptables -A INPUT -j ACCEPT  -p icmp -i eth0 --icmp-type  echo-request -d
10.0.0.1
iptables -A INPUT -j ACCEPT -p icmp -i eth0 --icmp-type  destination-unreachable
-d
10.0.0.1
```

Their rule listing will look like this:

```
ACCEPT      icmp --  0.0.0.0/0              10.0.0.1              icmp type 0
ACCEPT      icmp --  0.0.0.0/0              10.0.0.1              icmp type 8
ACCEPT      icmp --  0.0.0.0/0              10.0.0.1              icmp type 3
```

Ping operations need to be further controlled to avoid the ping-of-death security threat. You can do this several ways. One way is to deny any ping fragments. Ping packets are normally very small. You can block ping-of-death attacks by denying any ICMP packet that is a fragment. Use the **-f** option to indicate fragments.

```
iptables -A INPUT -p icmp -j DROP -f
```

Number	Name	Required By
0	echo-reply	ping
3	destination-unreachable	Any TCP/UDP traffic
5	redirect	Routing if not running routing daemon
8	echo-request	ping
11	time-exceeded	traceroute

Table 17-8: Common ICMP Packets

Another way is to limit the number of matches received for ping packets. You use the limit module to control the number of matches on the ICMP ping operation. Use **-m limit** to use the limit module, and **--limit** to specify the number of allowed matches. **1/s** will allow one match per second.

```
iptables -A FORWARD -p icmp --icmp-type echo-request -m limit --limit 1/s -j
ACCEPT
```

Controlling Port Access

If your system is hosting an Internet service, such as a Web or FTP server, you can use IPtables to control access to it. You can specify a particular service by using the source port (--sport) or destination port (--dport) options with the port that the service uses. IPtables lets you use names for ports such as **www** for the Web server port. The names of services and the ports they use are listed in the **/etc/services** file, which maps ports to particular services. For a domain name server, the port would be **domain**. You can also use the port number if you want, preceding the number with a colon. The following example accepts all messages to the Web server located at 192.168.0.43:

```
iptables -A INPUT -d 192.168.0.43 --dport www -j ACCEPT
```

You can also use port references to protect certain services and deny others. This approach is often used if you are designing a firewall that is much more open to the Internet, letting users make freer use of Internet connections. Certain services you know can be harmful, such as Telnet and NTP, can be denied selectively. For example, to deny any kind of Telnet operation on your firewall, you can drop all packets coming in on the Telnet port, 23. To protect NFS operations, you can deny access to the port used for the portmapper, 111. You can use either the port number or the port name.

```
# deny outside access to portmapper port on firewall.
iptables -A arriving  -j DROP -p tcp -i eth0  --dport 111
# deny outside access to telnet port on firewall.
iptables -A arriving  -j DROP -p tcp -i eth0  --dport telnet
```

The rule listing will look like this:

```
DROP      tcp  --  0.0.0.0/0     0.0.0.0/0     tcp dpt:111
DROP      tcp  --  0.0.0.0/0     0.0.0.0/0     tcp dpt:23
```

Common ports checked and their labels are shown here:

Service	Port Number	Port Label
Auth	113	auth
Finger	79	finger
FTP	21	ftp
NTP	123	ntp
Portmapper	111	sunrpc
Telnet	23	telnet
Web server	80	www

One port-related security problem is access to your X server ports that range from 6000 to 6009. On a relatively open firewall, these ports could be used to illegally access your system through your X server. A range of ports can be specified with a colon, as in 6000:6009. You can also use x11 for the first port, x11:6009. Sessions on the X server can be secured by using SSH, which normally accesses the X server on port 6010.

```
iptables -A arriving  -j DROP -p tcp -i eth0  --dport 6000:6009
```

Packet States: Connection Tracking

One of the more useful extensions is the state extension, which can easily detect tracking information for a packet. Connection tracking maintains information about a connection such as its source, destination, and port. It provides an effective means for determining which packets belong to an established or related connection. To use connection tracking, you specify the state module first with **-m state**. Then you can use the **--state** option. Here you can specify any of the following states:

State	Description
NEW	A packet that creates a new connection
ESTABLISHED	A packet that belongs to an existing connection
RELATED	A packet that is related to, but not part of, an existing connection, such as an ICMP error or a packet establishing an FTP data connection
INVALID	A packet that could not be identified for some reason
RELATED+REPLY	A packet that is related to an established connection, but not part of one directly

If you are designing a firewall that is meant to protect your local network from any attempts to penetrate it from an outside network, you may want to restrict packets coming in. Simply denying access by all packets is unfeasible because users connected to outside servers—say, on the Internet—must receive information from them. You can, instead, deny access by a particular kind of packet used to initiate a connection. The idea is that an attacker must initiate a connection from the outside. The headers of these kinds of packets have their SYN bit set on and their FIN and ACK bits empty. The state module's NEW state matches on any such SYN packet. By specifying a DROP target for such packets, you deny access by any packet that is part of an attempt to make a connection with your system. Anyone trying to connect to your system from the outside is unable to do so. Users on your local system who have initiated connections with outside hosts can still communicate with them. The following example will drop any packets trying to create a new connection on the **eth0** interface, though they will be accepted on any other interface:

```
iptables -A INPUT -m state --state NEW -i eth0 -j DROP
```

You can use the **!** operator on the **eth0** device combined with an ACCEPT target to compose a rule that will accept any new packets except those on the **eth0** device. If the **eth0** device is the only one that connects to the Internet, this still effectively blocks outside access. At the same time, input operation for other devices such as your localhost are free to make new connections. This kind of conditional INPUT rule is used to allow access overall with exceptions. It usually assumes that a later rule such as a chain policy will drop remaining packets.

```
iptables -A INPUT -m state --state NEW ! -i eth0 -j ACCEPT
```

The next example will accept any packets that are part of an established connection or related to such a connection on the **eth0** interface:

```
iptables -A INPUT -m state --state ESTABLISHED,RELATED -j ACCEPT
```

Tip: You can use the iptstate tool to display the current state table.

Specialized Connection Tracking: ftp, irc, Amanda, tftp.

To track certain kinds of packets, IPtables uses specialized connection tracking modules. These are optional modules that you have to have loaded manually. To track passive FTP connections, you would have to load the ip_conntrack_ftp module. To add NAT table support, you would also load the ip_nat_ftp module. For IRC connections, you use ip_conntrack_irc and ip_nat_irc. There are corresponding modules for Amanda (the backup server) and TFTP (Trivial FTP).

If you are writing your own iptables script, you would have to add **modprobe** commands to load the modules.

```
modprobe ip_conntrack ip_conntrack_ftp ip_nat_ftp
modprobe ip_conntrack_amanda ip_nat_amanda
```

Network Address Translation (NAT)

Network address translation (NAT) is the process whereby a system will change the destination or source of packets as they pass through the system. A packet will traverse several linked systems on a network before it reaches its final destination. Normally, they will simply pass the packet on. However, if one of these systems performs a NAT on a packet, it can change the source or destination. A packet sent to a particular destination could have its destination address changed. To make this work, the system also needs to remember such changes so that the source and destination for any reply packets are altered back to the original addresses of the packet being replied to.

NAT is often used to provide access to systems that may be connected to the Internet through only one IP address. Such is the case with networking features such as IP masquerading, support for multiple servers, and transparent proxying. With IP masquerading, NAT operations will change the destination and source of a packet moving through a firewall/gateway linking the Internet to computers on a local network. The gateway has a single IP address that the other local computers can use through NAT operations. If you have multiple servers but only one IP address, you can use NAT operations to send packets to the alternate servers. You can also use NAT operations to have your IP address reference a particular server application such as a Web server (transparent proxy). NAT tables are not implemented for ip6tables.

Adding NAT Rules

Packet selection rules for NAT operations are added to the NAT table managed by the **iptables** command. To add rules to the NAT table, you have to specify the NAT table with the -t option. Thus to add a rule to the NAT table, you would have to specify the NAT table with the **-t nat** option as shown here:

```
iptables -t nat
```

With the **-L** option, you can list the rules you have added to the NAT table:

```
iptables -t nat -L -n
```

Adding the **-n** option will list IP addresses and ports in numeric form. This will speed up the listing, as iptables will not attempt to do a DNS lookup to determine the hostname for the IP address.

Nat Targets and Chains

In addition, there are two types of NAT operations: source NAT, specified as SNAT target, and destination NAT, specified as DNAT target. SNAT target is used for rules that alter source addresses, and DNAT target, for those that alter destination addresses.

Three chains in the NAT table are used by the kernel for NAT operations. These are PREROUTING, POSTROUTING, and OUTPUT. PREROUTING is used for destination NAT (DNAT) rules. These are packets that are arriving. POSTROUTING is used for source NAT (SNAT) rules. These are for packets leaving. OUTPUT is used for destination NAT rules for locally generated packets.

As with packet filtering, you can specify source (**-s**) and destination (**-d**) addresses, as well as the input (**-i**) and output (**-o**) devices. The **-j** option will specify a target such as MASQUERADE. You would implement IP masquerading by adding a MASQUERADE rule to the POSTROUTING chain:

```
# iptables -t nat -A POSTROUTING -o eth0 -j MASQUERADE
```

To change the source address of a packet leaving your system, you would use the POSTROUTING rule with the SNAT target. For the SNAT target, you use the **--to-source** option to specify the source address:

```
# iptables -t nat -A POSTROUTING -o eth0 -j SNAT --to-source 192.168.0.4
```

To change the destination address of packets arriving on your system, you would use the PREROUTING rule with the DNAT target and the **--to-destination** option:

```
# iptables -t nat -A PREROUTING -i eth0 \
        -j DNAT --to-destination 192.168.0.3
```

Specifying a port lets you change destinations for packets arriving on a particular port. In effect, this lets you implement port forwarding. In the next example, every packet arriving on port 80 (the Web service port) is redirected to 10.0.0.3, which in this case would be a system running a Web server.

```
# iptables -t nat -A PREROUTING -i eth0 -dport 80 \
        -j DNAT --to-destination 10.0.0.3
```

With the TOS and MARK targets, you can mangle the packet to control its routing or priority. A TOS target sets the type of service for a packet, which can set the priority using criteria such as normal-service, minimize-cost, or maximize-throughput, among others.

The targets valid only for the NAT table are shown here:

SNAT	Modify source address, use `--to-source` option to specify new source address.
DNAT	Modify destination address, use `--to-destination` option to specify new destination address.
REDIRECT	Redirect a packet.
MASQUERADE	IP masquerading.
MIRROR	Reverse source and destination and send back to sender.
MARK	Modify the Mark field to control message routing.

Nat Redirection: Transparent Proxies

NAT tables can be used to implement any kind of packet redirection, a process transparent to the user. Redirection is communing used to implement a transparent proxy. Redirection of packets is carried out with the REDIRECT target. With transparent proxies, packets received can be automatically redirected to a proxy server. For example, packets arriving on the Web service port, 80, can be redirected to the Squid Proxy service port, usually 3128. This involves a command to redirect an packet, using the REDIRECT target on the PREROUTING chain:

```
# iptables -t nat -A PREROUTING -i eth1 --dport 80 -j REDIRECT --to-port 3128
```

Packet Mangling: the Mangle Table

The *packet mangling* table is used to actually modify packet information. Rules applied specifically to this table are often designed to control the mundane behavior of packets, like routing, connection size, and priority. Rules that actually modify a packet, rather than simply redirecting or stopping it, can be used only in the mangle table. For example, the TOS target can be used directly in the mangle table to change the Type of Service field to modifying a packet's priority. A TCPMSS target could be set to control the size of a connection. The ECN target lets you work around ECN black holes, and the DSCP target will let you change DSCP bits. Several extensions such as the ROUTE extension will change a packet, in this case, rewriting its destination, rather than just redirecting it.

The mangle table is indicated with the `-t mangle` option. Use the following command to see what chains are listed in your mangle table:

```
iptables -t mangle  -L
```

Several mangle table targets are shown here:

TOS	Modify the Type of Service field to manage the priority of the packet.
TCPMSS	Modify the allowed size of packets for a connection, enabling larger transmissions.
ECN	Remove ECN black hole information.
DSCP	Change DSCP bits.
ROUTE	Extension TARGET to modify destination information in the packet.

Note: The IPtables package is designed to be extensible, allowing customized targets to be added easily. This involves applying patches to the kernel and rebuilding it. See **www.netfilter.org** for more details, along with a listing of extended targets.

IPtables Scripts

Though you can enter IPtables rules from the shell command line, when you shut down your system, these commands will be lost. You will most likely need to place your IPtables rules in a script that can then be executed directly. This way you can edit and manage a complex set of rules, adding comments and maintaining their ordering.

An IPtables Script Example: IPv4

You now have enough information to create a simple IPtables script that will provide basic protection for a single system connected to the Internet. The following script, **myfilter**, provides an IPtables filtering process to protect a local network and a Web site from outside attacks. This example uses IPtables and IPv4 addressing. For IPv6 addressing you would use ip6tables, which has corresponding commands, except for the NAT rules, which would be implemented as mangle rules.

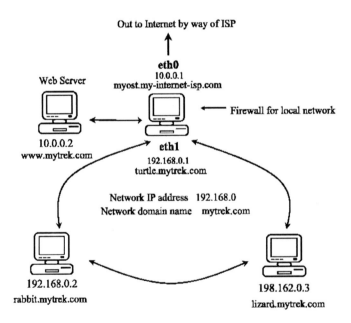

Figure 17-5: A network with a firewall

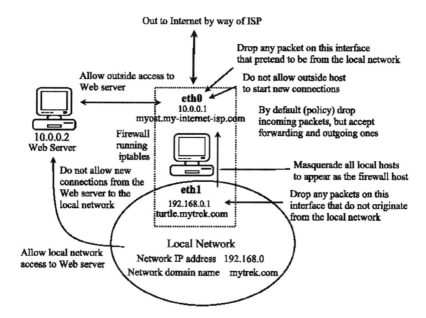

Figure 17-6: Firewall rules applied to a local network example

The script configures a simple firewall for a private network (check the IPtables HOWTO for a more complex example). If you have a local network, you could adapt this script to it. In this configuration, all remote access initiated from the outside is blocked, but two-way communication is allowed for connections that users in the network make with outside systems. In this example, the firewall system functions as a gateway for a private network whose network address is 192.168.0.0 (see Figure 17-5). The Internet address is, for the sake of this example, 10.0.0.1. The system has two Ethernet devices: one for the private network (**eth1**) and one for the Internet (**eth0**). The gateway firewall system also supports a Web server at address 10.0.0.2. Entries in this example that are too large to fit on one line are continued on a second line, with the newline quoted with a backslash.

The basic rules as they apply to different parts of the network are illustrated in Figure 17-6.

Initially, in the script you would clear your current IPtables with the flush option (-**F**), and then set the policies (default targets) for the non-user-defined rules. IP forwarding should also be turned off while the chain rules are being set:

```
echo 0 > /proc/sys/net/ipv4/ip_forward
```

Drop Policy

First, a DROP policy is set up for INPUT and FORWARD built-in IP chains. This means that if a packet does not meet a criterion in any of the rules to let it pass, it will be dropped. Then both IP spoofing attacks and any attempts from the outside to initiate connections (SYN packets) are rejected.

myfilter

```
Firewall Gateway system IP address is 10.0.0.1 using Ethernet device eth0
# Private network address is 192.168.0.0 using Ethernet device eth1
# Web site address is 10.0.0.2
# turn off IP forwarding
echo 0 > /proc/sys/net/ipv4/ip_forward
# Flush chain rules
iptables -F INPUT
iptables -F OUTPUT
iptables -F FORWARD
# set default (policy) rules
iptables -P INPUT DROP
iptables -P OUTPUT ACCEPT
iptables -P FORWARD ACCEPT

# IP spoofing, deny any packets on the internal network that have an external source address.
iptables -A INPUT -j LOG  -i eth1 \! -s 192.168.0.0/24
iptables -A INPUT -j DROP  -i eth1 \! -s 192.168.0.0/24
iptables -A FORWARD -j DROP  -i eth1 \! -s 192.168.0.0/24
# IP spoofing, deny any outside packets (any not on eth1) that have the source address of the
internal network
iptables -A INPUT -j DROP \! -i eth1 -s 192.168.0.0/24
iptables -A FORWARD -j DROP \! -i eth1 -s 192.168.0.0/24
# IP spoofing, deny any outside packets with localhost address
# (packets not on the lo interface (any on eth0 or eth1) that have the source address of
localhost)
iptables -A INPUT -j DROP  -i \! lo  -s 127.0.0.0/255.0.0.0
iptables -A FORWARD -j DROP  -i \! lo  -s  127.0.0.0/255.0.0.0

# allow all incoming messages for users on your firewall system
iptables -A INPUT -j ACCEPT  -i lo

# allow  communication to the Web server (address 10.0.0.2), port www
iptables -A INPUT  -j ACCEPT -p tcp -i eth0  --dport www -s 10.0.0.2
# Allow  established connections from Web servers to internal network
iptables -A INPUT -m state --state ESTABLISHED,RELATED -i eth0 -p tcp  --sport www -s
10.0.0.2 -d 192.168.0.0/24  -j ACCEPT
# Prevent new  connections from Web servers to internal network
iptables -A OUTPUT -m state --state  NEW -o eth0 -p tcp  --sport www -d 192.168.0.0/24  -j
DROP

# allow established and related outside communication to your system
# allow outside communication to the firewall, except for ICMP packets
iptables -A INPUT -m state --state ESTABLISHED,RELATED -i eth0 -p \! icmp -j ACCEPT
# prevent outside initiated connections
iptables -A INPUT -m state --state NEW -i eth0 -j DROP
iptables -A FORWARD -m state --state NEW -i eth0 -j DROP
# allow all local communication to and from the firewall on eth1  from the local network
iptables -A INPUT -j ACCEPT -p all -i eth1 -s 192.168.0.0/24
# Set up masquerading to allow internal machines access to outside network
iptables -t nat -A POSTROUTING -o eth0 -j MASQUERADE
# Accept ICMP Ping and Destination unreachable messages
# Others will be rejected by INPUT and OUTPUT DROP policy
iptables -A INPUT -j ACCEPT  -p icmp -i eth0 --icmp-type  echo-reply -d 10.0.0.1
iptables -A INPUT -j ACCEPT  -p icmp -i eth0 --icmp-type  echo-request -d 10.0.0.1
iptables -A INPUT -j ACCEPT -p icmp -i eth0 --icmp-type  destination-unreachable -d 10.0.0.1
# Turn on IP Forwarding
echo 1 > /proc/sys/net/ipv4/ip_forward
```

. Outside connection attempts are also logged. This is a very basic configuration that can easily be refined to your own needs by adding IPtables rules.iptables -P

```
INPUT DROP
iptables -P OUTPUT ACCEPT
iptables -P FORWARD ACCEPT
```

IP Spoofing

One way to protect the private network from the IP spoofing of any packets is to check for any outside addresses on the Ethernet device dedicated to the private network. In this example, any packet on device **eth1** (dedicated to the private network) whose source address is not that of the private network (`! -s 192.168.0.0`) is denied. Also, check to see if any packets coming from the outside are designating the private network as their source. In this example, any packets with the source address of the private network on any Ethernet device other than for the private network (**eth1**) are denied. The same strategy can be applied to the local host.

```
# IP spoofing, deny any packets on the internal network
# that has an external source address.
iptables -A INPUT -j LOG  -i eth1 \! -s 192.168.0.0/24
iptables -A INPUT -j DROP  -i eth1 \! -s 192.168.0.0/24
iptables -A FORWARD -j DROP  -i eth1 \! -s 192.168.0.0/24
# IP spoofing, deny any outside packets (any not on eth1)
# that have the source address of the internal network
iptables -A INPUT -j DROP \! -i eth1 -s 192.168.0.0/24
iptables -A FORWARD -j DROP \! -i eth1 -s 192.168.0.0/24
# IP spoofing, deny any outside packets with localhost address
# (packets not on the lo interface (any on eth0 or eth1)
# that have the source address of localhost)
iptables -A INPUT -j DROP  -i \! lo  -s  127.0.0.0/255.0.0.0
iptables -A FORWARD -j DROP  -i \! lo  -s  127.0.0.0/255.0.0.0
```

Then, you would set up rules to allow all packets sent and received within your system (localhost) to pass.

```
iptables -A INPUT -j ACCEPT  -i lo
```

Server Access

For the Web server, you want to allow access by outside users but block access by anyone attempting to initiate a connection from the Web server into the private network. In the next example, all messages are accepted to the Web server, but the Web server cannot initiate contact with the private network. This prevents anyone from breaking into the local network through the Web server, which is open to outside access. Established connections are allowed, permitting the private network to use the Web server.

```
# allow  communication to the Web server (address 10.0.0.2), port www
iptables -A INPUT  -j ACCEPT -p tcp -i eth0  --dport www -s 10.0.0.2
# Allow  established connections from Web servers to internal network
iptables -A INPUT -m state --state ESTABLISHED,RELATED -i eth0 \
  -p tcp  --sport www -s 10.0.0.2 -d 192.168.0.0/24  -j ACCEPT
# Prevent new  connections from Web servers to internal network
iptables -A OUTPUT -m state --state  NEW -o eth0 -p tcp \
  --sport www -d 192.168.0.1.0/24  -j DROP
```

Firewall Outside Access

To allow access by the firewall to outside networks, you allow input by all packets except for ICMP packets. These are handled later. The firewall is specified by the firewall device, **eth0**. First your firewall should allow established and related connections to proceed, as shown here. Then you would block outside access as described later.

```
# allow outside communication to the firewall,
# except for ICMP packets
iptables -A INPUT -m state --state ESTABLISHED,RELATED \
        -i eth0 -p \! icmp -j ACCEPT
```

Blocking Outside Initiated Access

To prevent outsiders from initiating any access to your system, create a rule to block access by SYN packets from the outside using the **state** option with NEW. Drop any new connections on the **eth0** connection (assumes only **eth0** is connected to the Internet or outside network).

```
# prevent outside initiated connections
iptables -A INPUT -m state --state NEW -i eth0 -j DROP
iptables -A FORWARD -m state --state NEW -i eth0 -j DROP
```

Local Network Access

To allow interaction by the internal network with the firewall, you allow input by all packets on the internal Ethernet connection, **eth1**. The valid internal network addresses are designated as the input source.

```
iptables -A INPUT -j ACCEPT -p all -i eth1 -s 192.168.0.0/24
```

Listing Rules

A listing of these **iptables** options shows the different rules for each option, as shown here:

```
# iptables -L
Chain INPUT (policy DROP)
target    prot opt source          destination
LOG       all  -- !192.168.0.0/24  anywhere         LOG level warning
DROP      all  -- !192.168.0.0/24  anywhere
DROP      all  -- 192.168.0.0/24   anywhere
DROP      all  -- 127.0.0.0/8      anywhere
ACCEPT    all  -- anywhere         anywhere
ACCEPT    tcp  -- 10.0.0.2         anywhere         tcp dpt:http
ACCEPT    tcp  -- 10.0.0.2         192.168.0.0/24   state RELATED,ESTABLISHED
                                                                 tcp spt:http
ACCEPT    !icmp -- anywhere        anywhere         state RELATED,ESTABLISHED
DROP      all  -- anywhere         anywhere         state NEW
ACCEPT    all  -- 192.168.0.0/24   anywhere
ACCEPT    icmp -- anywhere         10.0.0.1         icmp echo-reply
ACCEPT    icmp -- anywhere         10.0.0.1         icmp echo-request
ACCEPT    icmp -- anywhere         10.0.0.1         icmp destination-unreachable
Chain FORWARD (policy ACCEPT)
target    prot opt source          destination
```

```
DROP      all  --  !192.168.0.0/24   anywhere
DROP      all  --  192.168.0.0/24    anywhere
DROP      all  --  127.0.0.0/8       anywhere
DROP      all  --  anywhere          anywhere          state NEW

Chain OUTPUT (policy ACCEPT)
target   prot opt source        destination
DROP         tcp  --  anywhere       192.168.0.0/24   state NEW tcp spt:http
```

```
# iptables -t nat -L
Chain PREROUTING (policy ACCEPT)
target       prot opt source          destination
Chain POSTROUTING (policy ACCEPT)
target       prot opt source          destination
MASQUERADE  all  --  anywhere          anywhere
Chain OUTPUT (policy ACCEPT)
target       prot opt source        destination
```

User-Defined Rules

For more complex rules, you may want to create your own chain to reduce repetition. A common method is to define a user chain for both INPUT and FORWARD chains, so that you do not have to repeat DROP operations for each. Instead, you would have only one user chain that both FORWARD and INPUT chains would feed into for DROP operations. Keep in mind that both FORWARD and INPUT operations may have separate rules in addition to the ones they share. In the next example, a user-defined chain called arriving is created. The chain is defined with the **-N** option at the top of the script:

```
iptables -N arriving
```

A user chain has to be defined before it can be used as a target in other rules. So you have to first define and add all the rules for that chain, and then use it as a target. The arriving chain is first defined and its rules added. Then, at the end of the file, it is used as a target for both the INPUT and FORWARD chains. The INPUT chain lists rules for accepting packets, whereas the FORWARD chain has an ACCEPT policy that will accept them by default.

```
iptables -N arriving
iptables -F arriving
# IP spoofing, deny any packets on the internal network
# that has an external source address.
iptables -A arriving -j LOG  -i eth1 \! -s 192.168.0.0/24
iptables -A arriving -j DROP  -i eth1 \! -s 192.168.0.0/24
iptables -A arriving -j DROP \! -i eth1 -s 192.168.0.0/24
.........................
# entries at end of script
iptables -A INPUT -j arriving
iptables -A FORWARD -j arriving
```

A listing of the corresponding rules is shown here:

```
Chain INPUT (policy DROP)
target    prot opt source            destination
arriving  all  --  0.0.0.0/0          0.0.0.0/0
Chain FORWARD (policy ACCEPT)
target    prot opt source            destination
arriving  all  --  0.0.0.0/0          0.0.0.0/0
Chain arriving (2 references)
target    prot opt source            destination
LOG       all  --  !192.168.0.0/24   0.0.0.0/0        LOG flags 0 level 4
DROP      all  --  !192.168.0.0/24   0.0.0.0/0
DROP      all  --  192.168.0.0/24    0.0.0.0/0
```

For rules where chains may differ, you will still need to enter separate rules. In the **myfilter** script, the FORWARD chain has an ACCEPT policy, allowing all forwarded packets to the local network to pass through the firewall. If the FORWARD chain had a DROP policy, like the INPUT chain, then you may need to define separate rules under which the FORWARD chain could accept packets. In this example, the FORWARD and INPUT chains have different rules for accepting packets on the **eth1** device. The INPUT rule is more restrictive. To enable the local network to receive forwarded packets through the firewall, you could enable forwarding on its device using a separate FORWARD rule, as shown here:

```
iptables -A FORWARD -j ACCEPT -p all -i eth1
```

The INPUT chain would accept packets only from the local network.

```
iptables -A INPUT -j ACCEPT -p all -i eth1 -s 192.168.0.0/24
```

Masquerading Local Networks

To implement masquerading, where systems on the private network can use the gateway's Internet address to connect to Internet hosts, you create a NAT table (**-t nat**) POSTROUTING rule with a MASQUERADE target.

```
iptables -t nat -A POSTROUTING -o eth0 -j MASQUERADE
```

Controlling ICMP Packets

In addition, to allow ping and destination-reachable ICMP packets, you enter INPUT rules with the firewall as the destination. To enable ping operations, you use both echo-reply and echo-request ICMP types, and for destination unreachable, you use the destination-unreachable type.

```
iptables -A INPUT -j ACCEPT  -p icmp -i eth0 --icmp-type \
   echo-reply -d 10.0.0.1
iptables -A INPUT -j ACCEPT  -p icmp -i eth0 --icmp-type \
   echo-request -d 10.0.0.1
iptables -A INPUT -j ACCEPT -p icmp -i eth0 --icmp-type \
   destination-unreachable -d 10.0.0.1
```

At the end, IP forwarding is turned on again.

```
echo 1 > /proc/sys/net/ipv4/ip_forward
```

Simple LAN Configuration

To create a script to support a simple LAN without any Internet services like Web servers, you would just not include rules for supporting those services. You would still need FORWARD and POSTROUTING rules for connecting your local hosts to the Internet, as well as rules governing interaction between the hosts and the firewall. To modify the example script to support a simple LAN without the Web server, just remove the three rules governing the Web server. Leave everything else the same.

LAN Configuration with Internet Services on the Firewall System

Often, in the same system that functions as a firewall is also used to run Internet servers, like Web and FTP servers. In this case the firewall rules are applied to the ports used for those services. The example script dealt with a Web server running on a separate host system. If the Web server were instead running on the firewall system, you would apply the Web server firewall rules to the port that the Web server uses. Normally the port used for a Web server is 80. In the following example, the IPtables rules for the Web server have been applied to port www, port 80, on the firewall system. The modification simply requires removing the old Web server host address references, 10.0.0.2.

```
# allow  communication to the Web server, port www (port 80)
iptables -A INPUT  -j ACCEPT -p tcp -i eth0  --dport www
# Allow  established connections from Web servers to internal network
iptables -A INPUT -m state --state ESTABLISHED,RELATED -i eth0 \
   -p tcp  --sport www -d 192.168.0.0/24  -j ACCEPT
# Prevent new  connections from Web servers to internal network
iptables -A OUTPUT -m state --state  NEW -o eth0 -p tcp \
  --sport www -d 192.168.0.1.0/24 -j DROP
```

Similar entries could be set up for an FTP server. Should you run several Internet services, you could use a user-defined rule to run the same rules on each service, rather than repeating three separate rules per service. Working from the example script, you would use two defined rules, one for INPUT and one for OUTPUT, controlling incoming and outgoing packets for the services.

```
iptables -N inputservice
iptables -N outputservice
iptables -F inputservice
iptables -F outputservice
# allow  communication to the service
iptables -A inputservice  -j ACCEPT -p tcp -i eth0
# Allow  established connections from the service to internal network
iptables -A inputservice -m state --state ESTABLISHED,RELATED -i eth0 \
   -p tcp  -d 192.168.0.0/24  -j ACCEPT
# Prevent new  connections from service to internal network
iptables -A outputservice -m state --state  NEW -o eth0 -p tcp \
  -d 192.168.0.1.0/24 -j DROP
.........................
# Run rules for the Web server, port www (port 80)
iptables -A INPUT  --dport www -j inputservice
iptables -A INPUT  --dport www -j outputservice
# Run rules for the FTP server, port ftp (port 21)
iptables -A OUTPUT  --dport ftp -j inputservice
iptables -A OUTPUT  --dport ftp -j outputservice
```

IP Masquerading

On Linux systems, you can set up a network in which you can have one connection to the Internet, which several systems on your network can use. This way, using only one IP address, several different systems can connect to the Internet. This method is called *IP masquerading,* where a system masquerades as another system, using that system's IP address. In such a network, one system is connected to the Internet with its own IP address, while the other systems are connected on a local area network (LAN) to this system. When a local system wants to access the network, it masquerades as the Internet-connected system, borrowing its IP address.

IP masquerading is implemented on Linux using the IPtables firewall tool. In effect, you set up a firewall, which you then configure to do IP masquerading. Currently, IP masquerading supports all the common network services—as does IPtables firewall—such as Web browsing, Telnet, and ping. Other services, such as IRC, FTP, and RealAudio, require the use of certain modules. Any services you want local systems to access must also be on the firewall system because request and response actually are handled by services on that system.

You can find out more information on IP masquerading at the IP Masquerade Resource Web site at **ipmasq.webhop.net**. In particular, the Linux IP Masquerade mini-HOWTO provides a detailed, step-by-step guide to setting up IP masquerading on your system. IP masquerading must be supported by the kernel before you can use it. If your kernel does not support it, you may have to rebuild the kernel, including IP masquerade support, or use loadable modules to add it. See the IP Masquerade mini-HOWTO for more information.

With IP masquerading, as implemented on Linux systems, the machine with the Internet address is also the firewall and gateway for the LAN of machines that use the firewall's Internet address to connect to the Internet. Firewalls that also implement IP masquerading are sometimes referred to as *MASQ gates.* With IP masquerading, the Internet-connected system (the firewall) listens for Internet requests from hosts on its LAN. When it receives one, it replaces the requesting local host's IP address with the Internet IP address of the firewall and then passes the request out to the Internet, as if the request were its own. Replies from the Internet are then sent to the firewall system. The replies the firewall receives are addressed to the firewall using its Internet address. The firewall then determines the local system to whose request the reply is responding. It then strips off its IP address and sends the response on to the local host across the LAN. The connection is transparent from the perspective of the local machines. They appear to be connected directly to the Internet.

Masquerading Local Networks

IP masquerading is often used to allow machines on a private network to access the Internet. These could be machines in a home network or a small LAN, such as for a small business. Such a network might have only one machine with Internet access, and as such, only the one Internet address. The local private network would have IP addresses chosen from the private network allocations (10., 172.16., or 192.168.). Ideally, the firewall has two Ethernet cards: one for an interface to the LAN (for example, **eth1**) and one for an interface to the Internet, such as **eth0** (for dial-up ISPs, this would be **ppp0** for the modem). The card for the Internet connection (**eth0**) would be assigned the Internet IP address. The Ethernet interface for the local network (**eth1**, in this example) is the firewall Ethernet interface. Your private LAN would have a network address like 192.168.0. Its Ethernet firewall interface (**eth1**) would be assigned the IP address 192.168.0.1. In effect, the firewall interface lets the firewall operate as the local network's gateway. The firewall is then configured to masquerade any packets coming from the private network. Your LAN needs to have its own domain name server, identifying the machines on your network, including your firewall. Each local machine needs to have the firewall specified as its gateway. Try not to use IP aliasing to assign both the firewall and Internet IP addresses to the same physical interface. Use separate interfaces for them, such as two Ethernet cards, or an Ethernet card and a modem (**ppp0**).

Masquerading NAT Rules

In Netfilter, IP masquerading is a NAT operation and is not integrated with packet filtering as in IP Chains. IP masquerading commands are placed on the NAT table and treated separately from the packet-filtering commands. Use IPtables to place a masquerade rule on the NAT table. First reference the NAT table with the **-t nat** option. Then add a rule to the POSTROUTING chain with the **-o** option specifying the output device and the **-j** option with the MASQUERADE command.

```
iptables -t nat -A POSTROUTING -o eth0 -j MASQUERADE
```

IP Forwarding

The next step is to turn on IP forwarding, either manually or by setting the **net.ipv4.ip_forward** variable in the **/etc/sysctl.conf** file and running **sysctl** with the -p option. IP forwarding will be turned off by default. For IPv6, use **net.ipv6.conf.all.forwarding**. The **/etc/sysctl.conf** entries are shown here:

```
net.ipv4.ip_forward = 1
net.ipv6.conf.all.forwarding = 1
```

You then run **sysctl** with the -p option.

```
sysctl -p
```

You can directly change the respective forwarding files with an **echo** command as shown here:

```
echo 1 > /proc/sys/net/ipv4/ip_forward
```

For IPv6, you would to use the forwarding file in the corresponding **/proc/sys/net/ipv6** directory, **conf/all/forwarding**.

```
echo 1 > /proc/sys/net/ipv6/conf/all/forwarding
```

Masquerading Selected Hosts

Instead of masquerading all local hosts as the single IP address of the firewall/gateway host, you could use the NAT table to rewrite addresses for a few selected hosts. Such an approach is often applied to setups where you want several local hosts to appear as Internet servers. Using the DNAT and SNAT targets, you can direct packets to specific local hosts. You would use rules on the PREROUTING and POSTROUTING chains to direct input and output packets.

For example, the Web server described in the previous example could have been configured as a local host to which a DNAT target could redirect any packets originally received for 10.0.0.2. Say the Web server was set up on 192.168.0.5. It could appear as having the address 10.0.0.2 on the Internet. Packets sent to 10.0.0.2 would be rewritten and directed to 192.168.0.5 by the NAT table. You would use the PREROUTING chain with the **-d** option to handle incoming packets and POSTROUTING with the **-s** option for outgoing packets.

```
iptables -t nat -A PREROUTING -d 10.0.0.2  \
         --to-destination 192.168.0.5 -j DNAT
iptables -t nat -A POSTROUTING -s 192.168.0.5 \
         --to-source 10.0.0.2 -j SNAT
```

Tip: Bear in mind that with IPtables, masquerading is not combined with the FORWARD chain, as it is with IP Chains. So, if you specify a DROP policy for the FORWARD chain, you will also have to specifically enable FORWARD operation for the network that is being masqueraded. You will need both a POSTROUTING rule and a FORWARD rule.

ubuntu

Part 5: Shells

Shells
Files and Directories

18. Shells

The *shell* is a command interpreter that provides a line-oriented interactive and non-interactive interface between the user and the operating system. You enter commands on a command line; they are interpreted by the shell and then sent as instructions to the operating system (the command line interface is accessible from Gnome and KDE through a Terminal windows – Applications/Accessories menu). You can also place commands in a script file to be consecutively executed much like a program. This interpretive capability of the shell provides for many sophisticated features. For example, the shell has a set of file expansion characters that can generate filenames. The shell can redirect input and output, as well as run operations in the background, freeing you to perform other tasks.

Shell	Web Site
www.gnu.org/software/bash	BASH Web site with online manual, FAQ, and current releases
www.gnu.org/software/bash/manual/bash.html	BASH online manual
www.zsh.org	Z shell Web site with referrals to FAQs and current downloads.
www.tcsh.org	TCSH Web site with detailed support including manual, tips, FAQ, and recent releases
www.kornshell.com	Korn shell site with manual, FAQ, and references

Table 18-1: Linux Shells

Several different types of shells have been developed for Linux: the Bourne Again shell (BASH), the Korn shell, the TCSH shell, and the Z shell. All shells are available for your use, although the BASH shell is the default. You only need one type of shell to do your work. Ubuntu Linux includes all the major shells, although it installs and uses the BASH shell as the default. If you use the command line shell, you will be using the BASH shell unless you specify another. This chapter discusses the BASH shell, which shares many of the same features as other shells.

You can find out more about shells at their respective Web sites as listed in Table 18-1. Also, a detailed online manual is available for each installed shell. Use the **man** command and the shell's keyword to access them, **bash** for the BASH shell, **ksh** for the Korn shell, **zsh** for the Z shell, and **tsch** for the TSCH shell. For example, the command **man bash** will access the BASH shell online manual.

Note: You can find out more about the BASH shell at **www.gnu.org/software/bash**. A detailed online manual is available on your Linux system using the **man** command with the **bash** keyword.

The Command Line

The Linux command line interface consists of a single line into which you enter commands with any of their options and arguments. From GNOME or KDE, you can access the command line interface by opening a terminal window. Should you start Linux with the command line interface, you will be presented with a BASH shell command line when you log in.

By default, the BASH shell has a dollar sign (**$**) prompt, but Linux has several other types of shells, each with its own prompt (like **%** for the C shell). The root user will have a different prompt, the **#**. A shell *prompt,* such as the one shown here, marks the beginning of the command line:

```
$
```

You can enter a command along with options and arguments at the prompt. For example, with an **-l** option, the **ls** command will display a line of information about each file, listing such data as its size and the date and time it was last modified. In the next example, the user enters the **ls** command followed by a **-l** option. The dash before the **-l** option is required. Linux uses it to distinguish an option from an argument.

```
$ ls -l
```

If you wanted only the information displayed for a particular file, you could add that file's name as the argument, following the **-l** option:

```
$ ls -l mydata
-rw-r--r-- 1 chris weather 207 Feb 20 11:55 mydata
```

Tip: Some commands can be complex and take some time to execute. When you mistakenly execute the wrong command, you can interrupt and stop such commands with the interrupt key—CTRL-C.

You can enter a command on several lines by typing a backslash just before you press ENTER. The backslash "escapes" the ENTER key, effectively continuing the same command line to the next line. In the next example, the **cp** command is entered on three lines. The first two lines end in a backslash, effectively making all three lines one command line.

```
$ cp -i \
mydata \
/home/george/myproject/newdata
```

You can also enter several commands on the same line by separating them with a semicolon (;). In effect the semicolon operates as an execute operation. Commands will be executed in the sequence they are entered. The following command executes an `ls` command followed by a `date` command.

```
$ ls ; date
```

You can also conditionally run several commands on the same line with the `&&` operator. A command is executed only if the previous one is true. This feature is useful for running several dependent scripts on the same line. In the next example, the `ls` command is run only if the `date` command is successfully executed.

```
$ date && ls
```

TIP: Command can also be run as arguments on a command line, using their results for other commands. To run a command within a command line, you encase the command in back quotes, see Values from Linux Commands later in this chapter.

Command Line Editing

The BASH shell, which is your default shell, has special command line editing capabilities that you may find helpful as you learn Linux (see Table 18-2). You can easily modify commands you have entered before executing them, moving anywhere on the command line and inserting or deleting characters. This is particularly helpful for complex commands. You can use the CTRL-F or RIGHT ARROW key to move forward a character, or the CTRL-B or LEFT ARROW key to move back a character. CTRL-D or DEL deletes the character the cursor is on, and CTRL-H or BACKSPACE deletes the character before the cursor. To add text, you use the arrow keys to move the cursor to where you want to insert text and type the new characters. You can even cut words with the CTRL-W or ALT-D key and then use the CTRL-Y key to paste them back in at a different position, effectively moving the words. As a rule, the CTRL version of the command operates on characters, and the ALT version works on words, such as CTRL-T to transpose characters and ALT-T to transpose words. At any time, you can press ENTER to execute the command.

For example, if you make a spelling mistake when entering a command, rather than reentering the entire command, you can use the editing operations to correct the mistake. The actual associations of keys and their tasks, along with global settings, are specified in the **/etc/inputrc** file.

The editing capabilities of the BASH shell command line are provided by Readline. Readline supports numerous editing operations. You can even bind a key to a selected editing operation. Readline uses the **/etc/inputrc** file to configure key bindings. This file is read automatically by your **/etc/profile** shell configuration file when you log in. Users can customize their editing commands by creating an **.inputrc** file in their home directory (this is a dot file). It may be best to first copy the **/etc/inputrc** file as your **.inputrc** file and then edit it. **/etc/profile** will first check for a local **.inputrc** file before accessing the **/etc/inputrc** file. You can find out more about Readline in the BASH shell reference manual at **www.gnu.org/manual/bash**.

Command and Filename Completion

The BASH command line has a built-in feature that performs command line and file name completion. Automatic completions can be effected using the TAB key. If you enter an incomplete pattern as a command or filename argument, you can then press the TAB key to activate the command and filename completion feature, which completes the pattern. Directories will have a / attached to their name. If more than one command or file has the same prefix, the shell simply beeps and waits for you to enter the TAB key again. It then displays a list of possible command completions and waits for you to add enough characters to select a unique command or filename.

Movement Commands	Operation
CTRL-F, RIGHT-ARROW	Move forward a character
CTRL-B, LEFT-ARROW	Move backward a character
CTRL-A or HOME	Move to beginning of line
CTRL-E or END	Move to end of line
ALT-F	Move forward a word
ALT-B	Move backward a word
CTRL-L	Clear screen and place line at top
Editing Commands	**Operation**
CTRL-D or DEL	Delete character cursor is on
CTRL-H or BACKSPACE	Delete character before the cursor
CTRL-K	Cut remainder of line from cursor position
CTRL-U	Cut from cursor position to beginning of line
CTRL-W	Cut previous word
CTRL-C	Cut entire line
ALT-D	Cut the remainder of a word
ALT-DEL	Cut from the cursor to the beginning of a word
CTRL-Y	Paste previous cut text
ALT-Y	Paste from set of previously cut text
CTRL-Y	Paste previous cut text
CTRL-V	Insert quoted text, used for inserting control or meta (Alt) keys as text, such as CTRL-B for backspace or CTRL-T for tabs
ALT-T	Transpose current and previous word
ALT-L	Lowercase current word
ALT-U	Uppercase current word
ALT-C	Capitalize current word
CTRL-SHIFT-_	Undo previous change

Table 18-2: Command Line Editing Operations

For situations where you know there are likely multiple possibilities, you can just press the ESC key instead of two TABs. In the next example, the user issues a `cat` command with an incomplete filename. When the user presses the TAB key, the system searches for a match and, when it finds one, fills in the filename. The user can then press ENTER to execute the command.

```
$ cat pre tab
$ cat preface
```

The automatic completions also works with the names of variables, users, and hosts. In this case, the partial text needs to be preceded by a special character, indicating the type of name. A listing of possible automatic completions follows:

- Filenames begin with any text or /.

- Shell variable text begins with a $ sign.

- User name text begins with a ~ sign.

- Host name text begins with a @.

- Commands, aliases, and text in files begin with normal text.

Variables begin with a **$** sign, so any text beginning with a dollar sign is treated as a variable to be completed. Variables are selected from previously defined variables, like system shell variables. User names begin with a tilde (~). Host names begin with a @ sign, with possible names taken from the **/etc/hosts** file.For example, to complete the variable HOME given just $HOM, simple enter a tab character.

```
$ echo $HOM <tab>
$ echo $HOME
```

If you entered just an H, then you could enter two tabs to see all possible variables beginning with H. The command line is redisplayed, letting you complete the name.

```
$ echo $H <tab> <tab>
$HISTCMD $HISTFILE $HOME $HOSTTYPE HISTFILE  $HISTSIZE $HISTNAME
$ echo $H
```

Command (CTRL-R for listing possible completions)	Description
TAB	Automatic completion
TAB TAB or ESC	List possible completions
ALT-/, CTRL-R-/	Filename completion, normal text for automatic
ALT-$, CTRL-R-$	Shell variable completion, $ for automatic
ALT-~, CTRL-R-~	User name completion, ~ for automatic
ALT-@, CTRL-R-@	Host name completion, @ for automatic
ALT-!, CTRL-R-!	Command name completion, normal text for automatic

Table 18-3: Command Line Text Completion Commands

You can also specifically select the kind of text to complete, using corresponding command keys. In this case, it does not matter what kind of sign a name begins with.

For example, the ALT-~ will treat the current text as a user name. ALT-@ will treat it as a host name, and ALT-$, as a variable. ALT-! will treat it as a command. To display a list of possible completions, use the CTRL-X key with the appropriate completion key, as in CTRL-X-$ to list possible variable completions. See Table 18-3 for a complete listing.

History

The BASH shell keeps a list, called a *history list,* of your previously entered commands. You can display each command, in turn, on your command line by pressing the UP ARROW key. The DOWN ARROW key moves you down the list. You can modify and execute any of these previous commands when you display them on your command line.

Tip: The capability to redisplay a previous command is helpful when you've already executed a command you had entered incorrectly. In this case, you would be presented with an error message and a new, empty command line. By pressing the UP ARROW key, you can redisplay your previous command, make corrections to it, and then execute it again. This way, you would not have to enter the whole command again.

History Events

In the BASH shell, the *history utility* keeps a record of the most recent commands you have executed. The commands are numbered starting at 1, and a limit exists to the number of commands remembered—the default is 500. The history utility is a kind of short-term memory, keeping track of the most recent commands you have executed. To see the set of your most recent commands, type **history** on the command line and press ENTER. A list of your most recent commands is then displayed, preceded by a number.

```
$ history
1 cp mydata today
2 vi mydata
3 mv mydata reports
4 cd reports
5 ls
```

Each of these commands is technically referred to as an event. An *event* describes an action that has been taken—a command that has been executed. The events are numbered according to their sequence of execution. The most recent event has the highest number. Each of these events can be identified by its number or beginning characters in the command.

The history utility enables you to reference a former event, placing it on your command line and enabling you to execute it. The easiest way to do this is to use the UP ARROW and DOWN ARROW keys to place history events on your command line, one at a time. You needn't display the list first with **history**. Pressing the UP ARROW key once places the last history event on your command line. Pressing it again places the next history event on your command. Pressing the DOWN ARROW key places the previous event on the command line.

You can use certain control and meta keys to perform other history operations like searching the history list. A meta key is the ALT key, and the ESC key on keyboards that have no ALT key. The ALT key is used here. ALT-< will move you to the beginning of the history list; ALT-N will search it. CTRL-S and CTRL-R will perform incremental searches, display matching commands as you type in a search string. Table 18-4 lists the different commands for referencing the history list.

History Commands	Description
CTRL-N or DOWN ARROW	Moves down to the next event in the history list
CTRL-P or UP ARROW	Moves up to the previous event in the history list
ALT-<	Moves to the beginning of the history event list
ALT->	Moves to the end of the history event list
ALT-N	Forward Search, next matching item
ALT-P	Backward Search, previous matching item
CTRL-S	Forward Search History, forward incremental search
CTRL-R	Reverse Search History, reverse incremental search
fc *event-reference*	Edits an event with the standard editor and then executes it **Options** -l List recent history events; same as **history** command **-e** *editor event-reference* Invokes a specified editor to edit a specific event
History Event References	
! *event num*	References an event with an event number
! !	References the previous command
! *characters*	References an event with beginning characters
! ?*pattern***?**	References an event with a pattern in the event
! -*event num*	References an event with an offset from the first event
! *num-num*	References a range of events

Table 18-4: History Commands and History Event References

Tip: If more than one history event matches what you have entered, you will hear a beep, and you can then enter more characters to help uniquely identify the event.

You can also reference and execute history events using the **!** history command. The **!** is followed by a reference that identifies the command. The reference can be either the number of the event or a beginning set of characters in the event. In the next example, the third command in the history list is referenced first by number and then by the beginning characters:

```
$ !3
mv mydata reports
$ !mv my
mv mydata reports
```

You can also reference an event using an offset from the end of the list. A negative number will offset from the end of the list to that event, thereby referencing it. In the next example, the fourth command, **cd mydata**, is referenced using a negative offset, and then executed. Remember that you are offsetting from the end of the list—in this case, event 5—up toward the beginning of the list, event 1. An offset of 4 beginning from event 5 places you at event 2.

```
$ !-4
vi mydata
```

To reference the last event, you use a following !, as in !!. In the next example, the command !! executes the last command the user executed—in this case, **ls**:

```
$ !!
ls
mydata today reports
```

Filename Expansion: *, ?, [ ]

Filenames are the most common arguments used in a command. Often you may know only part of the filename, or you may want to reference several filenames that have the same extension or begin with the same characters. The shell provides a set of special characters that search out, match, and generate a list of filenames. These are the asterisk, the question mark, and brackets (*, ?, []). Given a partial filename, the shell uses these matching operators to search for files and expand to a list of filenames found. The shell replaces the partial filename argument with the expanded list of matched filenames. This list of filenames can then become the arguments for commands such as **ls**, which can operate on many files. Table 18-5 lists the shell's file expansion characters.

Matching Multiple Characters

The asterisk (*) references files beginning or ending with a specific set of characters. You place the asterisk before or after a set of characters that form a pattern to be searched for in filenames.

If the asterisk is placed before the pattern, filenames that end in that pattern are searched for. If the asterisk is placed after the pattern, filenames that begin with that pattern are searched for. Any matching filename is copied into a list of filenames generated by this operation.

In the next example, all filenames beginning with the pattern "doc" are searched for and a list generated. Then all filenames ending with the pattern "day" are searched for and a list is generated. The last example shows how the * can be used in any combination of characters.

```
$ ls
doc1 doc2 document docs mydoc monday tuesday
$ ls doc*
doc1 doc2 document docs
$ ls *day
monday tuesday
$ ls m*d*
monday
$
```

Filenames often include an extension specified with a period and followed by a string denoting the file type, such as **.c** for C files, **.cpp** for C++ files, or even **.jpg** for JPEG image files. The extension has no special status and is only part of the characters making up the filename. Using the asterisk makes it easy to select files with a given extension. In the next example, the asterisk is used to list only those files with a **.c** extension. The asterisk placed before the **.c** constitutes the argument for **ls**.

Common Shell Symbols	Execution
ENTER	Execute a command line.
;	Separate commands on the same command line.
`command`	Execute a command.
$ (*command*)	Execute a command.
[ ]	Match on a class of possible characters in filenames.
\	Quote the following character. Used to quote special characters.
|	Pipe the standard output of one command as input for another command.
&	Execute a command in the background.
!	History command.

File Expansion Symbols	Execution
*	Match on any set of characters in filenames.
?	Match on any single character in filenames.
[ ]	Match on a class of characters in filenames.

Redirection Symbols	Execution
>	Redirect the standard output to a file or device, creating the file if it does not exist and overwriting the file if it does exist.
>!	The exclamation point forces the overwriting of a file if it already exists.
<	Redirect the standard input from a file or device to a program.
>>	Redirect the standard output to a file or device, appending the output to the end of the file.

Standard Error Redirection Symbols	Execution
2>	Redirect the standard error to a file or device.
2>>	Redirect and append the standard error to a file or device.
2>&1	Redirect the standard error to the standard output.

Table 18-5: Shell Symbols

```
$ ls *.c
calc.c main.c
```

You can use * with the rm command to erase several files at once. The asterisk first selects a list of files with a given extension, or beginning or ending with a given set of characters, and then it presents this list of files to the rm command to be erased. In the next example, the rm command erases all files beginning with the pattern "doc":

```
$ rm doc*
```

Tip: Use the * file expansion character carefully and sparingly with the rm command. The combination can be dangerous. A misplaced * in an rm command without the -i option could easily erase all the files in your current directory. The -i option will first prompt the user to confirm whether the file should be deleted.

Matching Single Characters

The question mark (?) matches only a single incomplete character in filenames. Suppose you want to match the files **doc1** and **docA**, but not the file **document**. Whereas the asterisk will match filenames of any length, the question mark limits the match to just one extra character. The next example matches files that begin with the word "doc" followed by a single differing letter:

```
$ ls
doc1 docA document
$ ls doc?
doc1 docA
```

Matching a Range of Characters

Whereas the * and ? file expansion characters specify incomplete portions of a filename, the brackets ([]) enable you to specify a set of valid characters to search for. Any character placed within the brackets will be matched in the filename. Suppose you want to list files beginning with "doc", but only ending in *1* or *A*. You are not interested in filenames ending in *2* or *B,* or any other character. Here is how it's done:

```
$ ls
doc1 doc2 doc3 docA docB docD document
$ ls doc[1A]
doc1 docA
```

You can also specify a set of characters as a range, rather than listing them one by one. A dash placed between the upper and lower bounds of a set of characters selects all characters within that range. The range is usually determined by the character set in use. In an ASCII character set, the range "a-g" will select all lowercase alphabetic characters from *a* through *g,* inclusive. In the next example, files beginning with the pattern "doc" and ending in characters *1* through *3* are selected. Then, those ending in characters *B* through *E* are matched.

```
$ ls doc[1-3]
doc1 doc2 doc3
$ ls doc[B-E]
docB docD
```

You can combine the brackets with other file expansion characters to form flexible matching operators. Suppose you want to list only filenames ending in either a **.c** or **.o** extension, but no other extension. You can use a combination of the asterisk and brackets: `* [co]`. The asterisk matches all filenames, and the brackets match only filenames with extension **.c** or **.o**.

```
$ ls *.[co]
main.c  main.o  calc.c
```

Matching Shell Symbols

At times, a file expansion character is actually part of a filename. In these cases, you need to quote the character by preceding it with a backslash to reference the file. In the next example, the user needs to reference a file that ends with the **?** character, **answers?**. The **?** is, however, a file expansion character and would match any filename beginning with "answers" that has one or more characters. In this case, the user quotes the **?** with a preceding backslash to reference the filename.

```
$ ls answers\?
answers?
```

Placing the filename in double quotes will also quote the character.

```
$ ls "answers?"
answers?
```

This is also true for filenames or directories that have white space characters like the space character. In this case you could either use the backslash to quote the space character in the file or directory name, or place the entire name in double quotes.

```
$ ls My\ Documents
My Documents
$ ls "My Documents"
My Documents
```

Generating Patterns

Though not a file expansion operation, { } is often useful for generating names that you can use to create or modify files and directories. The braces operation only generates a list of names. It does not match on existing filenames. Patterns are placed within the braces and separated with commas. Any pattern placed within the braces will be used to generate a version of the pattern, using either the preceding or following pattern, or both. Suppose you want to generate a list of names beginning with "doc", but only ending in the patterns "ument", "final", and "draft". Here is how it's done:

```
$ echo doc{ument,final,draft}
document docfinal docdraft
```

Since the names generated do not have to exist, you could use the { } operation in a command to create directories, as shown here:

```
$ mkdir {fall,winter,spring}report
$ ls
fallreport springreport winterreport
```

Standard Input/Output and Redirection

The data in input and output operations is organized like a file. Data input at the keyboard is placed in a data stream arranged as a continuous set of bytes. Data output from a command or program is also placed in a data stream and arranged as a continuous set of bytes. This input data stream is referred to in Linux as the *standard input,* while the output data stream is called the *standard output.* There is also a separate output data stream reserved solely for error messages, called the *standard error* (see the section "Redirecting and Piping the Standard Error: >&, 2>" later in this chapter).

Because the standard input and standard output have the same organization as that of a file, they can easily interact with files. Linux has a redirection capability that lets you easily move data in and out of files. You can redirect the standard output so that, instead of displaying the output on a screen, you can save it in a file. You can also redirect the standard input away from the keyboard to a file, so that input is read from a file instead of from your keyboard.

When a Linux command is executed that produces output, this output is placed in the standard output data stream. The default destination for the standard output data stream is a device—in this case, the screen. *Devices,* such as the keyboard and screen, are treated as files. They receive and send out streams of bytes with the same organization as that of a byte-stream file. The screen is a device that displays a continuous stream of bytes. By default, the standard output will send its data to the screen device, which will then display the data.

For example, the `ls` command generates a list of all filenames and outputs this list to the standard output. Next, this stream of bytes in the standard output is directed to the screen device. The list of filenames is then printed on the screen. The `cat` command also sends output to the standard output. The contents of a file are copied to the standard output, whose default destination is the screen. The contents of the file are then displayed on the screen.

Redirecting the Standard Output: > and >>

Suppose that instead of displaying a list of files on the screen, you would like to save this list in a file. In other words, you would like to direct the standard output to a file rather than the screen. To do this, you place the output redirection operator, the greater-than sign (`>`) , followed by the name of a file on the command line after the Linux command. Table 18-6 lists the different ways you can use the redirection operators. In the next example, the output of the `ls` command is redirected from the screen device to a file:

```
$ ls -l *.c > programlist
```

The redirection operation creates the new destination file. If the file already exists, it will be overwritten with the data in the standard output. You can set the `noclobber` feature to prevent overwriting an existing file with the redirection operation. In this case, the redirection operation on an existing file will fail. You can overcome the `noclobber` feature by placing an exclamation point after the redirection operator. You can place the `noclobber` command in a shell configuration file to make it an automatic default operation. The next example sets the `noclobber` feature for the BASH shell and then forces the overwriting of the **oldarticle** file if it already exists:

```
$ set -o noclobber
$ cat myarticle >! oldarticle
```

Although the redirection operator and the filename are placed after the command, the redirection operation is not executed after the command. In fact, it is executed before the command. The redirection operation creates the file and sets up the redirection before it receives any data from the standard output. If the file already exists, it will be destroyed and replaced by a file of the same name. In effect, the command generating the output is executed only after the redirected file has been created.

Command	Execution
ENTER	Execute a command line.
;	Separate commands on the same command line.
command *opts args*	Enter backslash before carriage return to continue entering a command on the next line.
`command`	Execute a command.

Special Characters for Filename Expansion	Execution
*	Match on any set of characters.
?	Match on any single characters.
[]	Match on a class of possible characters.
\	Quote the following character. Used to quote special characters.

Redirection	Execution
command > filename	Redirect the standard output to a file or device, creating the file if it does not exist and overwriting the file if it does exist.
command < filename	Redirect the standard input from a file or device to a program.
command >> filename	Redirect the standard output to a file or device, appending the output to the end of the file.
command **2>** *filename*	Redirect the standard error to a file or device
command **2>>** *filename*	Redirect and append the standard error to a file or device
command **2>&1**	Redirect the standard error to the standard output in the Bourne shell.
command **>&** *filename*	Redirect the standard error to a file or device in the C shell.

Pipes	Execution
*command	command*	Pipe the standard output of one command as input for another command.

Table 18-6: The Shell Operations

In the next example, the output of the **ls** command is redirected from the screen device to a file. First the **ls** command lists files, and in the next command, **ls** redirects its file list to the **listf** file. Then the **cat** command displays the list of files saved in **listf**. Notice the list of files in **listf** includes the **listf** filename. The list of filenames generated by the **ls** command includes the name of the file created by the redirection operation—in this case, **listf**. The **listf** file is first created by the redirection operation, and then the **ls** command lists it along with other files. This file list output by **ls** is then redirected to the **listf** file, instead of being printed on the screen.

```
$ ls
mydata intro preface
$ ls > listf
$ cat listf
mydata intro listf preface
```

Tip: Errors occur when you try to use the same filename for both an input file for the command and the redirected destination file. In this case, because the redirection operation is executed first, the input file, because it exists, is destroyed and replaced by a file of the same name. When the command is executed, it finds an input file that is empty.

You can also append the standard output to an existing file using the **>>** redirection operator. Instead of overwriting the file, the data in the standard output is added at the end of the file. In the next example, the **myarticle** and **oldarticle** files are appended to the **allarticles** file. The **allarticles** file will then contain the contents of both **myarticle** and **oldarticle**.

```
$ cat myarticle >> allarticles
$ cat oldarticle >> allarticles
```

The Standard Input

Many Linux commands can receive data from the standard input. The standard input itself receives data from a device or a file. The default device for the standard input is the keyboard. Characters typed on the keyboard are placed in the standard input, which is then directed to the Linux command. Just as with the standard output, you can also redirect the standard input, receiving input from a file rather than the keyboard. The operator for redirecting the standard input is the less-than sign (**<**). In the next example, the standard input is redirected to receive input from the **myarticle** file, rather than the keyboard device (use CTRL-D to end the typed input). The contents of **myarticle** are read into the standard input by the redirection operation. Then the **cat** command reads the standard input and displays the contents of **myarticle**.

```
$ cat < myarticle
hello Christopher
How are you today
$
```

You can combine the redirection operations for both standard input and standard output. In the next example, the **cat** command has no filename arguments. Without filename arguments, the **cat** command receives input from the standard input and sends output to the standard output. However, the standard input has been redirected to receive its data from a file, while the standard output has been redirected to place its data in a file.

```
$ cat < myarticle > newarticle
```

Pipes: |

You may find yourself in situations in which you need to send data from one command to another. In other words, you may want to send the standard output of a command to another command, not to a destination file. Suppose you want to send a list of your filenames to the printer to be printed. You need two commands to do this: the **ls** command to generate a list of filenames and the `lpr` command to send the list to the printer. In effect, you need to take the output of the `ls` command and use it as input for the `lpr` command. You can think of the data as flowing from one command to another. To form such a connection in Linux, you use what is called a *pipe*. The *pipe operator* (| , the vertical bar character) placed between two commands forms a connection between them. The standard output of one command becomes the standard input for the other. The pipe operation receives output from the command placed before the pipe and sends this data as input to the command placed after the pipe. As shown in the next example, you can connect the `ls` command and the `lpr` command with a pipe. The list of filenames output by the `ls` command is piped into the `lpr` command.

```
$ ls | lpr
```

You can combine the **pipe** operation with other shell features, such as file expansion characters, to perform specialized operations. The next example prints only files with a **.c** extension. The `ls` command is used with the asterisk and ".c" to generate a list of filenames with the **.c** extension. Then this list is piped to the `lpr` command.

```
$ ls *.c | lpr
```

In the preceding example, a list of filenames was used as input, but what is important to note is that pipes operate on the standard output of a command, whatever that might be. The contents of whole files or even several files can be piped from one command to another. In the next example, the **cat** command reads and outputs the contents of the **mydata** file, which are then piped to the `lpr` command:

```
$ cat mydata | lpr
```

Linux has many commands that generate modified output. For example, the **sort** command takes the contents of a file and generates a version with each line sorted in alphabetic order. The **sort** command works best with files that are lists of items. Commands such as **sort** that output a modified version of its input are referred to as *filters*. Filters are often used with pipes. In the next example, a sorted version of **mylist** is generated and piped into the **more** command for display on the screen. Note that the original file, **mylist**, has not been changed and is not itself sorted. Only the output of **sort** in the standard output is sorted.

```
$ sort mylist | more
```

The standard input piped into a command can be more carefully controlled with the standard input argument (**-**). When you use the dash as an argument for a command, it represents the standard input.

19. Working with files and directories

In Linux, all files are organized into directories that, in turn, are hierarchically connected to each other in one overall file structure. A file is referenced not according to just its name, but also according to its place in this file structure. You can create as many new directories as you want, adding more directories to the file structure. The Linux file commands can perform sophisticated operations, such as moving or copying whole directories along with their subdirectories. You can use file operations such as `find`, `cp`, `mv`, and `ln` to locate files and copy, move, or link them from one directory to another. Desktop file managers, such as Konqueror and Nautilus used on the KDE and GNOME desktops, provide a graphical user interface to perform the same operations using icons, windows, and menus (see Chapters 8 and 9). This chapter will focus on the commands you use in the shell command line to manage files, such as `cp` and `mv`. However, whether you use the command line or a GUI file manager, the underlying file structure is the same.

Though not part of the Linux file structure, there are also special tools you can use to access Windows partitions and floppy disks. These follow much the same format as Linux file commands.

Archives are used to back up files or to combine them into a package, which can then be transferred as one file over the Internet or posted on an FTP site for easy downloading. The standard archive utility used on Linux and Unix systems is tar, for which several GUI front ends exist. You have several compression programs to choose from, including GNU zip (gzip), Zip, bzip, and compress.

Note: Linux also allows you to mount and access file systems used by other operating systems such as Unix or Windows. Linux itself supports a variety of different file systems such as ext2, ext3, and ReiserFS.

Linux Files

You can name a file using any letters, underscores, and numbers. You can also include periods and commas. Except in certain special cases, you should never begin a filename with a period. Other characters, such as slashes, question marks, or asterisks, are reserved for use as special characters by the system and should not be part of a filename. Filenames can be as long as

256 characters. Filenames can also include spaces, though to reference such filenames from the command line, be sure to encase them in quotes. On a desktop like GNOME or KDE you do not need quotes.

You can include an extension as part of a filename. A period is used to distinguish the filename proper from the extension. Extensions can be useful for categorizing your files. You are probably familiar with certain standard extensions that have been adopted by convention. For example, C source code files always have an extension of **.c**. Files that contain compiled object code have an **.o** extension. You can, of course, make up your own file extensions. The following examples are all valid Linux filenames. Keep in mind that to reference the last of these names on the command line, you would have to encase it in quotes as "New book review":

```
preface
chapter2
9700info
New_Revisions
calc.c
intro.bk1
New book review
```

Special initialization files are also used to hold shell configuration commands. These are the hidden, or dot, files, which begin with a period. Dot files used by commands and applications have predetermined names, such as the **.mozilla** directory used to hold your Mozilla data and configuration files. Recall that when you use `ls` to display your filenames, the dot files will not be displayed. To include the dot files, you need to use `ls` with the `-a` option. Dot files are discussed in more detail in Chapter 19.

The `ls -l` command displays detailed information about a file. First the permissions are displayed, followed by the number of links, the owner of the file, the name of the group the user belongs to, the file size in bytes, the date and time the file was last modified, and the name of the file. Permissions indicate who can access the file: the user, members of a group, or all other users. Permissions are discussed in detail later in this chapter. The group name indicates the group permitted to access the file object. The file type for **mydata** is that of an ordinary file. Only one link exists, indicating the file has no other names and no other links. The owner's name is **chris**, the same as the login name, and the group name is **weather**. Other users probably also belong to the **weather** group. The size of the file is 207 bytes, and it was last modified on February 20 at 11:55 A.M. The name of the file is **mydata**.

If you want to display this detailed information for all the files in a directory, simply use the `ls -l` command without an argument.

```
$ ls -l
-rw-r--r-- 1 chris weather 207 Feb 20 11:55 mydata
-rw-rw-r-- 1 chris weather 568 Feb 14 10:30 today
-rw-rw-r-- 1 chris weather 308 Feb 17 12:40 monday
```

All files in Linux have one physical format—a byte stream. A *byte stream* is just a sequence of bytes. This allows Linux to apply the file concept to every data component in the system. Directories are classified as files, as are devices. Treating everything as a file allows Linux to organize and exchange data more easily. The data in a file can be sent directly to a device such as a screen because a device interfaces with the system using the same byte-stream file format as regular files.

This same file format is used to implement other operating system components. The interface to a device, such as the screen or keyboard, is designated as a file. Other components, such as directories, are themselves byte-stream files, but they have a special internal organization. A directory file contains information about a directory, organized in a special directory format. Because these different components are treated as files, they can be said to constitute different *file types*. A character device is one file type. A directory is another file type. The number of these file types may vary according to your specific implementation of Linux. Five common types of files exist, however: ordinary files, directory files, first-in first-out pipes, character device files, and block device files. Although you may rarely reference a file's type, it can be useful when searching for directories or devices. Later in the chapter, you'll see how to use the file type in a search criterion with the `find` command to search specifically for directory or device names.

Although all ordinary files have a byte-stream format, they may be used in different ways. The most significant difference is between binary and text files. Compiled programs are examples of binary files. However, even text files can be classified according to their different uses. You can have files that contain C programming source code or shell commands, or even a file that is empty. The file could be an executable program or a directory file. The Linux `file` command helps you determine what a file is used for. It examines the first few lines of a file and tries to determine a classification for it. The `file` command looks for special keywords or special numbers in those first few lines, but it is not always accurate. In the next example, the `file` command examines the contents of two files and determines a classification for them:

```
$ file monday reports
monday: text
reports: directory
```

If you need to examine the entire file byte by byte, you can do so with the `od` (octal dump) command. The `od` command performs a dump of a file. By default, it prints every byte in its octal representation. However, you can also specify a character, decimal, or hexadecimal representation. The `od` command is helpful when you need to detect any special character in your file or if you want to display a binary file.

The File Structure

Linux organizes files into a hierarchically connected set of directories. Each directory may contain either files or other directories. In this respect, directories perform two important functions. A *directory* holds files, much like files held in a file drawer, and a directory connects to other directories, much as a branch in a tree is connected to other branches. Because of the similarities to a tree, such a structure is often referred to as a *tree structure*.

The Linux file structure branches into several directories beginning with a root directory, /. Within the root directory, several system directories contain files and programs that are features of the Linux system. The root directory also contains a directory called **/home** that contains the home directories of all the users in the system. Each user's home directory, in turn, contains the directories the user has made for his or her own use. Each of these can also contain directories. Such nested directories branch out from the user's home directory.

Note: The user's home directory can be any directory, though it is usually the directory that bears the user's login name. This directory is located in the directory named **/home** on your Linux system. For example, a user named **dylan** will have a home directory called **dylan** located in the system's **/home** directory. The user's home directory is a subdirectory of the directory called **/home** on your system.

Home Directories

When you log in to the system, you are placed within your home directory. The name given to this directory by the system is the same as your login name. Any files you create when you first log in are organized within your home directory. Within your home directory, however, you can create more directories. You can then change to these directories and store files in them. The same is true for other users on the system. Each user has his or her own home directory, identified by the appropriate login name. Users, in turn, can create their own directories.

You can access a directory either through its name or by making it your working directory. Each directory is given a name when it is created. You can use this name in file operations to access files in that directory. You can also make the directory your working directory. If you do not use any directory names in a file operation, the working directory will be accessed. The working directory is the one from which you are currently working. When you log in, the working directory is your home directory, usually having the same name as your login name. You can change the working directory by using the **cd** command to designate another directory as the working directory.

Pathnames

The name you give to a directory or file when you create it is not its full name. The full name of a directory is its *pathname*. The hierarchically nested relationship among directories forms paths, and these paths can be used to identify and reference any directory or file uniquely or absolutely. Each directory in the file structure can be said to have its own unique path. The actual name by which the system identifies a directory always begins with the root directory and consists of all directories nested below that directory.

In Linux, you write a pathname by listing each directory in the path separated from the last by a forward slash. A slash preceding the first directory in the path represents the root. The pathname for the **robert** directory is **/home/robert**. The pathname for the **reports** directory is **/home/chris/reports**. Pathnames also apply to files. When you create a file within a directory, you give the file a name. The actual name by which the system identifies the file, however, is the filename combined with the path of directories from the root to the file's directory. As an example, the pathname for **monday** is **/home/chris/reports/monday** (the root directory is represented by the first slash). The path for the **monday** file consists of the root, **home**, **chris**, and **reports** directories and the filename **monday**.

Pathnames may be absolute or relative. An *absolute pathname* is the complete pathname of a file or directory beginning with the root directory. A *relative pathname* begins from your working directory; it is the path of a file relative to your working directory. The working directory is the one you are currently operating in. Using the previous example, if **chris** is your working directory, the relative pathname for the file **monday** is **reports/monday**. The absolute pathname for **monday** is **/home/chris/reports/monday**.

The absolute pathname from the root to your home directory can be especially complex and, at times, even subject to change by the system administrator. To make it easier to reference, you can use a special character, the tilde (~), which represents the absolute pathname of your home directory. In the next example, from the **thankyou** directory, the user references the **monday** file in the home directory by placing a tilde and slash before **monday**:

```
$ pwd
/home/chris/letters/thankyou
$ cat ~/monday
raining and warm
$
```

You must specify the rest of the path from your home directory. In the next example, the user references the **monday** file in the **reports** directory. The tilde represents the path to the user's home directory, **/home/chris**, and then the rest of the path to the **monday** file is specified.

```
$ cat ~/reports/monday
```

Directory	Function
/	Begins the file system structure, called the *root*.
/home	Contains users' home directories.
/bin	Holds all the standard commands and utility programs.
/usr	Holds those files and commands used by the system; this directory breaks down into several subdirectories.
/usr/bin	Holds user-oriented commands and utility programs.
/usr/sbin	Holds system administration commands.
/usr/lib	Holds libraries for programming languages.
/usr/share/doc	Holds Linux documentation.
/usr/share/man	Holds the online Man files.
/var/spool	Holds spooled files, such as those generated for printing jobs and network transfers.
/sbin	Holds system administration commands for booting the system.
/var	Holds files that vary, such as mailbox files.
/dev	Holds file interfaces for devices such as the terminals and printers (dynamically generated by udev, do not edit).
/etc	Holds system configuration files and any other system files.

Table 19-1: Standard System Directories in Linux

System Directories

The root directory that begins the Linux file structure contains several system directories. The system directories contain files and programs used to run and maintain the system. Many contain other subdirectories with programs for executing specific features of Linux. For example, the directory **/usr/bin** contains the various Linux commands that users execute, such as **lpl**. The directory **/bin** holds system level commands. Table 19-1 lists the basic system directories.

Listing, Displaying, and Printing Files: ls, cat, more, less, and lpr

One of the primary functions of an operating system is the management of files. You may need to perform certain basic output operations on your files, such as displaying them on your screen or printing them. The Linux system provides a set of commands that perform basic file-management operations, such as listing, displaying, and printing files, as well as copying, renaming, and erasing files. These commands are usually made up of abbreviated versions of words. For example, the ls command is a shortened form of "list" and lists the files in your directory. The lpr command is an abbreviated form of "line print" and will print a file. The cat, less, and more commands display the contents of a file on the screen. Table 19-2 lists these commands with their different options. When you log in to your Linux system, you may want a list of the files in your home directory. The ls command, which outputs a list of your file and directory names, is useful for this. The ls command has many possible options for displaying filenames according to specific features.

Command or Option	Execution
ls	This command lists file and directory names.
cat *filenames*	This filter can be used to display a file. It can take filenames for its arguments. It outputs the contents of those files directly to the standard output, which, by default, is directed to the screen.
more *filenames*	This utility displays a file screen by screen. Press the SPACEBAR to continue to the next screen and **q** to quit.
less *filenames*	This utility also displays a file screen by screen. Press the SPACEBAR to continue to the next screen and **q** to quit.
lpr *filenames*	Sends a file to the line printer to be printed; a list of files may be used as arguments. Use the **-P** option to specify a printer.
lpq	Lists the print queue for printing jobs.
lprm	Removes a printing job from the print queue.

Table 19-2: Listing, Displaying, and Printing Files

Displaying Files: cat, less, and more

You may also need to look at the contents of a file. The cat and more commands display the contents of a file on the screen. The name cat stands for *concatenate*.

```
$ cat mydata
computers
```

The cat command outputs the entire text of a file to the screen at once. This presents a problem when the file is large because its text quickly speeds past on the screen. The more and less commands are designed to overcome this limitation by displaying one screen of text at a time. You can then move forward or backward in the text at your leisure. You invoke the more or `less` command by entering the command name followed by the name of the file you want to view (`less` is a more powerful and configurable display utility).

```
$ less mydata
```

When **more** or **less** invoke a file, the first screen of text is displayed. To continue to the next screen, you press the F key or the SPACEBAR. To move back in the text, you press the B key. You can quit at any time by pressing the Q key.

Printing Files: lpr, lpq, and lprm

With the printer commands such as `lpr` and `lprm`, you can perform printing operations such as printing files or canceling print jobs (see Table 19-2). When you need to print files, use the `lpr` command to send files to the printer connected to your system. In the next example, the user prints the **mydata** file:

```
$ lpr mydata
```

If you want to print several files at once, you can specify more than one file on the command line after the `lpr` command. In the next example, the user prints out both the **mydata** and **preface** files:

```
$ lpr mydata preface
```

Printing jobs are placed in a queue and printed one at a time in the background. You can continue with other work as your files print. You can see the position of a particular printing job at any given time with the `lpq` command, which gives the owner of the printing job (the login name of the user who sent the job), the print job ID, the size in bytes, and the temporary file in which it is currently held.

If you need to cancel an unwanted printing job, you can do so with the `lprm` command, which takes as its argument either the ID number of the printing job or the owner's name. It then removes the print job from the print queue. For this task, `lpq` is helpful, for it provides you with the ID number and owner of the printing job you need to use with `lprm`.

Managing Directories: mkdir, rmdir, ls, cd, pwd

You can create and remove your own directories, as well as change your working directory, with the `mkdir`, `rmdir`, and `cd` commands. Each of these commands can take as its argument the pathname for a directory. The `pwd` command displays the absolute pathname of your working directory. In addition to these commands, the special characters represented by a single dot, a double dot, and a tilde can be used to reference the working directory, the parent of the working directory, and the home directory, respectively. Taken together, these commands enable you to manage your directories. You can create nested directories, move from one directory to another, and use pathnames to reference any of your directories. Those commands commonly used to manage directories are listed in Table 19-3.

Creating and Deleting Directories

You create and remove directories with the `mkdir` and `rmdir` commands. In either case, you can also use pathnames for the directories. In the next example, the user creates the directory **reports**. Then the user creates the directory **articles** using a pathname:

```
$ mkdir reports
$ mkdir /home/chris/articles
```

You can remove a directory with the `rmdir` command followed by the directory name. In the next example, the user removes the directory **reports** with the `rmdir` command:

```
$ rmdir reports
```

Command	Execution
`mkdir` *directory*	Creates a directory.
`rmdir` *directory*	Erases a directory.
`ls -F`	Lists directory name with a preceding slash.
`ls -R`	Lists working directory as well as all subdirectories.
`cd` *directory name*	Changes to the specified directory, making it the working directory. **cd** without a directory name changes back to the home directory: **$ cd reports**
`pwd`	Displays the pathname of the working directory.
directory name / *filename*	A slash is used in pathnames to separate each directory name. In the case of pathnames for files, a slash separates the preceding directory names from the filename.
`. .`	References the parent directory. You can use it as an argument or as part of a pathname: **$ cd ..** **$ mv ../larisa oldarticles**
`.`	References the working directory. You can use it as an argument or as part of a pathname: **$ ls .**
`~/`*pathname*	The tilde is a special character that represents the pathname for the home directory. It is useful when you need to use an absolute pathname for a file or directory: **$ cp monday ~/today**

Table 19-3: Directory Commands

To remove a directory and all its subdirectories, you use the `rm` command with the `-r` option. This is a very powerful command and could easily be used to erase all your files. You will be prompted for each file. To simply remove all files and subdirectories without prompts, add the `-f` option. The following example deletes the **reports** directory and all its subdirectories:

```
rm -rf reports
```

Displaying Directory Contents

You have seen how to use the `ls` command to list the files and directories within your working directory. To distinguish between file and directory names, however, you need to use the `ls` command with the `-F` option. A slash is then placed after each directory name in the list.

```
$ ls
weather reports articles
$ ls -F
weather reports/ articles/
```

The `ls` command also takes as an argument any directory name or directory pathname. This enables you to list the files in any directory without first having to change to that directory. In the next example, the `ls` command takes as its argument the name of a directory, **reports**. Then the `ls` command is executed again, only this time the absolute pathname of **reports** is used.

```
$ ls reports
monday tuesday
$ ls /home/chris/reports
monday tuesday
$
```

Moving Through Directories

The `cd` command takes as its argument the name of the directory to which you want to change. The name of the directory can be the name of a subdirectory in your working directory or the full pathname of any directory on the system. If you want to change back to your home directory, you only need to enter the `cd` command by itself, without a filename argument.

```
$ cd props
$ pwd
/home/dylan/props
```

Referencing the Parent Directory

A directory always has a parent (except, of course, for the root). For example, in the preceding listing, the parent for **travel** is the **articles** directory. When a directory is created, two entries are made: one represented with a dot (.), and the other with double dots (. .). The dot represents the pathnames of the directory, and the double dots represent the pathname of its parent directory. Double dots, used as an argument in a command, reference a parent directory. The single dot references the directory itself.

You can use the single dot to reference your working directory, instead of using its pathname. For example, to copy a file to the working directory retaining the same name, the dot can be used in place of the working directory's pathname. In this sense, the dot is another name for the working directory. In the next example, the user copies the **weather** file from the **chris** directory to the **reports** directory. The **reports** directory is the working directory and can be represented with the single dot.

```
$ cd reports
$ cp /home/chris/weather .
```

The . . symbol is often used to reference files in the parent directory. In the next example, the `cat` command displays the **weather** file in the parent directory. The pathname for the file is the . . symbol followed by a slash and the filename.

```
$ cat ../weather
raining and warm
```

Tip: You can use the `cd` command with the `. .` symbol to step back through successive parent directories of the directory tree from a lower directory.

File and Directory Operations: find, cp, mv, rm, ln

As you create more and more files, you may want to back them up, change their names, erase some of them, or even give them added names. Linux provides you with several file commands that enable you to search for files, copy files, rename files, or remove files (see Tables 11-5). If you have a large number of files, you can also search them to locate a specific one. The commands are shortened forms of full words, consisting of only two characters. The `cp` command stands for "copy" and copies a file, `mv` stands for "move" and renames or moves a file, `rm` stands for "remove" and erases a file, and `ln` stands for "link" and adds another name for a file, often used as a shortcut to the original. One exception to the two-character rule is the `find` command, which performs searches of your filenames to find a file. All these operations can be handled by the GUI desktops, like GNOME and KDE.

Searching Directories: find

Once you have a large number of files in many different directories, you may need to search them to locate a specific file, or files, of a certain type. The `find` command enables you to perform such a search from the command line. The `find` command takes as its arguments directory names followed by several possible options that specify the type of search and the criteria for the search; it then searches within the directories listed and their subdirectories for files that meet these criteria. The `find` command can search for a file by name, type, owner, and even the time of the last update.

```
$ find directory-list -option criteria
```

Tip: From the GNOME desktop you can use the "Search" tool in the Places menu to search for files. From the KDE Desktop you can use the find tool in the file manager. Select find from the file manager (Konqueror) tools menu.

The `-name` option has as its criteria a pattern and instructs `find` to search for the filename that matches that pattern. To search for a file by name, you use the `find` command with the directory name followed by the `-name` option and the name of the file.

```
$ find directory-list -name filename
```

The `find` command also has options that merely perform actions, such as outputting the results of a search. If you want `find` to display the filenames it has found, you simply include the -`print` option on the command line along with any other options. The `-print` option is an action that instructs `find` to write to the standard output the names of all the files it locates (you can also use the `-ls` option instead to list files in the long format). In the next example, the user searches for all the files in the **reports** directory with the name **monday**. Once located, the file, with its relative pathname, is printed.

```
$ find reports -name monday -print
reports/monday
```

The `find` command prints out the filenames using the directory name specified in the directory list. If you specify an absolute pathname, the absolute path of the found directories will be output. If you specify a relative pathname, only the relative pathname is output. In the preceding example, the user specified a relative pathname, **reports**, in the directory list. Located filenames were output beginning with this relative pathname. In the next example, the user specifies an absolute pathname in the directory list. Located filenames are then output using this absolute pathname.

```
$ find /home/chris -name monday -print
/home/chris/reports/monday
```

Tip: Should you need to find the location of a specific program or configuration file, you could use `find` to search for the file from the root directory. Log in as the root user and use / as the directory. This command searched for the location of the `more` command and files on the entire file system: `find / -name more -print`.

Searching the Working Directory

If you want to search your working directory, you can use the dot in the directory pathname to represent your working directory. The double dots would represent the parent directory. The next example searches all files and subdirectories in the working directory, using the dot to represent the working directory. If you are located in your home directory, this is a convenient way to search through all your own directories. Notice the located filenames are output beginning with a dot.

```
$ find . -name weather -print
./weather
```

You can use shell wildcard characters as part of the pattern criteria for searching files. The special character must be quoted, however, to avoid evaluation by the shell. In the next example, all files with the **.c** extension in the **programs** directory are searched for and then displayed in the long format using the **-ls** action:

```
$ find programs -name '*.c' -ls
```

Locating Directories

You can also use the `find` command to locate other directories. In Linux, a directory is officially classified as a special type of file. Although all files have a byte-stream format, some files, such as directories, are used in special ways. In this sense, a file can be said to have a file type. The `find` command has an option called **-type** that searches for a file of a given type. The **-type** option takes a one-character modifier that represents the file type. The modifier that represents a directory is a **d**. In the next example, both the directory name and the directory file type are used to search for the directory called **travel**:

```
$ find /home/chris -name travel -type d -print
/home/chris/articles/travel
$
```

File types are not so much different types of files as they are the file format applied to other components of the operating system, such as devices. In this sense, a device is treated as a type of file, and you can use `find` to search for devices and directories, as well as ordinary files. Table 19-4 lists the different types available for the `find` command's **-type** option.

You can also use the find operation to search for files by ownership or security criteria, like those belonging to a specific user or those with a certain security context. The user option lets to locate all files belonging to a certain user. The following example lists all files that the user **chris** has created or owns on the entire system. To list those just in the users' home directories, you would use **/home** for the starting search directory. This would find all those in a user's home directory as well as any owned by that user in other user directories.

```
$ find / -user chris -print
```

Command or Option	Execution
find	Searches directories for files according to search criteria. This command has several options that specify the type of criteria and actions to be taken.
-name *pattern*	Searches for files with the *pattern* in the name.
-lname *pattern*	Searches for symbolic link files.
-group *name*	Searches for files belonging to the group *name*.
-gid *name*	Searches for files belonging to a group according to group ID.
-user *name*	Searches for files belonging to a user.
-uid *name*	Searches for files belonging to a user according to user ID.
-size *num*c	Searches for files with the size *num* in blocks. If **c** is added after *num*, the size in bytes (characters) is searched for.
-mtime *num*	Searches for files last modified *num* days ago.
-newer *pattern*	Searches for files modified after the one matched by *pattern*.
-context *scontext*	Searches for files according to security context (SE Linux).
-print	Outputs the result of the search to the standard output. The result is usually a list of filenames, including their full pathnames.
-type *filetype*	Searches for files with the specified file type. File type can be **b** for block device, **c** for character device, **d** for directory, **f** for file, or **l** for symbolic link.
-perm *permission*	Searches for files with certain permissions set. Use octal or symbolic format for permissions.
-ls	Provides a detailed listing of each file, with owner, permission, size, and date information.
-exec *command*	Executes command when files found.

Table 19-4: The find Command

Copying Files

To make a copy of a file, you simply give **cp** two filenames as its arguments (see Table 19-5). The first filename is the name of the file to be copied—the one that already exists. This is often referred to as the *source file.* The second filename is the name you want for the copy. This will be a new file containing a copy of all the data in the source file. This second argument is often referred to as the *destination file.* The syntax for the `cp` command follows:

```
$ cp source-file destination-file
```

In the next example, the user copies a file called **proposal** to a new file called **oldprop**:

```
$ cp proposal oldprop
```

You could unintentionally destroy another file with the `cp` command. The `cp` command generates a copy by first creating a file and then copying data into it. If another file has the same name as the destination file, that file is destroyed and a new file with that name is created. By default Ubuntu configures your system to check for an existing copy by the same name (`cp` is aliased with the `-i` option). To copy a file from your working directory to another directory, you only need to use that directory name as the second argument in the `cp` command. In the next example, the **proposal** file is overwritten by the **newprop** file. The **proposal** file already exists.

```
$ cp newprop proposal
```

You can use any of the wildcard characters to generate a list of filenames to use with `cp` or `mv`. For example, suppose you need to copy all your C source code files to a given directory. Instead of listing each one individually on the command line, you could use an `*` character with the **.c** extension to match on and generate a list of C source code files (all files with a **.c** extension). In the next example, the user copies all source code files in the current directory to the **sourcebks** directory:

```
$ cp *.c sourcebks
```

If you want to copy all the files in a given directory to another directory, you could use `*` to match on and generate a list of all those files in a `cp` command. In the next example, the user copies all the files in the **props** directory to the **oldprop** directory. Notice the use of a **props** pathname preceding the `*` special characters. In this context, **props** is a pathname that will be appended before each file in the list that `*` generates.

```
$ cp props/* oldprop
```

You can, of course, use any of the other special characters, such as `.`, `?`, or `[]`. In the next example, the user copies both source code and object code files (**.c** and **.o**) to the **projbk** directory:

```
$ cp *.[oc] projbk
```

When you copy a file, you may want to give the copy a different name than the original. To do so, place the new filename after the directory name, separated by a slash.

```
$ cp filename directory-name/new-filename
```

Moving Files

You can use the `mv` command either to rename a file or to move a file from one directory to another. When using `mv` to rename a file, you simply use the new filename as the second argument. The first argument is the current name of the file you are renaming. If you want to rename a file when you move it, you can specify the new name of the file after the directory name. In the next example, the **proposal** file is renamed with the name **version1**:

```
$ mv proposal version1
```

As with **cp**, it is easy for **mv** to erase a file accidentally. When renaming a file, you might accidentally choose a filename already used by another file. In this case, that other file will be erased. The **mv** command also has an **-i** option that checks first to see if a file by that name already exists.

You can also use any of the special characters to generate a list of filenames to use with **mv**. In the next example, the user moves all source code files in the current directory to the **newproj** directory:

```
$ mv *.c newproj
```

If you want to move all the files in a given directory to another directory, you can use * to match on and generate a list of all those files. In the next example, the user moves all the files in the **reports** directory to the **repbks** directory:

```
$ mv reports/* repbks
```

Note: The easiest way to copy files to a CD-R/RW or DVD-R/RW disc is to use the built-in Nautilus burning capability. Just insert a blank disk, open it as a folder, and drag and drop files on to it. You will be prompted automatically to burn the files.

Command	Execution
cp *filename filename*	Copies a file. **cp** takes two arguments: the original file and the name of the new copy. You can use pathnames for the files to copy across directories:
cp -r *dirname dirname*	Copies a subdirectory from one directory to another. The copied directory includes all its own subdirectories:
mv *filename filename*	Moves (renames) a file. The **mv** command takes two arguments: the first is the file to be moved. The second argument can be the new filename or the pathname of a directory. If it is the name of a directory, then the file is literally moved to that directory, changing the file's pathname:
mv *dirname dirname*	Moves directories. In this case, the first and last arguments are directories:
ln *filename filename*	Creates added names for files referred to as links. A link can be created in one directory that references a file in another directory:
rm *filenames*	Removes (erases) a file. Can take any number of filenames as its arguments. Literally removes links to a file. If a file has more than one link, you need to remove all of them to erase a file:

Table 19-5: File Operations

Copying and Moving Directories

You can also copy or move whole directories at once. Both **cp** and **mv** can take as their first argument a directory name, enabling you to copy or move subdirectories from one directory into another (see Table 19-5). The first argument is the name of the directory to be moved or copied, while the second argument is the name of the directory within which it is to be placed. The same pathname structure used for files applies to moving or copying directories.

You can just as easily copy subdirectories from one directory to another. To copy a directory, the `cp` command requires you to use the `-r` option. The `-r` option stands for "recursive." It directs the `cp` command to copy a directory, as well as any subdirectories it may contain. In other words, the entire directory subtree, from that directory on, will be copied. In the next example, the **travel** directory is copied to the **oldarticles** directory. Now two **travel** subdirectories exist, one in **articles** and one in **oldarticles**.

```
$ cp -r articles/travel oldarticles
$ ls -F articles
/travel
$ ls -F oldarticles
/travel
```

Erasing Files and Directories: the rm Command

As you use Linux, you will find the number of files you use increases rapidly. Generating files in Linux is easy. Applications such as editors, and commands such as `cp`, easily create files. Eventually, many of these files may become outdated and useless. You can then remove them with the `rm` command. The `rm` command can take any number of arguments, enabling you to list several filenames and erase them all at the same time. In the next example, the user erases the file **oldprop**:

```
$ rm oldprop
```

Be careful when using the `rm` command, because it is irrevocable. Once a file is removed, it cannot be restored (there is no undo). With the `-i` option, you are prompted separately for each file and asked whether to remove it. If you enter **y**, the file will be removed. If you enter anything else, the file is not removed. In the next example, the `rm` command is instructed to erase the files **proposal** and **oldprop**. The `rm` command then asks for confirmation for each file. The user decides to remove **oldprop,** but not **proposal**.

```
$ rm -i proposal oldprop
Remove proposal? n
Remove oldprop? y
$
```

Links: the ln Command

You can give a file more than one name using the `ln` command. You might want to reference a file using different filenames to access it from different directories. The added names are often referred to as *links*. Linux supports two different types of links, hard and symbolic. *Hard* links are literally another name for the same file, whereas *symbolic* links function like shortcuts referencing another file. Symbolic links are much more flexible and can work over many different file systems, whereas hard links are limited to your local file system. Furthermore, hard links introduce security concerns, as they allow direct access from a link that may have public access to an original file that you may want protected. Links are usually implemented as symbolic links.

Symbolic Links

To set up a symbolic link, you use the `ln` command with the `-s` option and two arguments: the name of the original file and the new, added filename. The `ls` operation lists both filenames, but only one physical file will exist.

```
$ ln -s original-file-name added-file-name
```

In the next example, the **today** file is given the additional name **weather**. It is just another name for the **today** file.

```
$ ls
today
$ ln -s today weather
$ ls
today weather
```

You can give the same file several names by using the `ln` command on the same file many times. In the next example, the file **today** is given both the names **weather** and **weekend**:

```
$ ln -s today weather
$ ln -s today weekend
$ ls
today weather weekend
```

If you list the full information about a symbolic link and its file, you will find the information displayed is different. In the next example, the user lists the full information for both **lunch** and **/home/george/veglist** using the `ls` command with the `-l` option. The first character in the line specifies the file type. Symbolic links have their own file type, represented by an **l**. The file type for **lunch** is **l**, indicating it is a symbolic link, not an ordinary file. The number after the term "group" is the size of the file. Notice the sizes differ. The size of the **lunch** file is only four bytes. This is because **lunch** is only a symbolic link—a file that holds the pathname of another file—and a pathname takes up only a few bytes. It is not a direct hard link to the **veglist** file.

```
$ ls -l lunch /home/george/veglist
lrw-rw-r-- 1 chris group 4 Feb 14 10:30 lunch
-rw-rw-r-- 1 george group 793 Feb 14 10:30 veglist
```

To erase a file, you need to remove only its original name (and any hard links to it). If any symbolic links are left over, they will be unable to access the file. In this case, a symbolic link would hold the pathname of a file that no longer exists.

Hard Links

You can give the same file several names by using the `ln` command on the same file many times. To set up a hard link, you use the `ln` command with no `-s` option and two arguments: the name of the original file and the new, added filename. The `ls` operation lists both filenames, but only one physical file will exist.

```
$ ln original-file-name added-file-name
```

In the next example, the **monday** file is given the additional name **storm**. It is just another name for the **monday** file.

```
$ ls
today
$ ln monday storm
$ ls
monday storm
```

To erase a file that has hard links, you need to remove all its hard links. The name of a file is actually considered a link to that file—hence the command **rm** that removes the link to the file. If you have several links to the file and remove only one of them, the others stay in place and you can reference the file through them. The same is true even if you remove the original link—the original name of the file. Any added links will work just as well. In the next example, the **today** file is removed with the **rm** command. However, a link to that same file exists, called **weather**. The file can then be referenced under the name **weather**.

```
$ ln today weather
$ rm today
$ cat weather
The storm broke today
and the sun came out.
$
```

Archiving and Compressing Files

Archives are used to back up files or to combine them into a package, which can then be transferred as one file over the Internet or posted on an FTP site for easy downloading. The standard archive utility used on Linux and Unix systems is tar, for which several GUI front ends exist. You have several compression programs to choose from, including GNU zip (gzip), Zip, bzip, and compress. Table 19-6 lists the commonly used archive and compressions applications.

Applications	Description
tar	Archive creation and extraction **www.gnu.org/software/tar/manual/tar.html**
FileRoller (Archive Manager)	GNOME front end for tar and gzip/bzip2
gzip	File, directory, and archive compression **www.gnu.org/software/gzip/manual/**
bzip2	File, directory, and archive compression **www.gnu.org/software/gzip/manual/**
zip	File, directory, and archive compression

Table 19-6: Archive and Compression Applications

Archiving and Compressing Files with File Roller

GNOME provides the File Roller tool (accessible from the Accessories menu, labeled Archive Manager) that operates as a GUI front end to archive and compress files, letting you perform Zip, gzip, tar, and bzip2 operation using a GUI interface. You can examine the contents of archives, extract the files you want, and create new compressed archives. When you create an archive, you determine its compression method by specifying its filename extension, such as **.gz** for gzip or **.bz2** for bzip2. You can select the different extensions from the File Type menu or enter the extension yourself. To both archive and compress files, you can choose a combined extension like .tar.bz2, which both archives with tar and compresses with bzip2. Click Add to add files to your archive. To extract files from an archive, open the archive to display the list of archive files. You can then click Extract to extract particular files or the entire archive.

Tip: File Roller can also be use to examine the contents of an archive file easily. From the file manager, right-click the archive and select Open With Archive Manager. The list of files and directories in that archive will be displayed. For subdirectories, double-click their entries. This method also works for RPM software files, letting you browse all the files that make up a software package.

Archive Files and Devices: tar

The tar utility creates archives for files and directories. With tar, you can archive specific files, update them in the archive, and add new files as you want to that archive. You can even archive entire directories with all their files and subdirectories, all of which can be restored from the archive. The tar utility was originally designed to create archives on tapes. (The term "tar" stands for tape archive. However, you can create archives on any device, such as a floppy disk, or you can create an archive file to hold the archive.) The tar utility is ideal for making backups of your files or combining several files into a single file for transmission across a network (File Roller is a GUI interface for tar). For more information on tar, check the man page or the online man page at **www.gnu.org/software/tar/manual/tar.html**.

Note: As an alternative to tar, you can use pax, which is designed to work with different kinds of Unix archive formats such as cpio, bcpio, and tar. You can extract, list, and create archives. The pax utility is helpful if you are handling archives created on Unix systems that are using different archive formats.

Displaying Archive Contents

Both file managers in GNOME and the K Desktop have the capability to display the contents of a tar archive file automatically. The contents are displayed as though they were files in a directory. You can list the files as icons or with details, sorting them by name, type, or other fields. You can even display the contents of files. Clicking a text file opens it with a text editor, and an image is displayed with an image viewer. If the file manager cannot determine what program to use to display the file, it prompts you to select an application. Both file managers can perform the same kinds of operations on archives residing on remote file systems, such as tar archives on FTP sites. You can obtain a listing of their contents and even read their readme files. The Nautilus file manager (GNOME) can also extract an archive. Right-click the Archive icon and select Extract.

Creating Archives

On Linux, tar is often used to create archives on devices or files. You can direct tar to archive files to a specific device or a file by using the **f** option with the name of the device or file. The syntax for the **tar** command using the **f** option is shown in the next example. The device or filename is often referred to as the archive name. When creating a file for a tar archive, the filename is usually given the extension **.tar**. This is a convention only and is not required. You can list as many filenames as you want. If a directory name is specified, all its subdirectories are included in the archive.

```
$ tar optionsf archive-name.tar directory-and-file-names
```

Commands	Execution
`tar` *options files*	Backs up files to tape, device, or archive file.
`tar` *options*f *archive_name filelist*	Backs up files to a specific file or device specified as *archive_name*. *filelist*; can be filenames or directories.
Options	
`c`	Creates a new archive.
`t`	Lists the names of files in an archive.
`r`	Appends files to an archive.
`U`	Updates an archive with new and changed files; adds only those files modified since they were archived or files not already present in the archive.
`--delete`	Removes a file from the archive.
`w`	Waits for a confirmation from the user before archiving each file; enables you to update an archive selectively.
`x`	Extracts files from an archive.
`m`	When extracting a file from an archive, no new timestamp is assigned.
`M`	Creates a multiple-volume archive that may be stored on several floppy disks.
`f` *archive-name*	Saves the tape archive to the file archive name, instead of to the default tape device. When given an archive name, the `f` option saves the tar archive in a file of that name.
`f` *device-name*	Saves a tar archive to a device such as a floppy disk or tape. **/dev/fd0** is the device name for your floppy disk; the default device is held in **/etc/default/tar-file**.
`v`	Displays each filename as it is archived.
`z`	Compresses or decompresses archived files using gzip.
`j`	Compresses or decompresses archived files using bzip2.

Table 19-7: File Archives: `tar`

To create an archive, use the `c` option. Combined with the `f` option, `c` creates an archive on a file or device. You enter this option before and right next to the `f` option. Notice no dash precedes a tar option. Table 19-7 lists the different options you can use with tar. In the next example, the directory **mydir** and all its subdirectories are saved in the file **myarch.tar**. In this example, the **mydir** directory holds two files, **mymeeting** and **party**, as well as a directory called **reports** that has three files: **weather**, **monday**, and **friday**.

```
$ tar cvf myarch.tar mydir
mydir/
mydir/reports/
mydir/reports/weather
mydir/reports/monday
mydir/reports/friday
mydir/mymeeting
mydir/party
```

Extracting Archives

The user can later extract the directories from the tape using the **x** option. The **xf** option extracts files from an archive file or device. The tar extraction operation generates all subdirectories. In the next example, the **xf** option directs **tar** to extract all the files and subdirectories from the tar file **myarch.tar**:

```
$ tar xvf myarch.tar
mydir/
mydir/reports/
mydir/reports/weather
mydir/reports/monday
mydir/reports/friday
mydir/mymeeting
mydir/party
```

You use the **r** option to add files to an already-created archive. The **r** option appends the files to the archive. In the next example, the user appends the files in the **letters** directory to the **myarch.tar** archive. Here, the directory **mydocs** and its files are added to the **myarch.tar** archive:

```
$ tar rvf myarch.tar mydocs
mydocs/
mydocs/doc1
```

Updating Archives

If you change any of the files in your directories you previously archived, you can use the **u** option to instruct tar to update the archive with any modified files. The **tar** command compares the time of the last update for each archived file with those in the user's directory and copies into the archive any files that have been changed since they were last archived. Any newly created files in these directories are also added to the archive. In the next example, the user updates the **myarch.tar** file with any recently modified or newly created files in the **mydir** directory. In this case, the **gifts** file was added to the **mydir** directory.

```
tar uvf myarch.tar mydir
mydir/
mydir/gifts
```

If you need to see what files are stored in an archive, you can use the **tar** command with the **t** option. The next example lists all the files stored in the **myarch.tar** archive:

```
tar tvf myarch.tar
drwxr-xr-x root/root 0 2000-10-24 21:38:18 mydir/
drwxr-xr-x root/root 0 2000-10-24 21:38:51 mydir/reports/
-rw-r--r-- root/root 22 2000-10-24 21:38:40 mydir/reports/weather
-rw-r--r-- root/root 22 2000-10-24 21:38:45 mydir/reports/monday
-rw-r--r-- root/root 22 2000-10-24 21:38:51 mydir/reports/friday
-rw-r--r-- root/root 22 2000-10-24 21:38:18 mydir/mymeeting
-rw-r--r-- root/root 22 2000-10-24 21:36:42 mydir/party
drwxr-xr-x root/root 0 2000-10-24 21:48:45 mydocs/
-rw-r--r-- root/root 22 2000-10-24 21:48:45 mydocs/doc1
drwxr-xr-x root/root 0 2000-10-24 21:54:03 mydir/
-rw-r--r-- root/root 22 2000-10-24 21:54:03 mydir/gifts
```

Note: To backup a files using several CD/DVD-ROMs, you would first create a split archive, one consisting of several files, using the -M option, the mulit-volume option. The tape size for an ISO DVD would be specified with the tape-length option, --tape-length=2294900.

Compressing Archives

The **tar** operation does not perform compression on archived files. If you want to compress the archived files, you can instruct tar to invoke the gzip utility to compress them. With the lowercase **z** option, tar first uses gzip to compress files before archiving them. The same **z** option invokes gzip to decompress them when extracting files.

```
$ tar czf myarch.tar.gz mydir
```

To use bzip instead of gzip to compress files before archiving them, you use the **j** option. The same **j** option invokes bzip to decompress them when extracting files.

```
$ tar cjf myarch.tar.bz2 mydir
```

Remember, a difference exists between compressing individual files in an archive and compressing the entire archive as a whole. Often, an archive is created for transferring several files at once as one tar file. To shorten transmission time, the archive should be as small as possible. You can use the compression utility gzip on the archive tar file to compress it, reducing its size, and then send the compressed version. The person receiving it can decompress it, restoring the tar file. Using gzip on a tar file often results in a file with the extension **.tar.gz**. The extension **.gz** is added to a compressed gzip file. The next example creates a compressed version of **myarch.tar** using the same name with the extension **.gz**:

```
$ gzip myarch.tar
$ ls
$ myarch.tar.gz
```

Instead of retyping the **tar** command for different files, you can place the command in a script and pass the files to it. Be sure to make the script executable. In the following example, a simple **myarchprog** script is created that will archive filenames listed as its arguments.

(5)myarchprog

tar cvf myarch.tar $*

A run of the **myarchprog** script with multiple arguments is shown here:

```
$ myarchprog mydata preface
mydata
preface
```

Archiving to Tape

If you have a default device specified, such as a tape, and you want to create an archive on it, you can simply use `tar` without the `f` option and a device or filename. This can be helpful for making backups of your files. The name of the default device is held in a file called **/etc/default/tar**. The syntax for the `tar` command using the default tape device is shown in the following example. If a directory name is specified, all its subdirectories are included in the archive.

```
$ tar option directory-and-file-names
```

In the next example, the directory **mydir** and all its subdirectories are saved on a tape in the default tape device:

```
$ tar c mydir
```

In this example, the **mydir** directory and all its files and subdirectories are extracted from the default tape device and placed in the user's working directory:

```
$ tar x mydir
```

Note: There are other archive programs you can use such as cpio, pax, and shar. However, tar is the one most commonly used for archiving application software.

File Compression: gzip, bzip2, and zip

Several reasons exist for reducing the size of a file. The two most common are to save space or, if you are transferring the file across a network, to save transmission time. You can effectively reduce a file size by creating a compressed copy of it. Anytime you need the file again, you decompress it. Compression is used in combination with archiving to enable you to compress whole directories and their files at once. Decompression generates a copy of the archive file, which can then be extracted, generating a copy of those files and directories. File Roller provides a GUI interface for these tasks. For more information on gzip, check the man page or the online man page at **www.gnu.org/software/gzip/manual/**. For bzip2 also check its man page or the online documentation at **www.bzip.org/docs.html.**

Compression with gzip

Several compression utilities are available for use on Linux and Unix systems. Most software for Linux systems uses the GNU gzip and gunzip utilities. The gzip utility compresses files, and gunzip decompresses them. To compress a file, enter the command `gzip` and the filename. This replaces the file with a compressed version of it with the extension **.gz**.

```
$ gzip mydata
$ ls
mydata.gz
```

To decompress a gzip file, use either `gzip` with the `-d` option or the command `gunzip`. These commands decompress a compressed file with the **.gz** extension and replace it with a decompressed version with the same root name but without the **.gz** extension. When you use gunzip, you needn't even type in the **.gz** extension; `gunzip` and `gzip` `-d` assume it. Table 19-8 lists the different gzip options.

```
$ gunzip mydata.gz
$ ls
mydata
```

Option	Execution
-c	Sends compressed version of file to standard output; each file listed is separately compressed: `gzip -c mydata preface > myfiles.gz`

-d	Decompresses a compressed file; or you can use gunzip:
	`gzip -d myfiles.gz`
	`gunzip myfiles.gz`

-h	Displays help listing.
-l *file-list*	Displays compressed and uncompressed size of each file listed: `gzip -l myfiles.gz.`
-r *directory-name*	Recursively searches for specified directories and compresses all the files in them; the search begins from the current working directory. When used with `gunzip`, compressed files of a specified directory are uncompressed.
-v *file-list*	For each compressed or decompressed file, displays its name and the percentage of its reduction in size.
-num	Determines the speed and size of the compression; the range is from –1 to –9. A lower number gives greater speed but less compression, resulting in a larger file that compresses and decompresses quickly. Thus –1 gives the quickest compression but with the largest size; –9 results in a very small file that takes longer to compress and decompress. The default is –6.

Table 19-8: The `gzip` Options

Tip: On your desktop, you can extract the contents of an archive by locating it with the file manager and double-clicking it. You can also right-click and choose Open with Archive Manager. This will start the File Roller application, which will open the archive, listing its contents. You can then choose to extract the archive. File Roller will use the appropriate tools to decompress the archive (bzip2, zip, or gzip) if compressed, and then extract the archive (tar).

You can also compress archived tar files. This results in files with the extensions **.tar.gz**. Compressed archived files are often used for transmitting extremely large files across networks.

```
$ gzip myarch.tar
$ ls
myarch.tar.gz
```

You can compress tar file members individually using the `tar z` option that invokes gzip. With the `z` option, tar invokes gzip to compress a file before placing it in an archive. Archives with members compressed with the `z` option, however, cannot be updated, nor is it possible to add to them. All members must be compressed, and all must be added at the same time.

The compress and uncompress Commands

You can also use the `compress` and `uncompress` commands to create compressed files. They generate a file that has a **.Z** extension and use a different compression format from gzip. The `compress` and `uncompress` commands are not that widely used, but you may run across **.Z** files occasionally. You can use the `uncompress` command to decompress a **.Z** file. The gzip utility is the standard GNU compression utility and should be used instead of `compress`.

Compressing with bzip2

Another popular compression utility is **bzip2**. It compresses files using the Burrows-Wheeler block-sorting text compression algorithm and Huffman coding. The command line options are similar to gzip by design, but they are not exactly the same. (See the bzip2 Man page for a complete listing.) You compress files using the `bzip2` command and decompress with `bunzip2`. The `bzip2` command creates files with the extension **.bz2**. You can use `bzcat` to output compressed data to the standard output. The `bzip2` command compresses files in blocks and enables you to specify their size (larger blocks give you greater compression). As when using gzip, you can use bzip2 to compress tar archive files. The following example compresses the **mydata** file into a bzip compressed file with the extension **.bz2**:

```
$ bzip2 mydata
$ ls
mydata.bz2
```

To decompress, use the `bunzip2` command on a bzip file:

```
$ bunzip2 mydata.bz2
```

Using Zip

Zip is a compression and archive utility modeled on PKZIP, which was used originally on DOS systems. Zip is a cross-platform utility used on Windows, Mac, MS-DOS, OS/2, Unix, and Linux systems. Zip commands can work with archives created by PKZIP and can use Zip archives. You compress a file using the `zip` command. This creates a Zip file with the **.zip** extension. If no files are listed, `zip` outputs the compressed data to the standard output. You can also use the - argument to have `zip` read from the standard input. To compress a directory, you include the `-r` option. The first example archives and compresses a file:

```
$ zip mydata
$ ls
mydata.zip
```

The next example archives and compresses the **reports** directory:

```
$ zip -r reports
```

A full set of archive operations is supported. With the `-f` option, you can update a particular file in the Zip archive with a newer version. The `-u` option replaces or adds files, and the

-**d** option deletes files from the Zip archive. Options also exist for encrypting files, making DOS-to-Unix end-of-line translations and including hidden files.

To decompress and extract the Zip file, you use the **unzip** command.

```
$ unzip mydata.zip
```

Appendix A: Getting Ubuntu

The Ubuntu Linux distribution installs a professional-level and very stable Linux system along with the KDE and GNOME GUI interfaces, flexible and easy-to-use system configuration tools, an extensive set of Internet servers, a variety of different multimedia applications, and thousands of Linux applications of all kinds. You can find recent information about Ubuntu at **www.ubuntu.com**.

Ubuntu tailors its installs by providing different CD/DVD install disc for different releases and versions. The LiveCD is not the only Ubuntu installation available. Ubuntu provides two other CDs, one designed for servers and the other provides specialized features like LVM and RAID. Alternate install also supports small installs with less than 320MB RAM, automated installs, customized OEM systems, and upgrading older releases that have no network access. The Wubi installation option will install a fully functional Ubuntu system on a virtual hard disk on Windows system. This is the easiest installation of Ubuntu and requires no hard disk partitioning.

- ➢ Desktop CD Install GNOME desktop with standard set of applications.

- ➢ Server install CD Install Ubuntu with set of standard servers

- ➢ Alternate CD Installs specialized features like LVM, RAID, encrypted file systems, small systems, and OEM configurations.

There is also an Install DVD that is meant to primarily install Ubuntu, and provides a large selection of software. The DVD can also serve as a Live DVD, and has the advantage of providing a large collection of installable software without needing network access to a repository.

Most Ubuntu software is available for download from the Ubuntu repository. Install disks are available also, either as smaller desktop only installs, or larger server installs. You normally use the Ubuntu Desktop Live CD to install Ubuntu. Ubuntu distribution strategy relies on install disks with a selected collection of software that can be later updated and enhanced from the very large collection of software on the Ubuntu repository. This means that the collection of software in an initial installation can be relatively small. Software on the Ubuntu repository is also continually updated, so any installation will likely have to undergo extensive updates from the repository.

With smaller install disks, you can quickly download and burn a Ubuntu install image. The Desktop Live CD is available from the GetUbuntu page on the Ubuntu Web site. There are 32 bit and 64 bit versions for all current releases. Both the desktop and Server versions are provided.

www.ubuntu.com/getubuntu

In addition, there are Alternate and Install DVD versions. These you can download ISO images for all versions directly from the following site.

`http://releases.ubuntu.com`

This site also includes the torrents for the versions, letting you use a BitTorrent client to download the CD or DVD image. Torrents are also listed at:

`http://torrent.ubuntu.com`

Also, there are several editions of Ubuntu that you can download from the respective edition Web site, as well as from the **http://releases.ubutu.com** and **http://cdimage.ubuntu.com**.

➢ **www.edubuntu.com**   Educational version

➢ **www.xubuntu.com**   Xfce desktop version

➢ **www.kubuntu.com**   KDE desktop version

➢ **http://wiki.ubuntu.com/Gobuntu**   Open Source only version

Additional community supported editions are also available like Kubuntu-4 with KDE release 4, mythbuntu for MythTV, and UbuntuStudio with image development software. You can download these, along with the other editions from

`http://cdimage.ubuntu.com`

Once you have the install image, you will need to burn it to a DVD or CD disk, which you can then use to install your system.

If you are a first time user, you may want to first run the Live CD to see how Ubuntu operates, before you decide to install. The Live-CD can run from system memory.

Check the Ubuntu install guide before installing at the following site, as well as Chapter 2 in this book.

`http://help.ubuntu.com`

Appendix B: Desktop Operations

There are several desktop operations that you may want to take advantage of when first setting up your desktop. These include setting up your personal information, burning CD/DVD disks, searching your desktop for files, and using removable media like USB drives, along with access to remote host.

Tip: With very large monitors and their high resolutions becoming more common, one feature users find helpful is the ability to increase the desktop font sizes. To increase the font size, open the Font panel on the Appearances preferences located in System | Preferences | Appearances menu. There you can change the font sizes used on your desktop.

GNOME International Clock: Time, Date, and Weather

The international clock applet is located on the top panel to the right. It displays the current time and date for your region, but can be modified to display the weather, as well as the time, date, and weather of any location in the world.

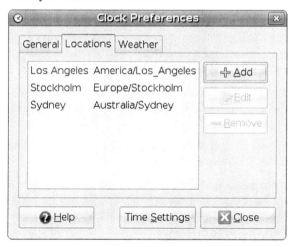

Figure B-1: Selecting a location on the international clock

To add a location, right-click on the time and select Preferences from the pop-up menu. The Clock Preferences window will display three panels: General, Location, and Weather. To ad a new location, click on the Add button on the Location panel. This opens a box where you can enter the name, timezone, and coordinates of the location. It is easier to just click the Find button and open an expandable tree of locations, starting with continent, then to region, country, and city (see Figure B-1).

On the Weather panel, you can specify the temperature and wind measures to use. The General panel you can set the clocks display options for the locations, whether to show weather, temperature, date and seconds.

Once you set the location for your own location, you will see a weather icon appear next to the time on the panel, showing you your current weather (see Figure B-2).

| ☁61 ℉ Thu Mar 27, 8:45 AM ||

Figure B-2: International clock with weather icon

To see the locations you have selected, click on the time displayed on the top panel (see Figure B-3). This opens a calendar, with Location label with an expandable arrow at the bottom. Click this arrow to display all your location, their time and weather. You home location will have a house icon next to it. A world map will show all your locations as red dots, with a blue house icon for your current home location. When you click on a location entry, its corresponding dot will blink for a few seconds. Each location will have a small globe weather icon, indicating the general weather, like sun or clouds. To see weather details, move your mouse over the weather icon. A pop-up dialog will display the current weather, temperature, wind speed, and time for sunrise and sunset. The clock icons for each location will be dark, grey, or bright depending on the time of day at that location.

You can easily change your home location, by click the Set button to the right the location you want made your home. You will see the home icon shift to the new location. This is helpful when traveling. Each location has a set button which will be hidden until you move your mouse over it, on the right side of the clock display.

To make any changes, you can click the Edit button next to the Locations label. This opens the Clock Preferences window where you can configure the display or add and remove locations.

The calendar will show the current date, but you can move to different months and years using the month and year scroll arrows at the top of the calendar.

To set the time manually, right-click on the time and select Adjust Date & Time (also from the General panel of the Clock Preferences window, click the Time Settings button). This opens a Time Settings window where you can enter the time and set the date. Use the month and year arrows on the calendar to change the month and year. To set the time for the entire system, click the Set System Time button

Figure B-3: International clock, full display

Configuring your personal information

To set up your personal information, including the icon to be used for your graphical login, you use the About Me preferences tool. On the Ubuntu GNOME desktop, select the About Me entry in the System | Preferences menu (System | Preferences | About Me). The About Me preferences dialog lets you set up personal information to be used with your desktop applications, as well as change your password (see Figure B-4). Each user can set up their own About Me personal information, including the icon or image they want to use to represent them.

Clicking on the image icon in the top left corner opens a browser where you can select a personal image. The Faces directory is selected by default displaying possible images. The selected image is displayed to the right on the browser. For a personal photograph you can select the Picture folder. This is the Pictures folder on your home directory. Should you place a photograph or image there, you could then select if for your personal image. The image will be use in the login screen when showing your user entry.

Should you want to change your password, you can click on the Change password button at the top right.

There are three panels: Contact, Addresses, and Personal Info. The Contact panel you enter email (home and work), telephone, and instant messaging addresses. On the Address panel you enter your home and work addresses, and on the Person Info panel you list your Web addresses and work information.

Figure B-4: About Me information: System | Preferences | About Me

Desktop Background

You use the Background panel on the Appearances tool to select or customize background image (see Figure B-5). To open this panel, you can either right click anywhere on the desktop background and select Change Desktop Background from the pop-up menu, or from the panel menus select System | Preferences | Appearances | and select the Background panel. Installed backgrounds are listed, with the current one selected. To add your own image, either drag and drop the image file to the Background panel tool, or click on the Add button to locate and select the image file. To remove an image, select it and click the Remove button.

Figure B-5: Choosing a desktop background, System | Preferences | Appearances

The style menu lets you choose different display options like centered, scaled, or tiled. A centered or scaled image will preserve the image proportions. Fill screen may distort it. Any space not filled, such as with a centered or scaled images, will be filled in with the desktop color. You can change the color if you wish, as well as make it a horizontal or vertical gradient (Colors menu). Colors are selected from a color wheel providing an extensive selection of possible colors.

Initially only the Ubuntu backgrounds are listed. Install the **gnome-background** package to add a collection of GNOME backgrounds. You can download more GNOME backgrounds from **art.gnome.org** and **www.gnome-look.org**.

TIP: You can set your screen resolution as well as screen orientation using the Monitor Resolution Settings utility accessible from System | Preferences | Screen Resolution. The utility supports RandR screen management features like screen rotation, resolution, and refresh rate.

Using Removable Devices and Media

Removable media such as CD and DVD discs, USB storage disks, digital cameras, and floppy disks will be displayed as icons on your desktop. These icons will not appear until you place the disks into their devices. To open a disk, double-click it to display a file manager window and the files on it.

Ubuntu now supports removable devices and media like digital cameras, PDAs, card readers, and even USB printers. These devices are handled automatically with an appropriate device interface set up on the fly when needed. Such hotplugged devices are identified, and where appropriate, their icons will appear in the file manager window. For example, when you connect a

USB drive to your system, it will be detected and displayed as storage device with its own file system. If you copied any files to the disk, be sure to unmount it first before removing it (right-click and select Unmount Volume).

Accessing File Systems, Devices, and Remote Hosts

The desktop will also display a Computer folder. Opening this folder will also list your removable devices, along with icons for your file system and network connections (see Figure B-6). The file system icon can be used to access the entire file system on your computer, starting from the root directory. Regular users will have only read access to many of these directories, whereas the root user will have full read and write access.

Opening Network will list any hosts on your system with shared directories, like Windows systems accessible with Samba. GNOME uses DNS-based service discovery to automatically detect these hosts. Opening a host's icons will list the shared directories available on that system. When opening a shared directory, you will be asked for a user and password, like the user and password for a directory owned by a Windows user. The first time you access a shared directory, you will also be asked to save this user and password in a keyring, which itself can be password protected. This allows repeated access without have to always enter the password.

Figure B-6: Removable devices, Computer folder, and shared network folders

Burning DVD/CDs with GNOME

With GNOME, burning data to a DVD or CD is a simple matter of dragging files to an open blank CD or DVD and clicking the Write To Disk button. When you insert a blank DVD/CD, a window will open labeled CD/DVD Creator. To burn files, just drag them to that window. All Read/Write discs, even if they are not blank, are also recognized as writable discs and opened up in a DVD/CD Creator window. Click Write To Disk when ready to burn a DVD/CD. A dialog will open. You can specify write speed, the DVD/CD writer to use (if you have more than one), and the disc label.

GNOME also supports burning ISO images. Just double-click the ISO image file or right-click the file and select Open With CD/DVD Creator. This opens the CD/DVD Creator dialog, which prompts you to burn the image. Be sure to first insert a blank CD or DVD into your CD/DVD burner. You can also burn DVD-Video disks.

For more complex DVD/CD burning you can use the Brasero DVD/CD burner (see Figure B-7). This is included with Ubuntu and is a GNOME project (Ubuntu main repository). Brasero supports drag and drop operations for creating Audio CDs. In particular, it can handle CD/DVD read/write discs, erasing discs. It also supports multi-session burns, adding data to DVD/CD disc. Initially Brasero will display a dialog with buttons for the type of project you want to do. You have the choice of creating a data or audio project, as well as copying a DVD/CD or burning a DVD/CD image file.

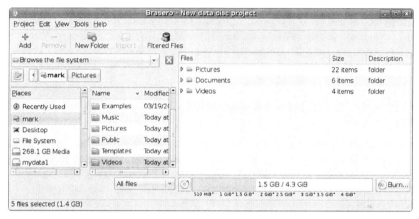

Figure B-7: Burning DVD/CD with Brasero

Searching files

On Ubuntu, there are two primary search tools available for your desktop, "Search for Files" and GNOME File Manager search. "Search for Files" is installed by default and will be accessible from Places | Search for Files, and the desktop menu. The GNOME file manager also provides its own search tool for quickly finding files.

Search for Files

The Search for Files tools performs basic file searching. It is just a GNOME front end for the Linux **grep**, **find**, and **locate** tools. Select Search for Files from the Places menu and enter the pattern to search for. File matching characters (wildcards) will help, like * for file name completion or [] to specify a range of possible characters or numbers.

Enter the pattern to search in the Name contains box, and then select the folder or file system to search from the Look in Folder pop up menu. The user home folder is selected by default. You can then elect to specify advanced options like the Contain text option for searching the contents of text files (**grep**), or additional file characteristics like the file date, size, or owner type (**find**). You can also use a regular expression to search file names.

GNOME File Manager Search

The GNOME file manager uses a different search tool, with the similar features. You enter a pattern to search, but you can also specify file types. Search begins from the folder opened, but you can specify other folder to search (Location option). Click the + button to add additional location and file type search parameters. In the browser mode, you can click on the Search button on the toolbar to make the URL box a Search box. Popup menus for location and file type will appear in the folder window, with + and - button to add or remove location and file type search parameters.

Gnome Power Management

For power management, Ubuntu uses the GNOME Power Manager, **gnome-power-manager**, which makes use of ACPI support provided by a computer to manage power use. The GNOME Power manager is configured with the Power Management Preferences window (**gnome-power-preferences**), accessible from System | Preferences | Power Management. Power management can be used to configure both a desktop and a laptop.

On a Laptop, the battery icon displayed on the panel will show how much power you have left, as well as when the battery become critical. It will also indicate an AC connection, as well as when the battery has recharged.

Tip: With the GNOME Screensaver Preferences you can control when the computer is considered idle and what screen saver to use if any. You can also control whether to lock the screen or not, when idle. Access the Screensaver Preferences from System | Preferences | Screensaver. To turn off the Screensaver by un-checking the "Activate screensaver when computer is idle" box.

For a desktop there are only two panels, On AC Power and General. On the On AC Power window you have two sleep options, one for the computer and one for the screen. You can put each to sleep after a specified interval of inactivity. On the General panel you set desktop features like actions to take when pressing the power button or whether to display the power icon. The AC power icon will show a plug image for desktops and a battery for laptops. The icon is displayed on the top panel.

To see how your laptop or desktop is performing with power, you can use Power statistics. Right-click on the Power Manager icon and select Power History. This runs the **gnome-power-statistics** tool. You may have to first choose to display the Power Manager icon in its General preferences.

To keep a measure of how much time you have left, you can use the Battery Charge Monitor applet. An icon will appear on your panel showing you how much time is left. The preferences let you specify features like showing time or percentage and when to notify of low charge.

Appendix C: Installing from a Desktop CD

If you are installing from the a Live CD/DVD, the Ubuntu operating system will start up in full live CD mode. To install, click on the Install icon on the desktop (see Figure C-1). If you are using the DVD, installation will begin immediately.

Figure C-1: Live CD (Desktop) with Install icon.

If you are installing from an Install DVD, the DVD will display an install menu (see Figure C-2).

Figure C-2: Welcome and Language

A Welcome screen will be displayed, with a Forward button on the lower-right corner. Once finished with a step, you click Forward to move on. In some cases you will be able to click a Back button to return to a previous step. On most screens, a link the lower left will display the Release Notes.

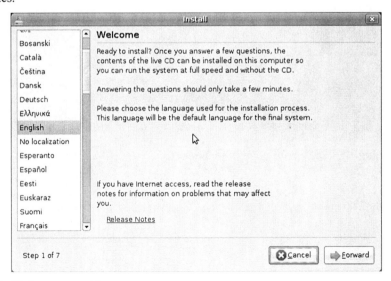

Figure C-3: Welcome and Language

On the Welcome screen you select the language to use in the sidebar scroll window. A default language will already be selected, usually English (see Figure C-3).

On the "Where are you?" screen, you have the option of setting the time by using a map to specify your location or by using Universal Coordinated Time (UTC) entries (see Figure C-4). The Time Zone tool uses a new map feature that expands first to your region to let you easily select your Zone. You can also select your time zone form the pop up menu directly.

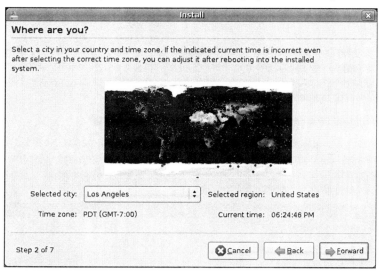

Figure C-4: Where Are You, Time zone

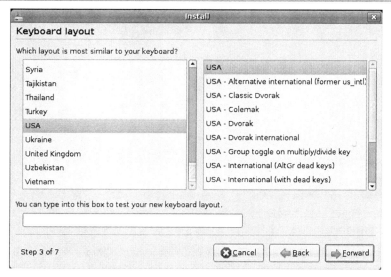

Figure C-5: Keyboard Layout

You will then be asked to select a keyboard—the default is already selected, such as U.S. English (see Figure C-5).

Then you will be asked to designate the Linux partitions and hard disk configurations you want to use on your hard drives. Ubuntu provides automatic partitioning options if you just want to use available drives and free space for your Linux system. To manually configure your hard disks, Ubuntu uses a very simple partitioning interface for setting up standard partitions. Unless you are using the Alternate install, LVM, RAID, and encrypted file systems are not supported during the install process.

No partitions will be changed or formatted until you select your packages later in the install process. You can opt out of the installation at any time until that point, and your original partitions will remain untouched. A default layout sets up a swap partition, a root partition of type ext3 (Linux native) for the kernel and applications.

First a dialog informs you that the partitioner is being started

If you have a single blank hard disk connected to your system, the partition screen will give you two options: Guided, using the entire disk, or Manual (see Figure C-6). The options will change according to the number of hard disk on your system. If you have several hard disks, they will be listed. You can also select the disk on which to install Ubuntu.

Figure C-6: Prepare disk space

Windows and Linux **/home** partitions will not be overwritten in a Guided partition. The Guided option, though, requires free space on your hard disk on which to install your system.

If you already have partitions set up on your hard disk, and want to overwrite existing Linux partitions, you should select the Manual option so you can edit those partitions, designating them for formatting and installation.

If you choose manual, then the partitioner interface starts up with the "Prepare partitions" screen, listing any existing partitions. Each hard disk is listed by its device name, such as sda for the first Serial ATA device. Then underneath the hard disk are its partitions and/or free space available (see Figure C-7). At the bottom of the screen are actions you can perform on partitions and free space: New Label, Edit, Delete, Undo changes to Partitions. When you select free space entry, the New button will become available. When you select an existing partition, the New Label, Edit, and Delete buttons become available, but not the New button. The "Undo changes to partitions button" is always available.

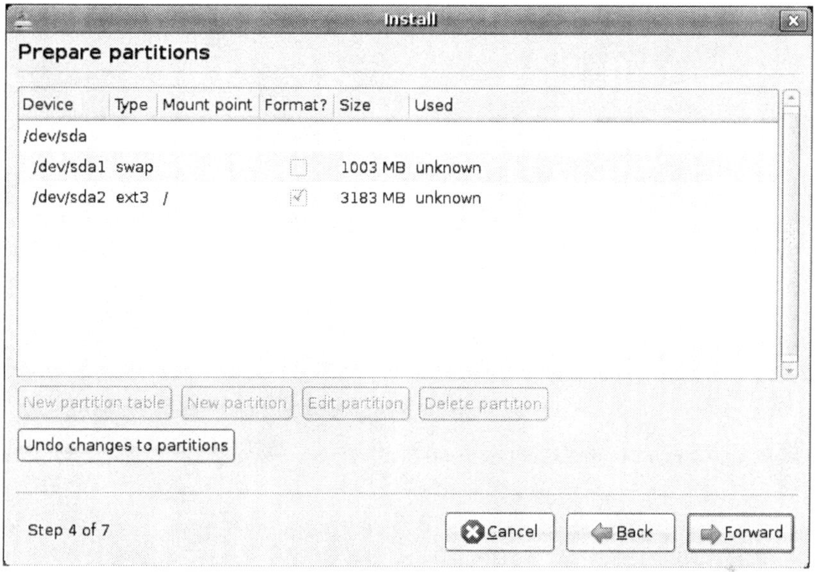

Figure C-7: Prepare Partitions

Your hard disk will be listed with the available free space. To create a new partition, select the free space entry for the hard disk and click the New button. A dialog opens with entries for the partition type (Primary or Logical), the size in megabytes, the location (beginning or end), the file system type (Use as), and the Mount point. For the root partition where you will install your system, the file system type would usually be **ext3**, and the root mount point is referenced with the / symbol (see Figure C-8).

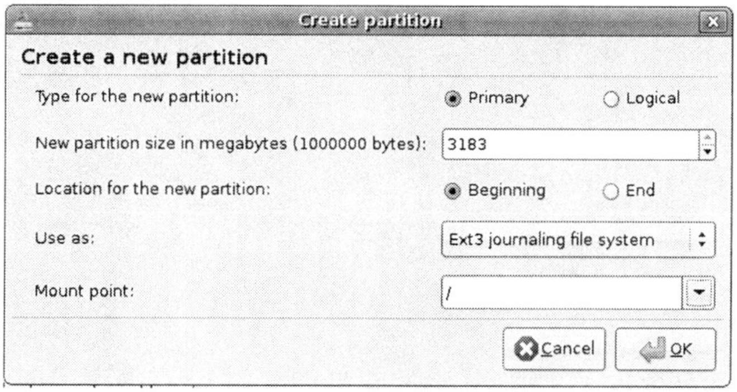

Figure C-8: New partition

For a swap partition you would select the swap as the file system type (Use as). Swap partitions have no mount point.

To edit an existing partition, click on its entry and click the Edit partition table button. A dialog opens with entries for the partition type (Use as), and the mount point (see Figure C-9). The / refers to the root mount point and is used to install your system.

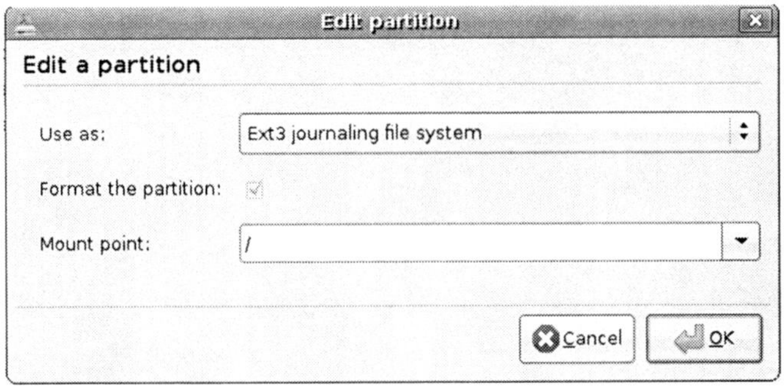

Figure C-9: Edit partition

To modify a partition, select it and then press enter. This opens a Disk Partition menu where you can

Use as - opens a menu where you can select the partition type, like ext3 for Linux partitions. Once you select a Use As, then entries appear for Format and mount point, as well as any mount options.Once you have created or edited a partition, you will see it appear in the Prepare partitions pane.

Partitions that will be formatted will be displayed. (see Figure C-10).

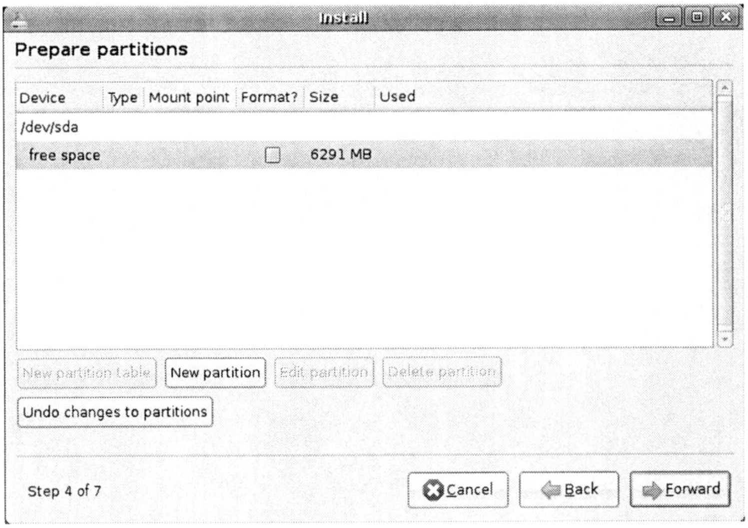

Figure C-10: Partitions with changes.

On the following screens you enter your name, your user log in name, that user's password (see Figure C-11). The user you are creating will have administrative access, allowing you to change your system configuration, add new users and printers, and install new software. You are also prompted if you need an HTTP proxy.

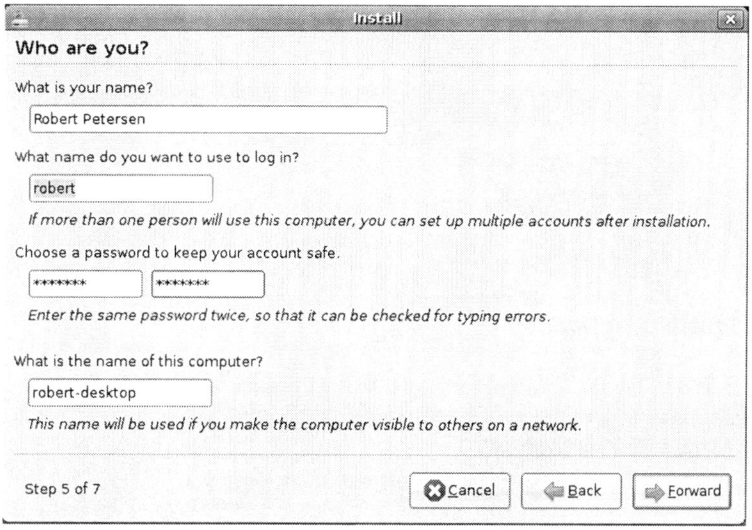

Figure C-11: Who are you?

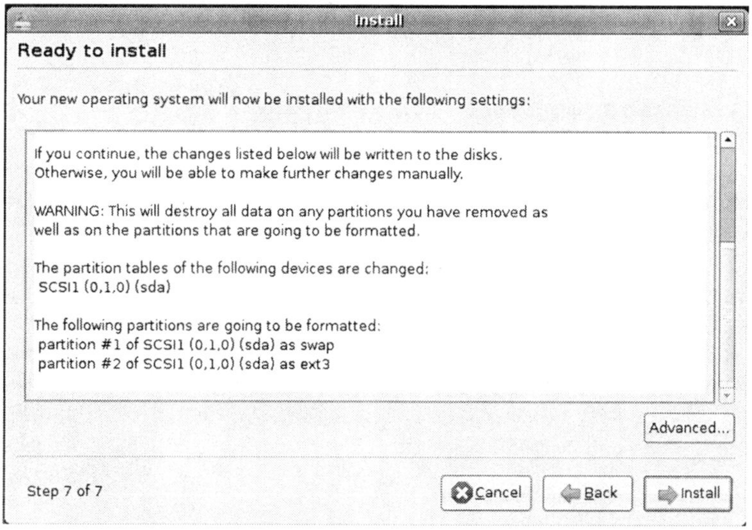

Figure C-12: Ready to Install

The Ready to Install window then lets you review the changes that will be made, especially the partitions that will be formatted. You can still cancel and back out at this time. Once you press the Install button, our partitions will be formatted and installation will begin (see Figure C-12).

The advanced option on this window will let you decide where to place the boot loader and whether to install it at all, or allow you to specify an HTTP proxy. The boot loader was automatically configured for you.

When you click Install, a progress screen is displayed showing install progress (see Figure C-13). You should not interrupt this for any reason. A standard set of packages from the CD are being installed.

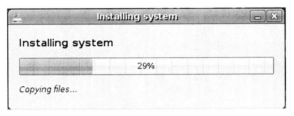

Figure C-13: Install progress

Once finished, the Installation complete dialog appears letting you to continue using the LiveCD to restart and reboot to the new installation (see Figure C-14). Your CD will be automatically ejected when your reboot.

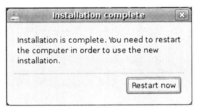

Figure C-14: Installation completed

When you restart, the GNOME Display Manager will manager will provide an interface for logging in, as well as shutting down.

Tip: If you already have a Linux system, you will most likely have several Linux partitions already. Some of these may be used for just the system software, such as the boot and root partitions. These should be formatted. Others may have extensive user files, such as a **/home** partition that normally holds user home directories and all the files they have created. You should *not* format such partitions.

Login and Logout

When your Ubuntu operating system starts up, the login screen will appear (see Figure C-15). You can then log in to your Linux system using a login name and a password for any of the users you have set up. An entry box will be displayed in the middle of the screen and labeled User. Just type in your user name and press ENTER. The label of the box will then change to password and the box will clear. Then enter your password and press ENTER.

Figure C-15: GDM login screen

On the login screen, the Options pop-up menu in the lower left corner lets Quit or Restart Linux.   The Sessions entry in this menu lets you choose what desktop graphical interface to use, such as KDE or GNOME. The Language entry lets you select a language to use.

When you finish, you can shut down your system. From GNOME, you can elect to shut down the entire system. If you log out from either GNOME or KDE and return to the login screen, you can click the Quit button to shut down.

Initial Configuration Tasks from the Desktop

There are a few configuration tasks you many want to configure right away. These include:

> The Date And Time - This configured using the world clock applet or the Date and Time configuration tool, date-admin (System | Administration | Date & Time). The world clock applet is on the right side of the top panel. Right-click on it and choose Preferences to configure.

> Create Users - This is handled by users-admin, System | Administration | Users and Groups.

> Sound Configuration - this is handled by PulseAudio, System | Preferences | Sound

> Firewall and Virus Projection: Use Firestarter for your firewall, System | Administration | Firewall. You can install ClamAV for virus protection and ClamTK for the interface, Applications | System Tools | Virus Scanner.

> Display configuration - If you are using a quality graphics card from Nvidia or ATI(AMD), you may want to install their vendor graphics hardware drivers for Linux. These drivers provide better support for Nvidia and ATI graphics cards. To install these

drivers just use the Hardware Drivers utility in the System | Administration window. If you want to configure these drivers yourself, you will also need their configuration interfaces. These you have to download using the Synaptic Package Manager. For Nvidia you would install the **nvdia-settings** package, and for ATI the **fglrx-control** package. Alternatively, if you want to still use the standard X.org drivers, but still have problems like detecting your monitor correctly, you can download an install the GNOME Screen and Graphics Preferences utility (**displayconfig-gtk**). You may have to start this from a terminal window with the command: **gksu displayconfig-gtk**.

Table Listing

Figure Listing

ubuntu

Index

Printed in the United States
132238LV00003B/243/P